THE JEWS

A TREASURY OF
ART AND LITERATURE

THE JEWS

A TREASURY OF
ART AND LITERATURE

Edited by Sharon R. Keller

Hugh Lauter Levin Associates, Inc.

Copyright © 1992, Hugh Lauter Levin Associates, Inc.
Design by Philip Grushkin
Photo research by Photo*search*, Inc., New York
Typeset by A & S Graphics, Inc., Wantagh, New York
Editorial production by Fair Street Productions/Photo*search*, Inc., New York
Color separations by Rainbow Graphic Arts
Printed in China
ISBN 0-88363-892-4

Selections from the Bible. *The Holy Scriptures.* © 1917 by The Jewish Publication Society of America.

"Second Book of the Maccabees." From *The Apocrypha*, Chapter 8, Verses 1–36. Translated by Edgar J. Goodspeed. © 1938, The University of Chicago Press.

Josephus. From *The Jewish War*, translated by G. A. Williamson (Penguin Books, 1959). Copyright © G. A. Williamson, 1959.

"Aboth (The Fathers)." From *The Mishnah*, translated by Herbert Danby. Oxford University Press, 1933. By permission of Oxford University Press.

"Sanhedrin 4:1–5." From *The Mishnah*, translated by Herbert Danby. Oxford University Press, 1933. By permission of Oxford University Press.

"Sanhedrin 37a; 38a." From *The Babylonian Talmud*, translated under the editorship of Rabbi I. Epstein. The Soncino Press, 1935.

"The Alphabet and the Creation." From *A Treasury of Judaism*, compiled and edited by Philip Birnbaum, 1962. Reprinted by permission of the Publishers, Hebrew Publishing Company, P.O. Box 157, Rockaway Beach, NY 11693. Copyright © 1962. All rights reserved.

Solomon ibn Gabirol. "Night Storm" and "Before I Was." From *The Penguin Book of Hebrew Verse*, edited by T. Carmi (Allen Lane, 1981), copyright © T. Carmi, 1981.

"Thirteen Principles of Faith." From *Siddur Tifereth Jehudah*, by A. Hyman Charlop, Hebrew Publishing Company, 1912. Reprinted by permission of the Publishers, Hebrew Publishing Company, P.O. Box 157, Rockaway Beach, NY 11693. Copyright © 1912. All rights reserved.

Moses ben Maimon. "Letter to Samuel ibn Tibbon." From *Islam: From the Prophet Mohammed to the Capture of Constantinople*, edited by Bernard Lewis. Copyright © 1974 by Bernard Lewis. Reprinted with permission from Walker and Company.

"Rabbi Moses ben Maimon and the Physicians: The Poison." From *Mimekor Yisrael (Selected Classical Jewish Folktales)*. Collected by Micha Joseph bin Gorion. Edited by Emanuel bin Gorion. Prepared by Dan Ben-Amos. Translated by I. M. Lask. © 1990 Indiana University Press.

From *The Zohar*, translated by Harry Sperling, Maurice Simon and Dr. Paul P. Levertoff. The Soncino Press, 1949.

Obadiah di Bertinoro. Excerpts from "Letters." From *Miscellany of Hebrew Literature*, translated by Adolf Neubauer, N. Trübner & Co., 1872. Publication of the Society of Hebrew Literature.

"The Edict of Expulsion." From *The History of the Jews of Spain and Portugal*, by E. H. Lindo. 1848.

A. Marx. "On the Expulsion of the Jews from Spain." From *Jewish Quarterly Review* (o.s.) Volume XX, 1908.

"The Former Marrano's Offering." From *Beyond Appearances: Stories from the Kabbalistic Ethical Writings* by Aryeh Wineman. (Originally published in *Mishnat hakhamim* by Moses Hagiz. Wandsbeck, 1733.) © 1988 The Jewish Publication Society.

Eldad the Danite. "The Lost Tribes of Israel," translated by Leo W. Schwarz. From *The Jewish Caravan*, edited by Leo W. Schwarz. Copyright 1935, © 1963, 1965 by Leo W. Schwarz. Reprinted by permission of Henry Holt and Company, Inc.

Benjamin of Tudela. From *The Itinerary of Benjamin of Tudela*, translated by Marcus Nathan Adler. 1964. Reprinted with permission of Feldheim Publishers.

Moses Dar'i. "Against the Rabbanites." From *Karaite Anthology*, translated by Leon Nemoy. (Yale Judaica Series, editor Julian Obermann. Vol. VII.) © 1952, Yale University Press.

"The Death of Moses." From *Falasha Anthology*, translated by Wolf Leslau. (Yale Judaica Series, editor Julian Obermann. Vol. VI.) © 1951, Yale University Press.

William Lempriere. *A Tour from Gibraltar to Tangier . . . Morrocco.* T. Dobson, 1794.

From *Jewish Self-Government in the Middle Ages*, by Louis Finkelstein, 1964. © The Jewish Theological Seminary of America.

Menasseh ben Israel. "Petition for Readmission of Jews to England." From *The Jew in the Medieval World*, by Jacob Marcus. Reprinted with the permission of the Hebrew Union College Press.

Nathan Hanover. "The Inner Life of the Jews in the Kingdom of Poland." From *Abyss of Despair*, translated by Abraham J. Mesch. Published by Bloch Publishing Company, New York, 1955. Reprinted with permission of Vellie Mesch (Mrs. Abraham J. Mesch).

Baruch Ben Gershon Marizo. "Shabtai Zvi." From *Out of Our People's Past*, edited by Walter Ackerman. United Synagogue of America, 1977. Reprinted by permission of Walter Ackerman.

Baruch Spinoza. "The God of Man's Making." From *The Road to Inner Freedom*, edited by Dagobert D. Runes. 1957. By permission of Philosophical Library, Inc.

Glückel of Hameln. "Zipporah's Unforgettable Marriage." From *The Memoirs of Glückel of Hameln*, translated by Marvin Lowenthal. Copyright 1932 by Harper & Brothers.

Israel Zangwill. "The Master of the Name." From *The Dreamers of the Ghetto*. The Jewish Publication Society of America, 1898.

Meyer Levin. "The Boy's Song." From *Classic Hassidic Tales (The Golden Mountain)* by Meyer Levin. 1932. (Originally published as *The Golden Mountain* by Behrman House; then as *Classic Hassidic Tales* by The Citadel Press). Reprinted by permission of Mrs. Meyer Levin.

Moses Mendelssohn. From *Jerusalem: A Treatise on Religious Power and Judaism*, translated by Isaac Leeser. Philadelphia, C. Sherman, 1852.

Napoleon Bonaparte. "The Proclamation and the Covering Letter." From *Napoleon and the Jews*, by Franz Kobler. 1976. Courtesy of the Leo Baeck Institute, New York.

"The Helmites Capture the Moon." From *The Wise Men of Helm*, by Solomon Simon. 1955. Published by Behrman House, Inc., West Orange, NJ 07052. Used with permission.

Pauline Wengeroff. "Memoirs of a Grandmother." From *The Golden Tradition: Jewish Life and Thought in Eastern Europe*, by Lucy Dawidowicz. Copyright © 1967 by Lucy Dawidowicz. Reprinted by permission of Henry Holt and Company, Inc.

David Frishman. "Three Who Ate." From *The Jewish Caravan*, edited by Leo W. Schwarz. Copyright 1935, © 1963, 1965 by Leo W. Schwarz. Reprinted by permission of Henry Holt and Company, Inc.

Sholom Aleichem. "On Account of a Hat," translated by Isaac Rosenfeld. From *A Treasury of Yiddish Stories*, by Irving Howe and Eliezer Greenberg. Copyright 1953, 1954, 1989 by Viking Penguin, renewed © 1981, 1982 by Irving Howe and Eva Greenberg. Used by permission of Viking Penguin, a division of Penguin Books USA Inc.

Alfred Dreyfus. *Five Years of My Life.* © 1901 by McClure, Phillips & Co.

Vladimir Medem. "Youth of a Bundist." Reprinted from *Commentary*, November 1950. Copyright © 1950 by the American Jewish Committee. All rights reserved.

I. L. Peretz. "The Golem." From *A Treasury of Yiddish Stories*, by Irving Howe and Eliezer Greenberg. Copyright 1953, 1954, 1989 by Viking Penguin; renewed © 1981, 1982 by Irving Howe and Eva Greenberg. Used by permission of Viking Penguin, a division of Penguin Books USA Inc.

Isaac Bashevis Singer. "The Last Demon." From *The Collected Stories*, by Isaac Bashevis Singer. Copyright © 1962, 1964, 1982 by Isaac Bashevis Singer. Reprinted by permission of Farrar, Straus & Giroux, Inc.

Hayyim Nahman Bialik. "Making the Crooked Straight." From *The Jewish Caravan*, edited by Leo W. Schwarz. Copyright 1935, © 1963, 1965 by Leo W. Schwarz. Reprinted by permission of Henry Holt and Company, Inc.

Marc Chagall. "What is a Jewish Artist." From *The Golden Tradition: Jewish Life and Thought in Eastern Europe*, by Lucy Dawidowicz. Copyright © 1967 by Lucy Dawidowicz. Reprinted by permission of Henry Holt and Company, Inc.

Sigmund Freud. "Jew-Hatred." From *Moses and Monotheism*, by Sigmund Freud. Copyright 1939 by Alfred A. Knopf, Inc. and renewed 1967 by Ernst L. Freud and Anna Freud. Reprinted by permission of the publisher.

"Petition to the Dutch West India Company." From *The Early History of the Jews in New York, 1654–1664*, by Samuel Oppenheim. Publication of the American Jewish Historical Society, Vol. 18 (1909), pp. 9–11.

Benjamin Rush. "Letter." From *On Love, Marriage, Children . . . and Death, Too*, collected and edited by Jacob R. Marcus. Society of Jewish Bibliophiles, 1965.

"Address of the Newport Congregation . . ." and "Washington's Reply." Reprinted from Publications of the American Jewish Historical Society, Vol. III, 1895.

Rebecca Samuel. "Letter." From *On Love, Marriage, Children . . . and Death, Too*, collected and edited by Jacob R. Marcus. Society of Jewish Bibliophiles, 1965.

Stephen Birmingham. "Mount Seligman." From *Our Crowd*, by Stephen Birmingham. Copyright © 1967 by Stephen Birmingham. Reprinted by permission of HarperCollins Publishers.

Abraham Kohn. "From His Diary." From "A Jewish Peddler's Diary," by Abram Vossen Goodman. *American Jewish Archives*, Vol. III, No. 3, June 1951.

Raphael Moses. *The Major Writes a Letter.* American Jewish Archives, reprinted 1967.

Emma Lazarus. "The Banner of the Jew." From *A Treasury of Jewish Poetry.* Crown Publishers, 1957.

Irving Howe. Excerpts from *World of Our Fathers*, copyright © 1976 by Irving Howe, reprinted by permission of Harcourt Brace Jovanovich, Inc.

Molly Picon. "The Marvels of Rezshishtchov." From *So Laugh a Little*, by Molly Picon and Ethel Clifford Rosenberg. Julian Messner, 1962. Reprinted by permission of the author and the author's agents, Scott Meredith Literary Agency, Inc., 845 Third Avenue, New York, NY 10022.

Abraham Cahan. From *The Rise of David Levinsky.* © 1917, Harper & Brothers.

From *A Bintel Brief*, by Isaac Metzker. Copyright © 1971 by Isaac Metzker. Forward and notes copyright © 1971 by Doubleday, a division of Bantam Doubleday Dell Publishing Group, Inc. Used by permission of Doubleday, a division of Bantam Doubleday Dell Publishing Group, Inc.

Kadia Molodowsky. "The Lost Shabes." From *The Tribe of Dina*, edited by Melanie Kaye/Kantrowicz and Irena Klepfisz. Copyright © 1986, 1989 by Melanie Kaye/Kantrowicz and Irena Klepfisz. Reprinted by permission of Beacon Press.

Harry Golden. Reprinted by permission of The Putnam Publishing Group from *Ess, Ess, Mein Kindt*, by Harry Golden. Copyright © 1966 by Harry Golden.

Sam Levenson. "Foods." From *Meet the Folks*, Citadel Press, 1951. Reprinted by permission of Sterling Lord Literistic, Inc. Copyright © 1951 by Sam Levenson.

Louis Brandeis. From *The Menorah Journal*, Vol. 1, No. 1, 1915.

Alfred Kazin. Excerpts from *A Walker in the City*, copyright 1951 and renewed 1979 by Alfred Kazin, reprinted by permission of Harcourt Brace Jovanovich, Inc.

Bernard Malamud. "The Loan." From *The Stories of Bernard Malamud*, by Bernard Malamud. Copyright © 1952 and renewal copyright © 1980 by Bernard Malamud. Reprinted by permission of Farrar, Straus & Giroux, Inc.

From *The Chosen*, by Chaim Potok. Reprinted by permission of the William Morris Agency, Inc., on behalf of the author. Copyright © 1967 by Chaim Potok.

Dan Jacobson. "The Example of Lipi Lippman." Reprinted from *Commentary* (November 1961), by permission, all rights reserved. Reprinted by permission of Dan Jacobson, copyright © 1961, 1964, 1991.

Mordecai Richler. From *Solomon Gursky Was Here*, by Mordecai Richler. Copyright © 1989 by Mordecai Richler. Reprinted by permission of Alfred A. Knopf, Inc.

Anne Roiphe. "Taking Down the Christmas Tree." From *Tikkun*, Vol. 4, No. 6, (Nov.–Dec. 1989), pp. 58–60. Reprinted with permission of *Tikkun*, a bimonthly Jewish critique of politics, culture and society based in Oakland, California.

André Schwartz-Bart. Reprinted with the permission of Atheneum, an imprint of Macmillan Publishing Company, from *The Last of the Just*, by André Schwartz-Bart. Translated from the French by Stephen Becker. Copyright © 1960 by Atheneum House, Inc. Copyright © 1959 by Editions du Seuil, Paris.

Anne Frank. From *Anne Frank: The Diary of a Young Girl*, by Anne Frank. Copyright 1952 by Otto H. Frank. Used by permission of Doubleday, a division of Bantam Doubleday Dell Publishing Group, Inc.

"Homesick" and "Terezin." From *Children's Drawings and Poems (Terezin 1942–44).* Statni Zidovské Muzeum v Praze (State Jewish Museum in Prague). Prague, 1957.

Elie Wiesel. Excerpt from *Night*, by Elie Wiesel. Copyright © 1960 by MacGibbon & Kee. Renewal copyright © 1988 by The Collins Publishing Group. Reprinted by permission of Hill and Wang, a division of Farrar, Straus & Giroux, Inc.

Primo Levi. "The Commander of Auschwitz." From *The Mirror Maker: Stories and Essays*, by Primo Levi, translated by Raymond Rosenthal. Copyright © 1989 by Schocken Books, Inc. Reprinted by permission of Schocken Books, published by Pantheon Books, a division of Random House, Inc.

Leslie Epstein. *King of the Jews.* Copyright © 1979 by Leslie Epstein. Available from Summit Books. Reprinted by permission of the author.

Simon Wiesenthal. From *The Murderers Among Us: The Simon Wiesenthal Memoirs*; copyright Simon Wiesenthal.

Theodor Herzl. From *The Jewish State*, 1946. By permission of *Midstream*, A Monthly Jewish Review.

Golda Meir. "First Days in Kibbutz Merhavia." From *Midstream*, Volume XVI, Number 5 (May 1970). By permission of *Midstream*, A Monthly Jewish Review.

S. Y. Agnon. "Fable of the Goat." From *Twenty-One Stories*, by S. Y. Agnon, edited by Nahum N. Glatzer. Copyright © 1970 by Schocken Books, Inc. Reprinted by permission of Schocken Books, published by Pantheon Books, a division of Random House, Inc.

Benjamin Tammuz. "Ahad Ha'am's Funeral." © Benjamin Tammuz. Translation © Institute for Translation of Hebrew Literature, Israel.

Chaim Weizmann. "The Rebirth of a Nation." From *The Letters and Papers of Chaim Weizmann*, Series B, Papers, Vol. II, Paper 91, pp. 672–680. By permission of The Weizmann Archives, Yad Chaim Weizmann (Weizmann National Memorial) Rehovot, Israel.

Albert Einstein. "The Jews of Israel." From *Out of My Later Years*, by Albert Einstein, 1950. Philosophical Library, Inc.

David Ben-Gurion. Excerpts from *Israel, A Personal History*, by David Ben-Gurion. Copyright © 1971 by the American Israel Publishing Co., Ltd. Reprinted by permission of HarperCollins Publishers.

Amos Oz. From *The Seventh Day: Soldiers' Talk About the Six-Day War.* Edited by Avraham Shapira. Published in the U.S. by Charles Scribners Sons. With permission of the author.

Bernard Isaacs. "Or Was it a Dream?" From *Selected Stories*, translated by Shoshona Perla. © 1968 by E. Lewin-Epstein, LTD., Publishers.

Edward Norden. "The Ingathering." Reprinted from *Commentary* (April 1991), by permission; all rights reserved. Reprinted with the permission of the author.

David Grossman. "The Spark and the Flute." Copyright © 1991 by The New York Times Company. Reprinted by permission.

CONTENTS

ACKNOWLEDGMENTS

I have availed myself of the advice, friendship, and support generously offered by many in the preparation of this volume. To all I am indebted. I will single out my parents and, most especially, my sister Eve and my brother-in-law David for the countless hours they spent in assisting me. I would also like to thank the Klau Library of the New York campus of the Hebrew Union College—Jewish Institute of Religion without whose collection this volume would have been impossible. My appreciation also goes to the publisher, Hugh Lauter Levin; to Rabbi Morrison D. Bial for reviewing the text; and to Rabbi Stephan Parnes for his help in editing the manuscript. The staff at Fair Street Productions/ Photo*search,* in particular Deborah Bull, Susan Wechsler, and Joanne Polster, deserves special acknowledgment for their helpful support and effort throughout this project. To all, my heartfelt thanks.

Sharon R. Keller

INTRODUCTION

The literary history of the Jews reflects the history of the Jewish people themselves. Jews have been called the "people of the book." Originally this referred to the fact that the Jewish religion is rooted in its founding document, the Hebrew Bible. Even today, as the major denominations of modern Judaism continue to flourish in diversity, each of them reaches back, though clearly with different interpretations and intentions, to the Torah (the Five Books of Moses), as well as to the writings of the Prophets and the Hagiographa. These writings define and ground Jewish practice and beliefs.

Even in the Hebrew Bible itself, it is clear that writing was conceived of as integral to the religious and cultural experience of the ancient Jews. The initial covenant made between them and the biblical God was formulated in writing. In one of the selections from Exodus presented in this book, Moses ascends Mount Sinai to meet the Lord and is presented with two tablets of stone inscribed by "the finger of God" Himself. The Ten Commandments that Moses thus receives are *written* and hence serve as perpetual testimony to the binding of God with His people.

Just as the covenant between man and God is written, so too is the covenant between divinely appointed kings and their subjects. The constitutional monarchy of Saul—the first king of Israel—was commemorated in a written document "placed before the Lord" by Samuel, the prophet who anointed both Saul and his successor, David. In the Hebrew Bible, therefore, writing is a sign of mutual and lasting commitment—religiously, between the people and their God; socially, among the people themselves.

Jews, however, are a "people of the book" in more than just the sense of connection to the Hebrew Bible. For the Jews, writing is not only a form of religious expression but also a means—perhaps the most potent means—of passing on a cultural heritage from one generation to the next. Other cultures have built their monuments in stone: the pyramids of Egypt, the Taj Mahal of India, the vast and spacious cathedrals of Europe. Jews, by contrast, have always built their monuments in words. Ever since the Temple of Solomon—the first temple—was destroyed, Jews have placed their foundations in the text rather than in institutions or persons. Although synagogues were built in various architectural forms and styles, for the most part their exteriors were relatively plain and their structures simple. Once inside and closer to the Torah the elaboration increases; the ark itself, where the Torah rests, becomes the focal point of the synagogue and is surrounded by splendorous fabrics, sometimes elaborately embellished.

Perhaps the Jewish commitment to text rather than to stone has something to do with the Jews' historical experience. As told in the selections from Genesis, Adam was exiled from Eden and Abraham was told to leave his homeland to search for his one God. Jews have always seen themselves as—and have had to be—wanderers. By and large, Jews have not stayed in one place for long periods of time; they were twice exiled from Israel and were driven from their homes around the world many times throughout the ages. They have had to leave, by choice or by force, the places of their fathers' births. Likewise, the objects used to commemorate Jewish customs often had to be left behind. Although they were utilitarian, ritual objects were customarily elaborate works of art that beautified and heightened the religious experience. Throughout Jewish history, ceremonial art of any value might have been sold to raise money or confiscated by rulers who recognized its sheer monetary value. Quite often, Jews had to depart rapidly and could only carry items essential for their survival.

Unlike the physical structures that testify to a people's "rootedness" to a particular place, the conceptual structures of texts can be carried, physically as well as spiritually, from place to place. Thus Jews have taken their texts with them—their laws, their ethics, their myths, their stories of ghetto life—and have passed this great literary heritage on to their children.

Text and image are often brought together by the artistic heritage of the Jews. Even though the biblical text *per se* has no inherent illustrations, there has been a continued tradition of illustrating stories from the Bible—ranging from the wall paintings in the synagogue of Dura Europas to works of contemporary artists like Larry Rivers. There is a long and varied tradition of decorating manuscripts with illuminated words, finely executed calligraphy, or with figures. In addition, ceremonial objects used to celebrate the rituals and customs of Jewish life are decorated with both pictorial representations and inscriptions and are fine works of art that greatly enhance the religious experience. For instance, Torah pointers made of silver, ivory, or other materials were designed to protect the words of the Torah from physical contact or obliteration and took the shape of the human hand; hence their name *yad* (Hebrew for "hand"). When a *yad* is used to keep one's place in the Torah text, the holiness or sacredness of the text being read is reinforced. Additionally, Torah mantles sewn from exquisitely woven textiles and decorated with elaborate ornamentation were appropriate to the sacred contents they protected.

The art chosen to illustrate this book is, for the most part, by Jewish artists. More importantly, though, the art reflects a personal interpretation of the Jewish experience. As does the literature, the art serves to bind successive generations one to another. While Jews of diverse cultures throughout the world have reflected aspects of their surrounding environment in their art, they have continually upheld and maintained their Jewish religious identity. Despite cultural differences, the desire to embellish or glorify the Jewish liturgical experience through artistic expression is a common factor of all Jewish communities throughout history.

The literary selections in this book attempt to display, however selectively, the richness and diversity of Jewish life as it has been expressed in Jewish literature. We have divided the selections into a number of categories that underscore not only the different time periods and geographical locations that define Jewish culture, but also document the unique aspects of Jewish traditions throughout the world. Most texts chosen for this volume celebrate Jewish life; traditions are recorded, recounted, and explored. But the literature also records the pain and the suffering, starting with the enslavement of the Israelites in Egypt, that has been part of Jewish history since it has been recorded.

The Hebrew Bible, the first product of Jewish literature, is the basis of both the religion and the culture of the Jewish people. It has been read as a book of strictly literal truths containing both the actual words of God and the words transmitted from God to His prophets; it has also been read as a social history of the Jewish people, starting with the creation of the world and continuing through to the beginning of the second commonwealth. The selections represented here show the diversity of biblical genres, including the earliest myths of Genesis (stories of creation, Abraham, Joseph and his brothers); the historical writings of Kings; and the exquisite poetry of Isaiah and the Psalmist. Biblical law, considered part of the foundation of much of Western legal and ethical tradition, expresses simple ethical truths, as exemplified by the legal formulations of Exodus and Leviticus chosen for this text.

One of the great collections of literature from the postbiblical period is the Talmud, from which we have chosen passages that illustrate the blending of the ethical and religious norms of Rabbinic Judaism with the legal and social organization of an ideally self-governing community. Thus, in the excerpt concerning laws for capital cases from *Sanhedrin*, the rabbis insert a beautiful homily on the sanctity of every human life, based on the omnipotent creative force of God. Talmudic texts, however, do not comprise the totality of Jewish literature during this period; there are important secular texts represented as well. Josephus, a Jewish apologist from the first century C.E., describes in moving detail the last stand of the revolutionaries at Masada, the scene of whose self-sacrifice can still be witnessed today near the Dead Sea in Israel.

Centuries later, Jewish life in the Muslim world witnessed a great flowering of literary, cultural, and artistic achievement. From the eleventh century onward, when the Jews of Christian Europe were subject to violent attacks and continual expulsions, the Jews of Spain and North Africa flourished and even made valuable contributions to non-Jewish society. Luminaries such as the philosopher Rabbi Moses ben Maimon and the poet Solomon ibn Gabirol won fame not only for their contributions to Jewish thought but also for their participation in secular society. We have included some of Ibn Gabirol's emotional liturgical poetry, as well as Maimonides's *Thirteen Principles of Faith*. The most celebrated of all the Jewish thinkers of this period, Maimonides was also the court physician to the vizier Saladin. In *Rambam and the Physicians,* the philosopher's important role in Muslim society and his fame as a physician is made clear; this folktale, handed down from generation to generation, has endured for hundreds of years.

Spain was unique among countries in the Middle Ages in that Jews, Christians, and Muslims coexisted in relative peace. When the Christians expanded into Spain in the eleventh century, they were at first tolerant of the existing Jewish communities; in fact, the Jews were instrumental in helping the Christians adjust to their new surroundings and even assisted with translations of Arabic texts. But the Golden Age of Spain that had led to artistic and religious freedoms eventually came to an end. Although there had been isolated incidents of intolerance and polemical disputations between Christians and Jews, none—until the end of the fourteenth century—resulted in the massacres or anti-Jewish uprisings that had plagued the rest of Christian Europe. The first widespread persecution of Spanish Jewry occurred in 1391, with the near-total destruction of many Jewish communities. For the first time in all of Jewish history, many Jews chose to become apostates rather than to martyr themselves for the sake of their religion. These new converts were never fully trusted as true adherents of Christianity, and consequently the fifteenth century saw a rise in Christian hostilities toward all Jews. By 1492, virulent anti-Jewish sentiments and the force of the Inquisition culminated in the expulsion of the Jews from Spain and all of her territories. The text of the expulsion edict is included in this book, and its effects on Spanish Jews are documented in the observations of a Jew living in Italy at the time of the Inquisition.

Large Diaspora communities did not, of course, begin with the expulsion of the Jews of Spain; rather, they began to form at the dispersion of exiles from Israel in biblical times, who spread from the initial Babylonian settlement to form communities all over the world. Jews who remained in many of these areas often became part of their new nation, adopting aspects of the culture as they adapted to their surroundings. Nonetheless, many of these communities—such as those in Iran, Iraq, Yemen, various North African countries, and Rome—maintained their own religious laws, customs, and traditions that differed from both those of the surrounding people and from other Jewish communities. For instance, the Ashkenazic Jews prohibit eating rice during Passover, whereas rice is a central part of the Seder meal in many Sephardic communities. A simple comparison between the Sephardic and the Ashkenazic liturgy shows that not even the prayer service is the same in all Jewish communities around the world. The Iranian tradition uses a different melody for the chanting of the Torah than do the communities from Europe, while the prophetical portion from the Bible read each week as part of the Sabbath service differs in the Sephardic and Ashkenazic traditions. Even the Torah scroll itself is different in the Ashkenazic and Sephardic communities, although the text remains the same. A Sephardic Torah scroll is encased in an elaborate standing case and is read from within the case in an upright position; in the Ashkenazic tradition, the scroll is kept covered with a cloth that is removed, and the scroll is layed flat prior to unrolling and reading. We have included examples of objects from both communities in this book.

The vast majority of Diaspora communities, such as those of Kaifeng (China), Yemen, and Bukhara, no longer exist as unique entities; expulsions, forced conversions, and economic concerns contributed to the dissolution of these historic settlements. In modern times, some groups of Jews, such as those living in Greece, fell victim to the Holocaust; others who survived persecution, ultimately relocated to Israel. The section entitled

"From Far-Off Lands," unlike the other sections in this book, does not confine itself to one period of history, but relates folk traditions of distant cultures throughout Jewish history. Descriptions of Jewish communities detailed by medieval travelers like Benjamin of Tudela are complemented by an excerpt from an eighteenth-century tour book by William Lempriere.

The art from these communities shows distinct cultural influences. Hence the manuscript page we have included from a Judeo-Persian Book of Conquest shows a clearly Near Eastern hand in the script style, as well as in the costumes of the men depicted. The synagogue wall from Persia, and the embroidered pillow cover from Istanbul, also show a distinct Muslim design influence. The text selections in this section include literature from the disparate communities themselves. The Karaite poem "Against the Rabbanites" and the Falasha funeral elegy that eloquently relates the story of the death of Moses are examples of literature intended for members of the homogeneous community. When they were first told, these stories were not thought of as literature that would traverse even the closest borders. Traditionally, such tales were recorded orally and transmitted generationally; it was not until their community members immigrated to Israel that many of the stories were finally added to the written record of the Jewish people.

Life in Medieval and Renaissance Europe presented Jewish communities with new struggles as well as with hopes fostered by false messiahs like Shabbatai Zevi. The Italian Jewish community of the fifteenth century had its own internal structure that facilitated good relations with the Christian community. In reading the piece on the Synod at Forli, we are given a clear picture of the rules and regulations that concerned Jewish leaders as they attempted to coexist within Italian society. These congenial relations, however, were short-lived; by the early sixteenth century Jews in Italy had been forced to live in ghettos and would soon witness public burnings of the Talmud. Such intolerance was not limited to the Catholic areas of Europe for the Protestant Reformation of the sixteenth century did not bring with it a newfound philo-Semitism.

Amsterdam, however, was unique among Jewish communities in seventeenth-century Europe. While the Jews in Poland and Ukraine suffered the Chmielnicki pogroms (described by Rabbi Nathan Hanover in *Yeven Metzulah*), which decimated nearly a quarter of the Jewish population, the Jews in Amsterdam continued to interact socially, economically, and intellectually with the Dutch Protestants who welcomed them into their communities. Many former *conversos*—Jews who had converted to Christianity during the Inquisition—flocked to the Netherlands after the Dutch won their independence from Spain in 1590, and often reasserted their Judaism. Baruch Spinoza came from one such family, as did Manasseh ben Israel. While Spinoza broke away from his Jewish heritage, and was ultimately excommunicated for his philosophical views, Manasseh ben Israel (1604–1657) tried to help Oliver Cromwell understand Judaism; he clarified common falsehoods, and ceaselessly petitioned that the Jews, who since 1290 had been expelled from England, be readmitted into the country. The text of this petition, reproduced in its entirety, became a necessary paving-stone for the future of the legal practice of Judaism on British soil.

The Enlightenment of the eighteenth century opened the ghetto gates throughout Europe and presented many European Jews with a challenge unknown to their ancestors: Could they maintain their Jewish heritage and still become a part of the ever-changing modern world? Could they assimilate into the cultural norms of the surrounding nations and still maintain some of their Jewish identity, or was that identity something that could and should be shed in the name of progress? Moses Mendelssohn, who has been called the first modern Jew, was by far the preeminent Jewish philosopher of the Enlightenment. In 1763 he submitted an essay to a competition held by the Prussian academy and was awarded first prize, while Immanuel Kant received an honorable mention. Mendelssohn felt that Judaism was indeed compatible with modern rational thought and that a total integration of the two systems was possible. He articulated these thoughts in his seminal work *Jerusalem,* a portion of which is reproduced in this volume. Two women authors who have been included, Kadia Molodowsky and Pauline Wengeroff, describe the tensions between the assimilationists and the traditionalists that ironically became one of the legacies of the Enlightenment.

The European Jewish community finally won full economic and political rights at the end of the eighteenth century. But despite the fact that many Jews moved to the cities, the *shtetl,* the small town of Eastern Europe/Russia, has become evocative of the era; its lifestyle and culture have been much romanticized in both the art and literature of the Jews. Hasidic tales, such as *The Boy's Song* and *The Master of the Name* bring the world of the *shtetl* close to the reader, while the small-town humor of the Helmites creates the image of pre-Holocaust Europe that is so familiar to readers today. Such bitter-sweet sentiment about *shtetl* life has also been immortalized by writers such as Sholem Aleichem, whose Tevya the dairyman perhaps represents the archetypal *shtetl* dweller.

By far the darkest moment in Jewish history was the Holocaust, the near-total annihilation of the European Jewish world. Surprisingly, both artistic and literary expression often served as a means of resistance. Anne Frank wrote her diary to record for herself the terrors of her isolated life with her family in an Amsterdam attic; today that diary is read by millions of people, Jews and non-Jews alike, who learn from her young words the history that too often escapes the history books—the quiet sufferings and aspirations of individual lives. The poetry by the children interned in Theresienstadt in Czechoslovakia is a vivid reminder that our society was willing to believe the Nazis, who in presenting Theresienstadt to the world as their "model settlement" for the Jews, attempted to hide plans for their extermination. The Holocaust literature we offer here includes both poetry and prose, first- and second-hand accounts, as well as fiction. Each piece is a testament to heroism; the Jewish people, although devastated, survived and continue to exist in some of the same countries that sought their annihilation.

The American community, the strongest Diaspora Jewish community of the second half of the twentieth century, started from humble beginnings. In 1654 a boat carrying twenty-three Jewish refugees arrived in New Amsterdam from Brazil. Portugal had expelled the Jews in 1497, and when it recaptured Brazil from the Dutch in the seventeenth century, the Jews who had settled there were forced to leave. Peter Stuyvesant was not at all welcoming, and, in fact, petitioned the Dutch West India Company for permission to deport these Jews. Ultimately the Dutch Jewish community interceded with the Dutch West India Company, and the new Jewish community was allowed to remain. Their petition, reprinted in this book, reminds us that the religious freedom we take for granted was not available to the Jews who first arrived.

Despite such prejudices, American Jewish communities grew in number and in strength during the colonial period, and by the Revolution there were already at least two thousand Jews in the new nation. The letters of Rebecca Samuel, Dr. Benjamin Rush, and the Newport Congregation document daily Jewish life in the early colonies. Jewish patriots like Uriah P. Levy, who was a naval Commodore, and Chaim Solomon, whom we show pictured with George Washington, steadfastly contributed to the cause of the Revolution. Levy, whose son's wedding Benjamin Rush attended, was responsible for the abolishment of flogging as a Naval punishment; Chaim Solomon spent his personal fortune selling and ultimately buying United States securities to help finance the new government.

The Jewish population grew dramatically in the years that followed; between 1820 and 1870 nearly 150,000 Jews immigrated to America from Germany. The hardships of making a living and adjusting to new, unfamiliar surroundings often became the subject of literary expression. A newly arrived immigrant, such as Abraham Kohn, often found himself in the unfamiliar role of a peddler, simply to survive. Kohn's extraordinary diary describes the difficulties and loneliness faced daily by newly arrived Jewish settlers. Such struggles are reflected in the text selections from this period. To escape from unfamiliar surroundings, these European immigrants often turned to the Yiddish theater for a nostalgic taste of home, which the text selection from Irving Howe's *World of Our Fathers* describes. The success and fame of the Yiddish theater, however, reached well beyond America's shores, as Molly Picon's image from a South American poster attests. The selections from *The Daily Forward*'s column *A Bintel Brief* that have been included in the book express the day-to-day, aggravating difficulties many people experienced in adjusting to the ways of the new world; while Molly Picon's *The Marvels of Rezshishtchov* relates how this famous star of the stage was constantly reminded by her grandmother of a better time and place. All these religious and secular tensions, idealized hopes for life in the new world, and idealized memories of the life left behind, contributed to the work and sentiment of American Jewish writers. Likewise, art by American Jewish artists such as Morris Hirschfield, Ben Shahn, or Larry Rivers sometimes drew on the folklore and liturgical traditions of Judaism for its inspiration.

While the Jewish-American population grew on the streets of lower Manhattan, modern Zionism was born on the shores of Europe. The blatant anti-Semitism of the Dreyfus affair in France instigated Theodor Herzl's call for the establishment of a Jewish national homeland, and that dream became a reality with the creation of the State of Israel in 1948. Since then, European and American Jews alike have supported the Jewish homeland. We have tried to include a variety of selections which describe their authors' feelings about Israel. From Chaim Weizmann's early hopes for peaceful coexistence between the Arabs and Jews of Palestine, expressed in his 1947 address to the United Nations; to Ben-Gurion's comments on the Six-Day War from his personal diary; to the article describing the successful rescue and relocation of thousands of Ethiopian Jews to Israel in 1991, it is clear that Zionism—though certainly embattled—continues to be a driving force in Jewish communities both within and outside Israel.

This book makes no claims to comprehensiveness. To sample all the seminal writings of Jewish thought and experience would require a library, not one volume. But that fact itself testifies to the importance and richness of Jewish literary expression. We have attempted not to complete the story of Jewish art and literature, but rather to begin it—to offer a sampling of the historically, culturally, and religiously varied works of art and writings that comprise and reflect the Jewish experience. This book is a treasury: we hope you will taste and be not satisfied but enticed.

THE BIBLE

GENESIS 1:1–2:3

The Creation of the World

This account of the creation of the world culminates with the creation of the first human beings, the crowning touch of God's work, and the observance of the first Sabbath, on which God ceased the work of creation. It is presented chronologically, emphasizing how God imposed order on chaos.

In the beginning God created the heaven and the earth. Now the earth was unformed and void, and darkness was upon the face of the deep; and the spirit of God hovered over the face of the waters. And God said: "Let there be light." And there was light. And God saw the light, that it was good; and God divided the light from the darkness. And God called the light Day, and the darkness He called Night. And there was evening and there was morning, one day.

And God said: "Let there be a firmament in the midst of the waters, and let it divide the waters from the waters." And God made the firmament, and divided the waters which were under the firmament from the waters which were above the firmament; and it was so. And God called the firmament Heaven. And there was evening and there was morning, a second day.

And God said: "Let the waters under the heaven be gathered together unto one place, and let the dry land appear." And it was so. And God called the dry land Earth, and the gathering together of the waters called He Seas; and God saw that it was good. And God said: "Let the earth put forth grass, herb yielding seed, and fruit-tree bearing fruit after its kind, wherein is the seed thereof, upon the earth." And it was so. And the earth brought forth grass, herb yielding seed after its kind, and tree bearing fruit, wherein is the seed thereof, after its kind; and God saw that it was good. And there was evening and there was morning, a third day.

And God said: "Let there be lights in the firmament of the heaven to divide the day from the night; and let them be for signs, and for seasons, and for days and years; and let them be for lights in the firmament of the heaven to give light upon the earth." And it was so. And God made the two great lights: the greater light to rule the day, and the lesser light to rule the night; and the stars. And God set them in the firmament of the heaven to give light upon the earth, and to rule over the day and over the night, and to divide the light from the darkness; and God saw that it was good. And there was evening and there was morning, a fourth day.

And God said: "Let the waters swarm with swarms of living creatures, and let fowl fly above the earth in the open firmament of heaven." And God created the great sea-monsters, and every living creature that creepeth, wherewith the waters swarmed, after its kind, and every winged fowl after its kind; and God saw that it was good. And God blessed them, saying: "Be fruitful, and multiply, and fill the waters in the seas, and let fowl multiply in the earth." And there was evening and there was morning, a fifth day.

And God said: "Let the earth bring forth the living creature after its kind, cattle, and creeping thing, and beast of the earth after its kind." And it was so. And God made the beast of the earth after its kind, and the cattle after their kind, and every thing that creepeth upon the ground after its kind; and God saw that it was good. And God said: "Let us make man in our image, after our likeness; and let them have dominion over the fish of

Sabbath Songs, Grace after Meals and Blessings. Prague, 1514. Ink on paper with hand-painted woodcuts. 5⅜ × 7⁷⁄₁₆" (13.6 × 18.8 cm). State Jewish Museum, Prague. *The text on this page, from one of the first Hebrew books printed in Prague, parallels the section from Genesis regarding God's resting on the seventh day of Creation. Observant Jews celebrate the Sabbath with a festive meal.*

the sea, and over the fowl of the air, and over the cattle, and over all the earth, and over every creeping thing that creepeth upon the earth." And God created man in His own image, in the image of God created He him; male and female created He them. And God blessed them; and God said unto them: "Be fruitful, and multiply, and replenish the earth, and subdue it; and have dominion over the fish of the sea, and over the fowl of the air, and over every living thing that creepeth upon the earth." And God said: "Behold, I have given you every herb yielding seed, which is upon the face of all the earth, and every tree, in which is the fruit of a tree yielding seed—to you it shall be for food; and to every beast of the earth, and to every fowl of the air, and to every thing that creepeth upon the earth, wherein there is a living soul, [I have given] every green herb for food." And it was so. And God saw every thing that He had made, and, behold, it was very good. And there was evening and there was morning, the sixth day.

And the heaven and the earth were finished, and all the host of them. And on the seventh day God finished His work which He had made; and He rested on the seventh day from all His work which He had made. And God blessed the seventh day, and hallowed it; because that in it He rested from all His work which God in creating had made.

GENESIS 2:4–3:24

The Garden of Eden

The story of the creation of Adam and Eve, the ancestors of all humanity, is set in the idyllic Garden of Eden. It is here that these first humans learn a lesson that results in their expulsion from the garden: moral transgressions remove one from a state of innocence and are not without consequence.

———————

These are the generations of the heaven and of the earth when they were created, in the day that the Lord God made earth and heaven.

No shrub of the field was yet in the earth, and no herb of the field had yet sprung up; for the Lord God had not caused it to rain upon the earth, and there was not a man to

COLORPLATE 3
Menorah from Excavated Synagogue at Eshtamua (Hebron area). 3rd century. Stone bas-relief. *The menorah, a seven-branched candelabrum, became the most important Jewish artistic motif. The Bible describes a menorah that was a prominent feature of the Tabernacle that was set up when the Israelites were wandering in the wilderness. A menorah was also a feature in the First and Second Temples in Jerusalem.*

COLORPLATE 4 *(opposite)*
Scenes from the Synagogue at Dura Europos. c. 245. Fresco. *The walls of the synagogue at Dura Europos, decorated with frescoes depicting biblical scenes, blend pagan elements with Persian and Greek influences. This fresco section from the west wall (located to the right of the Torah niche) contains a panel at the top that depicts the Ark of the Covenant in the land of the Philistines. The lower panel shows Pharaoh and the infancy of Moses.*

COLORPLATE 5
Hammath Tiberias, Floor from the Synagogue. 3rd–4th century. Mosaic. *Like the mosaic from Bet Alfa, this floor design represents the signs of the zodiac.*

COLORPLATE 6
Bet Alfa, Floor from the Synagogue. 3rd–4th century. Mosaic. *The synagogue at Bet Alfa was first excavated in 1929. The mosaic inscriptions at the entrance state that the mosaic floor was made during the reign of Emperor Justin (c. 518–527). There are three major panels. At the center of the panel reproduced here sits Helios, the Greek sun god, in his chariot. This cartouche is surrounded by the signs of the Zodiac, each with its Hebrew name above it. Busts of winged women, representing the seasons, adorn the four corners of this central panel.*

COLORPLATE 7
Gold-Glass Base of Vessel. Roman Catacombs, 4th century. Glass and gold leaf. ⅜ × 3⅞″ diameter
(.9 × 10 cm). Collection, Israel Museum, Jerusalem. Gift of Jacob Michael in memory of his wife
Erna Sondheimer–Michael.

COLORPLATE 8
Menorah from En-Gedi Synagogue. 6th
century. Bronze. Height: 5½″ (14 cm).
Collection, Israel Antiquities Authority.

COLORPLATE 9
Jewish Oil Lamp. Provenance unknown, 5–6th century. Bronze. 4⁵⁄₁₆ × 6½″ (11 × 16.5 cm).
Schloessinger Collection, Institute of Archaeology, Hebrew University, Jerusalem.

till the ground; but there went up a mist from the earth, and watered the whole face of the ground. Then the Lord God formed man of the dust of the ground, and breathed into his nostrils the breath of life; and man became a living soul. And the Lord God planted a garden eastward, in Eden; and there He put the man whom He had formed. And out of the ground made the Lord God to grow every tree that is pleasant to the sight, and good for food; the tree of life also in the midst of the garden, and the tree of the knowledge of good and evil. And a river went out of Eden to water the garden; and from thence it was parted, and became four heads. The name of the first is Pishon; that is it which compasseth the whole land of Havilah, where there is gold; and the gold of that land is good; there is bdellium and the onyx stone. And the name of the second river is Gihon; the same is it that compasseth the whole land of Cush. And the name of the third river is Tigris; that is it which goeth toward the east of Asshur. And the fourth river is the Euphrates. And the Lord God took the man, and put him into the garden of Eden to dress it and to keep it. And the Lord God commanded the man, saying: "Of every tree of the garden thou mayest freely eat; but of the tree of the knowledge of good and evil, thou shalt not eat of it; for in the day that thou eatest thereof thou shalt surely die."

And the Lord God said: "It is not good that the man should be alone; I will make him a help meet for him." And out of the ground the Lord God formed every beast of the field, and every fowl of the air; and brought them unto the man to see what he would call them; and whatsoever the man would call every living creature, that was to be the name thereof. And the man gave names to all cattle, and to the fowl of the air, and to every beast of the field; but for Adam there was not found a help meet for him. And the Lord God caused a deep sleep to fall upon the man, and he slept; and He took one of his ribs, and closed up the place with flesh instead thereof. And the rib, which the Lord God had taken from the man, made He a woman, and brought her unto the man. And the man said: "This is now bone of my bones, and flesh of my flesh; she shall be called Woman, because she was taken out of Man." Therefore shall a man leave his father and his mother, and shall cleave unto his wife, and they shall be one flesh. And they were both naked, the man and his wife, and were not ashamed.

Now the serpent was more subtle than any beast of the field which the Lord God had made. And he said unto the woman: "Yea, hath God said: Ye shall not eat of any tree of the garden?" And the woman said unto the serpent: "Of of the fruit of the trees of the garden we may eat; but of the fruit of the tree which is in the midst of the Garden, God hath said: Ye shall not eat of it, neither shall ye touch it, lest ye die." And the serpent said unto the woman: "Ye shall not surely die; for God doth know that in the day ye eat thereof, then your eyes shall be opened, and ye shall be as God, knowing good and evil." And when the woman saw that the tree was good for food, and that it was a delight to the eyes, and that the tree was to be desired to make one wise, she took of the fruit thereof, and did eat; and she gave also unto her husband with her, and he did eat. And the eyes of them both were opened, and they knew that they were naked; and they sewed fig-leaves together, and made themselves girdles. And they heard the voice of the Lord God walking in the garden toward the cool of the day; and the man and his wife hid themselves from the presence of the Lord God amongst the trees of the garden. And the Lord God called unto the man, and said unto him: "Where art thou?" And he said: "I heard Thy voice in the garden, and I was afraid, because I was naked; and I hid myself." And He said: "Who told thee that thou wast naked? Hast thou eaten of the tree, whereof I commanded thee that thou shouldest not eat?" And the man said: "The woman whom Thou gavest to be with me, she gave me of the tree, and I did eat." And the Lord God said unto the woman: "What is this thou hast done?" And the woman said: "The serpent beguiled me, and I did eat." And the Lord God said unto the serpent: "Because thou hast done this, cursed art thou from among all cattle, and from among all beasts of the field; upon thy belly shalt thou go, and dust shalt thou eat all the days of thy life. And I will put enmity between thee and the woman, and between thy seed and her seed; they shall bruise thy head, and thou shalt bruise their heel."

Unto the woman He said: "I will greatly multiply thy pain and thy travail; in pain thou shalt bring forth children; and thy desire shall be to thy husband, and he shall rule over thee."

And unto Adam He said: "Because thou hast hearkened unto the voice of thy wife, and hast eaten of the tree, of which I commanded thee, saying: Thou shalt not eat of it; cursed is the ground for thy sake; in toil shalt thou eat of it all the days of thy life. Thorns also and thistles shall it bring forth to thee; and thou shalt eat the herb of the field. In the sweat of thy face shalt thou eat bread, till thou return unto the ground; for out of it wast thou taken; for dust thou art, and unto dust shalt thou return." And the man called his wife's name Eve; because she was the mother of all living. And the Lord God made for Adam and for his wife garments of skins, and clothed them.

And the Lord God said: "Behold, the man is become as one of us, to know good and evil; and now, lest he put forth his hand, and take also of the tree of life, and eat, and live for ever." Therefore the Lord God sent him forth from the garden of Eden, to till the ground from whence he was taken. So He drove out the man; and He placed at the east of the garden of Eden the cherubim, and the flaming sword which turned every way, to keep the way to the tree of life.

REMBRANDT VAN RIJN. *Abraham Showing Hospitality to the Angel.* 1656. Etching. 6¼ × 5⅛" (16 × 13.1 cm).

GENESIS 12:1–9
Abram Answers God's Call

Abram (Abraham) and Sarai (Sarah) are the ancestors of the Hebrews. In this passage Abram answers a call from God to leave the world of his earlier life and to follow God to an unknown destination. Abram's faith in God and his separation from the world in which he was raised give rise to the view that he was also the father of monotheism.

Now the Lord said unto Abram: "Get thee out of thy country, and from thy kindred, and from thy father's house, unto the land that I will show thee. And I will make of thee a great nation, and I will bless thee, and make thy name great; and be thou a blessing. And I will bless them that bless thee, and him that curseth thee will I curse; and in thee shall all the families of the earth be blessed." So Abram went, as the Lord had spoken unto him; and Lot went with him; and Abram was seventy and five years old when he departed out of Haran. And Abram took Sarai his wife, and Lot his brother's son, and all their substance that they had gathered, and the souls that they had gotten in Haran; and they went forth to go into the land of Canaan; and into the land of Canaan they came. And Abram passed through the land unto the place of Shechem, unto the terebinth of Moreh. And the Canaanite was then in the land. And the Lord appeared unto Abram, and said: "Unto thy seed will I give this land"; and he builded there an altar unto the Lord, who appeared unto him. And he removed from thence unto the mountain on the east of Beth-el, and pitched his tent, having Beth-el on the west, and Ai on the east; and he builded there an altar unto the Lord, and called upon the name of the Lord. And Abram journeyed, going on still toward the South.

GENESIS 43:15–45:15
The Reunion of Joseph and His Brothers

The saga of Joseph and his brothers dramatically relates the complex familial rivalries and jealousies that prompt his brothers to sell him into slavery. This passage describes Joseph's encounter with his brothers after he was appointed to supervise the royal food supplies as a reward for interpreting the Pharaoh's dreams. His brothers arrive to buy grain and do not realize that this important Egyptian official is the brother they once plotted to kill. The entire Joseph cycle is a prelude to the enslavement and subsequent redemption of the Jews in Egypt, for it is Joseph's family that eventually multiplies to become the enslaved nation of Israel.

And the men took that present, and they took double money in their hand, and Benjamin; and rose up, and went down to Egypt, and stood before Joseph. And when Joseph saw Benjamin with them, he said to the steward of his house: "Bring the men into the house, and kill the beasts, and prepare the meat; for the men shall dine with me at noon." And the man did as Joseph bade; and the man brought the men into Joseph's house. And the men were afraid, because they were brought into Joseph's house; and they said: "Because

PHILIP EVERGOOD. *Joseph Sold into Slavery*. 20th century. Oil on canvas. 21 × 31½" (53.3 × 80 cm). Courtesy of private collection.

of the money that was returned in our sacks at the first time are we brought in; that he may seek occasion against us, and fall upon us, and take us for bondmen, and our asses." And they came near to the steward of Joseph's house, and they spoke unto him at the door of the house, and said: "Oh my lord, we came indeed down at the first time to buy food. And it came to pass, when we came to the lodging-place, that we opened our sacks, and, behold, every man's money was in the mouth of his sack, our money in full weight; and we have brought it back in our hand. And other money have we brought down in our hand to buy food. We know not who put our money in our sacks." And he said. "Peace be to you, fear not; your God, and the God of your father, hath given you treasure in your sacks; I had your money." And he brought Simeon out unto them. And the man brought the men into Joseph's house, and gave them water, and they washed their feet; and he gave their asses provender. And they made ready the present against Joseph's coming at noon; for they heard that they should eat bread there. And when Joseph came home, they brought him the present which was in their hand into the house, and bowed down to him to the earth. And he asked them of their welfare, and said: "Is your father well, the old man of whom ye spoke? Is he yet alive?" And they said: "Thy servant our father is well, he is yet alive." And they bowed the head, and made obeisance. And he lifted up his eyes, and saw Benjamin his brother, his mother's son, and said: "Is this your youngest brother of whom ye spoke unto me?" And he said: "God be gracious unto thee, my son." And Joseph made haste; for his heart yearned toward his brother; and he sought where to weep; and he entered into his chamber, and wept there. And he washed his face, and came out; and he refrained himself, and said: "Set on bread." And they set on for him by himself, and for them by themselves, and for the Egyptians, that did eat with him, by themselves; because the Egyptians might not eat bread with the Hebrews; for that is an abomination unto the Egyptians. And they sat before him, the first-born according to his birthright, and the youngest according to his youth; and the men marvelled one with another. And portions were taken unto them from before him; but Benjamin's portion was five times so much as any of theirs. And they drank, and were merry with him.

And he commanded the steward of his house, saying: "Fill the men's sacks with food, as much as they can carry, and put every man's money in his sack's mouth. And put my goblet, the silver goblet, in the sack's mouth of the youngest, and his corn money." And he did according to the word that Joseph had spoken. As soon as the morning was light, the men were sent away, they and their asses. And when they were gone out of the city, and were not yet far off, Joseph said unto his steward: "Up, follow after the men; and when thou dost overtake them, say unto them: Wherefore have ye rewarded evil for good? Is not this it in which my lord drinketh, and whereby he indeed divineth? ye have done evil in so doing." And he overtook them, and he spoke unto them these words. And they said unto him: "Wherefore speaketh my lord such words as these? Far be it from thy servants that they should do such a thing. Behold, the money, which we found in our sacks' mouths, we brought back unto thee out of the land of Canaan; how then should we steal out of thy lord's house silver or gold? With whomsoever of thy servants it be found, let him die, and we also will be my lord's bondmen." And he said: "Now also let it be according unto your words: he with whom it is found shall be my bondman; and ye shall be blameless." Then they hastened, and took down every man his sack to the ground, and opened every man his sack. And he searched, beginning at the eldest, and leaving off at the youngest; and the goblet was found in Benjamin's sack. Then they rent their clothes, and laded every man his ass, and returned to the city. And Judah and his brethren came to Joseph's house, and he was yet there; and they fell before him on the ground. And Joseph said unto them: "What deed is this that ye have done? know ye not that such a man as I will indeed divine?" And Judah said: "What shall we say unto my lord? what shall we speak? or how shall we clear ourselves? God hath found out the iniquity of thy servants; behold, we are my lord's bondmen, both we, and he also in whose hand the cup is found." And he said: "Far be it from me that I should do so; the man in whose hand the goblet is found, he shall be my bondman; but as for you, get you up in peace unto your father."

Then Judah came near unto him, and said: "Oh my lord, let they servant, I pray thee, speak a word in my lord's ears, and let not thine anger burn against they servant; for thou art even as Pharaoh. My lord asked his servants, saying: Have ye a father, or a brother? And we said unto my lord: We have a father, an old man, and a child of his old age, a little one; and his brother is dead, and he alone is left of his mother, and his father loveth him. And thou saidst unto thy servants: Bring him down unto me, that I may set mine eyes upon him. And we said unto my lord: The lad cannot leave his father; for if he should leave his father, his father would die. And thou saidst unto thy servants: Except your youngest brother come down with you, ye shall see my face no more. And it came to pass when we came up unto thy servant my father, we told him the words of my lord. And our father said: Go again, buy us a little food. And we said: We cannot go down; if our youngest brother be with us, then will we go down; for we may not see the man's face, except our youngest brother be with us. And thy servant my father said unto us: Ye know that my wife bore me two sons; and the one went out from me, and I said: Surely he is torn in pieces; and I have not seen him since; and if ye take this one also from me, and harm befall him, ye will bring down my gray hairs with sorrow to the grave. Now therefore when I come to thy servant my father, and the lad is not with us; seeing that his soul is bound up with the lad's soul; it will come to pass, when he seeth that the lad is not with us, that he will die; and thy servants will bring down the gray hairs of thy servant our father with sorrow to the grave. For thy servant became surety for the lad unto my father, saying: If I bring him not unto thee, then shall I bear the blame to my father for ever. Now therefore, let thy servant, I pray thee, abide instead of the lad a bondman to my lord; and let the lad go up with his brethren. For how shall I go up to my father, if the lad be not with me? lest I look upon the evil that shall come on my father."

W.T. Johnson, after an original by E. Grünewald.
Joseph and His Brothers. c. 1850. Engraving.

Then Joseph could not refrain himself before all them that stood by him; and he cried: "Cause every man to go out from me." And there stood no man with him, while Joseph made himself known unto his brethren. And he wept aloud; and the Egyptians heard, and the house of Pharaoh heard. And Joseph said unto his brethren: "I am Joseph; doth my father yet live?" And his brethren could not answer him; for they were affrighted at his presence. And Joseph said unto his brethren: "Come near to me, I pray you." And they came near. And he said: "I am Joseph your brother, whom ye sold into Egypt. And now be not grieved, nor angry with yourselves, that ye sold me hither; for God did send me before you to preserve life. For these two years hath the famine been in the land; and there are yet five years, in which there shall be neither plowing nor harvest. And God sent me before you to give you a remnant on the earth, and to save you alive for a great deliverance. So now it was not you that sent me hither, but God; and He hath made me a father to Pharaoh, and lord of all his house, and ruler over all the land of Egypt. Hasten ye, and go up to my father, and say unto him: Thus saith thy son Joseph: God hath made me lord of all Egypt; come down unto me, tarry not. And thou shalt dwell in the land of Goshen, and thou shalt be near unto me, thou, and thy children, and thy children's children, and thy flocks, and thy herds, and all that thou hast; and there will I sustain thee; for there are yet five years of famine; lest thou come to poverty, thou, and thy household, and all that thou hast. And, behold, your eyes see, and the eyes of my brother Benjamin, that it is my mouth that speaketh unto you. And ye shall tell my father of all my glory in Egypt, and of all that ye have seen; and ye shall hasten and bring down my father hither." And he fell upon his brother Benjamin's neck, and wept; and Benjamin wept upon his neck. And he kissed all his brethren, and wept upon them; and after that his brethren talked with him.

EXODUS 2:23–3:17

Moses and the Burning Bush

Moses was selected by God to lead the Israelites out of slavery in Egypt and to bring them to the land that had been promised to Abraham. Moses' experience at the burning bush is the first direct contact he had with God, an encounter that calls him to serve God. God explains the mission Moses is to undertake and what the Israelites should be told about their impending redemption.

And it came to pass in the course of those many days that the king of Egypt died; and the children of Israel sighed by reason of the bondage, and they cried, and their cry came up unto God by reason of the bondage. And God heard their groaning, and God remembered His covenant with Abraham, with Isaac, and with Jacob. And God saw the children of Israel, and God took cognizance of them.

Now Moses was keeping the flock of Jethro his father-in-law, the priest of Midian; and he led the flock to the farthest end of the wilderness, and came to the mountain of God, unto Horeb. And the angel of the Lord appeared unto him in a flame of fire out of the midst of a bush; and he looked, and, behold, the bush burned with fire, and the bush was not consumed. And Moses said: "I will turn aside now, and see this great sight, why the bush is not burnt." And when the Lord saw that he turned aside to see, God called unto him out of the midst of the bush, and said: "Moses, Moses." And he said: "Here am I." And He said: "Draw not nigh hither; put off thy shoes from off thy feet, for the place whereon thou standest is holy ground." Moreover He said: "I am the God of thy father, the God of Abraham, the God of Isaac, and the God of Jacob." And Moses hid his face; for he was afraid to look upon God. And the Lord said: "I have surely seen the affliction of My people that are in Egypt, and have heard their cry by reason of their taskmasters; for I know their pains; and I am come down to deliver them out of the hand of the Egyptians, and to bring them up out of that land unto a good land and a large, unto a land flowing with milk and honey; unto the place of the Canaanite, and the Hittite, and the Amorite, and the Perizzite, and the Hivite, and the Jebusite. And now, behold, the cry of the children of Israel is come unto Me; moreover I have seen the oppression wherewith the Egyptians oppress them. Come now therefore, and I will send thee unto Pharaoh, that thou mayest bring forth My people the children of Israel out of Egypt." And Moses said unto God: "Who am I, that I should go unto Pharaoh, and that I should bring forth the children of Israel out of Egypt?" And He said: "Certainly I will be with thee; and this shall be the token unto thee, that I have sent thee; when thou hast brought forth the people out of Egypt, ye shall serve God upon this mountain.' And Moses said unto God: "Behold, when I come unto the children of Israel, and shall say unto them: The God of your fathers hath sent me unto you; and they shall say to me: What is His name? what shall I say unto them?" And God said unto Moses: "I AM THAT I AM"; and He said: "Thus shalt thou say unto the children of Israel: I AM hath sent me unto you." And God said moreover unto Moses: "Thus shalt thou say unto the children of Israel: The Lord, the God of your fathers, the God of Abraham, the God of Isaac, and the God of Jacob, hath sent me unto you; this is My name for ever, and this is My memorial unto all generations. Go, and gather the elders of Israel together, and say unto them: The Lord, the God of your fathers, the God of Abraham, of Isaac, and of Jacob, hath appeared unto me, saying: I have surely remembered you, and seen that which is done to you in Egypt. And I have said: I will bring you up out of the affliction of Egypt unto the land of the Canaanite, and the Hittite, and the Amorite, and the Perizzite, and the Hivite, and the Jebusite, unto a land flowing with milk and honey. . . ."

EXODUS 12:29–32

The Israelites Go Free

The freeing of the Israelites from bondage in the land of Egypt is recalled continually in Jewish life. This section relates the tenth—and final—plague inflicted upon the Egyptians, the one that finally convinced Pharaoh to free the Israelites. The theme of redemption expressed here bound God and the Israelites to each other.

And it came to pass at midnight, that the Lord smote all the first-born in the land of Egypt, from the first-born of Pharaoh that sat on his throne unto the first-born of the captive that was in the dungeon; and all the first-born of cattle. And Pharaoh rose up in the night, he, and all his servants, and all the Egyptians; and there was a great cry in Egypt; for there was not a house where there was not one dead. And he called for Moses ad Aaron by night, and said: "Rise up, get you forth from among my people, both ye and the children of Israel; and go, serve the Lord, as ye have said. Take both your flocks and your herds, as ye have said, and be gone; and bless me also."

EXODUS 12:39–15:21

The Departure from Egypt

Even though Pharaoh eventually allowed the Israelites to leave, he sent his troops to pursue them after they fled. This selection describes their rapid departure and the lack of time for their bread to rise before it was baked. Consequently, unleavened bread, or matzot, *became their staple for the journey. Once the Israelites had crossed through the divided waters of the Red Sea (or, according to later translations, the Sea of Reeds), they were free to glorify the Lord with a new song of praise. Today Jews commemorate this release from bondage on Passover by eating the unleavened bread, as did their ancestors.*

And they baked unleavened cakes of the dough which they brought forth out of Egypt, for it was not leavened; because they were thrust out of Egypt, and could not tarry, neither had they prepared for themselves any victual. . . .

And Moses said unto the people: "Remember this day, in which ye came out from Egypt, out of the house of bondage; for by strength of hand the Lord brought you out from this place; there shall no leavened bread be eaten. This day ye go forth in the month Abib. And it shall be when the Lord shall bring thee into the land of the Canaanite, and the Hittite, and the Amorite, and the Hivite, and the Jebusite, which He swore unto thy fathers to give thee, a land flowing with milk and honey, that thou shalt keep this service in this month. Seven days thou shalt eat unleavened bread, and in the seventh day shall be a feast to the Lord. Unleavened bread shall be eaten throughout the seven days; and there shall no leavened bread be seen with thee, neither shall there be leaven seen with thee, in all thy borders. And thou shalt tell they son in that day, saying: It is because of that which the Lord did for me when I came forth out of Egypt. And it shall be for a

אנכי יהוה אלהיך
אשר הוצאתיך
מארץ מצרים
מבית עבדים

BEN SHAHN. *The First Commandment.* 1967. Watercolor and gold on paper. 32 × 26″ (81.3 × 66 cm). Kennedy Galleries, New York. © Estate of Ben Shahn/VAGA, New York. 1992.

sign unto thee upon thy hand, and for a memorial between thine eyes, that the law of the Lord may be in thy mouth; for with a strong hand hath the Lord brought thee out of Egypt. Thou shalt therefore keep this ordinance in its season from year to year.

And it shall be when the Lord shall bring thee into the land of the Canaanite, as He swore unto thee and to thy fathers, and shall give it thee, that thou shalt set apart unto the Lord all that openeth the womb; every firstling that is a male, which thou hast coming of a beast, shall be the Lord's. And every firstling of an ass thou shalt redeem with a lamb; and if thou wilt not redeem it, then thou shalt break its neck; and all the first-born of man among thy sons shalt thou redeem. And it shall be when thy son asketh thee in time to come, saying: What is this? that thou shalt say unto him: By strength of hand the Lord brought us out from Egypt, from the house of bondage; and it came to pass, when Pharaoh would hardly let us go that the Lord slew all the first-born in the land of Egypt, both the first-born of man, and the first-born of beast; therefore I sacrifice to the Lord all that openeth the womb, being males; but all the first-born of my sons I redeem. And it shall be for a sign upon thy hand, and for frontlets between thine eyes; for by strength of hand the Lord brought us forth out of Egypt."

And it came to pass, when Pharaoh had let the people go, that God led them not by the way of the land of the Philistines, although that was near; for God said: "Lest peradventure the people repent when they see war, and they return to Egypt." But God led the people about, by the way of the wilderness by the Red Sea; and the children of Israel went up armed out of the land of Egypt. And Moses took the bones of Joseph with him; for he had straitly sworn the children of Israel, saying: "God will surely remember you; and ye shall carry up my bones away hence with you." And they took their journey from Succoth, and encamped in Etham, in the edge of the wilderness. And the Lord went before them by day in a pillar of cloud, to lead them the way; and by night in a pillar of fire, to give them light; that they might go by day and by night: the pillar of cloud by day, and the pillar of fire by night, departed not from before the people.

And the Lord spoke unto Moses, saying: "Speak unto the children of Israel, that they turn back and encamp before Pi-hahiroth, between Migdol and the sea, before Baal-zephon, over against it shall ye encamp by the sea. And Pharaoh will say of the children of Israel: They are entangled in the land, the wilderness hath shut them in. And I will harden Pharaoh's heart, and he shall follow after them; and I will get Me honour upon Pharaoh, and upon all his host; and the Egyptians shall know that I am the Lord." And they did so. And it was told the king of Egypt that the people were fled; and the heart of Pharaoh and of his servants was turned towards the people, and they said: "What is this we have done, that we have let Israel go from serving us?" And he made ready his chariots, and took his people with him. And he took six hundred chosen chariots, and all the chariots of Egypt, and captains over all of them. And the Lord hardened the heart of Pharaoh king of Egypt, and he pursued after the children of Israel; for the children of Israel went out with a high hand. And the Egyptians pursued after them, all the horses and chariots of Pharaoh, and his horsemen, and his army, and overtook them encamping by the sea, beside Pi-hahiroth, in front of Baal-zephon. And when Pharaoh drew nigh, the children of Israel lifted up their eyes, and, behold, the Egyptains were marching after them; and they were sore afraid; and the children of Israel cried out unto the Lord. And they said unto Moses: "Because there were no graves in Egypt, hast thou taken us away to die in the wilderness? wherefore hast thou dealt thus with us, to bring us forth out of Egypt? Is not this the word that we spoke unto thee in Egypt, saying: Let us alone, that we may serve the Egyptians? For it were better for us to serve the Egyptians, than that we should die in the wilderness." And Moses said unto the people: "Fear ye not, stand still, and see the salvation of the Lord, which He will work for you to-day; for whereas ye have seen the Egyptians to-day, ye shall see them again no more for ever. The Lord will fight for you, and ye shall hold your peace."

And the Lord said unto Moses: "Wherefore criest thou unto Me? speak unto the children of Israel, that they go forward. And lift thou up thy rod, and stretch out they hand over the sea, and divide it; and the children of Israel shall go into the midst of the sea on dry ground. And I, behold, I will harden the hearts of the Egyptians, and they shall go in after them; and I will get Me honour upon Pharaoh, and upon all his host, upon his chariots, and upon his horsemen. And the Egyptians shall know that I am the Lord, when I have gotten Me honour upon Pharaoh, upon his chariots, and upon his horsemen." And the angel of God, who went before the camp of Israel, removed and went behind them; and the pillar of cloud removed from before them, and stood behind them; and it came between the camp of Egypt and the camp of Israel; and there was the cloud and the darkness here, yet gave it light by night there; and the one came not near the other all the night. And Moses stretched out his hand over the sea; and the Lord caused the sea to go back by a strong east wind all the night, and made the sea dry land, and the waters were divided. And the children of Israel went into the midst of the sea upon the dry ground, and the waters were a wall unto them on their right hand, and on their left. And the Egyptians pursued, and went in after them into the midst of the sea, all Pharaoh's horses, his chariots, and his horsemen. And it came to pass in the morning watch, that the Lord looked forth upon the host of the Egyptians through the pillar of fire and of cloud, and discomfited the host of the Egyptians. And He took off their chariot

Moses Crossing the Red Sea. 15th century. Woodcut from the Gutenberg Bible. *In this illustration from the famous early Bible, Moses is depicted as having horns. The horns have their origin in the Vulgate (Latin translation of the Bible), in which the verb "sent forth beams" is mistranslated as "horns."*

wheels, and made them to drive heavily; so that the Egyptians said: "Let us flee from the face of Israel; for the Lord fighteth for them against the Egyptians."

And the Lord said unto Moses: "Stretch out they hand over the sea, that the waters may come back upon the Egyptians, upon their chariots, and upon their horsemen." And Moses stretched forth his hand over the sea, and the sea returned to its strength when the morning appeared; and the Egyptians fled against it; and the Lord overthrew the Egyptians in the midst of the sea. And the waters returned, and covered the chariots, and the horsemen, even all the host of Pharaoh that went in after them in to the sea; there remained not so much as one of them. But the children of Israel walked upon dry land in the midst of the sea; and the waters were a wall unto them on their right hand, and on their left. Thus the Lord saved Israel that day out of the hand of the Egyptians; and Israel saw the Egyptians dead upon the sea-shore. And Israel saw the great work which the Lord did upon the Egyptians, and the people feared the Lord; and they believed in the Lord, and in His servant Moses.

Then sang Moses and the children of Israel this song unto the Lord, and spoke, saying:

I will sing unto the Lord, for He is highly exalted;
The horse and his rider hath He thrown into the sea.
The Lord is my strength and song, And He is become my salvation;
This is my God, and I will glorify Him;
My father's God, and I will exalt Him.
The Lord is a man of war,
The Lord is His name.
Pharaoh's chariots and his host hath He cast into the sea,
And his chosen captains are sunk in the Red Sea.
The deeps cover them—
They went down into the depths like a stone.
Thy right hand, O Lord, glorious in power,
They right hand, O Lord, dasheth in pieces the enemy.
And in the greatness of Thine excellency Thou overthrowest them that
    rise up against Thee;
Thou sendest forth Thy wrath, it consumeth them as stubble.
And with the blast of Thy nostrils the waters were piled up—
The floods stood upright as a heap;
The deeps were congealed in the heart of the sea.

The enemy said:
"I will pursue, I will overtake, I will divide the spoil;
My lust shall be satisfied upon them;
I will draw my sword, my hand shall destroy them."
Thou didst blow with Thy wind, the sea covered them;
They sank as lead in the mighty waters.
Who is like unto Thee, O Lord, among the mighty?
Who is like unto Thee, glorious in holiness,
Fearful in praises, doing wonders?
Thou stretchedst out Thy right hand—
The earth swallowed them.
Thou in Thy love hast led the people that Thou hast redeemed;
Thou hast guided them in Thy strength to Thy holy habitation.
The peoples have heard, they tremble;
Pangs have taken hold on the inhabitants of Philistia.
Then were the chiefs of Edom affrighted;
The mighty men of Moab, trembling taketh hold upon them;
All the inhabitants of Canaan are melted away.
Terror and dread falleth upon them;
By the greatness of Thine arm they are as still as a stone;
Till Thy people pass over, O Lord,
Till the people pass over that Thou hast gotten.
Thou bringest them in, and plantest them in the mountain of Thine
    inheritance,
The place, O Lord, which Thou hast made for Thee to dwell in,
The sanctuary, O Lord, which Thy hands have established.
The Lord shall reign for ever and ever.

For the horses of Pharaoh went in with his chariots and with his horsemen into the sea, and the Lord brought back the waters of the sea upon them; but the children of Israel walked on dry land in the midst of the sea.

And Miriam the prophetess, the sister of Aaron, took a timbrel in her hand; and all the women went out after her with timbrels and with dances. And Miriam sang unto them:

Sing ye to the Lord, for He is highly exalted:
The horse and his rider hath He thrown into the sea.

EXODUS 19:1–20:17

The Ten Commandments

In this famous biblical passage, Moses is told of the special covenant between God and the Jewish people, and his responsibility to carry God's words to the Israelites. The Ten Commandments are enumerated twice in the Pentateuch—in Exodus and in Deuteronomy—with slight variations between the two. The text from Exodus emphasizes the redemption motif initiated in the Exodus. Rabbinic tradition holds that despite the differences between the texts, God gave both in one utterance. The Ten Commandments have had a profound effect on western legal and moral traditions.

In the third month after the children of Israel were gone forth out of the land of Egypt, the same day came they into the wilderness of Sinai. And when they were departed from

Moses Receives the Tables of the Law; Moses Presents Them to the People. From the Bible of Montier-Grandval. Mid-9th century. Miniature on parchment. 16 × 11½" (40.6 × 29.2 cm). British Museum, London.

Rephidim, and were come to the wilderness of Sinai, they encamped in the wilderness; and there Israel encamped before the mount. And Moses went up unto God, and the Lord called unto him out of the mountain, saying: "Thus shalt thou say to the house of Jacob, and tell the children of Israel: Ye have seen what I did unto the Egyptians, and how I bore you on eagles' wings, and brought you unto Myself. Now therefore, if ye will hearken unto My voice indeed, and keep My covenant, then ye shall be Mine own treasure from among all peoples; for all the earth is Mine: and ye shall be unto Me a kingdom of priests, and a holy nation. These are the words which thou shalt speak unto the children of Israel." And Moses came and called for the elders of the people, and set before them all these words which the Lord commanded him. And all the people answered together, and said: "All that the Lord hath spoken we will do." And Moses reported the words of the people unto the Lord. And the Lord said unto Moses: "Lo, I come unto thee in a thick cloud, that the people may hear when I speak with thee, and may also believe thee for ever." And Moses told the words of the people unto the Lord. And the Lord said unto Moses: "Go unto the people, and sanctify them to-day and to-morrow, and let them wash their garments, and be ready against the third day; for the third day the Lord will come down in the sight of all the people upon mount Sinai. And thou shalt set bounds unto the people round about, saying: Take heed to yourselves, that ye go not up into the mount, or touch the border of it; whosoever toucheth the mount shall be surely put to death; no hand shall touch him, but he shall surely be stoned, or shot through; whether it be beast or man, it shall not live; when the ram's horn soundeth long, they shall come up to the mount." And Moses went down from the mount unto the people, and sanctified the people; and they washed their garments. And he said unto the people: "Be ready against the third day; come not near a woman." And it came to pass on the third day, when it was morning, that there were thunders and lightnings and a thick cloud upon the mount, and the voice of a horn exceeding loud; and all the people that were in the camp trembled. And Moses brought forth the people out of the camp to meet God; and they stood at the nether part of the mount. Now mount Sinai was altogether on smoke, because the Lord descended upon it in fire; and the smoke thereof ascended as the smoke of a furnace, and the whole mount quaked greatly. And when the voice of the horn waxed louder and louder, Moses spoke, and God answered him by a voice. And the Lord came down upon mount Sinai, to the top of the mount; and the Lord called Moses to the top of the mount; and Moses went up. And the Lord said unto Moses: "Go down, charge the people, lest they break through unto the Lord to gaze, and many of them perish. And let the priests also, that come near to the Lord, sanctify themselves, lest the Lord break forth upon them." And Moses said unto the Lord: "The people cannot come up to mount Sinai; for thou didst charge us, saying: Set bounds about the mount, and sanctify it." And the Lord said unto him: "Go, get thee down, and thou shalt come up, thou, and Aaron with thee; but let not the priests and the people break through to come up unto the Lord, lest He break forth upon them." So Moses went down unto the people, and told them.

And God spoke all these words, saying:

I am the Lord thy God, who brought thee out of the land of Egypt, out of the house of bondage.

Thou shalt have no other gods before me. Thou shalt not make unto thee a graven image, nor any manner of likeness, of any thing that is in heaven above, or that is in the earth beneath, or that is in the water under the earth; thou shalt not bow down unto them, nor serve them; for I the Lord thy God am a jealous God, visiting the iniquity of the fathers upon the children unto the third and fourth generation of them that hate Me; and showing mercy unto the thousandth generation of them that love Me and keep My commandments.

Thou shalt not take the name of the Lord thy God in vain; for the Lord will not hold him guiltless that taketh His name in vain.

Remember the sabbath day, to keep it holy. Six days shalt thou labour, and do all thy work; but the seventh day is a sabbath unto the Lord thy God, in it thou shalt not do any manner of work, thou, nor thy son, nor thy daughter, nor thy man-servant, nor thy maid-servant, nor thy cattle, nor thy stranger that is within thy gates; for in six days the Lord made heaven and earth, the sea, and all that in them is, and rested on the seventh day; wherefore the Lord blessed the sabbath day, and hallowed it.

Honour thy father and thy mother, that thy days may be long upon the land which the Lord thy God giveth thee.

Thou shalt not murder.

Thou shalt not commit adultery.

Thou shalt not steal.

Thou shalt not bear false witness against thy neighbour.

Thou shalt not covet thy neighbor's house; thou shalt not covet thy neighbour's wife, nor his man-servant, nor his maid-servant, nor his ox, nor his ass, nor any thing that is thy neighbour's.

And all the people perceived the thunderings, and the lightnings, and the voice of the horn, and the mountain smoking; and when the people saw it, they trembled, and stood afar off. And they said unto Moses: "Speak thou with us, and we will hear; but let not God speak with us, lest we die." And Moses said unto the people: "Fear not; for God is come to prove you, and that His fear may be before you, that ye sin not."

LEVITICUS 19:1-37
The Holiness Code

The book of Leviticus is primarily concerned with priestly matters and places great emphasis on ritual purity. This passage extends the idea of purity from the ritual to the moral realm. The second verse of this chapter, "You shall be holy; for I the Lord your God am holy," gives the rationale for the text that follows. The concept of imitatio dei *inspires people to follow such moral and ethical commands, for only by such imitation can man himself be made holy.*

And the Lord spoke unto Moses, saying: Speak unto all the congregation of the children of Israel, and say unto them:

Ye shall be holy; for I the Lord your God am holy. Ye shall fear every man his mother, and his father, and ye shall keep My sabbaths: I am the Lord your God. Turn ye not unto the idols, nor make to yourselves molten gods: I am the Lord your God.

And when ye offer a sacrifice of peace-offerings unto the Lord, ye shall offer it that ye may be accepted. It shall be eaten the same day ye offer it, and on the morrow; and if aught remain until the third day, it shall be burnt with fire. And if it be eaten at all on the third day, it is a vile thing; it shall not be accepted. But every one that eateth it shall bear his iniquity, because he hath profaned the holy thing of the Lord; and that soul shall be cut off from his people.

And when ye reap the harvest of your land, thou shalt not wholly reap the corner of thy field, neither shalt thou gather the gleaning of thy harvest. And thou shalt not glean thy vineyard, neither shalt thou gather the fallen fruit of thy vineyard; thou shalt leave them for the poor and for the stranger: I am the Lord your God. Ye shall not steal; neither shall ye deal falsely, nor lie one to another. And ye shall not swear by My name falsely, so that thou profane the name of thy God: I am the Lord. Thou shalt not oppress thy neighbour, nor rob him; the wages of a hired servant shall not abide with thee all night until the morning. Thou shalt not curse the deaf, nor put a stumbling-block before the

Copied by SIMHAH BEN SAMUEL HA-LEVI. Illustration at the end of Leviticus from the *Coburg Pentateuch.* 1385. Add. Ms. 19776. fol 72v. Vellum. 11⅜ × 8⅝" (28.9 × 21.9 cm). By permission of the British Library, London. *This 14th-century illustration of a teacher and his pupil displays the maxim from the Talmud "What is hateful to you, do not to your neighbor: that is the whole Torah, while the rest is commentary thereof."*

blind, but thou shalt fear thy God: I am the Lord. Ye shall do no unrighteousness in judgment; thou shalt not respect the person of the poor, nor favour the person of the mighty; but in righteousness shalt thou judge thy neighbour. Thou shalt not go up and down as a talebearer among thy people; neither shalt thou stand idly by the blood of thy neighbour: I am the Lord. Thou shalt not hate thy brother in thy heart; thou shalt surely rebuke thy neighbour, and not bear sin because of him. Thou shalt not take vengeance, nor bear any grudge against the children of thy people, but thou shalt love thy neighbour as thyself: I am the Lord. Ye shall keep My statutes. Thou shalt not let thy cattle gender with a diverse kind; thou shalt not sow thy field with two kinds of seed; neither shall there come upon thee a garment of two kinds of stuff mingled together. And whosoever lieth carnally with a woman, that is a bondmaid, designated for a man, and not at all redeemed, nor was freedom given her; there shall be inquisition; they shall not be put to death, because she was not free. And he shall bring his forfeit unto the Lord, unto the door of the tent of meeting, even a ram for a guilt-offering. And the priest shall make atonement for him with the ram of the guilt-offering before the Lord for his sin which he hath sinned; and he shall be forgiven for his sin which he hath sinned.

And when ye shall come into the land, and shall have planted all manner of trees for food, then ye shall count the fruit thereof as forbidden; three years shall it be as forbidden unto you; it shall not be eaten. And in the fourth year all the fruit thereof shall be holy, for giving praise unto the Lord. But in the fifth year may ye eat of the fruit thereof, that it may yield unto you more richly the increase thereof: I am the Lord your God. Ye shall not eat with the blood; neither shall ye practise divination nor soothsaying. Ye shall not round the corners of your heads, neither shalt thou mar the corners of thy beard. Ye shall not make any cuttings in your flesh for the dead, nor imprint any marks upon you: I am the Lord. Profane not thy daughter, to make her a harlot, lest the land fall into harlotry, and the land become full of lewdness. Ye shall keep My sabbaths, and reverence My sanctuary: I am the Lord. Turn ye not unto the ghosts, nor unto familiar spirits; seek them not out, to be defiled by them: I am the Lord your God. Thou shalt rise up before the hoary head, and honour the face of the old man, and thou shalt fear thy God: I am the Lord. And if a stranger sojourn with thee in your land, ye shall not do him wrong. The stranger that sojourneth with you shall be unto you as the home-born among you, and thou shalt love him as thyself; for ye were strangers in the land of Egypt: I am the Lord your God. Ye shall do no unrighteousness in judgment, in meteyard, in weight, or in measure. Just balances, just weights, a just ephah, and a just hin, shall ye have: I am the Lord your God, who brought you out of the land of Egypt. And ye shall observe all My statutes, and all Mine ordinances, and do them: I am the Lord.

DEUTERONOMY 6:1–25
The Observance of the Commandments

The Shema (Hear, O Israel . . . and upon thy gates), proclaiming allegiance to God, is considered the central article of faith of the Jewish people and serves an integral role in Jewish liturgy. It is recited daily in the morning and the evening, and its verses are inscribed on parchment and encased in mezuzot on the doorposts of Jewish homes. The words of the Shema are also encased within the boxes of the tefillin (phylacteries).

Now this is the commandment, the statutes, and the ordinances, which the Lord your God commanded to teach you, that ye might do them in the land whither ye go over to

זה המטרה ואהרן הטהץ שמן בנירות

COLORPLATE 10
Aaron Pouring Oil into One of the Lamps of the Menorah. Northern France, late 13th century. Add. ms. 11639 fol. 114r.
Vellum. 6⅜ × 4¾″ (16.2 × 12.1 cm). By permission of the British Library, London.

COLORPLATE 11 *(opposite)*
Workshop of the Scribe Hayyim. *Initial-Word Panel of Genesis.* From the *Schocken Bible.* 13th century. Ms. 14940 fol. 1v. Parchment. 8⅜ × 6″ (22 × 15 cm). Schocken Institute for Jewish Research of the Jewish Theological Seminary of America, Jerusalem. *This illuminated Bible contains thirty-five initial-word panels, one at the opening of each book of the Bible. In this opening page of Genesis, medallions with biblical illustrations surround the initial word.*

COLORPLATE 12
Moses Receiving and Bringing the Tables of the Law to His People. From the *Regensburg Pentateuch.* Germany, 1300. Ms. 1 80/52. Parchment. 9¹³⁄₁₆ × 7⁷⁄₁₆″ (24.5 × 18.5 cm). Collection, Israel Museum, Jerusalem. *The illustrations in this Pentateuch are noteworthy. Unlike most illuminations from South Germany at this time, the people are depicted here with human, rather than animal or distorted, heads.*

COLORPLATE 13
LEVI BAR ISAAC "HIJO" CARO. *Seated Figure Holding an Astrolabe.* From *Moreh Nevukhim (Guide for the Perplexed)* by Rabbi Moses ben Maimon (Maimonides). Barcelona, 1348. Cod. Hebr. 37 fol. 114r. Vellum. 7⅝ × 5¼″ (19.5 × 13.3 cm). Royal Library, Department of Hebraica and Judaica, Copenhagen. *The text is a Hebrew translation of Maimonides's manuscript, which was originally written in Arabic.*

COLORPLATE 14

Workshop of the Scribe Hayyim. *The Illuminated First Word of Deuteronomy.* From the *Duke of Sussex Pentateuch.* South Germany, c. 1300. Fine vellum. 9 × 6⅜" (22.8 × 16.2 cm). Add. ms. 15282 fol. 238v. By permission of the British Library, London. *An initial-word panel begins each of the five books in this beautifully illuminated Pentateuch from South Germany. This initial-word panel of the book of Deuteronomy features the word "eleh" (which begins the book of Deuteronomy) at its center, written in the square Ashkenazi script of this manuscript. Architectural motifs adapted from contemporary German churches surround the page. A six-pointed star, which at this time was not an exclusively Jewish symbol, appears below the initial word. Zoomorphic grotesques are another main feature of the decoration.*

COLORPLATE 15

Workshop of the Scribe Hayyim. *Full-Page Initial-Word Panel to the Book of Numbers.* From the *Duke of Sussex Pentateuch.* South Germany, c. 1300. Fine vellum. 9 × 6⅜" (22.8 × 16.2 cm). Add. ms. 15282 fol. 179v. By permission of the British Library, London. *In this opening page to the Book of Numbers, four monsters and four knights surround the first word. The knights carry banners representing four of the tribes of Israel: the lion symbolizes the tribe of Judah; the eagle stands for the tribe of Reuben; the bull represents Ephraim; and the serpent symbolizes the tribe of Dan.*

COLORPLATE 16 *(opposite)*

Initial-Word Panel Illumination Showing a Marriage Ceremony. From the *Hamburg Halakhah Miscellany.* Padua, 1476–1477. Codex Hebrew 337 (Scrin 132) fol. 75v. Vellum. 6 × 4½" (15.3 × 11.7 cm). Staats- und Universitätsbibliothek, Hamburg. *The Hamburg Halakhah Miscellany contains treatises on dietary laws and laws pertaining to women. In this wedding scene, the groom places a wedding ring on his bride's hand. A white circle, or Jewish badge, can be seen on the groom's coat.*

האיש אשר לא הלך בעצת רשעים ובדרך חטאים לא עמ
עמד ובמושכ לנים לא ישב כי אם בתורת יהוה חפצו וב

COLORPLATE 17
Ashrei Ha'ish (Blessed Is the Man), Initial-Word Panel of the Book of Psalms. From the *Rothschild Miscellany.* Northern Italy, 1450–1470. Vellum. 8¼ × 6⅝″ (21 × 16 cm). The Israel Museum, Jerusalem. *King David, the traditional author of the Psalter, is shown playing his lyre in the initial-word panel.*

COLORPLATE 18
Doctor Bleeding a Patient. From the *Cambridge Medical Miscellany.* 15th century. Vellum. 10⅝ × 8⅝″ (27 × 22 cm). Ms. Dd. 10.68 fol. 211r. By permission of the Syndics of Cambridge University Library, England. *Illustrated medical books were widespread among the Jews during the 14th and 15th centuries.*

COLORPLATE 20

Birds' Head Haggadah. Germany, c. 1300. Ms. 180/57. Vellum. 10⅝ × 7⅛″ (27 × 18.5 cm). Collection, Israel Museum, Jerusalem. *The Birds' Head Haggadah is the earliest extant illuminated German Haggadah. The illustrations, which are marginal for the most part, follow the text of the Haggadah; there is a full-page miniature at the beginning of the Haggadah and another at the end. The pages shown here are the hymn "Dayyeinu." The illustrations on the left-hand page depict Moses standing on Mount Sinai to receive two tablets from the hand of God; he passes five others (representing the Five Books of Moses) to the people below. On the right-hand page, figures gather manna and quails falling from heaven. The representation of the figures with animal heads is typical of South German manuscripts of the period.*

COLORPLATE 19 *(opposite)*

A Jew Touching the Mezuzah. From the *Rothschild Miscellany.* Northern Italy, 1450–1470. Vellum. 8¼ × 6⅝″ (21 × 16 cm). Ms. 180/51. Collection, Israel Museum, Jerusalem. *A mezuzah is affixed to the right doorpost at the entry to a Jewish home and is slanted so that the top of the mezuzah points inward toward the house. According to tradition, a person touches the mezuzah and then touches his fingers to his lips upon entering or leaving the home.*

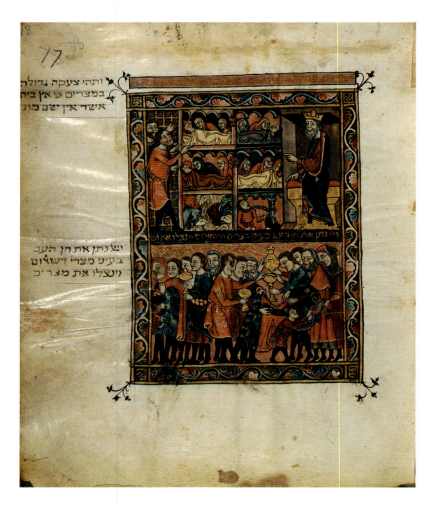

18
17

ותהי צעקה גדלה
במצרים כי אין בית
אשר אין שם מת

יש נתן את חן העב
בעיני מצרי וישלום
וינצלו את מצרים

COLORPLATES 21 AND 22

The Plagues of Egypt. From *The Rylands Haggadah.* Mid–14th century. Vellum. 11³⁄₁₆ × 9³⁄₁₆″ (28 × 23 cm). Rylands Hebrew Ms. 6 fols. 17v, 18r. Reproduced by courtesy of the Director and University Librarian, the John Rylands University Library of Manchester, England. *Unlike some other examples from this period, the iconography of the biblical illustrations in this Spanish Haggadah closely follows the story. The upper register on the page at the left and the scenes on the page at right depict three of the ten plagues inflicted upon the Egyptians: locusts, darkness, and the death of the Egyptian firstborn males. The bottom register on the left-hand page illustrates the Israelites collecting valuables from the Egyptians.*

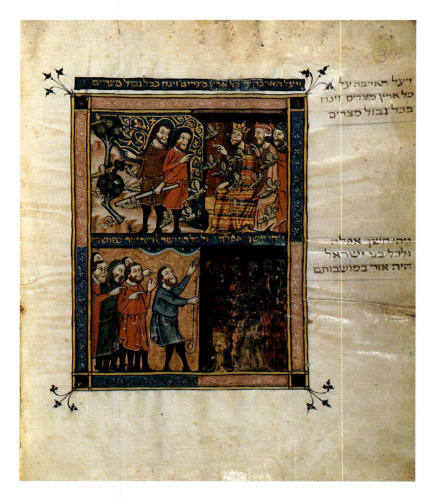

ויעל הארבה על כל ארץ מצרים וינח בכל גבול מצרים
כל ארץ מצרים וינח
בכל גבול מצרים

ויהי חשך אפלה
ולכל בני ישראל
היה אור במושבותם

COLORPLATE 23
A Hazzan in a Spanish Synagogue Reading the Haggadah. From the "Sister" to the *Golden Haggadah.*
Spain, 14th century. Or. ms. 2884 fol. 17v. Parchment. 9⅛ × 7½″ (23.3 × 19 cm). By permission
of the British Library, London.

אדמקרא שמת לחיות ולבהמות
אדם ואשתו ערומים

נחואשתו ובני יוצאים מן התיבה
ועהלך אל מבל חי מחברו
קיותאל מריים מעה

COLORPLATE 24

The Creation and Temptation of Eve. From the *Golden Haggadah*. Spain, c. 1320. Add. ms. 227210 fol. 2v. Vellum. 9¾ × 7¾″ (24.7 × 19.5 cm). By permission of the British Library, London. *The miniatures from this early Spanish Haggadah depict scenes from Genesis and Exodus. The scene at the upper left shows Eve emerging from the slumbering Adam, as well as Adam and Eve about to be cast out from the Garden of Eden.*

COLORPLATE 25

Initial-Word Panel of Psalm 114. From the *Kaufmann Haggadah.* Spain, late 14th century. Ms. A422
fol. 43r. Vellum. 8¾ × 7½" (22 × 19 cm). Library of the Hungarian Academy of Sciences,
Kaufmann Collection, Budapest. *Psalm 114 is one of the Psalms recited during the Passover Seder. In this
illumination from a 14th-century Spanish Haggadah, Moses leads the Israelites to freedom, while Pharaoh,
mounted on a horse on the far right, pursues them. The small dog in the left foreground recalls the verse "but
not a dog shall snarl at any of the Israelites" (Exodus 11:7).*

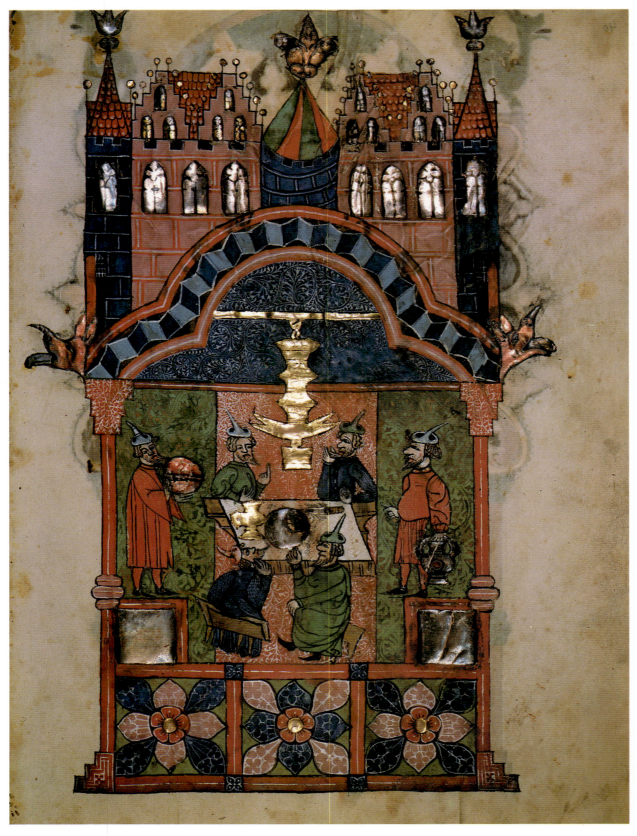

COLORPLATE 26
Passover Eve Table with Seated Men Reading the Haggadah. From the *Erna Michael Haggadah*. South Germany, early 15th century. Ms. 180/58 fol. 40. Vellum. 13¾ × 10⅛" (35 × 25.5 cm). The Israel Museum, Jerusalem. Gift to museum by Jakob Michael in memory of his wife Erna.

COLORPLATE 27 *(opposite)*
Baking of Matzot. From the *Rothschild Miscellany*. Northern Italy, 1470. Vellum. 8¼ × 6⅝" (21 × 16 cm). Israel Museum, Jerusalem.

פה רליטוש בל הדובל מית חמץ
בפסח מבתחלת ליל חדשה
עשיר ועד סוף יום יהוד ועבשלים מכן
בזודר חייבכיה שב כל מועל חמץ

הלמות חמץ ומצה
מהרמבם זצל

הזולך סרו סלפסה והאגרה

חורש יחוץ כרפס יחץ רחבר רחצה רופיונעה
מרור מך שלחן עוך טרוו בך והלל ברצה כל
יוחר

קרוס עבירה מכפא יבנב היו לחורץ נטילה הרחימן
צך יהנה רצך

מעבד פהה סרוך לוכתבת רוהשין לו יום יודע עד הריוסן וצבחיו וחבת
רחשוך ווזבן לו כס רוטשן

יוחר תפלת עובבת צריך עריך לתחתון עד שיהא ורדילה ורן יסבן מ
שלחן וחסרים כס לבב ה יוחר וירחר ורוב לסבן בך יוחר מייחרן לוכם
ונפבו המבל הבת יסרון גם הקעשה ונה הבל ריעות תרוסורעות ושם ור
ייזתה וויחתה שיט לה גבחוטב ישטרו תחלה בקעשה כר שתהין תחתור
ורין הכנרות השלישית וויחתה שיט לה בסירוכם ישרשם עליה והך
הכריות הרליעינצת גם יוחר בקעשה מרו הריחת רהייען מרור שהמל לוטך ובם ויחבך ר
יום קירבל יוו עשב מת טהרך לוך גם יהוף פה השט תבשילין ח
כבן ביום יעלה וחנום מבר מהחרוצב על יום חתיבה יחוחת בך
יה מה בל שם חרוסת גם יסרר לבחו רשו חורוץ בלי לבבל רושן
רטוכ לטול לבחול רב יריהם קהום שיסבר יחך בלח בבה וכל יוחר וריחר מוחו
למטן והרח התכרו מס רושטן והריחובבנב מסות ווזחיל הנבל תי
הבת ווהטרש

וזה נוסח הקידוש
שבת יוחר תל ... ...
ויכלו

יום הוו

COLORPLATE 28
Moses Leading the Israelites through the Red Sea. From the Haggadah in the *Hamburg Miscellany*. Mainz, 1427.
Vellum. $11\frac{7}{8} \times 9''$ (30 × 22 cm). Cod. Heb. 37 fol. 29v. Staats– und Universitätsbibliothek, Hamburg.

רבונו של עולם הריני מוחל לכל מי שהכעיס והקניט אותי
או שהטא כנגריבין בגופי בין ממוני בין בכבורי · בין
בכל אשר לי בין כאונס בין ברצון בין בשוגג בין במזיד בין בדבור
בין במעשה בין בגלגול זה בין בגלגול אחר לכל בר ישרא ולא יענש·
שוב ארם בסבתי : יהיר צונמרלפניך יי · אוא שלא אחטא ומה ש
שחטאתי מחוק ברחמיך הרבים ולא על יסורין ; יהיו לרצון אמרי
פי והגיון לבי לפניך יי צורי וגואלי ⁕

*Kriyat Shema, from
Seder Berachot. Vienna,
1724. Mic 8232.
Courtesy of the Jewish
Theological Seminary
of America, New York.*

possess it—that thou mightest fear the Lord thy God, to keep all His statutes and His commandments, which I command thee, thou, and thy son, and thy son's son, all the days of thy life; and that thy days may be prolonged. Hear therefore, O Israel, and observe to do it; that it may be well with thee, and that ye may increase mightily, as the Lord, the God of thy fathers, hath promised unto thee—a land flowing with milk and honey.

Hear, O Israel: the Lord our God, the Lord is one. And thou shalt love the Lord thy God with all thy heart, and with all thy soul, and with all thy might. And these words, which I command thee this day, shall be upon thy heart; and thou shalt teach them diligently unto thy children, and shalt talk of them when thou sittest in thy house, and when thou walkest by the way, and when thou liest down, and when thou risest up. And thou shalt bind them for a sign upon thy hand, and they shall be for frontlets between thine eyes. And thou shalt write them upon the door-posts of thy house, and upon thy gates.

And it shall be, when the Lord thy God shall bring thee into the land which He swore unto thy fathers, to Abraham, to Isaac, and to Jacob, to give thee—great and goodly cities, which thou didst not build, and houses full of all good things, which thou didst not fill, and cisterns hewn out, which thou didst not hew, vineyards and olive-trees, which thou didst not plant, and thou shalt eat and be satisfied—then beware lest thou forget the Lord, who brought thee forth out of the land of Egypt, out of the house of bondage. Thou shalt fear the Lord thy God; and Him shalt thou serve, and by His name shalt thou swear. Ye shall not go after other gods, of the gods of the peoples that are round about you; for a jealous God, even the Lord thy God, is in the midst of thee; lest the anger of the Lord thy God be kindled against thee, and He destroy thee from off the face of the earth.

Ye shall not try the Lord your God, as ye tried Him in Massah. Ye shall diligently keep the commandments of the Lord your God, and His testimonies, and His statutes, which He hath commanded thee. And thou shalt do that which is right and good in the sight of the Lord; that it may be well with thee, and that thou mayest go in and possess the good land which the Lord swore unto thy fathers, to thrust out all thine enemies from before thee, as the Lord hath spoken.

When thy son asketh thee in time to come, saying: "What mean the testimonies, and the statutes, and the ordinances, which the Lord our God hath commanded you?" then thou shalt say unto thy son: "We were Pharaoh's bondmen in Egypt; and the Lord brought us out of Egypt with a mighty hand. And the Lord showed signs and wonders, great and sore, upon Egypt, upon Pharaoh, and upon all his house, before our eyes. And He brought us out from thence, that He might bring us in, to give us the land which He swore unto our fathers. And the Lord commanded us to do all these statutes, to fear the Lord our God, for our good always, that He might preserve us alive, as it is at this day. And it shall be righteousness unto us, if we observe to do all this commandment before the Lord our God, as He hath commanded us."

I SAMUEL 17:42–18:2
David and Goliath

David's courageous victory continues to stand as a metaphor for the triumph of faith over evil. The passage relates how the young insignificant lad has no qualms about fighting the great Philistine warrior Goliath in the name of the Lord God of Israel. The victorious David is eventually annointed as the second king of Israel.

And when the Philistine looked about, and saw David, he disdained him; for he was but a youth, and ruddy, and withal of a fair countenance. And the Philistine said unto David: "Am I a dog, that thou comest to me with staves?" And the Philistine cursed David by his god. And the Philistine said to David: "Come to me, and I will give thy flesh unto the fowls of the air, and to the beasts of the field." Then said David to the Philistine: "Thou comest to me with a sword, and with a spear, and with a javelin; but I come to thee in the name of the Lord of hosts, the God of the armies of Israel, whom thou hast taunted. This day will the Lord deliver thee into my hand; and I will smite thee, and take thy head from off thee; and I will give the carcasses of the host of the Philistines this day unto the fowls of the air, and to the wild beasts of the earth; that all the earth may know that there is a God in Israel; and that all this assembly may know that the Lord saveth not with sword and spear; for the battle is the Lord's, and He will give you into our hand." And it came to pass, when the Philistine arose, and came and drew nigh to meet

David, that David hastened, and ran toward the army to meet the Philistine. And David put his hand in his bag, and took thence a stone, and slung it, and smote the Philistine in his forehead; and the stone sank into his forehead, and he fell upon his face to the earth. So David prevailed over the Philistine with a sling and with a stone, and smote the Philistine, and slew him; but there was no sword in the hand of David. And David ran, and stood over the Philistine, and took his sword, and drew it out of the sheath thereof, and slew him, and cut off his head therewith. And when the Philistines saw that their mighty man was dead, they fled. And the men of Israel and of Judah arose, and shouted, and pursued the Philistines, until thou comest to Gai, and to the gates of Ekron. And the wounded of the Philistines fell down by the way to Shaaraim, even unto Gath, and unto Ekron. And the children of Israel returned from chasing after the Philistines, and they spoiled their camp. And David took the head of the Philistine, and brought it to Jerusalem; but he put his armour in his tent.

And when Saul saw David go forth against the Philistine, he said unto Abner, the captain of the host: "Abner, whose son is this youth?" and Abner said: "As thy soul liveth, O king, I cannot tell." And the king said: "Inquire thou whose son the stripling is." And as David returned from the slaughter of the Philistine, Abner took him, and brought him before Saul with the head of the Philistine in his hand. And Saul said to him: "Whose son art thou, thou young man?" And David answered: "I am the son of thy servant Jesse the Beth-lehemite."

And it came to pass, when he had made an end of speaking unto Saul, that the soul of Jonathan was knit with the soul of David, and Jonathan loved him as his own soul. And Saul took him that day, and would let him go no more home to his father's house.

David and Goliath. c. 1280. Vellum. Illustration from North French Miscellany. Add. ms. 11639 fol. 523v. By permission of the British Library, London.

I KINGS 6:1–38; 7:13–51

Solomon Builds the Temple

The Temple built by King Solomon was destroyed by the Babylonians in 586 B.C.E. The building of this important structure, described in detail in this passage, took seven years. It was magnificent, not only in its architecture, but also in its embellishments and adornments. It served as the "House of God," and Jews were commanded to visit it on pilgrimage festivals.

And it came to pass in the four hundred and eightieth year after the children of Israel were come out of the land of Egypt, in the fourth year of Solomon's reign over Israel, in the month Ziv, which is the second month, that he began to build the house of the Lord. And the house which king Solomon built for the Lord, the length thereof was threescore cubits, and the breadth thereof twenty cubits, and the height thereof thirty cubits. And the porch before the temple of the house, twenty cubits was the length thereof, according to the breadth of the house; and ten cubits was the breadth thereof before the house. And for the house he made windows broad within, and narrow without. And against the wall of the house he built a side-structure round about, against the walls of the house round about, both of the temple and of the Sanctuary; and he made side-chambers round about; the nethermost story of the side-structure was five cubits broad, and the middle was six cubits broad, and the third was seven cubits broad; for on the outside he made rebatements in the wall of the house round about, that the beams should not have hold in the walls of the house.—For the house, when it was in building, was built of stone made ready at the quarry; and there was neither hammer nor axe nor any tool of iron heard in the house, while it was in building.—The door for the lowest row

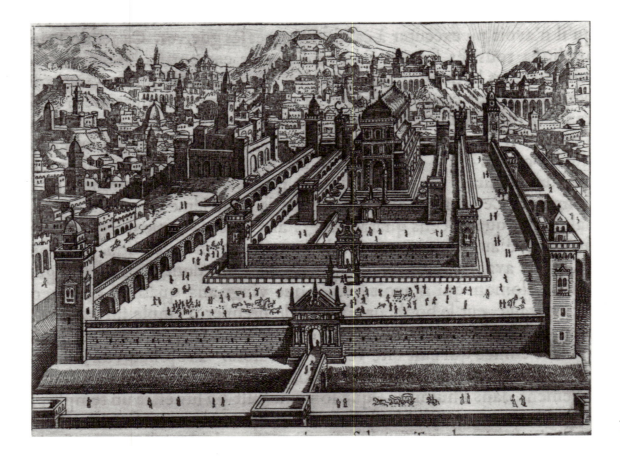

Second Temple at Jerusalem. 19th century. Woodcut.

of chambers was in the right side of the house and they went up by winding stairs into the middle row, and out of the middle into the third. So he built the house, and finished it; and he covered in the house with planks of cedar over beams. And he built the stories of the side-structure against all the house, each five cubits high; and they rested on the house with timber of cedar.

And the word of the Lord came to Solomon, saying: "As for this house which thou art building, if thou wilt walk in My statutes, and execute Mine ordinances, and keep all My commandments to walk in them; then will I establish My word with thee, which I spoke unto David thy father; in that I will dwell therein among the children of Israel, and will not forsake My people Israel."

So Solomon built the house, and finished it. And he built the walls of the house within with boards of cedar; from the floor of the house unto the joists of the ceiling, he covered them on the inside with wood; and he covered the floor of the house with boards of cypress. And he built twenty cubits on the hinder part of the house with boards of cedar from the floor unto the joists; he even built them for himself within, for a Sanctuary, even for the most holy place. And the house, that is, the temple before [the Sanctuary], was forty cubits long. And the cedar on the house within was carved with knops and open flowers; all was cedar; there was no stone seen. And he prepared the Sanctuary in the midst of the house within, to set there the ark of the covenant of the Lord. And before the Sanctuary which was twenty cubits in length, and twenty cubits in breadth, and twenty cubits in the height thereof, overlaid with pure gold, he set an altar, which he covered with cedar. So Solomon overlaid the house within with pure gold; and he drew chains of gold across the wall before the Sanctuary; and he overlaid it with gold. And the whole house he overlaid with gold, until all the house was finished; also the whole altar that belonged to the Sanctuary he overlaid with gold.

And in the Sanctuary he made two cherubim of olive-wood, each ten cubits high. And five cubits was the one wing of the cherub, and five cubits the other wing of the cherub; from the uttermost part of the one wing unto the uttermost part of the other were ten cubits. And the other cherub was ten cubits; both the cherubim were of one measure and one form. The height of the one cherub was ten cubits, and so was it of the other cherub. And he set the cherubim within the inner house; and the wings of the cherubim were stretched forth, so that the wing of the one touched the one wall, and the wing of the other cherub touched the other wall; and their wings touched one another in the midst of the house. And he overlaid the cherubim with gold.

And he carved all the walls of the house round about with carved figures of cherubim and palm-trees and open flowers, within and without. And the floor of the house he overlaid with gold, within and without. And for the entrance of the Sanctuary he made doors of olive-wood, the door-posts within the frame having five angles. And as for the two doors of olive-wood, he carved upon them carvings of cherubim and palm-trees and open flowers, and overlaid them with gold; and he spread the gold upon the cherubim, and upon the palm-trees. So also made he for the entrance of the temple door-posts of olive-wood, within a frame four-square; and two doors of cypress-wood; the two leaves of the one door were folding, and the two leaves of the other door were folding. And he carved thereon cherubim and palm-trees and open flowers; and he overlaid them with gold fitted upon the graven work. And he built the inner court with three rows of hewn stone, and a row of cedar beams.

In the fourth year was the foundation of the house of the Lord laid, in the month Ziv. and in the eleventh year, in the month Bul, which is the eighth month, was the house finished throughout all the parts thereof, and according to all the fashion of it. So was he seven years in building it.

And king Solomon sent and fetched Hiram out of Tyre. He was the son of a widow of the tribe of Naphtali, and his father was a man of Tyre, a worker in brass; and he was filled with wisdom and understanding and skill, to work all works in brass. And he came to king Solomon, and wrought all his work.

Thus he fashioned the two pillars of brass, of eighteen cubits high each; and a line of twelve cubits did compass it about; [and so] the other pillar. And he made two capitals of molten brass, to set upon the tops of the pillars; the height of the one capital was five cubits, and the height of the other capital was five cubits. He also made nets of checker-work, and wreaths of chain-work, for the capitals which were upon the top of the pillars: seven for the one capital, and seven for the other capital. And he made the pillars; and there were two rows round about upon the one network, to cover the capitals that were upon the top of the pomegranates; and so did he for the other capital. And the capitals that were upon the top of the pillars in the porch were of lily-work, four cubits. And there were capitals above also upon the two pillars, close by the belly which was beside the network; and the pomegranates were two hundred, in rows round about upon each capital. And he set up the pillars at the porch of the temple; and he set up the right pillar, and called the name thereof Jachin; and he set up the left pillar, and called the name thereof Boaz. And upon the top of the pillars was lily-work; so was the work of the pillars finished.

And he made the molten sea of ten cubits from brim to brim, round in compass, and the height thereof was five cubits; and a line of thirty cubits did compass it round about. And under the brim of it round about there were knops which did compass it, for ten cubits, compassing the sea round about; the knops were in two rows, cast when it was cast. It stood upon twelve oxen, three looking toward the north, and three looking toward the west, and three looking toward the south, and three looking toward the east; and the sea was set upon them above, and all their hinder parts were inward. And it was a handbreath thick; and the brim thereof was wrought like the brim of a cup, like the flower of a lily; it held two thousand baths.

And he made the ten bases of brass; four cubits was the length of one base, and four cubits the breadth thereof, and three cubits the height of it. And the work of the bases was on this manner: they had borders; and there were borders between the stays; and on the borders that were between the stays were lions, oxen, and cherubim; and upon the stays it was in like manner above; and beneath the lions and oxen were wreaths of hanging work. And every base had four brazen wheels, and axles of brass; and the four feet thereof had undersetters; beneath the laver were the undersetters molten, with wreaths at the side of each. And the mouth of it within the crown and above was a cubit high; and the mouth thereof was round after the work of a pedestal, a cubit and a half; and also upon the mouth of it were gravings; and their borders were foursquare, not round. And the four wheels were underneath the borders; and the axletrees of the wheels were in the base; and the height of a wheel was a cubit and half a cubit. And the work of the wheels was like the work of a chariot wheel; their axletrees, and their felloes, and their spokes, and their naves, were all molten. And there were four undersetters at the four corners of each base; the undersetters thereof were of one piece with the base itself. And in the top of the base was there a round compass of half a cubit high; and on the top of the base the stays thereof and the borders thereof were of one piece therewith. And on the plates of the stays thereof, and on the borders thereof, he graved cherubim, lions, and palm-trees, according to the space of each, with wreaths round about. After this manner he made the ten bases; all of them had one casting, one measure, and one form.

And he made ten lavers of brass: one laver contained forty baths; and every laver was four cubits; and upon every one of the ten bases one laver. And he set the bases, five on the right side of the house, and five on the left side of the house; and he set the sea on the right side of the house eastward, toward the south.

And Hiram made the pots, and the shovels, and the basins.

So Hiram made an end of doing all the work that he wrought for king Solomon in the house of the Lord: the two pillars, and the two bowls of the capitals that were on the top of the pillars; and the two networks to cover the two bowls of the capitals that were on the top of the pillars; and the four hundred pomegranates for the two networks, two rows of pomegranates for each network, to cover the two bowls of the capitals that were upon the top of the pillars; and the ten bases, and the ten lavers on the bases; and the one sea, and the twelve oxen under the sea; and the pots, and the shovels, and the basins;

even all these vessels, which Hiram made for king Solomon, in the house of the Lord, were of burnished brass. In the plain of the Jordan did the king cast them, in the clay ground between Succoth and Zarethan. And Solomon left all the vessels unweighed, because they were exceeding many; the weight of the brass could not be found out. And Solomon made all the vessels that were in the house of the Lord: the golden altar, and the table whereupon the showbread was, of gold; and the candlesticks, five on the right side, and five on the left, before the Sanctuary, of pure gold; and the flowers, and the lamps, and the tongs, of gold; and the cups, and the snuffers, and the basins, and the pans, and the fire-pans, of pure gold; and the hinges, both for the doors of the inner house, the most holy place, and for the doors of the house, that is, of the temple, of gold.

Thus all the work that king Solomon wrought in the house of the Lord was finished.

HANS HOLBEIN THE YOUNGER. *Isaiah Weeping over Jerusalem. (Judah's Rebellion)* from *Icones Historiarum Veteris Testamenti.* Lyons, 1547. Woodcut/ printed book. 2⅞ × 3⅜″ (7.3 × 8.6 cm). Miriam and Ira D. Wallach Division of Art, Prints and Photographs. The New York Public Library, Astor, Lenox and Tilden Foundations.

ISAIAH 2:1–4
A Vision of Peace

Isaiah was an eighth-century prophet who saw the nations of the world as just tools in the hands of God. He called upon the people to live just and moral lives, and he felt that failure to live such lives would result in punishment by God. This chapter is famous for its fourth verse, containing a vision of future peace. These words still carry a powerful message and have been inscribed on a wall directly across from United Nations headquarters in New York City.

The word that Isaiah the son of Amoz saw concerning Judah and Jerusalem.

> And it shall come to pass in the end of days,
> That the mountain of the Lord's house shall be established as the top of
> the mountains,
> And shall be exalted above the hills;
> And all nations shall flow unto it.

And many peoples shall go and say:
  "Come ye, and let us go up to the mountain of the Lord,
To the house of the God of Jacob;
And He will teach us of His ways,
And we will walk in His paths."
For out of Zion shall go forth the law,
And the word of the Lord from Jerusalem.
And He shall judge between the nations,
And shall decide for many peoples;
And they shall beat their swords into plowshares,
And their spears into pruning-hooks;
Nation shall not lift up sword against nation,
Neither shall they learn war any more.

EZEKIEL 37:1–14

The Vision of the Dry Bones

Ezekiel, one of the great literary prophets, lived and worked during the time of the Babylonian Exile (early sixth century B.C.E.). In the vision in this passage, Ezekiel speaks of a regeneration of the people Israel, thus providing a message of hope to those in Exile, many of whom had lost all hope of being restored to their homeland.

The hand of the Lord was upon me, and the Lord carried me out in a spirit, and set me down in the midst of the valley, and it was full of bones; and He caused me to pass by them round about, and, behold, there were very many in the open valley; and, lo, they were very dry. And He said unto me: "Son of man, can these bones live?" And I answered: "O Lord God, Thou knowest." Then He said unto me: "Prophesy over these bones, and say unto them: O ye dry bones, hear the word of the Lord: Thus saith the Lord God unto these bones: Behold, I will cause breath to enter into you, and ye shall live. And I will lay sinews upon you, and will bring up flesh upon you, and cover you with skin, and put breath in you, and ye shall live; and ye shall know that I am the Lord." So I prophesied as I was commanded; and as I prophesied, there was a noise, and behold a commotion, and the bones came together, bone to its bone. And I beheld, and, lo, there were sinews upon them, and flesh came up, and skin covered them above; but there was no breath in them. Then said He unto me: "Prophesy unto the breath, prophesy, son of man, and say to the breath: Thus saith the Lord God: Come from the four winds, O breath, and breathe upon these slain, that they may live." So I prophesied as He commanded me, and the breath came into them, and they lived, and stood up upon their feet, an exceeding great host. Then He said unto me: "Son of man, these bones are the whole house of Israel; behold, they say: Our bones are dried up, and our hope is lost; we are clean cut off. Therefore prophesy, and say unto them: Thus saith the Lord God: Behold, I will open your graves, and cause you to come up out of your graves, O My people; and I will bring you into the land of Israel. And ye shall know that I am the Lord, when I have opened your graves, and caused you to come up out of your graves, O My people. And I will put My spirit in you, and ye shall live, and I will place you in your own land; and ye shall know that I the Lord have spoken, and performed it, saith the Lord."

Ezekiel's Vision of the Resurrection. Fresco from the Synagogue of Dura Europos, Syria. 3rd century. 63¾ × 161¹³⁄₁₆″ (162 × 411 cm). Courtesy of Yale University Art Gallery, New Haven. Dura Europos Collection.

PSALM 137

By the Rivers of Babylon

This Psalm is a poignant expression of the feelings of those who were exiled to Babylon. Their captors taunted them, demanding that the captives sing "one of the songs of Zion." They could not sing; they could only mourn and look ahead to the day that God will punish those who destroyed Jerusalem.

By the rivers of Babylon,
There we sat down, yea, we wept,
When we remembered Zion.
Upon the willows in the midst thereof
We hanged up our harps.
For there they that led us captive asked of us words of song,
And our tormentors asked of us mirth:
"Sing us one of the songs of Zion."
How shall we sing the Lord's song
In a foreign land?
If I forget thee, O Jerusalem,
Let my right hand forget her cunning.
Let my tongue cleave to the roof of my mouth,
If I remember thee not;
If I set not Jersualem
Above my chiefest joy.

Remember, O Lord, against the children of Edom
The day of Jersualem;
Who said: "Rase it, rase it,
Even to the foundation thereof."
O daughter of Babylon, that art to be destroyed;
Happy shall he be, that repayeth thee
As thou hast served us.
Happy shall he be, that taketh and dasheth thy little ones
Against the rock.

ESTHER 3:1–4:3; 7:1–8:17
The Rise and Fall of Haman

The Book of Esther is one of the Five Scrolls, or Megillot, in the Bible. Set in the Persian Empire, it recounts the tale of how Haman, chief minister of King Ahasuerus, plots to exterminate the Jews because Mordecai, a Jew, failed to kneel and bow down to him. Esther, Ahasuerus's queen, learns of this scheme, and devises a means to unmask the evil Haman and his devious plan. The subsequent downfall of Haman and ultimate victory of the Persian Jews is commemorated by the holiday of Purim.

After these things did king Ahasuerus promote Haman the son of Hammedatha the Agagite, and advanced him, and set his seat above all the princes that were with him. And all the king's servants, that were in the king's gate, bowed down, and prostrated themselves before Haman; for the king had so commanded concerning him. But Mordecai bowed not down, nor prostrated himself before him. Then the king's servants, that were in the king's gate, said unto Mordecai: "Why transgressest thou the king's command-

Mordecai and Esther Panel. Fresco from the Synagogue of Dura Europos. 3rd century. 64³⁄₁₆ × 154⁵⁄₁₆" (163 × 392 cm). Courtesy of Yale University Art Gallery, New Haven. Dura Europos Collection.

ment?" Now it came to pass, when they spoke daily unto him, and he hearkened not unto them, that they told Haman, to see whether Mordecai's words would stand; for he had told them that he was a Jew. And when Haman saw that Mordecai bowed not down, nor prostrated himself before him, then was Haman full of wrath. But it seemed contemptible in his eyes to lay hands on Mordecai alone; for they had made known to him the people of Mordecai; wherefore Haman sought to destroy all the Jews that were throughout the whole kingdom of Ahasuerus, even the people of Mordecai. In the first month, which is the month Nisan, in the twelfth year of king Ahasuerus, they cast pur, that is, the lot, before Haman from day to day, and from month to month, to the twelfth month, which is the month Adar.

And Haman said unto king Ahasuerus: "There is a certain people scattered abroad and dispersed among the peoples in all the provinces of thy kingdom; and their laws are diverse from those of every people; neither keep they the king's laws; therefore it profiteth not the king to suffer them. If it please the king, let it be written that they be destroyed; and I will pay ten thousand talents of silver into the hands of those that have the charge of the king's business, to bring it into the king's treasuries." And the king took his ring from his hand, and gave it unto Haman the son of Hammedatha the Agagite, the Jews' enemy. And the king said unto Haman: "The silver is given to thee, the people also, to do with them as it seemeth good to thee."

Then were the king's scribes called in the first month, on the thirteenth day thereof, and there was written, according to all that Haman commanded, unto the king's satraps, and to the governors that were over every province, and to the princes of every people; to every province according to the writing thereof, and to every people after their language; in the name of king Ahasuerus was it written, and it was sealed with the king's ring. And letters were sent by posts into all the king's provinces, to destroy, to slay, and to cause to perish, all Jews, both young and old, little children and women, in one day, even upon the thirteenth day of the twelfth month, which is the month Adar, and to take the spoil of them for a prey. The copy of the writing, to be given out for a decree in every province, was to be published unto all the peoples, that they should be ready against that day. The posts went forth in haste by the king's commandment, and the decree was given out in Shushan the castle; and the king and Haman sat down to drink; but the city of Shushan was perplexed.

Now when Mordecai knew all that was done, Mordecai rent his clothes, and put on sackcloth with ashes, and went out into the midst of the city, and cried with a loud and a bitter cry; and he came even before the king's gate; for none might enter within the king's gate clothed with sackcloth. And in every province, whithersoever the king's commandment and his decree came, there was great mourning among the Jews, and fasting, and weeping, and wailing; and many lay in sackcloth and ashes.

★　　★　　★

So the king and Haman came to banquet with Esther the queen. And the king said again unto Esther on the second day at the banquet of wine: "Whatever thy petition, queen Esther, it shall be granted thee; and whatever thy request, even to the half of the kingdom, it shall be performed." Then Esther the queen answered and said: "If I have found favour in thy sight, O king, and if it please the king, let my life be given me at my petition, and my people at my request; for we are sold, I and my people, to be destroyed, to be slain, and to perish. But if we had been sold for bondmen and bondwomen, I had held my peace for the adversary is not worthy that the king be endamaged."

Then spoke the king Ahasuerus and said unto Esther the queen: "Who is he, and where is he, that durst presume in his heart to do so?" And Esther said: "An adversary and an enemy, even this wicked Haman." Then Haman was terrified before the king and the queen. And the king arose in his wrath from the banquet of wine and went into the palace garden; but Haman remained to make request for his life to Esther the queen; for he saw that there was evil determined against him by the king. Then the king returned out of the palace garden into the place of the banquet of wine; and Haman was fallen upon the couch whereon Esther was. Then said the king: "Will he even force the queen before me in the house?" As the word went out of the king's mouth, they covered Haman's face. Then said Harbonah, one of the chamberlains that were before the king: "Behold also, the gallows fifty cubits high, which Haman hath made for Mordecai, who spoke good for the king, standeth in the house of Haman." And the king said: "Hang him thereon." So they hanged Haman on the gallows that he had prepared for Mordecai. Then was the king's wrath assuaged.

On that day did the king Ahasuerus give the house of Haman the Jews' enemy unto Esther the queen. And Mordecai came before the king; for Esther had told what he was unto her. And the king took off his ring, which he had taken from Haman, and gave it unto Mordecai. And Esther set Mordecai over the house of Haman.

And Esther spoke yet again. . . . And she said: "If it please the king, and if I have found favour in his sight, and the thing seem right before the king, and I be pleasing in his eyes, let it be written to reverse the letters devised by Haman the son of Hammedatha the Agagite, which he wrote to destroy the Jews that are in all the king's provinces; for how can I endure to see the evil that shall come unto my people? or how can I endure to see the destruction of my kindred?"

Then the king Ahasuerus said unto Esther the queen and to Mordecai the Jew: "Behold, I have given Esther the house of Haman, and him they have hanged upon the gallows, because he laid his hand upon the Jews. Write ye also concerning the Jews, as it liketh you, in the king's name, and seal it with the king's ring; for the writing which is written in the king's name, and sealed with the king's ring, may no man reverse."

★　★　★

And Mordecai went forth from the presence of the king in royal apparel of blue and white, and with a great crown of gold, and with a robe of fine linen and purple; and the city of Shushan shouted and was glad. The Jews had light and gladness, and joy and honour. And in every province, and in every city, whithersoever the king's commandment and his decree came, the Jews had gladness and joy, a feast and a good day.

POSTBIBLICAL LITERATURE

II MACCABEES 8:1–36

Judah Leads His Followers to Victory

The Second Book of Maccabees, originally written in Greek, is not included in the Bible but appears in the postbiblical collection known as the Apocrypha, or "Outside Books." It gives a clear message that the suffering of the people is divine recompense for their sin. The book deals almost exclusively with the deeds of Judah Maccabee, who, with his brothers, waged a successful war against the troops of Antiochus IV in 165 B.C.E. The cleansing and rededication of the Temple was marked by a special celebration and is commemorated each year by the lighting of the Hanukkah menorah during the festival of Hanukkah.

Judas Maccabeus. France, 16th century. Enameled plaque. 3¹¹⁄₁₆″ (9.3 cm) diameter. Musée d'Ecouen. *This portrait by a 16th-century French artist portrays the Jewish hero as a strong, dignified leader.*

But Judas, who was called Maccabeus, and his followers secretly entered the villages and called on their kinsmen to join them, and by enlisting those who had clung to the Jewish religion, they mustered as many as six thousand. And they called upon the Lord to look upon the people who were oppressed by all men and to have pity on the sanctuary which had been profaned by the godless, and to have mercy on the city which was being ruined and would soon be leveled with the ground, and to hearken to the blood that cried to them, and to remember the lawless destruction of the innocent babies and the blasphemies uttered against his name, and to hate their wickedness. And as soon as Maccabeus got them organized, the heathen found him irresistible, for the wrath of the Lord now turned to mercy. He would go unexpectedly to towns and villages and set fire to them, and in recovering advantageous positions and putting to flight not a few of the enemy, he found the nights especially favorable for such attacks. And the country rang with talk of his valor.

When Philip saw that the man was gaining ground little by little, and that his successful advances were becoming more frequent, he wrote to Ptolemy, the governor of Coelesyria and Phoenicia, to support the king's side. And he promptly selected Nicanor, the son of Patroclus, one of the king's chief Friends and sent him, putting him in command of not less than twenty thousand heathen of various nationalities, to wipe out the whole race of Judea. And he associated with him Gorgias, a general and a man of experience in military service. But Nicanor resolved by taking the Jews captive to make up for the king the tribute which he owed to the Romans, which amounted to two thousand talents. And he immediately sent to the coast towns, inviting them to buy Jewish slaves, and promising to deliver them at ninety for a talent, little expecting the judgment from the Almighty that was to overtake him.

When news of Nicanor's advance reached Judas, and when he informed his followers of the arrival of the army, those who were cowardly and doubtful about the judgment of God ran away and took themselves off. And others sold everything they had left and besought the Lord together to deliver those who had been sold in advance by the impious Nicanor; if not for their own sakes, for the sake of the agreements made with their forefathers, and because they had been called by his revered and glorious name. And Maccabeus gathered his men together, to the number of six thousand, and exhorted them not to be panic-stricken at the enemy, or to fear the vast multitude of the heathen who were coming against them wrongfully, but to fight nobly, keeping before their eyes the lawless outrage they had committed against the holy place, and the tormenting of the derided city, and besides, the destruction of their ancestral mode of life. "For they," he said, "trust in arms and daring, but we trust in the Almighty God, for he is able with a mere nod to strike down not only our enemies but the whole world."

★　　★　　★

And the Almighty was their ally, and they slaughtered more than nine thousand of the enemy, and wounded and disabled most of Nicanor's army, and forced them all to flee. And they captured the money of those who had come to buy them. And after pursuing them for a considerable distance, they were obliged to turn back because of the time of day; for it was the day before the sabbath, and for that reason they could not prolong their pursuit of them. But after collecting the enemy's arms and stripping them of their spoils, they busied themselves about the sabbath, fervently blessing and thanking the Lord who had preserved them to see that day, because he had begun to show them mercy. After the sabbath, they gave some of the spoils to the wounded and to the widows and orphans and divided the rest with their children. When they had accomplished this, they made a common supplication, and besought the merciful Lord to be wholly reconciled to his slaves.

When they encountered the forces of Timotheus and Bacchides, they killed more than twenty thousand of them, and obtained possession of some exceedingly high strongholds, and they divided a great amount of plunder, giving shares equal to their own to the wounded and orphans and widows, and also to the older people as well. And they carefully collected all their own arms and deposited them in the advantageous places, and the rest of the spoils they carried to Jerusalem. And they killed the cavalry commander of Timotheus' forces, a most impious man, who had greatly injured the Jews. And in celebrating their victory in the city of their forefathers, they burned those who had set fire to the sacred gates, and Callisthenes, who had taken refuge in a cottage; so he received the proper reward for his impious conduct. But the thrice-accursed Nicanor, who had brought the thousand slave-dealers to buy the Jews, after being humbled through the Lord's help by those whom he had thought of no account, took off his fine clothes and going alone like a runaway across country reached Antioch, having been supremely successful—in destroying his army! So the man who had undertaken to secure tribute for the Romans by the capture of the people of Jerusalem proclaimed that the Jews had a champion, and that the Jews were invulnerable because of their way of life, because they followed the laws laid down by him.

Flavius Josephus

FROM THE JEWISH WAR

The Fall of Masada

Josephus (c. 38–c. 100), famed as an historian, as well as a Jewish traitor to Rome, served as commander of Jewish forces in the Galilee during the beginning of the revolt against Rome (66 C.E.). Josephus was captured and subsequently won the friendship of both Vespasian and Titus and the hatred of the Jewish populace. After the fall of Jersualem, Josephus traveled to Rome and was granted Roman citizenship and a royal pension. His historical works have contributed greatly to our knowledge of Jewish matters at this time.

But Eleazar had no intention of slipping out himself, or of allowing anyone else to do so. He saw his wall going up in flames; he could think of no other means of escape or heroic endeavour; he had a clear picture of what the Romans would do to men, women, and children if they won the day; and death seemed to him the right choice for them all.

Making up his mind that in the circumstances this was the wisest course, he collected the toughest of his comrades and urged it upon them in a speech of which this was the substance:

"My loyal followers, long ago we resolved to serve neither the Romans nor anyone else but only God, who alone is the true and righteous Lord of men: now the time has come that bids us prove our determination by our deeds. At such a time we must not disgrace ourselves: hitherto we have never submitted to slavery, even when it brought no danger with it: we must not choose slavery now, and with it penalties that will mean the end of everything if we fall alive into the hands of the Romans. For we were the first of all to revolt, and shall be the last to break off the struggle. And I think it is God who has given us this privilege, that we can die nobly and as free men, unlike others who were unexpectedly defeated. In our case it is evident that daybreak will end our resistance, but we are free to choose an honourable death with our loved ones. This our enemies cannot prevent, however earnestly they may pray to take us alive; nor can we defeat them in battle.

"From the very first, when we were bent on claiming our freedom but suffered such constant misery at each other's hands and worse at the enemy's, we ought perhaps to have read the mind of God and realized that His once beloved Jewish race had been sentenced to extinction. For if He had remained gracious or only slightly indignant with us, He would not have shut His eyes to the destruction of so many thousands or allowed His most holy City to be burnt to the ground by our enemies. We hoped, or so it would seem, that of all the Jewish race we alone would come through safe, still in possession of our freedom, as if we had committed no sin against God and taken part in no crime—we who had taught the others! Now see how He shows the folly of our hopes, plunging us into miseries more terrible than any we had dreamt of. Not even the impregnability of our fortress has sufficed to save us, but though we have food in abundance, ample supplies of arms, and more than enough of every other requisite, God Himself without

Aerial view of Masada. 1980. Photograph.

a doubt has taken away all hope of survival. The fire that was being carried into the enemy lines did not turn back of its own accord towards the wall we had built: these things are God's vengeance for the many wrongs that in our madness we dared to do to our own countrymen.

"For those wrongs let us pay the penalty not to our bitterest enemies, the Romans, but to God—by our own hands. It will be easier to bear. Let our wives die unabused, our children without knowledge of slavery: after that, let us do each other an ungrudging kindness, preserving our freedom as a glorious winding-sheet. But first let our possessions and the whole fortress go up in flames: it will be a bitter blow to the Romans, that I know, to find our persons beyond their reach and nothing left for them to loot. One thing only let us spare—our store of food: it will bear witness when we are dead to the fact that we perished, not through want but because, as we resolved at the beginning, we chose death rather than slavery. . . .

"Come! while our hands are free and can hold a sword, let them do a noble service! Let us die unenslaved by our enemies, and leave this world as free men in company with our wives and children. That is what the Law ordains, that is what our wives and children demand of us, the necessity God has laid on us, the opposite of what the Romans wish—they are anxious none of us should die before the town is captured. So let us deny the enemy their hoped-for pleasure at our expense, and without more ado leave them to be dumbfounded by our death and awed by our courage."

Eleazar had many more arguments to urge, but all his listeners cut him short and full of uncontrollable enthusiasm made haste to do the deed. As if possessed they rushed off, everyone anxious to be quicker than the next man, and regarding it as proof positive of manliness and wisdom not to be found among the last: so irresistible a desire had seized them to slaughter their wives, their little ones, and themselves. It might have been thought that as they approached their task their determination would have weakened; but they clung resolutely to the purpose they had formed while listening to the appeal, and while they all retained feelings of personal affection, reason, which had urged what was best for their dear ones, won the day. For at the very moment when with streaming eyes they embraced and caressed their wives, and taking their children in their arms pressed upon them the last, lingering kisses, hands other than their own seemed to assist them and they carried out their purpose, the thought of the agonies they would suffer at the hands of the enemy consoling them for the necessity of killing them. In the end not a man failed to carry out his terrible resolve, but one and all disposed of their entire families, victims of cruel necessity who with their own hands murdered their wives and children and felt it to be the lightest of evils!

Unable to endure any longer the horror of what they had done, and thinking they would be wronging the dead if they outlived them a moment longer, they quickly made one heap of all they possessed and set it on fire; and when ten of them had been chosen by lot to be the executioners of the rest, every man lay down beside his wife and children where they lay, flung his arms round them, and exposed his throat to those who must perform the painful office. These unflinchingly slaughtered them all, then agreed on the same rule for each other, so that the one who drew the lot should kill the nine and last of all himself: such perfect confidence they all had in each other that neither in doing nor in suffering would one differ from another. So finally the nine presented their throats, and the one man left till last first surveyed the serried ranks of the dead, in case amidst all the slaughter someone was still left in need of his hand; then finding that all had been dispatched set the palace blazing fiercely, and summoning all his strength drove his sword right through his body and fell dead by the side of his family. Thus these men died supposing that they had left no living soul to fall into the hands of the Romans; but an old woman escaped, along with another who was related to Eleazar, in intelligence and education superior to most women, and five little children. They had hidden in the conduits that brought drinking-water underground while the rest were intent upon the suicide-pact. These numbered 960, women and children included. The tragedy was enacted on 15th of Xanthicos.

COLORPLATE 29

Fathnama (Book of the Conquest). Persia, 17th century. Paper. 11¼ × 8″ (28.6 × 20.3 cm). Or. ms. 13704 fol. 31v. By permission of the British Library, London. *The Book of Conquest, written in Judeo-Persian (the Persian language written in Hebrew letters) paraphrases the narratives in the biblical books of Joshua, Samuel, and Ruth. In this scene from Joshua, seven men blowing rams' horns are circling the walls of the city of Jericho.*

COLORPLATE 30
AARON WOLF of Jevíčo (Gewitsch). *Circumcision Book.* Vienna, 1728. Ink and gouache on parchment. 5⁹⁄₁₆ × 3⅜″ (14.4 × 9.5 cm). State Jewish Museum, Prague.

COLORPLATE 31 *(opposite)*
MOSES LEIB BEN WOLF of Trebitsch. *Seder in an 18th-Century Bohemian Home.* Frontispiece to the "Sister" of the *Van Geldern Haggadah.* 1716–1717. Mss. 444.1. Hebrew Union College Library—Jewish Institute of Religion, Cincinnati.

COLORPLATE 32

SOLOMON ALEXANDER HART. *The Feast of the Rejoicing of the Law at the Synagogue in Leghorn, Italy.* 1850. Oil on canvas. 55⅝ × 68¾″ (141.3 × 174.6 cm). The Jewish Museum, New York. Gift of Mr. and Mrs. Oscar Gruss. *Solomon Hart, like other 19th-century British artists who traveled as part of the "Grand Tour," visited Italy and documented the sites he saw. In this romanticized canvas, he depicts a procession during the celebration of Simhat Torah in the synagogue at Leghorn (Livorno), whose lavish interior he observed while traveling through Italy.*

COLORPLATE 35
Attributed to GEORGE EMANUEL OPITZ. *Dedication of a Synagogue in Alsace.* 1820. Oil on canvas.
24½ × 35½" (62.2 × 90.2 cm). The Jewish Museum, New York.

COLORPLATE 33 *(opposite, above)*
Anonymous artist of the Bohemian school in Eastern Europe. *Jewish Wedding.* 18th century.
Oil on canvas. 34⁷⁄₁₆ × 47⅝" (87.5 × 121 cm). Collection, Israel Museum, Jerusalem.

COLORPLATE 34 *(opposite, below)*
EMANUEL DE WITTE. *Interior of the Portuguese Synagogue in Amsterdam.* c. 1680. Oil on canvas.
43¼ × 49¼" (108 × 123 cm). Collection, Israel Museum, Jerusalem. *The Portuguese Synagogue in Amsterdam, built 1671–1675, was one of the earliest and most beautiful in Europe.*

COLORPLATE 36
MORITZ OPPENHEIM. *The Kindling of the Hanukkah Lights.* 1880. Oil on canvas. $27^{11}/_{16} \times 22^{1}/_{2}''$ (70.4 × 57.2 cm). Collection, Israel Museum, Jerusalem.

Gravestone with figures of a man with his son and two daughters, and Palmyrene inscription. 2nd–3rd century. The Metropolitan Museum of Art, New York. Purchase, Funds from Various Donors, 1902 (02.29.1). This family relief underscores the continuity of Jewish laws, traditions, and culture that pass from one generation to the next.

ABOTH 1:14, 18; 4:12, 17; 5:21
Sayings of the Fathers

The Mishnah is the codification of Jewish law compiled by Rabbi Judah the Patriarch c. 200 C.E. The tractate known as Aboth differs from the rest of the Mishnah in that it does not contain laws. The statements contained in Aboth are pithy expressions of the ideology of the rabbis. The custom of reading from "Ethics of the Fathers" on Saturday afternoon can be traced as far back as the ninth century. This custom has led to the inclusion of Aboth in many modern prayer books.

He [Hillel] used to say: If I am not for myself who is for me? and being for mine own self what am I? and if not now, when?

Rabban Simeon b. Gamaliel said: By three things is the world sustained: by truth, by judgement, and by peace, as it is written, *Execute the judgement of truth and peace.*

R. Eleazar b. Shammua said: Let the honour of thy disciple be as dear to thee as thine own and as the honour of thy companion, and the honour of thy companion as the fear of thy teacher, and the fear of thy teacher as the fear of Heaven.

He used to say: Better is one hour of repentance and good works in this world than the whole life of the world to come; and better is one hour of bliss in the world to come than the whole life of this world.

He used to say: At five years old [one is fit] for the Scripture, at ten years for the Mishnah, at thirteen for [the fulfilling of] the commandments, at fifteen for the Talmud, at eighteen for the bride-chamber, at twenty for pursuing [a calling], at thirty for authority, at forty for discernment, at fifty for counsel, at sixty for to be an elder, at seventy for grey hairs, at eighty for special strength, at ninety for bowed back, and at a hundred a man is as one that has [already] died and passed away and ceased from the world.

SANHEDRIN 4:1–5
Court Procedures

This portion of the Mishnaic tractate Sanhedrin discusses some of the procedures for trying both capital and non-capital cases. The passage quoted here ends by pointing out that God created each person as a unique individual and that every single life is as valuable as the lives of an entire world.

4. 1. Non-capital and capital cases are alike in examination and inquiry, for it is written, *Ye shall have one manner of law*. In what do non-capital cases differ from capital cases? Non-capital cases [are decided] by three and capital cases by three and twenty [judges]. Non-capital cases may begin either with reasons for acquittal or for conviction, but capital cases must begin with reasons for acquittal and may not begin with reasons for conviction. In non-capital cases they may reach a verdict either of acquittal or of conviction by the decision of a majority of one; but in capital cases they may reach a verdict of acquittal by the decision of a majority of one, but a verdict of conviction only by the decision of a majority of two. In non-capital cases they may reverse a verdict either [from conviction] to acquittal or [from acquittal] to conviction; but in capital cases they may reverse a verdict [from conviction] to acquittal but not [from acquittal] to conviction. In non-capital cases all may argue either in favour of conviction or of acquittal; but in capital cases all may argue in favour of acquittal but not in favour of conviction. In non-capital cases he that

Drawn after life by
Bernard Picart. *The Manner of Holding up the Law in the Sight of All the People before They Begin to Read It.* 18th century. Engraving.

had argued in favour of conviction may afterward argue in favour of acquittal, or he that had argued in favour of acquittal may afterward argue in favour of conviction; in capital cases he that had argued in favour of conviction may afterward argue in favour of acquittal, but he that had argued in favour of acquittal cannot afterward change and argue in favour of conviction. In non-capital cases they hold the trial during the daytime and the verdict may be reached during the night; in capital cases they hold the trial during the daytime and the verdict also must be reached during the daytime. In non-capital cases the verdict, whether of acquittal or of conviction, may be reached the same day; in capital cases a verdict of acquittal may be reached on the same day, but a verdict of conviction not until the following day. Therefore trials may not be held on the eve of a Sabbath or on the eve of a Festival-day.

2. In non-capital cases concerning uncleanness and cleanness [the judges declare their opinion] beginning from the eldest, but in capital cases they begin from [them that sit at] the side. All [of the family stocks] are qualified to try non-capital cases; but all are not qualified to try capital cases, but only priests, levites, and Israelites that may give [their daughters] in marriage into the priestly stock.

3. The Sanhedrin was arranged like the half of a round threshing-floor so that they all might see one another. Before them stood the two scribes of the judges, one to the right and one to the left, and they wrote down the words of them that favoured acquittal and the words of them that favoured conviction. R. Judah says: There were three: one wrote down the words of them that favoured acquittal, and one wrote down the words of them that favoured conviction, and the third wrote down the words both of them that favoured acquittal and of them that favoured conviction.

4. Before them sat three rows of disciples of the Sages, and each knew his proper place. If they needed to appoint [another as a judge], they appointed him from the first row, and one from the second row came into the first row, and one from the third row came into the second; and they chose yet another from the congregation and set him in the third row. He did not sit in the place of the former, but he sat in the place that was proper for him.

5. How did they admonish the witnesses in capital cases? They brought them in and admonished them, [saying,] "Perchance ye will say what is but supposition or hearsay or at secondhand, or [ye may say in yourselves], We heard it from a man that was trustworthy. Or perchance ye do not know that we shall prove you by examination and inquiry? Know ye, moreover, that capital cases are not as non-capital cases: in non-capital cases a man may pay money and so make atonement, but in capital cases the witness is answerable for the blood of him [that is wrongfully condemned] and the blood of his posterity [that should have been born to him] to the end of the world. For so have we found it with Cain that slew his brother, for it is written, *The bloods of thy brother cry*. It says not 'The blood of thy brother', but *The bloods of thy brother*—his blood and the blood of his posterity. (Another saying is: *Bloods of thy brother*—because his blood was cast over the trees and stones.) Therefore but a single man was created in the world, to teach that if any man has caused a single soul to perish from Israel Scripture imputes it to him as though he had caused a whole world to perish; and if any man saves alive a single soul from Israel Scripture imputes it to him as though he had saved alive a whole world. Again [but a single man was created] for the sake of peace among mankind, that none should say to his fellow, 'My father was greater than thy father'; also that the heretics should not say, 'There are many ruling powers in heaven'. Again [but a single man was created] to proclaim the greatness of the Holy One, blessed is he; for man stamps many coins with the one seal and they are all like one another; but the King of kings, the Holy One, blessed is he, has stamped every man with the seal of the first man, yet not one of them is like his fellow. Therefore every one must say, For my sake was the world created. And if perchance ye would say, Why should we be at these pains?—was it not once written, *He being a witness, whether he hath seen or known, [if he do not utter it, then shall he bear his iniquity]*? And if perchance ye would say, Why would we be guilty of the blood of this man?—was it not once written, *When the wicked perish there is rejoicing?*"

SANHEDRIN 37a; 38a

On the Creation of Man

The redaction of the Mishnah prompted the rabbis to study its teachings carefully in order to understand the principles of the law contained therein. Over the following centuries the rabbis studied the text itself, its connection with the written Torah and oral traditions, and its connections to rabbinic teachings that stemmed from the same period as the teachings in the Mishnah but which were not included in it. The Gemara is the text that sets forth the studies that followed the publication of the Mishnah. Here a portion of the Mishnah that was cited in the preceding section is accompanied by a comment on it from the Gemara.

MISHNAH

For this reason was man created alone, to teach thee that whosoever destroys a single soul of Israel, scripture imputes [guilt] to him as though he had destroyed a complete world; and whosoever preserves a single soul of Israel, scripture ascribes [merit] to him as though he had preserved a complete world. Furthermore, [he was created alone] for the sake of peace among men, that one might not say to his fellow, "My father was greater than thine," and that the minim might not say, "There are many ruling powers in heaven"; again, to proclaim the greatness of the Holy One, blessed be He: for if a man strikes many coins from one mould, they all resemble one another, but the Supreme King of kings, the Holy One, blessed be He, fashioned every man in the stamp of the first man, and yet not one of them resembles his fellow. Therefore every single person is obliged to say: The world was created for my sake.

GEMARA

Our Rabbis taught: Adam was created [last of all beings] on the eve of Sabbath. And why?—Lest the Sadducees say: The Holy One, blessed be He, had a partner [viz., Adam] in His work of creation. Another answer is: In order that, if a man's mind becomes [too] proud, he may be reminded that the gnats preceded him in the order of creation. Another answer is: That he might immediately enter upon the fulfilment of a precept. Another answer is: That he might straightway go in to the banquet. The matter may be compared to a king of flesh and blood who built palaces and furnished them, prepared a banquet, and *thereafter* brought in the guests. For it is written: *Wisdom hath builded her house, she hath hewn out her seven pillars. She hath prepared her meat, she hath mingled her wine, she hath also furnished her table. She hath sent forth her maidens, she calleth upon the highest places of the city. Wisdom hath builded her house,*—this is the attribute of the Holy One, blessed be He, who created the world by wisdom. *She hath hewn out her seven pillars,*—these are the seven days of creation. *She hath prepared her meat, she hath mingled her wine, she hath also furnished her table,*—these are the seas and the rivers and all the other requirements of the world. *She hath sent forth her maidens, she calleth,*—this refers to Adam and Eve.

THE ALPHABET AND THE CREATION

This midrash, or commentary on a biblical text, teaches that the alphabet was created prior to the creation of the world. Each letter of the Hebrew alphabet, here given in reverse alphabetical order, petitions God for the privilege of being the letter that initiates the creation. The letter beth *is chosen* (bereshith, *"in the beginning"*) *because it begins the word* barukh, *or "blessed," the word by which God is praised.*

When God was about to create the world, each of the twenty-two letters of the Hebrew alphabet pleaded: "Create the world through me!"

The letter Tav said: "O Lord of the universe, may it be thy will to create the world through me; it is through me that thou wilt give the Torah to Israel." God replied: "No, because in days to come I shall place you as a sign of death upon the foreheads of men."

The Shin pleaded: "Lord of the universe, create thy world through me; thy own name *Shaddai* begins with me." Unfortunately, it is also the first letter of *sheker*, falsehood, and that disqualified it.

The Resh had no better luck, because it was the initial letter of *ra*, evil.

The Koof was rejected because *kelalah*, curse, outweighs the advantage of being the first in *Kadosh*, the Holy One.

In vain did the Tsadde draw attention to *Tsaddik*, the Righteous One; there was *tsaroth*, misfortunes, to testify against it.

The Peh had *podeh*, Redeemer, to its credit; but *pesha*, transgression, discredited it.

The Ayin was declared unfit because, though it begins *anavah*, humility, it performs the same service for *erwah*, immorality.

The Samekh said: "O Lord, may it be thy will to begin the creation with me, for thou art called *somekh*, the Upholder of all that fall." But God replied: "You are needed right where you are; you must continue to uphold all that fall."

The Nun introduces *ner*, lamp, the lamp of the Lord, which is the spirit of men, but it also brings to mind the lamp of the wicked which will be put out by God.

The Mem starts *melekh*, king, one of the titles of God. But as it is the first letter of *mehumah*, confusion, it had no chance of achieving its desire.

The Lamed advanced the argument that it was the first letter of *luhoth*, the celestial tablets of the Ten Commandments. It forgot that the tablets were dashed to pieces by Moses.

The Kaf was sure of victory: *kisseh*, the throne of God, *kavod*, his honor, and *kether*, his crown, all begin with it. God had to remind it that he would clap his hands, *kaf*, in despair over the misfortunes of Israel.

The Yod seemed to be the proper letter for the beginning of creation on account of its association with *Yah*, God; but *yetser ha-ra*, the evil impulse, begins with it too.

The Teth is identified with *tov*, good. However, permanent good is reserved for the world to come.

The Heth is the first letter of *hanun*, the Gracious One; but this advantage is offset by its place in the word for sin, *hattath*.

Zayin was disqualified because it is the word for weapon, the doer of mischief.

Wav and Hey compose the Ineffable Name of God; they are therefore too exalted to be pressed into the service of a mundane world.

Daleth stands for *din*, justice; but justice untempered by mercy would bring the world to ruin.

The Gimmel would not do, because *gemul*, retribution, starts with it.

When the claims of all these letters had been disposed of, the Beth stepped before the Holy One, blessed be he, and pleaded: Lord of the universe, may it be thy will to create thy world through me, since all the inhabitants of the world will give praise daily unto thee through me, for it is written: "Blessed (*barukh*) be the Lord forever." God at once granted the petition of Beth, and created the world through it, and so it is written: "*Bereshith*, in the beginning, God created the heaven and the earth."

The only letter that had refrained from making any claims was the modest Alef, and God rewarded it later for its humility by giving it the first place in the Ten Commandments, which begin with *Anokhi*.

MEDIEVAL AND RENAISSANCE TIMES

Solomon ibn Gabirol
TWO POEMS

Solomon ibn Gabirol (c. 1020–c. 1057) considered himself to be a native of Malagá, yet it is uncertain if he was actually born there. A philosopher, he also wrote both secular and religious poetry. As a testament to his poetic genius, many of Gabirol's liturgical poems have been included not only in Sephardic prayer books, but also in those of the Ashkenazi and Karaite communities.

NIGHT STORM

I am the man who braced himself and will not desist until he fulfils his vow— whose heart recoiled from his heart, whose spirit scorned to dwell in his flesh, who chose wisdom even as a youth—though he be tested seven times in the crucible of Time, though it pull down whatever he has built, though it uproot whatever he has planted and breach all his barriers.

As I slept—and the skies were spotless—the radiant, pure-hearted moon led me over the paths of wisdom and, as he led me, instructed me in his light. And I, fearing some misfortune, was filled with pity for his light, as a father for his first-born son.

Then the wind assailed the moon with sailing clouds, and they covered his face with a mask. It was as if the wind craved for streams of rain and pressed upon the clouds to make them flow. The skies robed themselves in darkness. It seemed as if the moon had died, and the cloud had buried him. And all the other clouds of heaven wept for him, as the people of Aram wept for the son of Beor.

Then the night put on an armour-plate of darkness; thunder, with a spear of lightning, pierced it; and the lightning flew about the skies, as if it were jousting with the night, spreading its wings like a bat; the ravens of the dark fled when they saw it. And God closed in my thoughts. He barred my heart's desire from all sides. He bound my heart with ropes of darkness. Yet it arose like a warrior breaking out of a siege.

But I dare not hope, my friends, for the light of the moon, which has turned into pitch-black darkness, as though the clouds were jealous of my soul and therefore deprived me of his light. And when I chance to see his face revealed, I rejoice like a slave who sees that his master remembers him. When a mortal wages war, his spear is beaten down; and when he tries to run, his steps falter. And even the man whose spirit dwells in the shining heavens—misfortune overtakes him.

Before I was, Your enduring love came to me, O You who make being out of nothingness, and You created me. Who was it that designed my form? Who cast my body in a crucible and then made it congeal? Who was it that breathed into me the breath of life? Who opened the belly of Sheol and brought me forth? Who has been my guide from boyhood to this day? Who taught me wisdom and showed me wonders? Yes, I am like clay in Your hands. Truly, it was You, not I, that made me. And so I shall confess my guilt; nor shall I say, "It was the serpent who conspired to deceive me." How could I ever conceal my sin from You? Even before I was, Your enduring love came to me!

Judah Halevi
TO ISRAEL IN EXILE

Judah Halevi (c. 1075–c. 1114,) born and raised in Muslim Spain, received his education in both Hebrew and Arabic. Although trained as a physician, he won particular fame as a poet and philosopher. His best known work, The Kuzari, *describes the conversion of the king of the Khazars to Judaism, and took Halevi twenty years to complete. During that time, he decided to make* aliyah, *the journey to Israel, but he apparently died in Egypt before reaching his final destination. His great love for the land of Zion is evident in this poem, translated by Rabbi Morrison David Bial.*

He sleeps, but His heart is awake, burning and raging.
Arise, wake and go forth;
    walk in the light of My presence.
Rise and ride on! A star has risen for you.
He who has lain in the pit has ascended to the top of Sinai.
Let them not preen their souls,
    those who say, "Zion is desolate!"—
    for there is My heart and there are My eyes.
I reveal Myself and I conceal Myself,
    I rage, I consent—
but who will show more compassion than I for My children?

Moses Maimonides
THIRTEEN PRINCIPLES OF FAITH

Rambam is the common acronym of Rabbi Moses ben Maimon (1135–1204), the foremost rabbinic authority and philosopher of the posttalmudic era. As a rabbi and a scholar, Maimonides summarized his understanding of Judaism in thirteen principles that he felt every member of the Jewish community should accept. Although they were never accepted as binding or definitive, these articles have found a home in many prayer books, both in the credal form seen here and in poetic form (as, for instance, in the popular hymn Yigdal*). Many victims of the Holocaust recited the words as a statement of faith and act of protest when they faced their death.*

I believe with perfect faith that the Creator, blessed be His name, is the Author and Guide of everything that has been created, and that He alone has made, does make, and will make all things.

I believe with perfect faith that the Creator, blessed be His name, is a Unity, and that there is no unity in any manner like unto his, and that He alone is our God, who was, is, and will be.

I believe with perfect faith that the Creator, blessed be His name, is not a body, and that He is free from all the accidents of matter, and that He has not any form whatsoever.

I believe with perfect faith that the Creator, blessed be His name, is the first and the last.

I believe with perfect faith that to the Creator, blessed be His name, and to Him alone, it is right to pray, and that it is not right to pray to any being besides Him.

I believe with perfect faith that all the words of the prophets are true.

I believe with perfect faith that the prophecy of Moses our teacher, peace be unto him, was true, and that he was the chief of the prophets, both of those that preceded and of those that followed him.

I believe with perfect faith that the whole Law, now in our possession, is the same that was given to Moses our teacher, peace be unto him.

MOSES MAIMONIDES. *Mishneh Torah.* c. 1180. Vellum. The Jewish National and University Library, Jerusalem. *The inscription asks, "How much I love your Torah. All day long I talk about it."*

I believe with perfect faith that this Law will not be changed and that there will never be any other law from the Creator, blessed be His name,

I believe with perfect faith that the Creator, blessed be His name, knows every deed of the children of men, and all their thoughts, as it is said, It is he that fashioneth the hearts of them all, that giveth heed to all their deeds.

I believe with perfect faith that the Creator, blessed be His name, rewards those that keep his commandments, and punishes those that transgress them.

I believe with perfect faith in the coming of the Messiah, and though he tarry, I will wait daily for his coming.

I believe with perfect faith that there will be a resurrection of the dead at the time when it shall please the Creator, blessed be His name, and exalted be the remembrance of him for ever and ever.

Moses Maimonides

LETTER TO SAMUEL IBN TIBBON
A Day in the Life of a Court Physician

Samuel ibn Tibbon (c. 1160–c. 1230) wrote to Maimonides to seek his assistance in translating Maimonides' Guide of the Perplexed *into Hebrew from the Arabic original. Ibn Tibbon expressed his desire to meet with Maimonides, but Maimonides wrote that such a meeting would not be possible because of his difficult daily schedule.*

I live in Fusṭāṭ, and the king lives in Cairo, and between the two places there is a distance of two Sabbath day's journey [about 1 1/2 miles]. With the king I have a very heavy program. It is impossible for me not to see him first thing every day. If he suffers any indisposition, or if any of his sons or concubines falls sick, I cannot leave Cairo, and I spend most of my day in the palace. It may also happen that one or two of his officers fall sick, and I must attend to them. In short, I go to Cairo early every morning, and if there is no mishap and nothing new, I return to Fusṭāṭ in the afternoon, and certainly not before then. By then I am hungry, and I find the anterooms all filled with people: Gentiles and Jews, great and small, judges and bailiffs, friends and enemies, a mixed multitude, who await the moment of my return. I dismount from my beast and wash my hands and go to them to soothe them and placate them and beg them to excuse me and wait while I eat a quick meal, my only one in the whole day. Then I go out to treat them and write prescriptions and instructions for their illnesses. They come and go without a break until night, and sometimes, I swear by my faith in the Torah, until two hours of the night or more. I talk to them and instruct them and converse with them, lying on my back from exhaustion. By nightfall I am so worn out that I cannot speak. In fine, no Jew can speak to me or keep company with me or have private conversation with me except on the Sabbath. Then all or most of the congregation come to me after prayers, and I instruct the community on what they should do throughout the week, and they read for a while until noon, and then they go their way; some of them return and read again between the afternoon and evening prayers.

This is how I spend the day.

FROM MIMEKOR YISRAEL

"Rabbi Moses ben Maimon and the Physicians: The Poison"

Mimekor Yisrael, a collection of Jewish folk-tales gleaned from classical sources, medieval folklore books, and other later works, was published in Germany during and just after the First World War. This tale focuses on Moses Maimonides, the Rambam, as a physician rather than as a philosopher or Jewish scholar.

_____

It is told that the Rambam, Rabbi Moses ben Maimon, may he rest in peace, was a minister of a king of Spain who raised him up above all his other ministers on account of his wisdom. For he was versed in all knowledge, and particularly in the knowledge of remedies; so the king loved him very much. In due course and by reason of the great honor the king showed him, the other ministers began to envy him and denounce him to the king, so that he fled away to Egypt. And he knew the Arabic language perfectly, but did not know the Chaldean and Median languages.

While he was in Egypt, he took disciples from Alexandria and Damascus and established a great Yeshiva, and his fame spread afar. His wisdom was widely known among the Jews but concealed from the Gentiles, because he was not familiar with those languages. So he chose to study the languages of Chaldea and the Hagarenes, and within seven years he had mastered those tongues too, and his fame became known throughout the land. Then the king of Egypt took him to be a physician.

Now in Egypt it was the custom for the sultan to be seated on his royal throne on certain days, and he had seven levels of seats representing the seven sciences of those times; and the great sages and ministers used to be seated upon them. Now the king did not know on which of these levels to seat the Rambam, for he found that he was wiser than all the sages in all the sciences and fields of knowledge. And by reason of his great modesty the rabbi never wished to take his seat on any of these levels.

Now after the ministers and sages of the king who took their place on these levels saw the great honor and affection which the king bestowed upon him, they envied him exceedingly and spoke misleadingly to the king regarding him. In due course they began to discuss the science of medicine in his presence, after having arranged among themselves that whoever overcame the other would be the greatest and wisest of the physicians.

They agreed to accept a drug which the Rambam would prepare for them, while he accepted the drug that they would prepare for him, and they all would drink it off in the presence of the king. But they insisted that the Rambam should drink the potion that they prepared for him first, and only afterwards would they drink. And he agreed to this.

Now on the appointed day the Rambam told his pupils of this matter, and it seemed very wrong to them. But he laughed at them and instructed them as to all the remedies and treatments which he would need before and after drinking, and they prepared all these very carefully. Then the disciples proclaimed a fast and prayed to the Lord for their master, while he went to the king. There the physicians gave him a goblet of poison which he drank, returning home at once. His disciples did all that he had instructed them, and the Lord was with him, and he was healed.

Now on the third day he also appeared before the king, bearing poison with him. The men there were astonished and wondered how the Jew had been preserved; yet in their own despite they had to drink, and ten of them perished in the presence of the king. And the king was indeed astonished at him and honored him even more than he had done before. So the rabbi became most highly honored and glorified in the eyes of the king and the ministers, while the faces of his foes turned black as the sides of a cooking pot; and he lived henceforth in peace.

King and Seer. 1450.
Watercolor. 6 × 4″
(15.2 × 10.1 cm).
Mss. Opp. 154. fols.
44v and 45r. Bodleian
Library, Oxford. *This
manuscript is a copy of a
13th-century Spanish
collection of fables written
by a physician and
Hebrew writer, Isaac ben
Solomon ibn Abi
Sahulah.*

FROM THE ZOHAR
The Torah and Her Lovers

*The Zohar, or Book of Splendor, is the central literary work of the Kabbalah, the esoteric teachings
of Judaism and Jewish mysticism. The work portrays itself as the teaching of Simeon bar Yohai,
a great scholar of the second century. The majority of the text is arranged according to the weekly
Torah portions, but there are many digressions.*

When the ancient one had reached this point he paused, and the two rabbis prostrated
themselves before him, wept and said: "Had we come into this world only in order to
hear these thy words from thy mouth it were sufficient." Said he: "Associates, I did not
begin to speak to you merely in order to tell you what I have told up till now, for, surely,
an old man like myself would not limit himself to one saying, making a noise like a single
coin in a jug. How many human beings live in confusion of mind, beholding not the
way of truth whose dwelling is in the Torah, the Torah which calls them day by day to
herself in love, but alas, they do not even turn their heads! It is indeed as I have said, that
the Torah lets out a word, and emerges for a little from her sheath, and then hides herself
again. But she does this only for those who understand and obey her. She is like unto a
beautiful and stately damsel, who is hidden in a secluded chamber of a palace and who
has a lover of whom no one knows but she. Out of his love for her he constantly passes
by her gate, turning his eyes towards all sides to find her. She, knowing that he is always
haunting the palace, what does she do? She opens a little door in her hidden palace,
discloses for a moment her face to her lover, then swiftly hides it again. None but he
notices it; but his heart and soul, and all that is in him are drawn to her, knowing as he
does that she has revealed herself to him for a moment because she loves him. It is the
same with the Torah, which reveals her hidden secrets only to those who love her. She

knows that he who is wise of heart daily haunts the gates of her house. What does she do? She shows her face to him from her palace, making a sign of love to him, and straightway returns to her hiding place again. No one understands her message save he alone, and he is drawn to her with heart and soul and all his being. Thus the Torah reveals herself momentarily in love to her lovers in order to awaken fresh love in them. Now this is the way of the Torah. At first, when she begins to reveal herself to a man, she makes signs to him. Should he understand, well and good, but if not, then she sends for him and calls him 'simpleton,' saying to her messengers: 'Tell that simpleton to come here and converse with me,' as it is written: 'Whoso is a simpleton let him turn in hither' (Prov. IX, 4). When he comes to her she begins to speak to him, first from behind the curtain which she has spread for him about her words suitable to his mode of understanding, so that he may progress little by little. This is called 'Derasha' (Talmudic casuistry, namely the derivation of the traditional laws and usages from the letter of Scripture). Then she speaks to him from behind a thin veil of a finger mesh, discoursing riddles and parables—which go by the name of Haggadah. When at last he is familiar with her she shows herself to him face to face and converses with him concerning all her hidden mysteries and all the mysterious ways which have been secreted in her heart from time immemorial. Then such a man is a true adept in the Torah, a 'master of the house,' since she has revealed to him all her mysteries, withholding and hiding nothing. She says to him: 'Seest thou the sign, the hint, which I gave thee at first, how many mysteries it contains?' He realizes then that nothing may be added to nor taken from the words of the Torah, not even one sign or letter. Therefore men should follow the Torah with might and main in order that they may become her lovers, as has been described.' "

Obadiah ben Abraham Yare di Bertinoro
LETTER TO HIS FATHER
1488

Bertinoro (c. 1450–before 1516) is the author of a standard commentary on the Mishnah, which is often printed along with the text in most editions. He is also well known for his rabbinical work with the Jewish community of Jerusalem. In 1485, he traveled through his native Italy before leaving for Rhodes, Egypt, and the land of Israel in 1487. His observations, recorded here, offer a rich description of the Jewish, Samaritan, and Karaite communities of the countries he visited. Bertinoro reached Jerusalem in 1488 and was eventually buried there on the Mount of Olives.

On the first day of the ninth month (Sivan, 1486), after having arranged all matters in my place of residence, Citta di Castello, I repaired to Rome, and thence to Naples, where I arrived on the 12th of Sivan, and where I tarried for a long time, not finding any vessel such as I wished. I went to Salerno, where I gave gratuitous instruction for at least four months, and then returned to Naples.

In the fourth month, on the fast-day (the 17th of Thammuz) 1487, I set out from Naples, in the large and magnificent ship Messen Belanez (?) together with eight other Jews; it was five days, however, before we reached Palermo, owing to a calm.

Palermo is the chief town of Sicily, and contains about 850 Jewish families, all living in one street which is situated in the best part of the town. They are artisans—such as copper-smiths and iron-smiths, porters and peasants, and are despised by the Christians because they wear tattered garments. As a mark of distinction they are obliged to wear a piece of red cloth, about the size of a gold coin, fastened on the breast. The royal tax falls heavily on them, for they are obliged to work for the king at any employment that is given them; they have to draw ships to the shore, to construct dykes, and so on. They are also employed in administering corporal punishment and in carrying out the sentence of death. . . .

On the eve of Sukoth, 5248 (the feast of Tabernacles) a French galley came to Palermo, on its way to Alexandria. The worthy Meshulam of Volturna was in it, with his servant, and I rejoiced to travel in his company. The night after Sabbath Bereshith we embarked, and on Sunday at mid-day we left Palermo. All day and night we had a favourable wind, so that in the morning we were close to the Pharos of Messina; we got safely past this, and were in Messina on Monday at noon. This town is a place of trade for all nations; ships come here from all parts; for Messina lies in the middle of the Pharos, so that ships from the east and the west pass it by, and its harbour is the only one of its kind in the world; the largest vessels may here come close to the shore. Messina is not so large as Palermo, neither has it such good openings; but the town is very beautiful and has a strong fortress. There are about 400 Jewish families in it, living quietly in a street of their own; they are richer than those in Palermo, and are almost all artisans; there are only a few merchants among them. They have a Synagogue with a porch, open above, but enclosed on the four sides, and in the middle of it is a well with spring water. There is an administration consisting of persons who are chosen every year; and this, as well as other arrangements resembles that of the Jews of Palermo. . . .

On the eleventh of Marcheshwan (October) we left Messina to go to Rhodes; we were joined in the ship by a Jewish merchant from Sucari, with his servant, three Jewish leatherworkers from Syracuse, and a Sephardic Jew with his wife, two sons, and two daughters, so that together we were fourteen Jewish souls on board. We passed the Pharos in safety, sailed through the Gulf of Venice, and thus reached the Archipelago. The Archipelago is full of small islands. Corfu, Candia, Negropont, Rhodes, and Cyprus, are reckoned among its islands; and, altogether, it is said to contain about 300 inhabited and uninhabited islands. For four days we had a favourable wind; on the fourth day, towards evening we were thrown back by a storm, and could only escape the fury of the waves by remaining in a little natural harbour in the mountains, into which we were thrown; these mountains are full of St. John's bread and myrtle-trees, and here we remained for three days.

After three days, on Sunday the 18th of Marcheshwan, we left this place and came within 60 miles of Rhodes. All the way we saw islands on both sides, and the Turkish mountains were also visible. But we were driven back 80 miles; and the ship had to cast anchor on the shores of the island Longo, which is under the dominion of Rhodes, and there we had to remain ten days, for the wind was unfavourable. . . .

The inhabitants of Rhodes welcomed us gladly, for the master of our ship was a friend and relative of the Governor. The chief men of the Jewish community of Rhodes soon came to our ship, and received us with kindness; for the merchant Meshulam, who had been with us in the ship, was the brother of the physician, R. Nathan, the most distinguished man among the Jews of Rhodes. A fine room, provided with all necessaries, was assigned to me; while the other Jews, who accompanied me were accommodated as well as it was possible, for the Jewish house in Rhodes had been almost entirely destroyed by the siege of the Turks, under their first Emperor, undertaken by him in the year of his death. No one who has not seen Rhodes, with its high and strong walls, its firm gates and battlements, has ever seen a fortress. The Turkish Emperor, in the year of his death, sent a besieging army against it, bombarded the town with a multitude of stones, which are still to be seen there, and in this way threw down the walls surrounding the Jewish street and destroyed the houses. The Jews here have told me that when the Turks got into the town they killed all before them until they came to the door of the Synagogue, when God brought confusion among them, so that they began at once to flee, and slew one another. On account of this miracle the Governor built a church on the spot, and gave the Jews another building instead of it. While I was in Rhodes, he granted them 100 ducats from the revenues of the town, to build a new synagogue.

Not many Jews have remained in Rhodes; altogether there are twenty-two families, all poor, who subsist with difficulty on vegetables, not eating bread or meat, for they never slaughter, nor do they buy any wine for fear of getting into disputes with the Greeks who dwell there. When they buy in the market, they touch nothing that belongs to the Greeks; and they observe the law against wine just as strictly as that against pork. The Jews here are all very intelligent and well-educated; they speak a pure dialect, and are very moral and polite; even the tanners are neatly dressed and speak with propriety. They all allow their hair to grow long, and are beautiful in person. Nowhere are there more beautiful women than in Rhodes; they occupy themselves in doing all kinds of handiwork for the Acomodoren (the nobles of the land), and in this way support their husbands. The Acomodoren hold the Jews in high esteem, often coming into their houses to chat awhile with the women who work there. . . .

In Alexandria there are about 25 families and two old synagogues. One is very large and somewhat damaged, the other is smaller. Most pray in the smaller, because it bears the name of the prophet Elijah; and it is said that he once appeared to somebody in the south-east corner, where a light is now kept constantly burning. I have been told that 20 years ago he again appeared to an old man; God alone knows the truth. In all Arabian countries no man enters the synagogue with shoes on his feet; even in paying a visit the shoes are left outside, at the door; and everybody sits on the ground on mats or carpets.

Alexandria is a very large town, surrounded with a wall, and encircled by the sea, though two-thirds of it are now destroyed, and many houses uninhabited. The inhabited courts are paved with mosaic; peach and date-trees are in the middle of them. All the houses are large and beautiful, but the inhabitants are few on account of the unhealthy atmosphere, which has prevailed here for many years. It is said that those who are not accustomed to the air, and remain long here, die, or at least fall sick. Most of the inhabitants are subject to diseases of the eye. Merchants come from all parts, and at present there are four consuls here; for Venice, Genoa, Catalonia, and Ancona; and the merchants of all nations have to treat with them. The Christians are obliged to shut themselves in their houses.

I spent seven days in Alexandria, leaving my effects which were very few, in the large ship, which was still detained in Bukari by the calm. It happened just at this time that there was a man in Alexandria who had made a vow to celebrate the passover-feast in Jerusalem with his wife and two sons; I joined myself to him, and travelled with him on camels. I commissioned R. Moshe Grasso to bring my things from the large ship, and to send them to me at Cairo. At Rosetta on the Nile we got into a ship. On both sides of the Nile there are towns and villages, which are beautiful, large and populous, but all unfortified. We remained two days in Fuah, because the wind was not favourable; it is a large and beautiful place, and fish and vegetables can be got almost for nothing. We came next to Bulak, which already forms the beginning of Cairo. On the Nile I saw the large species of frog, which the natives call *El Timsah,* (the crocodile); it is larger than a bear, and spots are visible on its skin. The ship's crew say that there are some twice this size— the frogs which have remained from the time of Moses, as Maimonides mentions in his commentary. The Nile is wide, and its waters are very sweet, but troubled; the part where we sailed forms merely a branch, for the other goes to Damietta, where it flows into the sea. . . .

In Cairo there are now about 700 Jewish families; of these 50 are Samaritans, called also Cutheans; 150 are Karaites, and the rest Rabbanites. The Samaritans have only the five books of Moses; and their mode of writing differs from ours, the sacred writing. Maimonides remarks that this writing was customary among the Israelites before the time of the Assyrian exile, as already related in the Tract Sanhedrim; but their language is like ours. Wherever the tetragrammaton occurs in scripture, they write Ashima; they are an abomination to the Jews because they offer up sacrifices and frankincense on Mount

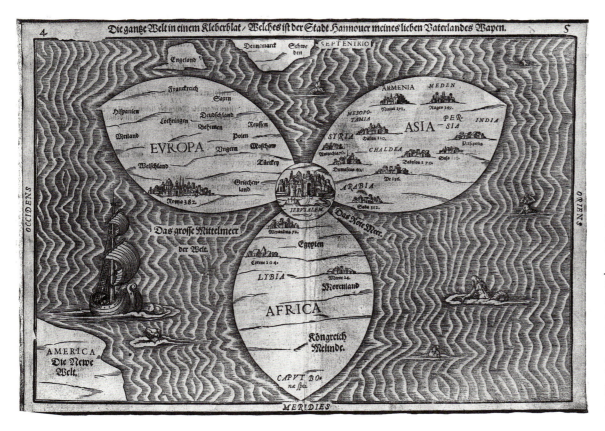

Die gantze Welt in einem Kleeberblat / Welches ist der Stadt Hannouer meines lieben Vaterlandes Wapen.

HEINRICH BUNTING.
*Map of the World in
Cloverleaf Form with
Jerusalem in the Center,*
from H. Bunting,
*Itinerarium Sacrae
Scripturae.* Helmstadt,
1581. Woodcut. 11 13/16
× 14 15/16" (30 × 38
cm). Collection of
Teddy Kollek.
Photograph, Israel
Museum, Jerusalem.

Gerizim. Many of them left Cairo with us to bring the passover-offering to Mount Gerizim, for they have a temple there; they celebrate the Sabbath from the midnight of Friday till the midnight of Saturday. There are very few of them in existence now: it is said scarcely 500 families altogether.

The Karaim, as you know, do not believe the words of our sages; but they are familiar with the Bible. . . . I have seen some of their commentaries, such as that of Japhet, which is quoted by Ibn-Ezra, and those of R. Aaron, the Karaite; every day they make new explanations of the Thora, and maintain that even a fundamental law which has been established by the Ancients, may be altered if it does not appear to one of their wise men now living to agree with the text of the Bible, and they decide everything by the letter of the Thora. In all this they do not consider that either old or living scholars do any wrong. . . .

In Cairo there are about fifty families of forced apostates (New Christians), from Spain, who have all done penance; they are mostly poor, having left their possessions, their parents, and relatives, and come here to seek shelter under the wings of the Lord God of Israel. Among the Jews in Cairo there are money-changers and merchants; for the country is large, and some branch of industry is open to every one. For trade there is no better place in the world than Cairo; it is easy to grow rich; hence one meets there with innumerable foreigners of all nations and languages. You may go out by night as well as by day, for all the streets are lighted with torches; the people sleep on the ground before the shop. The Jew can buy everything that is necessary such as meat, cheese, fish, vegetables, and in general, all that he requires, for everything is sold in the Jews' street; this is the case also in Palermo, but there it is not the same as in Cairo, for in the latter place the Jews cook at home only for the Sabbath, since men as well as women are occupied during the whole week, and can therefore buy everything at the market. Wood is very dear; a load of wood, not so large as the load of a pair of mules, costs upwards of two-thirds of a ducat, and even more; meat and fruit are also dear; the former is very good however, especially the tail of the sheep. The Karaites do not eat this, for according to them it belongs to that kind of fat which the Thora has forbidden. I have seen nothing cheap in Cairo except onions of the Nile, leek, melons, gourds, and vegetables. Bread is cheap in years of plenty—it is made in the form of a cake, and is kneaded very soft.

The wilderness between Egypt and Palestine is not large, for from one day's journey to another there are places of encampment for the camels, erected principally for travellers; yet it is all sand, and no vegetation whatever is to be seen except date-trees in certain well-known places. Water is found after every two days' journey, sometimes even after one day's journey, but it is rather brackish.

In the wilderness we came to Arish, said to be the former Succoth. The caravans going through the wilderness either encamp at mid-day and journey in the evening till midnight; or travel from midnight into the third part of the day; this depends on the will of those who have charge of the caravans. Generally speaking, they travel by night rather than by day.

Thus we journeyed from place to place in the wilderness, till we came to Gaza, without misadventure. Gaza is the first town that we found on coming out of the wilderness leading to the land of the Philistines. It is a large and beautiful city, of the same size as Jerusalem, but without walls; for among all the places under Egyptian dominion, which now extends over Palestine, the country of the Philistines, and Syria, Alexandria is the only one surrounded by walls. If the account of the Jews living there be correct, I saw in Gaza the ruins of the building that Samson pulled down on the Philistines. We remained four days in Gaza; there is now a Rabbi from Germany there, by name Rabbi Moses, of Prague, who fled thither from Jerusalem; he insisted on my going to his house, and I was obliged to stay with him all the time I was in Gaza. On the Sabbath all the wardens were invited to dine with us. Cakes of grapes and fruit were brought; we partook of several glasses before eating, and were joyful.

On Sunday, the 11th of Nissan (April), we journeyed from Gaza on asses; we came within two miles of Hebron, and there spent the night. On Monday we reached Hebron, a small town on the slope of the mountain, called by the Turks, Chalil. It is divided into two parts, one beside the Cave of the Patriarchs; the other opposite, a bow-shot farther away. I was in the Cave of Machpelah, over which a mosque has been built; and the Arabs hold the place in high honour. All the kings of the Arabs come here to repeat their prayers; but neither a Jew nor an Arab can enter the cave itself, where the real graves of the Patriarchs are; the Arabs remain above, and let down burning torches into it through a window, for they keep a light always burning there. All who come to pray leave money, which they throw into the cave through the window; when they wish to take the money out, they let down a young man, who is unmarried, by a rope, to bring it up—so I have been told by the Jews who live there. All Hebron with its fields and neighbourhood belongs to the cave; bread and lentil, or some other kind of pulse, is distributed to the poor every day, without distinction of faith, and this is done in honour of Abraham. Without, in the wall of the cave, there is a small opening, said to have been made just after the burial of Abraham; and there the Jews are allowed to pray, but none may come within the walls of the cave. At this little window I offered up my prayers. On the summit of the opposite mountain is a large cave, said to be the grave of Jesse, the father of David. We went there also to pray on the same day. Between the grave of Jesse and the Cave of the Patriarchs is a well, which the Arabs call the well of Isaac, said to have belonged to the patriarch Isaac. Near to Hebron, between rocks, there is a spring of fresh water, distinguished as the well of Sarah. Hebron has many vineyards and olive-trees, and contains at the present time twenty families, all Rabbanites, half of whom are descendants of the forced Apostates who have recently returned to their faith.

On Tuesday morning, the 13th of Nissan, we left Hebron, which is a day's journey distant from Jerusalem, and came on as far as Rachel's tomb, where there is a round, vaulted building in the open street. We got down from our asses and prayed at the grave, each one according to his ability. On the right hand of the traveller to Jerusalem lies the hill on which Bethlehem stands; this is a small village, about half a mile from Rachel's grave, and the Catholic priests have a church there. . . .

Jerusalem is for the most part desolate and in ruins. I need not repeat that it is not

COLORPLATE 37
JEAN-LEON GERÔME. *The Wailing Wall*. 1880. Oil on canvas. 28¾ × 23⁷⁄₁₆″ (73 × 59.5 cm).
Collection, Israel Museum, Jerusalem.

COLORPLATE 38
Artist unknown. *Saul Levi Löwenstam* 1780. Oil on panel. 8¼ × 6¼″ (21 × 16 cm).
Jewish Historical Museum, Amsterdam.

צורת הרב זה מוהרר יהונתן דצלאבר רקס אלשנא המבורג ואנזיבעק

COLORPLATE 39

Artist unknown. *Rabbi Yehonatan Eybeschütz*. 19th century. Oil on canvas. 20¹³⁄₁₆ × 16⁷⁄₁₆″ (52 × 41 cm). Sir Isaac and Lady Edith Wolfson Museum, Hechal Schlomo, Jerusalem. *Eybeschütz was a well-known talmudist and kabbalist from Prague. He subsequently became rabbi of the "Three Communities"— Altona, Hamburg, and Wandsbek.*

COLORPLATE 40

MORITZ DANIEL OPPENHEIM. *Lavater and Lessing Visiting Moses Mendelssohn*. 1856. Oil on canvas.
33 × 28″ (83.8 × 71.1 cm). Judah L. Magnes Museum, Berkeley.

COLORPLATE 41
TELEMACO SIGNORINI. *Il Ghetto a Firenze (The Ghetto in Florence)*. 1882. Oil on canvas.
37½ × 25⅝″ (95 × 65 cm). Galleria Nazionale d'Arte Moderna, Rome.

COLORPLATE 42

Portion of a Synagogue Wall, Persia. 16th century. Faience tile mosaic. 104 × 186″ (264.2 × 472.4 cm). The Jewish Museum, New York. Gift of Adele and Dr. Harry G. Friedman, Lucy and Henry Moses, Miriam Schaar Schloessinger, Florence Sutro Anspacher, Lucille and Samuel Lemberg, John S. Lawrence, Louis A. Oresman, and Khalil Rabenou. *This mosaic wall of glazed tiles displays the floral and geometric designs, color, and style typical of*

Islamic architecture and design. The Sephardim traditionally house their Torah scrolls in rigid upright containers, and the niches on this wall were used to hold the Torah cases when they were not in use. Verses from the Psalter are inscribed in Hebrew at the top of the wall: "But I through Your abundant love, enter your house; I bow down in awe at Your holy temple" (Psalm 5:8); "This is the gateway to the Lord, the righteous shall enter through it" (Psalm 118:20).

COLORPLATE 43
"Aron Kodesh" from the Vittorio Veneto Synagogue, Italy. 1701. Carved and gilt wood. Width: 11¼'
(34.4 m). Collection, Israel Museum, Jerusalem. Transferred and installed in the museum with the
help of Jakob Michael, N.Y., in memory of his wife Erna Sondheimer Michael.

surrounded by walls; its inhabitants, I am told, number about 4,000 families. As for Jews, about 70 families of the poorest class have remained; there is scarcely a family that is not in want of the commonest necessaries; one who has bread for a year is called rich. Among the Jewish population there are many aged, forsaken widows from Germany, Spain, Portugal, and other countries, so that there are seven women to one man.

Ferdinand and Isabella of Spain
EDICT OF EXPULSION OF THE JEWS

Spain had been an intellectual and cultural center of Jewish life for centuries. Prior to the expulsion of 1492, Jews played a significant role in affairs of state. King Ferdinand and Queen Isabella ordered the eviction of all the Jews from their territories because they feared that the Jews were subverting Catholicism and enticing Christians to apostatize.

Whereas, having been informed that in these our kingdoms, there were some bad Christians who judaized and apostatized from our holy catholic faith, the chief cause of which was the communication of Jews with Christians; at the Cortes we held in the city of Toledo in the year 1480, we ordered the said Jews in all the cities, towns, and places in our kingdoms and dominions, to separate into Jewries and places apart, where they should live and reside, hoping by their separation alone to remedy the evil. Furthermore, we have sought and given orders, that inquisition should be made in our said kingdoms, which, as is known, for upwards of twelve years has been, and is done, whereby many guilty persons have been discovered, as is notorious. And as we are informed by the inquisitors, and many other religious, ecclesiastical, and secular persons, that great injury has resulted, and does result, and it is stated, and appears to be, from the participation, society, and communication they held and do hold with Jews, who it appears always endeavour in every way they can to subvert our holy catholic faith, and to make faithful Christians withdraw and separate themselves therefrom, and attract and pervert them to their injurious opinions and belief, instructing them in the ceremonies and observances of their religion, holding meetings where they read and teach them what they are to believe and observe according to their religion. . . .

Notwithstanding we were informed of the major part of this before, and we knew the certain remedy for all these injuries and inconveniences was to separate the said Jews from all communication with Christians, and banish them from all our kingdoms, yet we were desirous to content ourselves by ordering them to quit all the cities, towns, and places of Andalusia, where, it appears, they had done the greatest mischief, considering that would suffice, and that those of other cities, towns and places would cease to do and commit the same.

But as we are informed that neither that, nor the execution of some of the said Jews, who have been guilty of the said crimes and offences against our holy Catholic faith, has been sufficient for a complete remedy to obviate and arrest so great an opprobrium and offence to the Catholic faith and religion.

And as it is found and appears, that the said Jews, wherever they live and congregate, daily increase in continuing their wicked and injurious purposes; to afford them no further opportunity for insulting our holy Catholic faith, and those whom until now God has been pleased to preserve, as well as those who had fallen, but have amended and are brought back to our holy mother church, which, according to the weakness of our human nature and the diabolical suggestion that continually wages war with us, may easily occur, unless the principal cause of it be removed, which is to banish the said Jews from our kingdoms.

And when any serious and detestable crime is committed by some persons of a college or university, it is right that such college or university should be dissolved and annihilated, and the lesser suffer for the greater, and one be punished for the other; and those that disturb the welfare and proper living of cities and towns, that by contagion may injure others, should be expelled therefrom, and even for lighter causes that might be injurious to the state, how much more then for the greatest, most dangerous, and contagious of crimes like this.

Therefore we, by and with the counsel and advice of some prelates and high noblemen of our kingdoms, and other learned persons of our council, having maturely deliberated thereon, resolve to order all the said Jews and Jewesses to quit our kingdoms, and never to return or come back to them, or any of them. Therefore we command this our edict to be issued, whereby we command all Jews and Jewesses, of whatever age they may be, that live, reside, and dwell in our said kingdoms and dominions, as well natives as those who are not, who in any manner or for any cause may have come to dwell therein, that by the end of the month of July next, of the present year 1492, they depart from all our said kingdoms and dominions, with their sons, daughters, man-servants, maid-servants, and Jewish attendants, both great and small, of whatever age they may be; and they shall not presume to return to, nor reside therein, or in any part of them, either as residents, travellers, or in any other manner whatever, under pain that if they do not perform and execute the same, and are found to reside in our said kingdoms and dominions, or should in any manner live therein, they incur the penalty of death, and confiscation of all their property to our treasury, which penalty they incur by the act itself, without further process, declaration, or sentence. . . .

THE EXPULSION FROM SPAIN AS SEEN BY A JEW IN ITALY

In 1492, when King Ferdinand and Queen Isabella issued the edict expelling Jews from Spain, the Jews faced a difficult time. They had to completely abandon a country in which they had lived for centuries. Although they could convert to Christianity and remain, the majority fled. This account, probably written by an Italian Jew in April or May of 1495 enumerates the problems the Spanish Jews had not only in fleeing Spain but in traveling to, and relocating in, other Jewish communities.

And in the year 5252 (1492) the Lord visited the remnant of his people a second time, and exiled them in the days of King Ferdinand. After the king had captured the city of Granada from the Ishmaelites, and it had surrendered to him on the 8th of January of the year just mentioned, he ordered the expulsion of all the Jews in all parts of his kingdom— in the kingdoms of Castile, Catalonia, Aragon, Galicia, Majorca, Minorca, the Basque provinces, the islands of Sardinia and Sicily, and the kingdom of Valencia. Even before that the queen had expelled them from the kingdom of Andalusia. The king gave them three months' time to leave in. It was announced in public in every city on the first of May, which happened to be the 19th day of the Omer, and the term ended on the day before the 9th of Ab. The number of the exiled was not counted, but, after many inquiries, I found that the most generally accepted estimate is 50,000 families, or, as others say,

53,000. They had houses, fields, vineyards, and cattle, and most of them were artisans. . . .

In the course of the three months' respite granted them they endeavoured to effect an arrangement permitting them to stay on in the country, and they felt confident of success. Their representatives were the Rabbi, Don Abraham Senior, the leader of the Spanish congregations, who was attended by a retinue on thirty mules, and R. Meïr, the secretary to the king, and Don Isasc Abarbanel, who had fled to Castile from the King of Portugal, and then occupied an equally prominent position at the Spanish royal court, the very one who was expelled, went to Naples, and was highly esteemed by the King of Naples. The aforementioned great Rabbi, R. Isaac of Leon, used to call this Don Abraham Senior Soné Or (Hater of Light), because he was a heretic, and the end proved that he was right, as he was converted to Christianity at the age of eighty, he and all his family, and R. Meïr with him. Don Abraham had arranged the nuptials between the king and the queen. The queen was the heiress to the throne, and the king one of the Spanish nobility. On account of this Don Abraham was appointed leader of the Jews, but not with their consent. The agreement permitting them to remain in the country on the payment of a large sum of money was almost completed when it was frustrated by the interference of an official, who referred to the story of the Cross. Then the queen gave an answer to the representatives of the Jews, similar to the saying of King Solomon: "The king's heart is in the hand of the Lord, as the rivers of water. He turneth it withersoever he will." She said furthermore: "Do you believe that this comes upon you from us? The Lord hath put this thing into the heart of the king." Then they saw that there was evil determined against them by the king, and they gave up the hope of remaining. But the time had become short, and they had to hasten their exodus from Spain. They sold their houses, their landed estates, and their cattle for very small prices, to save themselves. The king did not allow them to carry silver and gold out of his country, so that they were compelled to exchange their silver and gold for merchandise of cloths and skins and other things.

One hundred and twenty thousand of them went to Portugal, according to a compact which a prominent man, Don Vidal bar Benveniste del Cavalleria, had made with the king of Portugal, and they paid one ducat for every soul, and the fourth part of all the merchandise they had carried thither; and he allowed them to stay in his country six months. This king acted much worse toward them than the king of Spain, and after the six months had elapsed he made slaves of all those that remained in his country, and banished seven hundred children to a remote island to settle it, and all of them died. Some say that there were double as many. Upon them the Scriptural word was fulfilled: "Thy sons and thy daughters shall be given unto another people," &c. He also ordered the congregation of Lisbon, his capital, not to raise their voice in their prayers, that the Lord might not hear their complaining about the violence that was done unto them.

Many of the exiled Spaniards went to Mohammedan countries, to Fez, Tlemçen and the Berber provinces, under the king of Tunis. Most of the Moslems did not allow them into their cities, and many of them died in the fields from hunger, thirst, and lack of everything. The lions and bears, which are numerous in this country, killed some of them while they lay starving outside of the cities. A Jew in the kingdom of Tlemçen, named Abraham, the viceroy who ruled the kingdom, made part of them come to this kingdom, and he spent a large amount of money to help them. The Jews of Northern Africa were very charitable toward them. A part of those who went to Northern Africa, as they found no rest and no place that would receive them, returned to Spain, and became converts, and through them the prophecy of Jeremiah was fulfilled: "He hath spread a net for my feet, he hath turned me back." For, originally, they had all fled for the sake of the unity of God; only a very few had become converts throughout all the boundaries of Spain; they did not spare their fortunes, yea, parents escaped without having regard to their children.

When the edict of expulsion became known in the other countries, vessels came from Genoa to carry away the Jews. The crews of these vessels, too, acted maliciously and meanly toward the Jews, robbed them, and delivered some of them to the famous pirate of that time, who was called the Corsair of Genoa. To those who escaped and arrived at Genoa the people of the city showed themselves merciless, and oppressed and robbed them, and the cruelty of their wicked hearts went so far that they took the infants from the mothers' breasts.

Many ships with Jews, especially from Sicily, went to the city of Naples on the coast. The king of this country was friendly to the Jews, received them all, and was merciful towards them, and he helped them with money. The Jews that were at Naples supplied them with food as much as they could, and sent around to the other parts of Italy to collect money to sustain them. The Marranos in this city lent them money on pledges without interest; even the Dominican Brotherhood acted mercifully toward them. But all this was not enough to keep them alive. Some of them died by famine, others sold their children to Christians to sustain their life. Finally, a plague broke out among them, spread to Naples, and very many of them died, so that the living wearied of burying the dead.

Part of the exiled Spaniards went over sea to Turkey. Some of them were thrown into the sea and drowned, but those who arrived there the king of Turkey received kindly, as they were artisans. He lent them money to settle many of them on an island, and gave them fields and estates.

A few of the exiles were dispersed in the countries of Italy, in the city of Ferrara, in the counties of Romagna, le Marche, and Patrimonium, and in Rome.

Before the expulsion the king of Spain had stretched forth his hand against the Marranos, and investigated their secrets, because they observed part of the laws secretly, and he had ordered the Jews in every city to proclaim in the synagogues that whoever knew of any Marrano who gave oil to the lighting of the synagogue, or money for any holy purpose, must reveal his name on penalty of excommunication. Thus the preachers made proclamation in the synagogues in the presence of the royal officials, and they adjured the people with the formula: "If he did not utter it" . . . and with the order of the king to inform against them; and they decreed the ban against everybody who would not give information. Oh, how that sword of excommunication wrought havoc among the Spanish Jews, who wherever they turned found hardship and misfortune! By means of this accusation the Spanish king had many thousands of the Marranos burned, and confiscated their fortunes without number, using the money for the war against Granada. It seems that this was from the Lord to destroy these Marranos, who halted between two opinions, as if they had made a new law for themselves. Their end shows that they did not sanctify the name of the Lord in the hour of their death. When the asked them in which religion they wanted to die they chose Christianity, in order to die an easier death, and they died with a cross in their hands. Only a few of them died as Jews, and of these few most were women.

Moses Hagiz

FROM MISHNAT HAKHAMIM

The Former Marrano's Offering

Marranos were Jews who, to escape persecution, outwardly accepted Christianity. This story comes from an early eighteenth-century work that includes legends such as this one, not found in any other book. The Ari referred to in the story, Rabbi Isaac ben Solomon Ashkenazi Luria (1534–1572), was a seminal kabbalistic thinker whose ideas were extremely influential.

In the days of the Ari—may his memory be for a blessing—it once happened that one of the Marranos who had come from Portugal to the holy city of Safed in the Upper Galilee—may it be built speedily in our days—heard the rabbi of that holy community preach concerning the shewbread that was offered in the Temple from week to week. And it appears that the rabbi sighed during his sermon and, very distressed, said, "And now, due to our many iniquities, we have no such means to enable the divine abundance to descend upon our world."

Hearing this, that former Marrano went home and, in his whole-hearted and simple way, told his wife to prepare for him, at least on Fridays, two rolls of bread waved thirteen times, kneaded in purity, beautifully formed, and baked till done in the oven, as he wished to offer them before the ark of the Lord—perhaps God would favor him by accepting them and consuming them as a burnt offering. His wife did just as he had commanded. And each Friday he would bring those two rolls of bread before the ark of the Lord and would pray and plead before Him that He willingly accept them and eat them, that He might find them tasty and fragrant, and so forth, pleading as a child seeking his father's favor. And he would place the rolls there and leave.

Now the sexton came and took the two rolls without inquiring or questioning from where they had come or who had brought them, and he ate them, delighting in them as one rejoices in the yield of the harvest. Later, at the hour of the evening prayer, that God-fearing man would run to the ark of the Lord, and as he did not find the rolls his heart was full of joy and he went and said to his wife, "Praise to God, may He be blessed, who has not rejected the gift of a poor man, but has already accepted the bread and has eaten it while it is yet warm. For the sake of God, be not careless in preparing them, but be very diligent. For since we have nothing else with which to honor Him and we note that He delights in these rolls, it is our duty to please Him with them." And he persisted in this practice for some time.

One Friday it happened that the congregation's rabbi, whose sermon had prompted the man to bring the rolls, was standing at the reading desk reviewing the Sabbath sermon he would deliver the following day, and he saw that man come, as was his good custom, with the rolls and approach the holy ark. The man began to arrange his words and petitions as he was accustomed to do and because of his overflowing enthusiasm and his sense of joy in bringing his present before God he was unaware that the rabbi was standing by the reading desk.

The rabbi remained silent, observing all that the man did and listening to all that he spoke, and then he became angry and called out to him in rebuke, "Idiot! Does our God eat or drink? Beyond any doubt it is the sexton who takes them, while you are of the opinion that it is God who receives them. It is a terrible error to ascribe any corporeality to God—may He be blessed—who has no body and no bodily image." He went on speaking in this manner until the sexton came, as was his custom, to take the rolls. And as the rabbi saw him he called out to him, "Thank this man, Why have you come? And who took the two rolls that this man has been bringing each Friday here in the holy congregation?" The sexton then confessed what he had done.

Upon hearing this, the man who had brought the offering began to cry. And he asked the rabbi to forgive him for he had misunderstood his sermon and thought he was performing a mitzvah, whereas, in truth, according to the rabbi's words, he was actually committing a transgression.

In the aftermath of all this, a special messenger from the Ari—may his memory be for a blessing—came to the rabbi and told him, in the name of holy Rabbi, "Go home and put your affairs in order, for tomorrow during the course of your sermon you shall die. The decree has already gone out concerning this."

The rabbi was terrified. He went to the Ari to inquire of him the nature of his sin and transgression. And the Ari—may his memory be for a blessing—answered him, "I have heard that it is because you withheld pleasure from God. For from that day on which the Temple was destroyed, God has not experienced such delight as when this former Marrano, in the simplicity of his heart, would bring his two rolls and offer them before His ark, thinking that God—may He be blessed—accepted them from him. And because you stopped him from bringing them, it is decreed irrevocably that you shall die."

The rabbi, who had given that sermon, went and put the affairs of his household in order. And on the holy Sabbath, at the time he was to preach, he died, just as the man of God, the Ari—may his memory be for a blessing—had told him.

FROM FAR-OFF LANDS

Eldad the Danite

FROM LETTER TO THE JEWS OF SPAIN

"The Lost Tribes of Israel"

Eldad the Danite was a late ninth-century traveler whose origins are virtually unknown to us today, except for the fact that he claimed to be descended from the tribe of Dan. He is thought to have visited the Jews of Babylonia, North Africa, and Spain. He told about the Ten Tribes and their continued independent existence. Although the historical authenticity of Eldad's accounts has been questioned by both ancient and modern scholars, it is believed that some of his descriptions were based on actual Jewish rulers and kingdoms, such as the Khazar kingdom.

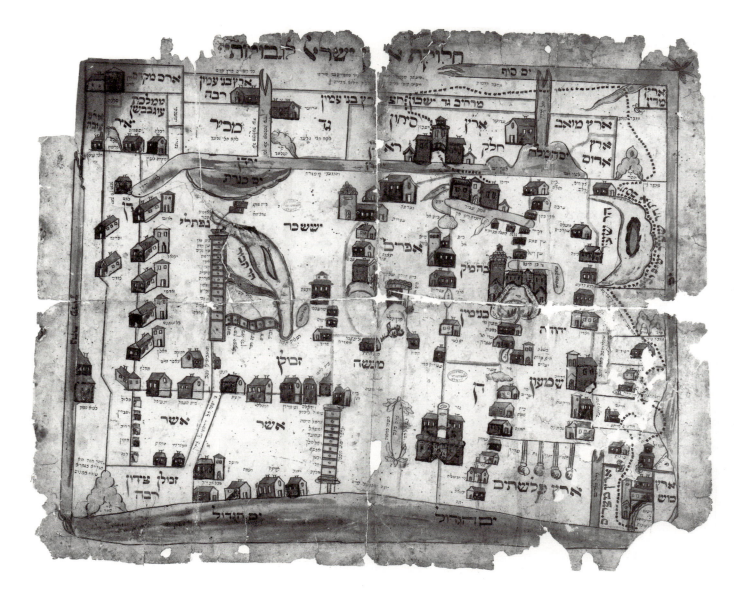

My departure from the other side of the rivers of Ethiopia was in the following manner.

I and a Jew of the tribe of Asher boarded a small ship to trade with the seamen and alas! at midnight, the Lord caused a strong gale to blow up and the ship was wrecked. Now the Lord had prepared a piece of the wreckage and I seized upon it and my companion, seeing this, also took hold of it, and we went up and down with it, until the sea cast us forth among a people called the Romaranus. And they dwelt in one of the seven kingdoms of Ethiopia and they are black Ethiopians, very tall, without raiment upon their bodies; cannibals, like the beasts of the field.

Now when we came to their country, they seized us, and seeing that my companion was fat and delectable, they slaughtered and ate him, and he cried aloud: "Alas for me, that I should have known this people and the Ethiopians should eat my flesh," but me they put aside, for I was sick on the ship, and they put me in chains until I should grow healthy and fat. And they brought me delicious and fattening food, but forbidden according to our Law, but I ate nothing and hid the food, but when they asked me whether I had eaten, I answered and said, "Yes, I have eaten."

And I was among them a long time until God, blessed be He, performed a miracle for me, for a great army came upon them from another place, who plundered and slaughtered more of them, and took me away with the captives. And those wicked men were fire-worshippers and every morning built a great fire and bowed down and lay prostrate before it. And I dwelt among them four years until on a certain day they brought me to a place called Azania.

And a Jewish merchant of the tribe of Issachar found me and bought me for thirty-

Division of the Land of Israel within its Borders, i.e. a Map of Israel Divided among the Tribes. 19th century. Paper. 146½ × 27½" (372 × 70 cm). Eran Laor Cartographic Collection, The Jewish National and University Library, Jerusalem. This map was copied from the original drawn by Rabbi Elijah ben Solomon Zalman (the "Vilna Gaon"), c. 1802.

two pieces of gold, and brought me back to his country. They live in the mountains of the sea-coast and are ruled by the Medes and the Persians, and they fulfil the command, "the book of this law shall not depart from thy mouth." The yoke of power is not upon them but they live under the yoke of the Law. There are among them military leaders but they fight with no man, except to protect the Law. They dwell in prosperity and peace and among them are no troublemakers and no evil happenings. They live in a land ten days' journey by ten days, and they have much cattle and camels and asses and slaves, but they do not rear horses. They have no weapons, except the knife for the slaughter of animals, and among them extortion and robbery do not exist, and even if they should find garments or money on a public road, they would not stretch forth their hands to take them. But near them dwell wicked men, fire-worshippers, who take their own mothers and sisters to wife, but our tribes they do not hurt nor help. And they have a Judge, and I inquired about him and they said his name was Nahshon, and they practice the four death penalties—burning, beheading, stoning, and strangling—in the execution of criminals. They speak the Hebrew and Persian tongues. . . .

And in our country we have a tradition among us that we are the children of the captivity, the tribes of Judah and the tribe of Benjamin, living under the dominion of idolators in an unclean land, that we were scattered under the Romans who destroyed our Holy Temple, and under the Greeks and the Mohammedans, may their sword pierce their own heart and may their bones be broken!

We also have an ancient tradition, handed down from father to son, that we are descendants of the tribe of Dan and in those early days we were tent-dwellers in the land of Israel and among all the tribes of Israel there were none like unto us in strength and valor. And when Jeroboam, the son of Nebat, who caused Israel to sin and made two golden calves, caused a revolt, and brought about the division of the Kingdom of David, the tribes gathered together and said, "Let us arise and fight against Rehoboam and against Jersualem." But the Danites answered, "Why should we fight with our brothers and with the son of our lord David, king of Israel and Judah? God forbid that we should do such a thing!" Then answered the elders of Israel, "In all the tribes of Israel there are no mighty ones like the tribe of Dan. Arise, therefore, and fight with the tribe of Judah." But the Danites refused, saying, "By the life of our father Dan, we will not fight with our brothers, and we will not shed their blood." Whereupon the tribe of Dan took their swords and lances and bows and made ready to depart from the land of Israel, for we saw that we could not remain any longer, and said, "Let us depart now and find a resting-place, for if we wait until the end, we, too, may perish." And then we took counsel and decided to go down to Egypt to lay waste the land and destroy its inhabitants but after deliberation among our princes and nobles we took counsel to go down but not by the way our fathers went and not to lay waste the land but only to pass over the land to cross the river Pishon to Ethiopia. And behold, when we came near to Egypt, all the people trembled and their hearts melted, and sent messengers to us asking, "War or peace?" And we answered, "Peace; we will pass over your country to the river Pishon and there we will find a resting-place for ourselves." But they did not believe us and all the Egyptians were on guard until we passed through their land and arrived in Ethiopia; and we found it a good and fertile land and in it there were fields and vineyards and gardens. The Ethiopians could not prevent our tribe from dwelling with them for we seized the land by force and, because we wished to slay all of them, they had to pay us tribute, and we dwelt with them many years and became fruitful and multiplied and had great riches. . . .

And this is my name and genealogy, Eldad Ben Mahali Ben Ezekiel Ben Hezikiah Ben Aluk Ben Abner Ben Shemayah Ben Hater Ben Hur Ben Elkanah Ben Hillel Ben Tobias Ben Pedath Ben Ainon Ben Naaman Ben Taam Ben Taami Ben Onani Ben Gaul Ben Shalom Ben Caleb Ben Omram Ben Dumain Ben Obadiah Ben Abraham Ben Joseph Ben Moses Ben Jacob Ben Kappus Ben Ariel Ben Asher Ben Job Ben Shallum Ben Clihu Ben Ahaliab Ben Ahisamah Ben Hushim Ben Dan Ben Jacob our Patriarch, peace upon him and all Israel.

And these letters prince Eldad sent to Spain in the year 883.

Benjamin of Tudela
FROM SEFER HA-MASSA'OT *(Book of Travels)*

All we know about this greatest of all medieval Jewish travelers is gleaned from his Book of Travels. *It is assumed that Benjamin began his journey—which lasted no less than five years and maybe as long as fourteen—either in 1159 or 1167, and that he returned to Spain in 1172 or 1173. His account of the Jews of Baghdad, from which this excerpt is taken, is the longest and most comprehensive in his work.*

In Bagdad there are about 40,000 Jews, and they dwell in security, prosperity and honour under the great Caliph, and amongst them are great sages, the heads of Academies engaged in the study of the law. In this city there are ten Academies. At the head of the great Academy is the chief rabbi R. Samuel, the son of Eli. He is the head of the Academy Gaon Jacob. He is a Levite, and traces his pedigree back to Moses our teacher. The head of the second Academy is R. Hanania his brother, warden of the Levites; R. Daniel is the head of the third Academy; R. Elazar the scholar is the head of the fourth Academy; and R. Elazar, the son of Zemach, is the head of the order, and his pedigree reaches to Samuel the prophet, the Korahite. He and his brethren know how to chant the melodies as did the singers at the time when the Temple was standing. He is head of the fifth Academy. R. Hisdai, the glory of the scholars, is head of the sixth Academy. R. Haggai is head of the seventh Academy. R. Ezra is the head of the eighth Academy. R. Abraham, who is called Abu Tahir, is the head of the ninth Academy. R. Zakkai, the son of Bostanai the Nasi, is the head of the Sium. These are the ten Batlanim, and they do not engage in any other work than communal administration; and all the days of the week they judge the Jews their countrymen, except on the second day of the week, when they all appear before the chief rabbi Samuel, the head of the Yeshiba Gaon (Jacob), who in conjunction with the other Batlanim judges all those that appear before him. And at the head of them all is Daniel the son of Hisdai, who is styled "Our Lord the Head of the Captivity of all Israel." He possesses a book of pedigrees going back as far as David, King of Israel. The Jews call him "Our Lord, Head of the Captivity," and the Mohammedans call him "Saidna ben Daoud," and he has been invested with authority over all the congregations of Israel at the hands of the Emir al Muminim, the Lord of Islam. For thus Mohammed commanded concerning him and his descendants; and he granted him a seal of office over all the congregations that dwell under his rule, and ordered that every one, whether Mohammedan or Jew, or belonging to any other nation in his dominion, should rise up before him (the Exilarch) and salute him, and that any one who should refuse to rise up should receive one hundred stripes.

And every fifth day when he goes to pay a visit to the great Caliph, horsemen, Gentiles as well as Jews, escort him, and heralds proclaim in advance, "Make way before our Lord, the son of David, as is due unto him," the Arabic words being "Amilu tarik la Saidna ben Daud." He is mounted on a horse, and is attired in robes of silk and embroidery with a large turban on his head, and from the turban is suspended a long white cloth adorned with a chain upon which the cipher of Mohammed is engraved. Then he appears before the Caliph and kisses his hand, and the Caliph rises and places him on a throne which Mohammed had ordered to be made for him, and all the Mohammedan princes who attend the court of the Caliph rise up before him. And the Head of the Captivity is seated on his throne opposite to the Caliph, in compliance with the command of Mohammed to give effect to what is written in the law—"The sceptre shall not depart from Judah nor a law-giver from between his feet, until he come to Shiloh: and to him shall the gathering of the people be." The authority of the Head of the Captivity extends over all the communities of Shinar, Persia, Khurasan and Sheba which is El-Yemen, and Diyar Kalach (Bekr) and the land of Aram Naharaim (Mesopotamia), and over the dwellers in the mountains of Ararat and the land of the Alans, which is a land surrounded by mountains and has no outlet except by the iron gates which Alexander made, but which were afterwards broken. Here are the people called Alani. His authority extends also over the land of Siberia, and the communities in the land of the Togarmim unto the mountains of Asveh and the land of Gurgan, the inhabitants of which are called Gurganim who dwell by the river Gihon, and these are the Girgashites who follow the Christian religion. Further it extends to the gates of Samarkand, the land of Tibet, and the land of India. In respect of all these countries the Head of the Captivity gives the communities power to appoint Rabbis and Ministers who come unto him to be consecrated and to receive his authority. They bring him offerings and gifts from the ends of the earth. He owns hospices, gardens and plantations in Babylon, and much land inherited from his fathers, and no one can take his possessions from him by force. He has a fixed weekly revenue arising from the hopsices of the Jews, the markets and the merchants, apart from that which is brought to him from far-off lands. The man is very rich, and wise in the Scriptures as well as in the Talmud, and many Israelites dine at his table every day.

At his installation, the Head of the Captivity gives much money to the Caliph, to the Princes and the Ministers. On the day that the Caliph performs the ceremony of investing him with authority, he rides in the second of the royal equipages, and is escorted from the palace of the Caliph to his own house with timbrels and fifes. The Exilarch appoints the Chiefs of the Academies by placing his hand upon their heads, thus installng them in their office. The Jews of the city are learned men and very rich.

In Bagdad there are twenty-eight Jewish Synagogues, situated either in the city itself or in Al-Karkh on the other side of the Tigris; for the river divides the metropolis into two parts. The great synagogue of the Head of the Captivity has columns of marble of various colours overlaid with silver and gold, and on these columns are sentences of the Psalms in golden letters. And in front of the ark are about ten steps of marble; on the topmost step are the seats of the Head of the Captivity and of the Princes of the House of David. The city of Bagdad is twenty miles in circumference, situated in a land of palms, gardens and plantations, the like of which is not to be found in the whole land of Shinar. People come thither with merchandise from all lands. Wise men live there, philosophers who know all manner of wisdom, and magicians expert in all manner of witchcraft.

Thence it is two days to Gazigan which is called Resen. It is a large city containing about 5,000 Jews. In the midst of it is the Synagogue of Rabbah—a large one. He is buried close to the Synagogue, and beneath his sepulchre is a cave where twelve of his pupils are buried.

Thence it is a day's journey to Babylon, which is the Babel of old. The ruins thereof are thirty miles in extent. The ruins of the palace of Nebuchadnezzar are still to be seen there, but people are afraid to enter them on account of the serpents and scorpions. Near at hand, within a distance of a mile, there dwell 3,000 Israelites who pray in the Synagogue of the Pavilion of Daniel, which is ancient and was erected by Daniel. It is built of hewn stones and bricks. Between the Synagogue and the Palace of Nebuchadnezzar is the furnace into which were thrown Hananiah, Mishael, and Azariah, and the site of it lies in a valley known unto all.

Thence it is five parasangs to Hillah, where there are 10,000 Israelites and four Synagogues: that of R. Meir, who lies buried before it; the Synagogue of Mar Keshisha, who is buried in front of it; also the Synagogue of Rab Zeiri, the son of Chama, and the Synagogue of R. Mari; the Jews pray there every day.

Thence it is four miles to the Tower of Babel, which the generation whose language was confounded built of the bricks called Agur. The length of its foundation is about two miles, the breadth of the tower is about forty cubits, and the length thereof two hundred cubits. At every ten cubits' distance there are slopes which go round the tower by which one can ascend to the top. One can see from there a view twenty miles in extent, as the land is level. There fell fire from heaven into the midst of the tower which split it to its very depths.

Ketubbah. Crimea, 1769. Courtesy of the Library of the Jewish Theological Seminary of America, NY. *This wedding contract represents a marriage in the 18th-century Karaite community in the Crimea.*

Moses Dar'i

AGAINST THE RABBANITES

The Karaite sect is thought to have originated around the ninth century in Babylonian Jewish communities. Some would place its origins in the eighth century; others claim its origins are even earlier. Karaites do not recognize the authority of the rabbinic oral tradition or Talmud but rather rely solely on the biblical text. Moses ben Abraham Dar'i, who lived no earlier than the middle of the twelfth century, was an Egyptian Karaite descended from a Spanish family. He is considered the greatest medieval Karaite poet.

God forbid that I should join a wicked people to walk along their path;
Or that I should give heed to their lying jeers or to their scoffing;

Or that I should turn to the false claims of their books or to their vanity;
Or that I should study the ordinances of their Mishnah, invented by
    themselves.
Rather do I deny that it is a tradition and a secret commanded by the
    Rock to His congregation on Mount Sinai to cherish these false
    things,
And I believe only in the written Law given by God to His own people;
One Law, to which I add nothing; one rule, to which I assign no second.

THE DEATH OF MOSES
A Midrash of the Ethiopian Jews

This text, translated from Ge'ez, probably dates from the fourteenth or fifteenth century and was traditionally recited at the cemetery during funeral services. The moving descriptions of Moses's farewells to his mother and to his wife and children are followed by a humorous description of the preparation of his final resting place.

———————————

And every Friday Moses put on burial clothes and purified himself for the arrival of the Angel of Death. After a time Moses forgot about the day [of his death] and ascended Mt. Sinai and prayed to God. Then the Angel of Death appeared and stood before him as a young man of the children of Israel and said to him: "Peace upon thee, Moses!" When Moses heard the voice of the Angel of Death his throat contracted, his tongue was tied, he was unable to utter a word, his knees trembled, and he fell on his face. Then he rose and said to the Angel of Death: "Who art thou that said to me: 'Peace be upon thee!' I never heard a voice which frightened me as does thine." The Angel of Death said to Moses: "Dost thou not know me? Hearken, Moses, to what I tell thee: I am the one who is tasted by women and children; the one who destroys houses and builds graves until the coming of the end of the world. I am Suryāl, the Angel of Death." Moses said to the Angel of Death: "What hast thou come to do?" The Angel of Death said to Moses: "I came to take thy soul and to bring her before God." Moses said to the Angel of Death: "I adjure thee by the God who sent thee not to take my soul until the third hour of the morning, until I shall go to my wife and children." God said to the Angel of Death: "Leave him until his time does arrive." The Angel left him until his time arrived and sat shaded from the sun.

    Moses descended from Mt. Sinai and arrived at a parting of the ways; one road led to his wife and one to his mother. He stood between them and thought to himself: Should I go to my wife or to my mother? While he was so thinking he heard a voice from Heaven, saying: "Go first to thy mother." And he went to his mother. When he arrived at the door he called: "Open to me." His mother came, opened the door, and saw that the face of her son was sad and his body withered. She said to him: "What has befallen thee, my son? Did the shepherds come to tell thee that thy cattle got lost, or what is it that has happened to thee?" Moses said to his mother: "Who calls me but God, and who frightens me but Death?" His mother said to him: "Will he who spoke with God face to face and mouth to mouth die?" He said to his mother: "Yes, he will die; all the prophets died. Rise, put thy left foot at my left side, stretch out both thy hands and pray to God that He may ease the bitterness of death." She did what he told her and he kissed her. He parted from her and wept with a great weeping. She said: "Let us not believe in the fashion of this world, and let us look for what is in Heaven."

When Moses went to his wife his spirit fainted, his body withered, and he knew not his way. He arrived at the door and said to her: "I am Moses, open to me." She arose and opened to him. Moses entered, and she saw that his face was pale and his heart faint. She said to him: "What has befallen thee, my beloved, that thy heart is faint and thy body withered? Hast thou lost thy camels or thy wealth?" Moses said to his wife: "Who calls me but God, and who frightens me but Death?" His wife said to him: "Will he who spoke with God die?" He said to her: "Yes, he will die, Abraham died, and all the prophets died." And Moses said to his wife: "Where are my children?" His wife said to him: "They sleep in their beds." Moses said to his wife: "Bring them to me." And she wept with a great weeping. She went, weeping, and said to the children: "Go to your father before he dies, for you shall see him no more." She awakened them from their sleep and brought them, holding their hands in her right and left hands, and said to them: "Weep over your father, for you and he must part." They said to her: "Where is our father?" She brought them to their father and said to them: "Look well at your father until you be satisfied, for soon you will be parted." When they saw their father they fell on their faces and wept with a great weeping. Moses wept with them, and said to them: "We part from upon the earth." His wife said to him: "Shall we see one another then no more?" He put his younger son Eleazar on his right knee and his older son Gershom on his left and he blessed them. He said to them: "Now we part." They said: "Now that we part from our father, even he who loved us will deliver us [to others], and he who hates us will banish us." When Moses heard his children's words he wept, and Heaven and earth wept with him. God said to Moses: "What makes thee cry? Is it because thou leavest the earth or because thou fearest death?" Moses said to God: "My two children and my wife do make me cry. Her father, Jethro, died; my brother, Aaron, died too; and if I die, to whom will I leave them?" God said to Moses: "When thou wast born and thy mother Jochabed hid thee in a box and threw thee out upon the sea, did I forget thee then? I closed the mouth of Pharaoh, the king of Egypt, and made it so that his mouth could utter no words, and I made thee so that Tarmut, Pharaoh's daughter, loved thee much and called thee: 'My child,' and thou didst stay forty years. And now rise and take thy rod and smite the Red Sea." Moses arose and smote the sea. Then he went out of the sea and found a big stone that rolled. God said to Moses: "Strike this stone that rolls." And he struck the stone, and the stone burst asunder. He found in the stone a small worm eating green grass that said: "Blessed be God who did not forget me until this day, while I was in the depths of the sea." God said to Moses: "Dost thou not see that I forgot not the worm while he lived hidden in a rolling stone in the sea? And dost thou think that I shall forget thy children when they pray to me? Thy children will be my security. And now, kiss thy children and thy wife, because those who will take thy soul away draw nigh, and thou wilt enter here no more." His wife embraced him, and she wept with a great weeping, and Moses wept with her. Then he went out of his house, and he left his wife and children. He walked with a faint heart and a pale face and did not know which way to walk. He met three handsome young men digging a grave. He said to them: "Peace upon you, and may God's peace be with you." Then he said to them: "For whom do you dig this grave?" They said to him: "We dig it for a man beloved of God." Moses said to them: "If you dig for a man beloved of God I shall help you and shall dig with you." When they had finished the grave Moses said to them: "Bring the corpse that we should bury." The young men said—and they were angels in the appearance of men—"We are afraid that the place will be too small for him whom we would bury, and he is like thee in size, length, and appearance; now enter the grave and measure it for us." Moses entered the grave and he found there the Angel of Death. The Angel of Death said to Moses: "Peace upon thee, Moses, son of Amram." Moses said to the Angel of Death: "May the greeting return to thee." So Moses died, and the angels buried him.

William Lempriere

FROM A TOUR FROM GIBRALTER TO TANGIER, . . . AND THENCE OVER MOUNT ATLAS, TO MOROCCO

On Moroccan Jews

This excerpt comes from a traveler's tour book published in England at the close of the eighteenth century. It offers a picturesque description of the dress and mores of the Moroccan Jews the author encountered on his journey.

———————

The Jews in most parts of this empire live entirely separate from the Moors; and though in other respects oppressed, are allowed the free exercise of their religion. Many of them, however, to avoid the arbitrary treatment which they constantly experience, have become converts to the Mahometan faith; upon which they are admitted to all the privileges of Moors, though they lose their real estimation in the opinion of both sects.

After a drawing by Jean-Baptiste Vanmour. *Jewish Woman Bringing Her Merchandise for Sale to the Women of the Harem Who Are Not Permitted to Go Out.* 1714. Etching. Collection of Israel Museum, Jerusalem. Gift of Victor Klagsbald.

In most of the sea port towns, and particularly at Tetuan and Tangier, the Jews have a tolerable smattering of Spanish; but at Morocco, Tarudant, and all the inland towns, they can only speak Arabic and a little Hebrew. They nearly follow the customs of the Moors, except in their religious ceremonies; and in that particular they are by far more superstitious than the European Jews.

The Jews of Barbary shave their heads close, and wear their beards long; their dress indeed, altogether, differs very little from that of the Moors (which I shall hereafter describe) except in being obliged to appear externally in black. For which purpose they wear a black cap, black slippers, and instead of the *haick* worn by the Moors, substitute the *alberoce,* a cloak made of black wool, which covers the whole of the under dress. The Jews are not permitted to go out of the country, but by an express order from the emperor; nor are they allowed to wear a sword, or ride a horse, though they are indulged in the use of mules. This arises from an opinion prevalent among the Moors that a horse is too noble an animal to be employed in the service of such infidels as Jews.

The dress of the Jewish women consists of a fine linen shirt, with large and loose sleeves, which hang almost to the ground; over the shirt is worn a *Caftan,* a loose dress made of woollen cloth, or velvet, of any colour, reaching as low as the hips, and covering the whole of the body, except the neck and breast, which are left open, and the edges of the *Caftan,* as worn by the Jewesses of Morocco, are embroidered with gold. In addition to these is the *geraldito,* or petticoats, made of fine green woollen cloth, the edges and corners of which are sometimes embroidered with gold. They are fastened by a broad sash of silk and gold, which surrounds the waist, and the ends of it are suffered to hang down behind in an easy manner. This is the dress they wear in the house, but when they go abroad, they throw over it the haick. The unmarried women wear their hair plaited in different folds, and hanging down behind. They have a very graceful and becoming method of putting a wreath of wrought silk round the head, and tying it behind in a bow. This dress sets off their features to great advantage, and distinguishes them from the married women, who cover their heads with a red silk handkerchief, which they tie behind, and over it put a silk sash, leaving the ends to hang loose on their backs. None of the Jewish women use stockings, but wear red slippers, curiously embroidered with gold. They wear very large gold ear-rings at the lower part of the ears, and at the upper three small ones set with pearls or precious stones. Their necks are loaded with beads, and their fingers with small gold or silver rings. Round each wrist and ankle they wear large solid silver bracelets; and the rich have gold and silver chains suspended from the sash behind.

Their marriages are celebrated with much festivity for sometime previous to the ceremony, and the intended bride, with all her female relations, go through the form of having their faces painted red and white, and their hands and feet stained yellow, with an herb named *henna*. A variety of figures are marked out on them with a needle, and then this herb, which is powdered and mixed with water into a paste, is worked into the holes made by the needle, and these marks continue on the hands and feet for a long space of time. Upon the death of a Jew (before and after burial) all the female relations, with other women hired for the purpose, assemble in the room of the deceased, and for several days lament his loss by most dreadful shrieks and howlings, and tearing their cheeks and hair.

The Jewesses of this empire in general are very beautiful and remarkably fair. They marry very young, and when married, though they are not obliged to hide their faces in the street, yet at home they are frequently treated with the same severity as the Moorish women. Like the Moors, the Jewish men and women at Morocco eat separate; and the unmarried women are not permitted to go out, except upon particular occasions, and then always with their faces covered.

A disposition for intrigue in the female sex is always found to accompany tyrannical conduct and undue restraint on the part of ours; and this disposition is again made the excuse for the continuance of these restraints. Thus the effect becomes a cause, and when women cease to be the guardians of their own honour, they derive no credit from the preservation of it, and incur in their own estimation but little disgrace by its loss. The Jews allege, in extenuation of their severity, the licentious inclinations and artful dispositions of their women, and that a single act of criminality in a daughter would be an effectual bar to her ever forming a legal connection. The same objection not being so applicable to their married women, they are permitted to go out without restraint. Indeed many of their husbands, from interested motives, are too apt to connive at a conduct, which, in other countries, would infallibly bring down upon them well-merited contempt.

EUROPE BEFORE THE EIGHTEENTH CENTURY

Synod at Forli (1418)
ORDINANCES

Many of Europe's Jewish communities had an internal government that controlled the everyday affairs of its people and acted as liaison between the Jewish community and civil and Church officials. The ordinances approved at Forli (Italy) in 1418 were an extension of ordinances passed at Bologna two years earlier. The Jewish communities levied taxes on themselves, sought protection and reaffirmation of their rights from the pope, and passed sumptuary laws to govern public appearances and private celebrations.

We, the undersigned, gathered here at Forli, on Wednesday the thirteenth of Sivan, corresponding to the eighteenth of May, of the year 5178, to discuss the communal affairs of the Italian Jews. We then examined the ordinances which had been passed at Bologna in the month of Tebet, 5176. The following is an extract of those ordinances:

"Whereas critical times appear to be approaching, and the Jewish communities are in need of wise and learned men to lead them so as to prevent any catastrophe, therefore have we, the undersigned, selected general commissioners in the communities of Rome, Padua, Ferrara, Bologna, and the districts of Romagna and Toscana whose duty it shall be to guard the interests of the communities during the coming ten years. If in their opinion necessity should arise for an assembly of their members they shall gather, and their council shall be empowered to levy such taxes on the communities as the situation will require. The collection shall, however, follow the methods used in collecting the general tax. The moneys collected shall be placed with Benjamin b. Menahem of Corinaldo. The commissioners shall be authorized to disburse these collected funds as they will think necessary.

"If for some reasons any commissioner will find it impossible to attend the meeting, he shall appoint a representative to act in his place. This representative must be acceptable to the other members of the council, and when thus accepted he shall be clothed in all the authority and power of his principal. . .

COLORPLATE 44
Torah Case. Kaifeng, China, 17th century. Wood, red lacquer. Gilt. Bronze hinges. Height: 30″
(76.2 cm). From the Collection of Hebrew Union College Skirball Museum, Los Angeles.

COLORPLATE 45
Curtain for the Torah Ark (Parokhet). Padua, 1550. Wool, knotted. 54½ × 44¼″ (139 × 112.5 cm).
Comunità Ebraica, Padua.

COLORPLATE 46

Torah Curtain (Parokhet) and Valance.
Bratislava, 1832–1833. Yellow silk;
embroidered with gold and silver metallic
and silk thread, appliquéd with colored
silver foils, sequins, studs, shell; hung with
silver bells. Curtain: 93 × 58″ (236.2 ×
147.4 cm). Valance: 26 × 69½″ (66 × 176.6
cm). Collection, Congregation Emanu-El of
the City of New York. Gift of Ludwig
Vogelstein, 1929. *The ark, which houses the
Torah scrolls, is the central focus of a synagogue.
A curtain, often made of sumptuous fabric and
embroidered with metallic thread, covers the ark,
separating and protecting the sacred texts.
Traditionally, when the curtain is opened and the
scrolls are exposed, the congregation stands as a
sign of respect. Both curtains here are embellished
with the Lions of Judah supporting the crown.*

COLORPLATE 47

Torah Curtain and Valance. Menden, Germany,
1785. Silk damask background with metallic
embroidery and padded appliqués of silk velvet.
67 × 55″ (170.2 × 139.7 cm).

COLORPLATE 48 *(opposite)*
Torah Mantle (Me'il).
Tangiers, 19th century.
Velvet appliquéd with gold
embroidery. Sir Isaac and
Lady Edith Wolfson
Museum, Hechal Shlomo,
Jerusalem. *When not being
read, the Torah is always kept
covered. Elaborate Torah covers
were often commissioned and
then donated to a synagogue in
memory of the deceased or to
celebrate a special occasion.*

COLORPLATE 49
*Torah Mantle, Shield,
Rimmonim.* Turkey, late 19th
century. *Mantle:* Velvet
embroidered with metallic
and silk threads. $36\frac{5}{8} \times 19\frac{11}{16}$
$\times 10\frac{5}{8}''$ (93 × 50 × 27 cm).
The Jewish Museum, New
York. The H. Ephraim and
Mordecai Benguiat Family
Collection; *Shield:* Silver:
cast, repoussé, engraved,
parcel-gilt, and nielloed. $11\frac{7}{16}$
$\times 10''$ (29 × 25.4 cm).
Division of Community Life,
National Museum of
American History,
Smithsonian Institution.
154.990; *Rimmonim (left):*
Silver, raised, repoussé,
ajouné, and engraved. $15\frac{5}{8} \times$
$4\frac{3}{8}''$ (38.9 × 11.1 cm); *(right):*
Silver: raised, engraved,
ajouné, and stamped. $15\frac{3}{8} \times$
$4\frac{1}{2}''$ (39 × 11.5 cm). Both,
The Jewish Museum, New
York. Gift of Dr. Harry G.
Friedman.

COLORPLATE 50 (from top to bottom)
Torah Binder (Wimpel).
United States, 1855.
Multicolored paint on glazed
cotton. 8½ × 144″ (21.6 ×
366 cm). Collection,
Congregation Emanu-El of
the City of New York.

Torah Binder (Wimpel).
United States, 1858. Dark
blue and red colors on linen.
6 × 138⅞″ (15.3 × 352.7
cm). Collection,
Congregation Emanu-El of
the City of New York.

Torah Binder (Wimpel).
United States, 1844.
Multicolored paint on linen.
8½ × 134½″ (21.6 × 341.6
cm). Collection,
Congregation Emanu-El of
the City of New York.

Torah Binder (Wimpel).
United States, 1852.
Multicolored paint on linen.
8¾ × 138″ (22.3 × 350.8
cm). Collection,
Congregation Emanu-El of
the City of New York.

A Torah wimpel, or binder, is
used to tie the two sides of a
Torah scroll together before
placing the Torah cover over the
scrolls. Wimpels were often made
from a baby's swaddling cloth
and were sometimes decorated
with the words from a prayer
that expressed the parents' wish
that the newborn infant might
grow up to study Torah, get
married, and do good deeds.

COLORPLATE 51 *(from top to bottom)*
Torah Binder (Wimpel). Brocade. 64¾ × 6¾″ (164.5 × 17 cm). Israel Museum, Jerusalem; *Torah Binder (Wimpel).* Brocade. 59⅞ × 7½″ (152 × 19 cm). Israel Museum, Jerusalem; *Torah Binder (Wimpel).* Silk, multicolored silk-thread embroidery. Chain stitch. 44½ × 6″ (113 × 15.5 cm). Israel Museum, Jerusalem; *Torah Binder (Wimpel).* Linen, reversible multicolored silk-thread embroidery. 33¹³⁄₁₆ × 7″ (86 × 18 cm). Israel Museum, Jerusalem; *Torah Binder (Wimpel).* Satin, couched metal-thread embroidery. 46¼ × 7½″ (117.5 × 19 cm). Israel Museum, Jerusalem. *Sephardic Torah binders were generally very decorative and displayed the name of a woman. Mothers traditionally donated the binders to the synagogue after childbirth.*

COLORPLATE 52
Miniature Torah Scroll with Two Mantles. Late 17th–19th century. Scroll: Moravia, late 17th century.
Vellum. Height: 4¹⁄₁₆″ (10.2 cm); Handles and Finials: East European, possibly Ukraine. Late 19th
century. Silver: embossed and engraved. Height: 9¼″ (23.5 cm). Box: wood, velvet covered, brass
fittings. 4¼ × 11⅞ × 6¾″ (10.7 × 30.4 × 17.2 cm). Collection, Congregation Emanu-El of the
City of New York. Gift of Judge Irving Lehman, 1945.

"We have further decided that if the Commission shall find that it must incur certain expenditures, the Communities of Rome and the vicinity shall not be obliged to contribute more than a fair proportion of the amount needed." Thus far the said Ordinance.

When we realized that there was need for the Commission to take action, we sent invitations to the above-mentioned commissioners to assemble here at Forli; some of them came in person and some are represented here by proxies. After a long discussion it has been decided that we ought at least to send to the Pope a committee to ask his protection for ourselves and our people, and to beg of him to issue a new *Privilegi*, and to re-affirm the old rights which we enjoyed under former Popes.

In order to cover the expenses involved in this matter and other necessary communal affairs, we have decided that the following taxes shall be levied:

A tax on the communities of one ducat and a half for every thousand ducats of property whether in houses, land or currency belonging to their members in accordance with the method of collecting the general taxes.

A tax of a ducat and a half for each family from all those whose property is valued at five hundred ducats or more. Because this is not merely a matter of defending our property but our very lives, it were perhaps proper that it should be distributed equally on all the members of the community. We have therefore decided that everyone possessing five hundred ducats or less but more than one hundred shall pay besides his share in the above-mentioned property tax (of one and a half ducats per thousand, which is collected from the communities) an additional ducat for the family tax. Whoever is possessed of less than one hundred ducats is urged to pay a ducat as family tax if possible, but in any case must contribute half a ducat to the fund.

No one shall be exempt of the above tax except those who must be supported from charity. . . .

All the Communities and their officers shall unite to compel every Jew to pay his share of the tax in accordance with the regulations. They make make use for this purpose of any methods that they may deem proper. . . .

Every community shall have a local Commission who will look after the needs of that community, and such a commission shall have the authority to make ordinances and regulations for its community. . . .

In order that we may carry ourselves in modesty and humbleness before the Lord, our God, and to avoid arousing the envy of the Gentiles, we decree that until the end of the above-mentioned term (ten years, 1416–1426) no Jew or Jewess shall be permitted to make a *foderato-cinto,* unless it be black, and that the sleeves shall be open and that the sleeves shall have no silk lining whatever on them. Those who already possess such cloaks (*foderato-cinto*) of any color other than black, may continue to wear them, provided the sleeves are not open, and the cloaks are closed both in the front and back.

Neither shall any man or woman wear any cloak of sabel or ermine or mixed fur or of red material of mixed color or of muslin or of violet color. However, a cloak lined with fur may be worn, if none of the fur is placed on the outer covering of the cloak.

Women's cloaks which have already been made with open sleeves and are lined with fur, may be worn within the house but not in public, unless the sleeves are sewn or the cloaks are worn under an overcoat, so that the cloak cannot be seen at all. Also the coats of women which are lined with fur, must so far as possible be so made so as not to show the fur.

No man shall be permitted to wear a silk or velvet *giubetta* (cloak) except in such manner that is completely concealed. Neither shall women wear any silk or velvet dress except in such manner that it is completely concealed. Neither shall they wear any dress having fringes attached to it other than at the opening of the neck or the sleeves.

No woman shall wear any necklace on her neck or a gold hairnet on her head unless it be concealed except that newly-married brides may wear golden hair-nets unconcealed for thirty days after the wedding; after that time they must wear the veil over the net. No girdle which has a silver buckle more than six ounces in weight, or which is covered with velvet in any form, shall be worn by men in public.

No more than one gold ring may be worn by a man, but the ring may be placed on any finger. Women shall under no circumstances wear more than two or three rings.

Neither shall women wear a girdle or belt the silver of which weighs more than ten ounces.

The fine for the transgression of any of these provisions regarding the use of clothes and ornaments shall be ten Bolognini of silver or their value for the treasury of the city for each offense. Men shall be held responsible for the infractions of these rules by their wives. If anyone will refuse to obey the ordinances, the community shall refuse to admit him to *minyan* or to read the Torah or to perform the *Gelilah*.

We have also decreed that it shall be prohibited for more than three ladies and two maids to walk together in the streets except in the performance of some religious duty. Nor shall it be permitted for women to promenande through the streets and avenues except on festival days, when they shall be limited in the said manner. Men shall be held responsible for the observance of this section by their wives as in the case of the dresses.

Neither shall men be permitted to walk in large groups or gather at the parting of the roads, or before the synagogues in groups of more than six, except in the performance of a religious duty. The fine for the infraction of this section shall be set by the commissioners.

From the end of this month of Sivan, 178, till the end of the year 186, no Jew shall be permitted to invite to a banquet more than twenty men and ten women and five girls. This number shall include both the people of the city and those without, but shall not include relatives as close as second cousins.

If a bride arrives from another city on horse, she may be escorted by no more than ten Jews on horseback and four men on foot. If she come by boat she may be escorted to the place of the wedding by no more than twelve Jews or Jewesses.

At feasts of circumcision only ten Jews and five Jewesses may be invited in addition to the relatives. In this matter, too, relatives as near as second cousins shall not be counted toward the limited number.

Any infraction of these provisions shall be punished by a fine of one ducat to the treasury of the city. . . .

The local commissioners in every city and province shall have authority to add other ordinances than these for their respective jurisdictions. A copy of these ordinances shall be made in each city and they shall be placed either in the synagogue or in the ark so that anyone may read them.

Written and signed in the year 1576.

William Shakespeare
FROM THE MERCHANT OF VENICE
Shylock's Speech

William Shakespeare's play The Merchant of Venice, *written in 1596, has been translated into, and performed, in both Hebrew and Yiddish. The portrayal of Shylock as a bloodthirsty Jewish usurer, "the very devil incarnation," is only slightly modified by this famous speech.*

I am a Jew. Hath not a Jew eyes? Hath not a Jew hands, organs, dimensions, senses, affections, passions?—fed with the same food, hurt with the same weapons, subject to

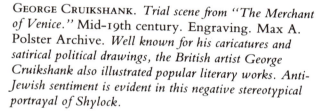

GEORGE CRUIKSHANK. *Trial scene from "The Merchant of Venice."* Mid-19th century. Engraving. Max A. Polster Archive. *Well known for his caricatures and satirical political drawings, the British artist George Cruikshank also illustrated popular literary works. Anti-Jewish sentiment is evident in this negative stereotypical portrayal of Shylock.*

the same diseases, healed by the same means, warmed and cooled by the same winter and summer as a Christian is? If you prick us, do we not bleed? If you tickle us, do we not laugh? If you poison us, do we not die? And if you wrong us, shall we not revenge? If we are like you in the rest, we will resemble you in that. If a Jew wrong a Christian, what is his humility? Revenge! If a Christian wrong a Jew, what should his sufferance be by Christian example? Why revenge! The villainy you teach me I will execute, and it shall go hard but I will better the instruction.

Menasseh ben Israel

PETITION FOR READMISSION OF JEWS TO ENGLAND

On July 18, 1290, Edward I ordered the expulsion of the Jews of England by All Saints Day. More than 350 years later, Oliver Cromwell encouraged Rabbi Menassah ben Israel (1604–1657) to petition for the readmission of the Jews to the country. Although the request was not granted, by the end of the seventeenth century, Judaism could once again be legally practiced in England.

These are the boons and the favors which I, Menasseh ben Israel, in the name of my Hebrew nation, beseech of your most serene Highness, and may God prosper you and give you much success in all your undertakings. Such is the wish and desire of your humble servant.

I. The first thing which I ask of your Highness is that our Hebrew nation be received and admitted into this mighty republic under the protection and care of your Highness like the citizens themselves, and for greater security in the future I entreat your Highness, if it is agreeable to you, to order all your commanders and generals to defend us on all occasions.

II. That it please your Highness to allow us public synagogues, not only in England, but also in all other conquered places which are under the power of your Highness, and to allow us to exercise our religion in all details as we should.

III. That we should be allowed to have a plot or cemetery outside the city for burying our dead without being molested by anyone.

IV. That it be allowed us to trade freely in all sorts of merchandise just like every one else.

V. That (in order that those who come in shall do so for the benefit of the citizens and live without doing harm or causing trouble to any one) your most serene Highness should appoint a person of prominence to inform himself of those who enter and to receive their passports. He should be informed of those who arrive and should oblige them to take an oath to be faithful to your Highness in this country.

VI. And in order that the justices of the peace should not at all be bothered with litigation and quarrels which may arise among those of our nation, we ask that your most serene Highness grant the liberty to the rabbi of associating with himself two Jewish clergymen in order to adjust and to judge all the disputes at law in conformity with the Mosaic code, with the privilege, nevertheless, of appealing a sentence to the civil judges. The sum to which the party will have been condemned must first be deposited, however.

JOHN RUSLEN. *Lord Mayor's Tray.* 1708–1709. Silver: repoussé and engraved. 21⅜ × 26½ × 3¼" (54.3 × 67.3 × 8.3 cm). Jewish Museum, New York. Gift of Mrs. Felix M. Warburg. *This silver tray was offered to the Lord Mayor of London by the Congregation Bevis Marks. The central panel depicts the seal of the congregation—a Tent of Assembly in the wilderness.*

VII.   That if, peradventure, there should be any laws against our Jewish nation, then first and before all things they should be revoked so that by this means it should be possible for us to live with greater security, under the safeguard and protection of your most serene Highness.

If your most serene Highness grants us these things we will always be most attached to you and under obligations to pray to God for the prosperity of your Highness and of your illustrious and most sage Council. May it be His will to grant much success to all the undertakings of your most serene Highness. Amen.

Nathan Hanover

FROM ABYSS OF DESPAIR
"The Inner Life of the Jews in the Kingdom of Poland"

Having escaped the Chmielnicki massacres of 1648–1652 in Polish-ruled Ukraine, Nathan of Hanover wandered through Poland, Germany, and Holland before settling in Italy in 1653. Yeven Metzulah chronicles these pogroms, both from eyewitness accounts, as well as from hearsay evidence. This work is especially noteworthy because it presents a portrait of Jewish life in seventeenth-century Poland

And now I will begin to describe the practices of the Jews in the Kingdom of Poland, which were founded on principles of righteousness and steadfastness.

It is said in Tractate Aboth: Simon the Just was one of the last survivors of the Great Synagogue. He used to say: "Upon three things the world is based: Upon the Torah, upon divine service, and upon the practice of charity." Rabban Simeon, the son of Gamaliel said: "By three things is the world preserved: by truth, by judgment and by peace." All the six pillars upon which the world rests were in existence in the Kingdom of Poland.

The Pillar of the Torah: Matters that are well known need no proof, for throughout the dispersions of Israel there was nowhere so much learning as in the Kingdom of Poland. Each community maintained academies, and the head of each academy was given an ample salary so that he could maintain his school without worry, and that the study of the Torah might be his sole occupation. The head of the academy did not leave his house the whole year except to go from the house of study to the synagogue. Thus he was engaged in the study of the Torah day and night. Each community maintained young men and provided for them a weekly allowance of money that they might study with the head of the academy. And for each young man they also maintained two boys to study under his guidance, so that he would orally discuss the Gemara (Talmud), the commentaries of Rashi, and the Tosafoth, which he had learned, and thus he would gain experience in the subtlety of Talmudic argumentation. The boys were provided with food from the community benevolent fund or from the public kitchen. If the community consisted of fifty householders it supported not less than thirty young men and boys. One young man and two boys would be assigned to one householder. And the young man ate at his table as one of his sons. Although the young man received a stipend from the community, the householder provided him with all the food and drink that he needed. Some of the more charitable householders also allowed the boys to eat at their table, thus three persons would be provided with food and drink by one householder the entire year. . . .

The program of study in the Kingdom of Poland was as follows: The term of study consisted of the period which required the young men and the boys to study with the head of the academy in the academy. In the summer it extended from the first day of the month of Iyar till the fifteenth day of the month Ab, and in the winter, from the first day of the month of Cheshvan, till the fifteenth day of the month of Shevat. After the fifteenth of Shevat or the fifteenth of Ab, the young men and the boys were free to study wherever they preferred. From the first day of Iyar till the Feast of Weeks, and in the winter from the first day of Cheshvan till Chanukkah, all the students of the academy studied Gemara, the commentaries of Rashi and Tosafoth, with great diligence. Each day they studied a halachah—one page of Gemara with the commentaries of Rashi and Tosafoth is called a halachah. . . .

In the summer they would not leave the academy before noon. From the Feast of Weeks till the New Year, and from Chanukkah till Passover, the head of the academy would not engage in so many discussions. He would study with the scholars the Codes such as the Arbaah Turim (the Four Rows) and their commentaries. With young men he would study Rav Alfas and other works. In any case, they also studied Gemara, Rashi, and Tosafoth, till the first day of Ab or the fifteenth day of Shevat. From then on until Passover or the New Year they studied the codes and similar works only. Some weeks prior to the fifteenth day of Ab or the fifteenth day of Shevat, the head of the academy would honor each student to lead in the discussions in his stead. The honor was given both to the scholars and the students. They would present the discussion, and the head of the academy would listen and then join in the disputation. This was done to excercise their intellect. The same tractate was studied throughout the Kingdom of Poland in the proper sequence of the Six Orders.

After that [the fifteenth of Ab or the fifteenth of Shevat] the head of the academy, together with all his students, the young men and the boys, journeyed to the fair. In the summer they travelled to the fair of Zaslaw and to the fair of Jaroslaw; in the winter to the fairs of Lwow and Lublin. There the young men and boys were free to study in any academy they preferred. Thus at each of the fairs hundreds of academy heads, thousands of young men, and tens of thousands of boys, and Jewish merchants, and Gentiles like the sand on the shore of the sea, would gather. For people would come to the fair from one end of the world to the other. Whoever had a son or daughter of marriageable age went to the fair and there arranged a match. For there was ample opportunity for everyone to find his like and his mate. Thus hundreds and sometimes thousands of such matches would be arranged at each fair. And Jews, both men and women, walked about the fair, dressed in royal garments. For they were held in esteem in the eyes of the rulers and in the eyes of the Gentiles, and the children of Israel were many like the sand of the sea, but now, because of our sins, they have become few. May the Lord have mercy upon them. . . .

The Pillar of Divine Service: At this time prayer has replaced (sacrificial) service, as it is written: "So we will render for bullocks, the offering of our lips." Prayers were "set upon sockets of fine gold." At the head was the fellowship of those who rose before dawn, called "Shomrim La Boker," "they that watch for the morning," to pray and to mourn over the destruction of the Temple. With the coming of dawn the members of the Chevra Tehillim would rise to recite Psalms for about an hour before prayers. Each week they would complete the recitation of the entire Book of Psalms. And far be it, that any man should oversleep the time of prayer in the morning and not go to the synagogue, except for unusual circumstances. When a man went to the synagogue, he would not depart thence to his business until he had heard some words of the Law expounded by a scholar or a passage from the commentary of Rashi on the Torah, the Prophets, the Hagiographa, the Mishah or some laws of ritual, whatever his heart desired to learn; for in all synagogues there were many groups of scholars who taught others in the synagogue immediately after evening and morning prayers. They would observe: "They shall go from strength to strength, every one of them appeareth before God in Zion."

The Pillar of Charity: There was no measure for the dispensation of charity in the

Polish Jews. Illustration from *Yeven Metzulah (Abyss of Despair)* showing typical clothes of Polish Jews during the 16th and 17th century, as well as Sabbath attire for women.

Kingdom of Poland, especially as regards hospitality. If a scholar or preacher visited a community, even one which had a system of issuing communal tickets to be offered hospitality by a householder, he did not have to humiliate himself to obtain a ticket, but went to some community leader and stayed wherever he pleased. The community beadle then came and took his credentials to collect funds to show it to the synagogue official or the community leader for the month, and they gave an appropriate gift which was delivered by the beadle in dignified manner. He was then the guest of the householder for as many days as he desired. Similarly all other transients who received tickets, would be the guests of a householder, whose turn it was by lot, for as many days as he wished. A ticket was good for at least three days. The guest was given food and drink, morning, noon and evening. If they wished to depart they would be given provisions for the road, and they would be conveyed by horse and carriage from one community to another. If young men or boys or older men or unmarried girls, came from distant places, they would be forthwith furnished with garments. Those who wanted to work at a trade would be apprenticed to a tradesman, and those who wanted to be servants in a house would be assigned to serve in a house. Those who wanted to study would be provided with a teacher, and afterwards, when he became an important young man, a rich man would take him to his house and give him his daughter in marriage as well as several thousand gold pieces for a dowry, and he would clothe him in royal garments—for who is royalty? The scholars. After the wedding he would send him away from his home to study in great academies. When he returned home after two or three years, his father-in-law would maintain an academy for him in his home and he would spend much money among the householders who were prominent scholars that they should attend his academy for a number of years, until he also will become a head of an academy in some community. Even if the lad was not yet an important student at that time but had a desire to study, enabling him to become a scholar after he had studied, there would at times come a rich man who had a young daughter, and give him food and drink and clothes, and all his needs, as he would to his own son, and he would hire a teacher for him until he was ready with his studies, then he would give him his daughter in marriage. There is no greater benevolence than this. Similarly there were very praiseworthy regulations for poor unmarried girls in every province. No poor girl reached the age of eighteen without being married, and many pious women devoted themselves to this worthy deed. May the Lord recompense them and have compassion upon the remnant of Israel.

The Pillar of Justice was in the Kingdom of Poland as it was in Jerusalem before the destruction of the Temple, when courts were set up in every city, and if one refused to be judged by the court of his city he went to the nearest court, and if he refused to be judged by the nearest court, he went before the great court. For in every province there was a great court. Thus in the capital city of Ostrog there was the great court for Volhynia and the Ukraine, and in the capital city of Lwow there was the great court for [Little]

Russia. There were thus many communities each of which had a great court for its own province.

If two important communities had a dispute between them, they would let themselves be judged by the heads of the council of Four Lands (may their Rock and Redeemer preserve them) who would be in session twice a year. One leader would be chosen from each important community, added to these, were six great scholars from the land of Poland, and these were known as the Council of Four Lands. They would be in session during every fair in Lublin between Purim and Passover, and during every fair at Jaroslaw in the month of Ab or Elul. The leaders of the Four Lands were like the Sanhedrin in the Chamber of Hewn Stones. They had the authority to judge all Israel in the Kingdom of Poland, to establish safeguards, to institute ordinances, and to punish each man as they saw fit. Each difficult matter was brought before them and they judged it. And the leaders of the Four Lands selected judges from the provinces to relieve their burden, and these were called judges of the provinces. They attended to cases involving money matters. Fines, titles, and other difficult laws were brought before the leaders of the Four Lands, may their Rock and Redeemer preserve them. Never was a dispute among Jews brought before a Gentile judge or before a nobleman, or before the King, may his glory increase, and if a Jew took his case before a Gentile court he was punished and chastised severely, to observe: "Even our enemies themselves being judges."

The Pillar of Truth: Every community appointed men in charge of weights and measures, and of other business dealings, so that everything would be conducted according to truth and trustworthiness.

The Pillar of Peace: For it is said: "The Lord will give strength unto His people; the Lord will bless His people with peace." There was in Poland so much interest in learning that no three people sat down to a meal without discussing the words of Torah, for throughout the repast everyone indulged in debating matters of the Law and puzzling passages in the Midrashim, in order to observe: "Thy law is my inmost parts." And the Holy One blessed be He, recompensed them so that even when they were in the land of their enemies, He did not despise them and did not break his covenant with them. And wherever their feet trod the ground among our brothers of the House of Israel they were treated with great generosity, above all, our brethren of the House of Israel who were in distress and in captivity among the Tartars. For the Tartars led them to Constantinople, a city that was a mother in Israel, and to the famed city of Salonica, and to other communities in Turkey and Egypt, and in Barbary and other provinces of Jewish dispersion where they were ransomed for much money, as mentioned above. To this day they have not ceased to ransom prisoners that are brought to them each day. The Lord recompense them.

Baruch ben Gershon Marizo
FROM ZICHRON L'BNEI YISROEL
Shabtai Zvi

The virulent anti-Semitism of the mid-seventeenth century probably gave rise to the acceptance of Shabbateanism, the movement named for Shabbetai Zevi (1626–1670), whose followers believed him to be the Messiah. The movement gave both the educated and common people palpable hope for the future. Even after his (possibly forced) conversion to Islam in 1666, many Jews refused to give up their dream of the imminent arrival of the Messiah.

Crown of Zevi from *Tikkun Keri'a Lekol Laila Ve-Yom.* Amsterdam, 1666. Printed book. Courtesy of the Library of the Jewish Theological Seminary of America, New York.

i.   After that he began to behave in a strange manner and to comport himself contrary to the laws of God and His Torah. He implored others to follow his example. On Thursday, which was the third day of Chanukkah, he went to the Synagogue dressed in royal garb and began to chant the prayers in a fashion which caused wonderment among all those who heard him . . . On the Sabbath he went to the synagogue of the Portuguese. Because many of them did not believe that he was the Messiah, they closed the doors of the synagogue and refused to let him enter. Greatly angered by this he sent for an axe and began pounding on the door—all on the Sabbath—until they opened the door. He entered the synagogue . . . and began to chant: he continued with his chanting until the time for the morning prayers had passed. He said to the congregation. "Today there is no need for you to pray: say only the *Sh'ma* without either the blessings before or after. Then he took a *Chumash* out of his bag and declared that it was holier than the Scroll of the Law . . . And even though he did all these stranges things, he became known as the King Messiah and the vast majority of the Jews believed him . . .

In the month of Sh'vat our master donned a royal garb of fine gold, in one hand he carried a *Chumash* and in the other a golden scepter, like those carried by the great kings. He left his house followed by 500 Jews who went after him through the streets of Smyrna shouting, "Long live the king our master! Long live our master the king!"

And the Turks who saw all this said nothing; instead they bowed and kneeled before even. Even though the matter was known to the Pasha and Cadi and to all those in authority in the city, nothing was said and no harm or injury was done to the Jews.

After that many came to believe—men, women, and children . . . and they all declared, "Shabtai Zvi is the Messiah of the God of Jacob!"

And then our master, may his glory increase, decreed . . . that the 9th day of Av should be celebrated as a great holiday. When that decree arrived in Constantinople, even though there were many there who believed in him, there were many doubts as to whether or not such an extraordinary thing should be done . . . all the learned men of the city turned to God and beseeched him in prayer asking that He guide them in their way and instruct them as to what to do. They all got together and drew lots. On one lot there was inscribed "holiday" and on the other was written "fast". The lots were put in a box and drawn three times. Each time the "holiday" was drawn . . . That year Tisha B'Av was celebrated as a great holiday.

And this was the decree of our Lord!

ii.   "To my brethren and people . . . men, women and children in every country . . . and place to which the word of the king and his decree reach . . . I do decree that the 9th day of Av shall be a day of feasting and joy, a day of eating and drinking . . . a day for lights and candles and singing . . . for that is the day on which was born Shabtai Zvi, your king . . . and on that day you shall pray as follows:

And thou hast given us in love, O Lord our God, holidays for gladness, festivals and seasons for rejoicing. Thou hast granted us this Feast of Consolation, the Season of the Birth of our King, our Messiah, Shabtai Zvi, as a holy convocation, commemorating our liberation from Egypt . . . The saying of David the son of Jesse . . . the Messiah of the God of Jacob . . . Shabtai Zvi."

Baruch Spinoza

FROM THE ETHICS

The God of Man's Making

Baruch Spinoza (1632–1677), a Dutch philosopher, may be considered the father of modern biblical criticism because he applied scientific inquiry and rationalism to religious ideas. His unorthodox religious views were considered blasphemous, prompting the Sephardic community of Amsterdam to excommunicate him in 1656.

God is, and acts solely by the necessity of His own nature, He is the free cause of all things. All things are in God, and so depend on him, and without Him they could neither exist nor be conceived; lastly, all things are predetermined by God, not through his free will or absolute wish, but from the very nature of God or infinite power.

Yet there remain misconceptions not a few, which might and may prove very grave hindrances to the understanding of the concatenation of things. I have thought it worth while to bring these misconceptions before the bar of reason.

All such opinions spring from the notion commonly entertained that all things in nature act as men themselves act, namely, with an end in view. It is accepted as certain that God Himself directs all things to a definite goal (for it is said that God made all things for man, and man that he might worship Him). I will, therefore, consider this opinion, asking first, why it obtains general credence, and why all men are naturally so prone to adopt it? secondly, I will point out its falsity; and, lastly, I will show how it has given rise to prejudices about good and bad, right and wrong, praise and blame, order and confusion, beauty and ugliness, and the like. However, this is not the place to deduce these misconceptions from the nature of the human mind.

All men are born ignorant of the causes of things, all have the desire to seek for what is useful to them, and they are conscious of such desire. Herefrom it follows, first, that men think themselves free inasmuch as they are conscious of their volitions and desires, and never even dream, in their ignorance, of the causes which have disposed them so to wish and desire. Secondly, that men do all things for an end, namely, for that which is useful to them, and which they seek. Thus it comes to pass that they only look for a knowledge of the final causes of events, and when these are learned, they are content, as having no cause for further doubt. If they cannot learn such causes from external sources, they are compelled to turn to considering themselves, and reflecting what end would have induced them personally to bring about the given event, and thus they necessarily judge other natures by their own. Further, as they find in themselves and outside themselves many means which assist them not a little in their search for what is useful, for instance, eyes for seeing, teeth for chewing, herbs and animals for yielding food, the sun for giving light, the sea for breeding fish, etc., they come to look on the whole of nature as a means of obtaining such conveniences. Now as they are aware that they found these conveniences and did not make them, they think they have cause for believing that some other being has made them for their use.

As they look upon things as means, they cannot believe them to be self-created; but, judging from the means which they are accustomed to prepare for themselves, they are bound to believe in some ruler or rulers of the universe endowed with human freedom, who have arranged and adapted everything for human use. They are bound to estimate the nature of such rulers (having no information on the subject) in accordance with their own nature, and therefore they assert that the gods ordained everything for the use of man, in order to bind man to themselves and obtain from him the highest honor.

Hence also it follows that everyone thought out for himself, according to his abilities, a different way of worshipping God, so that God might love him more than his fellows, and direct the whole course of nature for the satisfaction of his blind cupidity and insatiable avarice. Thus the prejudice developed into superstition, and took deep root in the human mind; and for this reason everyone strove most zealously to understand and explain the final causes of things; but in their endeavor to show that nature does nothing in vain, *i.e.,* nothing which is useless to man, they only seem to have demonstrated that nature, the gods, and men are all made together.

Consider, I pray you, the result: among the many helps of nature they were bound to find some hindrances, such as storms, earthquakes, diseases, etc.: so they declared that such things happen because the gods are angry at some wrong done them by men, or at some fault committed in their worship. Experience day by day protested and showed by infinite examples that good and evil fortunes fall to the lot of pious and impious alike. . . . They therefore laid down as an axiom, that God's judgments far transcend human understanding. Such a doctrine might well have sufficed to conceal the truth from the human race for all eternity, if mathematics had not furnished another standard of verity in considering solely the essence and properties of figures without regard to their final causes. . . .

I have now explained my first point. There is no need to show at length that *nature has no particular goal in view, and final causes are mere human figments*. However, I will add a few remarks in order to overthrow the doctrine of a final cause utterly.

This doctrine does away with the perfection of God: for, if God acts for an object, He necessarily desires something which He lacks. Certainly, theologians and metaphysicians draw a distinction between the object of want and the object of assimilation; still they confess that God made all things for the sake of Himself, not for the sake of creation. They are unable to point to anything prior to creation, except God Himself, as an object for which God should act, and are therefore driven to admit (as they clearly must), that God lacked those things for whose attainment He created means, and further that He desired them.

We must not omit to notice that the followers of this doctrine, anxious to display their talent in assigning final causes, have imported a new method of argument in proof of their theory—namely, a reduction, not to the impossible, but to ignorance; thus showing that they have no other method of exhibiting their doctrine. . . . So they will pursue their questions from cause to cause, till at last you take refuge in the will of God—in other words, the sanctuary of ignorance. So, again, when they survey the frame of the human body, they are amazed; and being ignorant of the causes of so great a work of art, conclude that it has been fashioned, not mechanically, but by divine and supernatural skill, and has been so put together that one part shall not hurt another.

Hence anyone who seeks for the true causes of miracles, and strives to understand natural phenomena as an intelligent being, and not to gaze at them like a fool, is set down and denounced as an impious heretic by those whom the masses adore as the interpreters of nature and the gods. Such persons know that, with the removal of ignorance, the wonder which forms their only available means for proving and preserving their authority would vanish also. But I now quit this subject, and pass on to my third point.

After men persuaded themselves that everything which is created is created for their sake, they were bound to consider as the chief quality in everything that which is most useful to themselves, and to account those things the best of all which have the most beneficial effect on mankind. Further, they were bound to form abstract notions for the explanation of the nature of things, such as goodness, badness, order, confusion, warmth, cold, beauty, deformity, and so on; and from the belief that they are free agents arose the further notions, praise and blame, sin and merit.

Everything which conduces to health and the worship of God they have called good, everything which hinders these objects they have styled bad; and inasmuch as those who do not understand the nature of things do not verify phenomena in any way, but merely imagine them after a fashion, and mistake their imagination for understanding, such persons firmly believe that there is an order in things, being really ignorant both of things and their own nature.

When phenomena are of such a kind that the impression they make on our senses requires little effort of imagination, and can consequently be easily remembered, we say that they are well-ordered; if the contrary, that they are ill ordered or confused. Further,

Spinoza's Excommunication from the Sephardic Community, Issued on July 27, 1656. Collection, Portuguese Jewish Community, Amsterdam.

as things which are easily imagined are more pleasing to us, men prefer order to confusion—as though there were any order in nature, except in relation to our imagination—and say that God has created all things in order; thus, without knowing it, attributing imagination to God, unless, indeed, they would have it that God foresaw human imagination, and arranged everything so that it should be most easily imagined.

If this be their theory, they would not, perhaps, be daunted by the fact that we find an infinite number of phenomena, far surpassing our imagination, and very many others which confound its weakness.

The other abstract notions are nothing but modes of imagining, in which the imagination is differently affected, though they are considered by the ignorant as the chief attributes of things, inasmuch as they believe that everything was created for the sake of themselves; and, according as they are affected by it, style it good or bad, healthy or rotten and corrupt . . . We need no longer wonder that there have arisen all the controversies we have witnessed, and finally skepticism: for, although human bodies in many respects agree, yet in very many others they differ; so that what seems good to one seems bad to another; what is pleasing to one displeases another, and so on.

I need not further enumerate, because the fact is sufficiently well known. It is commonly said: "So many men, so many minds; everyone is wise in his own way; brains differ as completely as palates." All of which proverbs show that men judge of things according to their mental disposition, and rather imagine than understand: for, if they understood phenomena, they would, as mathematics attest, be convinced, if not attracted, by what I have urged.

All the explanations commonly given of nature are mere modes of imagining, and do not indicate the true nature of anything, but only the constitution of the imagination; and, although they have names, as though they were entities, existing externally in the imagination, I call them entities imaginary rather than real; and, therefore, all arguments against us drawn from abstractions are easily rebutted.

Many argue in this way. If all things follow from a necessity of the absolutely perfect nature of God, why are there so many imperfections in nature? such, for instance, as things corrupt to the point of putridity, loathsome deformity, confusion, evil, sin etc. But these reasoners are, as I have said, easily confuted, for the perfection of things is to be reckoned only from their own nature and power; things are not more or less perfect, according as they delight or offend human senses, or according as they are serviceable or repugnant to mankind. To those who ask why God did not so create all men that they should be governed only by reason, I give no answer but this: because matter was not lacking to Him for the creation of every degree of perfection from highest to lowest; or, more strictly, because the laws of His nature are so vast as to suffice for the production of everything conceivable by an infinite intelligence.

Such are the misconceptions I have undertaken to note; if there are any more of the same sort, everyone may easily dissipate them for himself with the aid of a little reflection.

Glückel of Hameln

FROM THE MEMOIRS OF GLÜCKEL OF HAMELN

Zipporah's Wedding

At age 46, after the death of her first husband, Glückel (1645–1724), a Jewish woman living in central Europe, began to write her memoirs. She was the mother of twelve children, had a solid traditional education, and ran her husband's business after he died. In the reminiscences presented here, Glückel describes in detail the wedding of her daughter Zipporah, offering the reader an intimate glimpse into daily Jewish life in the seventeenth century.

Our business prospered. And Zipporah, my eldest child, was now a girl of almost twelve. Whereat Loeb Hamburger in Amsterdam, the son of Reb Amschel, proposed her marriage to Kossmann, the son of Elias Cleve, of blessed memory.

My husband was accustomed to travel to Amsterdam twice a year, and now, after writing the marriage broker he was coming to see what could be done, he set forth six weeks in advance of his usual time. The country was at war and Elias Cleve had left his home in Cleves and moved with his people to Amsterdam. . . .

Well, my blessed husband concluded the match with the rich Elias Cleve and settled on our daughter a dowry of 2200 Reichsthalers in Dutch money. They fixed the wedding for a year and a half later in Cleves. My husband likewise undertook to contribute 100 Reichsthalers towards the wedding expenses.

When time for the marriage drew near, I with a babe at my breast, my husband, my daughter Zipporah the bride, our Rabbi Meir, who is now the rabbi of Friedberg, a maidservant and our man Elegant Sam—in sum, a great retinue—set forth for the wedding.

We sailed from Altona in company with Mordecai Cohen, Meir Ilius and Aaron Todelche. I cannot begin to tell what a merry voyage it was. And after a gay and delightful trip we arrived safely in Amsterdam. . . .

Then came the great preparations for the wedding. At that time, Prince Frederick was in Cleves. His older brother, Prince Elector Karl, still lived, and Prince Frederick was then a young lord about thirteen years of age. Not long after, Karl died and Frederick in turn became Prince Elector. Prince Maurice of Nassau and other titled personages and great lords were likewise in Cleves, and they all signified their desire to witness the nuptials.

Naturally, Elias Cleve, the father of the groom, made fitting preparations for such notable guests. On the marriage day, immediately after the wedding, there was spread a lavish collation of all kinds of sweetmeats and fine imported wines and fruits. You can readily picture the bustle and excitement, and how Elias Cleve and his people set themselves to wait upon and cater to their distinguished company. There was not even time to deliver and count over the dowries, as is customary. So we placed our own dowry in a pouch and sealed it, and Elias Cleve did likewise, that we might tally the sum after the wedding was over.

As the bridal pair were led beneath the *chuppah* [wedding canopy] out it came that in the confusion we had forgotten to write the marriage contract! What was to be done? Nobility and princes were already at hand and they were all agog to see the ceremony. Whereat Rabbi Meir declared that the groom should appoint a bondsman to write out the contract immediately after the wedding. Then the rabbi read a set-contract from a book. And so the couple were joined.

After the ceremony, all the distinguished guests were ushered into Elias Cleve's enormous salon with its walls of leather tooled in gold. There stood the mighty table laden with dainties fit for a king. And the company were served according to their rank.

My son Mordecai was then a child of about five; there was not a prettier boy in all the world, and we had him dressed in his neatest and best. All the nobility wanted to eat him up on the spot, and the Prince in particular, God heighten his fame! never let go his hand.

When the guests of honour had eaten of the fruit and cakes and had done justice to the wine, the table was cleared and removed. Then appeared masked performers who bowed prettily and played all manner of entertaining pranks. They concluded their performance with a truly splendid Dance of Death.

BERNARD PICART.
Wedding of Ashkenazi Jews. 1712. Engraving.
Jewish Historical Museum, Amsterdam.

A number of prominent Sephardim likewise attended the wedding, among them one Mocatta, a jeweller, who wore a beautiful small gold watch set with diamonds and worth no less than 500 Reichsthalers. Elias Cleve wanted to buy the little watch from Mocatta for a gift to the Prince. But a good friend who was standing by said to him, «What for?— why give the young Prince such a costly present? If, to be sure, he were already Prince Elector, well and good.» But, as I have said, the Prince Elector died soon after, and our young prince succeeded to the title and now his is Elector himself. And after that, every time Elias Cleve met his prudent friend he cast it in his teeth. In truth, if Elias Cleve had given the little watch, the young Prince would have always remembered it, for great lords never forget such things. But there is no point in grumbling over what is past.

As it was, the young Prince and Prince Maurice and all the noble-born guests departed in great content, and never a Jew received such high honour in a hundred years. And the wedding was brought to a happy end.

EUROPE SINCE THE EIGHTEENTH CENTURY

Israel Zangwill
FROM DREAMERS OF THE GHETTO
"The Master of the Name"

Israel Zangwill (1864–1926) was a British author of international fame, whose play, "The Melting Pot," enjoyed an extended run on Broadway. The Jewish and immigrant experience figure prom-

inently in Zangwill's works. In Dreamers of the Ghetto, *written in 1898, he sketches the lives of some major Jewish figures.*

It was April ere I began to draw near my destination. The roads were still muddy and marshy; but in that happy interval between the winter gray and the summer haze the breath of spring made the world beautiful. The Stri river sparkled, even the ruined castles looked gay, while the pleasure-grounds of the lords of the soil filled the air with sweet scents. One day, as I was approaching a village up a somewhat steep road, a little gray-haired man driving a wagon holding some sacks of flour passed me, whistling cheerfully. We gave each other the "Peace" salutation, knowing ourselves brother Jews, if only by our furred caps and ear-curls. Presently, in pity of his beast, I saw him jump down and put his shoulder to the wheel; but he had not made fifty paces when his horse slipped and fell. I hastened up to help him extricate the animal; and before we had succeeded in setting the horse on his four feet again, the driver's cheeriness under difficulties had made me feel quite friendly towards him.

"Satan is evidently bent upon disturbing my Passover," said he, "for this is the second time that I have tried to get my Passover flour home. My good wife told me that we had nothing to eat for the festival, so I felt I must give myself a counsel. Out I went with my slaughtering-knife into the villages on the north—no, don't be alarmed, not to kill the inhabitants, but to slaughter their Passover poultry."

"You are a *Shochet* (licensed killer)," said I.

"Yes," said he; "among other things. It would be an intolerable profession," he added reflectively, "were it not for the thought that since the poor birds have to be killed, they are better off in my hands. However, as I was saying, I killed enough poultry to buy Passover flour; but before I got it home the devil sent such a deluge that it was all spoilt. I took my knife again and went out into the southern villages, and now, here am I in another quandary. I only hope I sha'n't have to kill my horse too."

"No, I don't think he is damaged," said I, as the event proved.

When I had helped this good-natured little man and his horse to the top of the hill, he invited me to jump into the cart if my way lay in his direction.

"I am in search of the Baal Shem," I explained.

"Indeed," said he; "he is easily to be found."

"What, do you know the Baal Shem?" I cried excitedly.

He seemed amused at my agitation. His black eyes twinkled. "Why, everybody in these parts knows the Baal Shem," said he.

"How shall I find him, then?" I asked.

He shrugged his shoulders. "You have but to step up into my cart."

"May your strength increase!" I cried gratefully; "you are going in his direction?"

He nodded his head.

I climbed up the wheel and plumped myself down between two flour-sacks. "Is it far?" I asked.

He smiled. "Nay, if it was far I should scarcely have asked you up."

Then we both fell silent. For my part, despite the jolting of the vehicle, the lift was grateful to my spent limbs, and the blue sky and the rustling leaves and the near prospect of at last seeing the Baal Shem contributed to lull me into a pleasant languor. But my torpor was not so deep as that into which my new friend appeared to fall, for though as we approached a village another vehicle dashed towards us, my shouts and the other driver's cries only roused him in time to escape losing a wheel.

"You must have been thinking of a knotty point of Torah (Holy Law)," said I.

"Knotty point," said he, shuddering; "it is Satan who ties those knots."

"Oho," said I, "though a *Shochet,* you do not seem fond of rabbinical learning."

"Where there is much study," he replied tersely, "there is little piety."

At this moment, appositely enough, we passed by the village Beth-Hamidrash,

COLORPLATE 53
POSEN. *Schiff Set of Torah Ornaments. Torah Shield, Finials, and Pointer.* Frankfurt, 1890. Gilded silver, embossed and chased; castings, enameling, lapis, semiprecious stones, niello; ivory on pointer. *Shield (Tas):* 15¾ × 11⅜″ (40 × 29 cm); *Finials (Rimmonim):* 18 × 10½″ (45.8 × 26.7 cm); *Pointer (Yad):* 12″ (30.5 cm) long. Collection, Congregation Emanu-El of the City of New York. Gift of Jacob H. and Therese Schiff, 1890.

COLORPLATE 54

ZACHARIAS WAGNER. *Torah Shield (Tas).* Augsberg, c. 1715. Silver: repoussé, cast, engraved and gilt. 16⅝ × 11¹⁵⁄₁₆″ (42.2 × 30.3 cm). The Jewish Museum, New York. Gift of Dr. Harry G. Friedman. *Torah shields or breastplates sometimes serve as labels to indicate the place to which the Torah scroll was rolled. The central rectangle of this shield indicates that the scroll was rolled to the appropriate place for Shabbat Nahamu, the Sabbath after the fast day of the ninth of Av.*

COLORPLATE 55 *(opposite)*

POSEN. *Schiff Set of Torah Ornaments. Torah Shield (Tas).* Frankfurt, 1890. Gilded silver, embossed and chased; castings, enameling, lapis, semiprecious stones, niello. 15¾ × 11⅜″ (40 × 29 cm). Collection, Congregation Emanu-El of the City of New York. Gift of Jacob H. and Therese Schiff, 1890.

COLORPLATE 59
Bloomingdale Torah Crowns. New York, 1891. Gilded brass, cutout work, appliqué, colored stones. Heights: 12″ (30.5 cm); 21″ (53.3 cm); 20½″ (52 cm). Collection, Congregation Emanu-El of the City of New York. Gift of Lyman G. Bloomingdale in memory of his brother Samuel, 1891. *Torah Crowns, like Rimmonim, decorate the finials of Torah spindles.*

COLORPLATE 60 *(opposite)*
Torah Finials (Rimmonim). Morocco, 19th century. Silver: cast and engraved; enamel. 11 × 3⁵⁄₁₆″ (28 × 8.5 cm). Sir Isaac and Lady Edith Wolfson Museum, Hechal Shlomo, Jerusalem. *The word "rimmonim" comes from the Hebrew for "pomegranates." These finials were used to adorn the staves of the Torah scroll.*

COLORPLATE 61
Torah Crown. Venice, 1752. Silver: embossed, chiseled, engraved and incised, cast and gilt; red-orange coral. 8¼ × 10⅝″ (21 × 27 cm). Comunità Israelitica, Florence.

whence loud sounds of "pilpulistic" (wire-drawn) argument issued. The driver clapped his palms over his ears.

"It is such disputants," he cried with a grimace, "who delay the redemption of Israel from exile."

"How so?" said I.

"Satan induces these Rabbis," said he, "to study only those portions of our holy literature on which they can whet their ingenuity. But from all writings which would promote piety and fear of God he keeps them away."

I was delighted and astonished to hear the *Shochet* thus deliver himself, but before I could express my acquiescence, his attention was diverted by a pretty maiden who came along driving a cow.

"What a glorious creature!" said he, while his eyes shone.

"Which?" said I laughingly. "The cow?"

"Both," he retorted, looking back lingeringly.

"I understand now what you mean by pious literature," I said mischievously: "the Song of Solomon."

He turned on me with strange earnestness, as if not perceiving my irony. "Ay, indeed," he cried; "but when the Rabbis do read it, they turn it into a bloodless allegory, Jewish demons as they are! What is the beauty of yonder maiden but an emanation from the divine? The more beautiful the body, the more shiningly it leads us to the thought of God."

I was much impressed with this odd fellow, whom I perceived to be an original.

"But that's very dangerous doctrine," said I; "by parity of reasoning you would make the lust of the flesh divine."

"Everything is divine," said he.

"Then feasting would be as good for the soul as fasting."

"Better," said the driver curtly.

I was disconcerted to find such Epicurean doctrines in a district where, but for my experience of Baer, I should have expected to see the ascetic influence of the Baal Shem predominant. "Then you're not a follower of the Baal Shem?" said I tentatively.

"No, indeed," said he, laughing.

He had got me into such sympathy with him—for there was a curious attraction about the man—that I felt somehow that, even if the Baal Shem *were* an ascetic, I should still gain nothing from him, and that my long journey would have been made in vain, the green pastures and the living waters being still as far off as ever from my droughty soul.

We had now passed out of the village and into a thick pine-wood with a path scarcely broad enough for the cart. Of a sudden the silence into which we again fell was broken by piercing screams for "Help" coming from a copse on the right. Instantly the driver checked the horse, jumped to the ground, and drew a long knife from his girdle.

"'Tis useful to be a *Shochet*," he said grimly, as he darted among the bushes.

I followed in his footsteps and a strange sight burst upon us. A beautiful woman was struggling with two saturnine-visaged men dressed as Rabbis in silken hose and mantles. One held her arms pinned to her sides, while the other was about to plunge a dagger into her heart.

"Hold!" cried the *Shochet*.

The would-be assassin fell back, a startled look on his narrow fanatical face.

"Let the woman go!" said the driver sternly.

In evident consternation the other obeyed. The woman fell forward, half-fainting, and the driver caught her.

"Be not afraid," he said. "And you, murderers, down at my feet and thank me that I have saved you your portion in the World-To-Come."

"Nay, you have lost it to us," said the one with the dagger. "For it was the vengeance of Heaven we were about to execute. Know that this is our sister, whom we have discovered to be a wanton creature, that must bring shame upon our learned house and into our God-fearing town. Whereupon we and her husband held a secret Beth-Din, and resolved, according to the spirit of our ancient Law, that this plague-spot must be cleansed out from Israel for the glory of the Name."

"The glory of the Name!" repeated the driver, and his eyes flamed. "What know you of the glory of the Name?"

Both brothers winced before the passion of his words. They looked at each other strangely and uneasily, but answered nothing.

"How dare you call any Jewess a plague-spot?" went on the driver. "Is any sin great enough to separate us irredeemably from God, who is in all things? Pray for your sister if you will, but do not dare to sit in judgment upon a fellow-creature!"

The woman burst into loud sobs and fell at his feet.

"They are right! they are right!" she cried. "I am a wicked creature. It were better to let me perish."

The driver raised her tenderly. "Nay, in that instant you repented," he said, "and one instant's repentance wins back God. Henceforward you shall live without sin."

"What! you would restore her to Brody?" cried the elder brother—"to bring the wrath of Heaven upon so godly a town. Be you who you may, saint or devil, that is beyond your power. Her husband assuredly will not take her back. With her family she cannot live."

"Then she shall live with mine," said the *Shochet*. "My daughter dwells in Brody. I will take her to her. Go your ways."

They stood disconcerted. Presently the younger said: "How know we we are not leaving her to greater shame?"

The old man's face grew terrible.

"Go your ways," he repeated.

They slunk off, and I watched them get into a two-horsed carriage, which I now perceived on the other side of the copse. I ran forward to give an arm to the woman, who was again half-fainting.

"Said I not," said the old man musingly, "that even the worst sinners are better than these Rabbis? So blind are they in the arrogance of their self-conceit, so darkened by their pride, that their very devotion to the Law becomes a vehicle for their sin."

We helped the woman gently into the cart. I climbed in, but the old man began to walk with the horse, holding its bridle, and reversing its direction.

"Aren't you jumping up?" I asked.

"We are going up now, instead of down," he said, smiling. "Brody sits high, in the seat of the scornful."

A pang of shame traversed my breast. What! I was riding and this fine old fellow was walking! But ere I could offer to get down, a new thought increased my confusion. I, who was bent on finding the Baal Shem, was now off on a side-adventure to Brody. And yet I was loath to part so soon with my new friend. And besides, I told myself, Brody was well worth a visit. The reputation of its Talmudical schools was spread over the kingdom, and although I shared the old man's repugnance to them my curiosity was alert. And even on the Baal Shem's account I ought to go there. For I remembered now that his early life had had many associations with the town, and that it was his wife's birthplace. So I said, "How far is Brody?"

"Ten miles," he said.

"Ten miles!" I repeated in horror.

"Ten miles," he said musingly, "and ten years since I set foot in Brody."

I jumped down. "'Tis I must walk, not you," I said.

"Nay," said he good-humoredly. "I perceive neither of us can walk. Those sacks must play Jonah. Out with them."

"No," I said.

"Yes," he insisted, laughing. "Did I not say Satan was determined to spoil my Passover? The third time I shall have better luck perhaps."

I protested against thus causing him so much loss, and offered to go and find the Baal Shem alone, but he rolled out the flour-bags, laughing, leaving one for the woman to lie against.

"But your wife will be expecting them," I remarked, as the cart proceeded with both of us in our seats.

"She will be expecting me, too," he said, smiling ruefully. "However, she has faith in God. Never yet have we lacked food. Surely He who feedeth the ravens—" He broke off with a sudden thought, leapt down, and ran back.

"What is it?" I said.

I saw him draw out his knife again and slit open the sacks. "The birds shall keep Passover," he called out merrily.

The woman was still sobbing as he climbed to his place, but he comforted her with his genial and heterodox philosophy.

"'Tis a device of Satan," he said, "to drive us to despondency, so as to choke out the God-spark in us. Your sin is great, but your Father in Heaven awaits you, and will rejoice as a King rejoices over a princess redeemed from captivity. Every soul is a whole Bible in itself. Yours contains Sarah and Ruth as well as Jezebel and Michal. Hitherto you have developed the Jezebel in you; strive now to develop the Sarah." With such bold consolations he soothed her, till the monotonous movement of the cart sent her into a blessed sleep. Then he took out a pipe and, begging permission of me, lighted it. As the smoke curled up his face became ecstatic.

"I think," he observed musingly, "that God is more pleased with this incense of mine than with all the prayers of all the Rabbis."

This shocked even me, fascinated though I was. Never had I met such a man in all Israel. I shook my head in half-serious reproof. "You are a sinner," I said.

"Nay, is not smoking pleasurable? To enjoy aright aught in God's creation is to praise God. Even so, is not to pray the greatest of all pleasures?"

"To pray?" I repeated wonderingly. "Nay, methinks it is a heavy burden to get through our volumes of prayer."

"A burden!" cried the old man. "A burden to enter into relation with God, to be reabsorbed into the divine unity. Nay, 'tis a bliss as of bridegroom with bride. Whoso does not feel this joy of union—this divine kiss—has not prayed."

"Then have I never prayed," I said.

"Then 'tis you that are the sinner," he retorted, laughing.

His words struck me into a meditative silence. It was towards twilight when our oddly-encountered trio approached the great Talmudical centre. To my surprise a vast crowd seemed to be waiting at the gates.

"It is for me," said the woman hysterically, for she had now awakened. "My brothers have told the elders. They will kill you. O save yourself."

"Peace, peace," said the old man, puffing his pipe.

As we came near we heard the people shouting, and nearer still made out the sounds. Was it? Yes, I could not be mistaken. "The Baal Shem! The Baal Shem!"

My heart beat violently. What a stroke of luck was this! "The Baal Shem is there!" I cried exultantly.

The woman grew worse. "The Baal Shem!" she shrieked. "He is a holy man. He will slay us with a glance."

"Peace, my beautiful creature," said the driver. "You are more likely to slay him with a glance."

This time his levity grated on me. I peered eagerly towards the gates, striving to make out the figure of the mighty Saint!

The dense mob swayed tumultuously. Some of the people ran towards out cart. Our horse had to come to a stand-still. In a trice a dozen hands had unharnessed him, there was an instant of terrible confusion in which I felt that violence was indeed meditated, then I found our cart being drawn forward as in triumph by contesting hands, while in my ears thundered from a thousand throats, "The Baal Shem! The Baal Shem!" Suddenly I looked with an incredible suspicion at the old man, smoking imperturbably at my side.

"'Tis indeed a change for Brody," he said, with a laugh that was half a sob.

A faintness blotted out the whole strange scene—the town-gates, the eager faces, the gesticulating figures, the houses, the frightened woman at my side.

It was the greatest surprise of my life.

Kindling the Sabbath Lights. Amsterdam, 1723. Woodcut. Sir Isaac and Lady Edith Wolfson Museum, Hechal Shlomo, Jerusalem. *The lighting of the Sabbath lights is a ritual that marks the beginning and end of the Sabbath. This illustration is from an 18th-century Dutch book of customs.*

Meyer Levin

FROM CLASSIC HASSIDIC TALES
"The Boy's Song"

Judaism has a traditional fixed liturgy, but this Hassidic story suggests that heartfelt prayers can traverse the expanse between heaven and Earth, even if those prayers are not uttered in intelligible words.

The Enemy did not forswear the battle, but came out openly and spread his iron wings between the earth and heaven. The wings were as thick as a mountain is high, and all through they were made of heavy iron. He wrapped his wings around the earth as he would enclose it within the two cups of his hand.

On earth, all was darkness. The wings of the Enemy pressed forever closer to the earth, and crushed the spirits of men.

When Rabbi Israel was about to enter into a synagogue, he stopped outside the door and said, "I cannot go in there. There is no room for me to enter."

But the chassidim said, "There are not many people in the synagogue."

"The house is filled from the ground to the roof with prayers! said the Master.

But as he saw the chassidim taking pride because of his words, he said, "Those prayers are all dead prayers. They have no strength to fly to heaven. They are crushed, they lie one on top of the other, the house is filled with them."

And he returned to Medzibuz.

He felt the weight of the wings of the Enemy pressing ever closer upon him. He sought for a way to pierce that iron cloud, and make a path to Heaven.

Not far from Medzibuz there lived a Jewish herdsman. This man had an only son, the boy was twelve years old but so slow-witted that he could not remember the alphabet. For several years the Jew had sent his son to the cheder, but as the boy could not remember anything, the father ceased to send him to the school, and instead sent him into the fields to mind the cows.

The boy took a reed and made himself a flute, and sat all day long in the grass, playing upon his flute.

But when the boy reached his thirteenth birthday, his father said, "After all, he must be taught some shred of Jewishness." So he said to the lad, "Come, we will go to the synagogue for the holidays."

He got in his wagon, and drove his son to Medzibuz, and bought him a cap and new shoes. And all that time, David carried his flute in his pocket.

His father took him to the synagogue of Rabbi Israel.

They sat together among the other men. The boy was very still.

Then the moment came for the prayer of mussaf to be said. David saw the men all about him raise their little books, and read out of them in praying, singing voices. He saw his father do as the other men did. Then David pulled at his father's arm.

"Father," he said, "I too want to sing. I have my flute in my pocket. I'll take it out, and sing."

But his father caught his hand. "Be still" he whispered. "Do you want to make the Rabbi angry? Be still!"

David sat quietly on the bench.

Until the prayer of mincha, he did not move. But when the men arose to repeat the mincha prayer the boy also arose, "Father," he said, "I too want to sing!"

His father whispered quickly. "Where have you got your fife?"

"Here in my pocket."

"Let me see it."

David drew out his fife, and showed it to his father. His father seized it out of his hand. "Let me hold it for you," he said.

David wanted to cry, but was afraid, and remained still.

At last came the prayer of neilah. The candles burned trembling in the evening wind, and the hearts of the worshippers trembled as the flames of the candles. All through the house was the warmth of holiness, and the stillness as before the Presence. Then the outspread palms of the Rabbi were raised over them, and the words of the eighteen benedictions were spoken.

The boy could hold back his desire no longer. He seized the flute from his father's hand, set it to his mouth, and began to play his music.

A silence of terror fell upon the congregation. Aghast, they looked upon the boy; their backs cringed, as if they waited instantly for the walls to fall upon them.

But a flood of joy came over the countenance of Rabbi Israel. He raised his spread palms over the boy David.

"The cloud is pierced and broken!" cried the Master of the Name," and evil is scattered from over the face of the earth!"

Solomon Simon

FROM THE WISE MEN OF HELM

"The Helmites Capture the Moon"

Chelm, a community in Poland, has earned a unique place in Jewish folklore because of the supposed naiveté of its residents—ironically referred to as the "wise men of Chelm." In this tale the Chelmites devise a plan for making their community a very rich town indeed.

In spite of their hardships, the Helmites remained a pious folk and never ceased to worship God. When the nights were bright and the moon was new, they stood outdoors beneath the open sky, and with faces upturned, chanted the traditional blessings.

Gimpel prayed along with them, but as befits the leading citizen of Helm, his mind was occupied with the more pressing earthly problems.

"What will happen to Helm?" he brooded. "Things are getting worse and worse. I must think of something soon." Rocking in prayer as pious Jews do, he gazed up at the bright moon. Suddenly, like a thunderbolt, he sprang up joyfully.

"Helmites, we are saved!" he cried.

Caught at the end of their payers, the astonished Helmites froze with the last words on the tips of their tongues.

"Helmites, give heed! We will capture the moon!" roared Gimpel.

"Capture the moon?" they repeated in utter amazement.

"Yes! You know that all good Jews must pray to the new moon each month. So here's what we'll do. We'll take down the moon, wrap it up carefully and hide it in our Synagogue. Then all the Jews from all over the world will have to come to us to pray to the moon. And by charging them all a small fee—nothing excessive, of course—we'll become the richest town in the world. All our problems will be solved."

"Helmites, we have a wizard amongst us. Sometimes we forget how much we owe him!" they cried to one another.

"Yes, we'll roll in riches," cried some others, "but don't forget, we'll give poor folks a piece of the moon for nothing."

"Wait," added Gimpel. "I haven't finished. I have more ideas. After we've kidnapped the moon, we'll wash it and scrub it and clean off its stains so that it will shine brighter and clearer. Then we'll comb it and polish it and rent it out to all the big cities, and instead of using lanterns to light their streets at night, they can put up one bright, neat, well-washed moon. That'll save them lots of money and we'll amass a fortune."

"We are saved," chorused the Helmites, and they praised the Lord for having blessed them with Gimpel and his wisdom.

Suddenly, a small voice was heard. "I don't like to make a pest of myself," it said, "but would you mind telling me how we're going to get hold of the moon?" Everyone looked in the direction of the voice and there, sure enough, shaking with fright at his own boldness stood Berel the Beadle.

"How would *you* do it, Berel?" said Gimpel mockingly.

Berel was silent for a moment, then he offered timidly. "Well, we could collect all the ladders in Helm, tie them together, lean this great, long ladder against the Synagoguge and—" to appease them, he added, "let me scramble up to lift the moon out of the sky."

"Just as I thought, the village fool has spoken," decreed Gimpel, whereupon all the Helmites took this as a signal to laugh uproariously. "Come tomorrow night and you'll see how it, *will* be done," Gimpel concluded.

Poor Berel said to himself, "Why did I have to open my big mouth?"

The next evening, the market place was black with people. Not a Helmite was missing, and even the Rabbi was there, all wondering how Gimpel was going to perform the miracle. In the sky the moon shone brightly.

They had not long to wait. Gimpel soon arrived, followed by two Helmites carrying a tubful of red beet soup. After them came two more Helmites carrying a sack, a rope, and some sealing wax.

Halting in the center of the square, Gimpel commanded:

"Put the tub of red borsht here?"

The two Helmites obeyed.

Gimpel raised his voice so that all could hear:

"Helmites, lift up your eyes and behold! High above the moon is shining in the dark blue sky. Now look down into the tub of beet soup."

Thereupon the twelve foremost citizens approached and looked into the tub of red borsht.

ANONYMOUS. *Blessing Said for the Appearances of the New Moon*. After 1911. Oil on canvas. The Jewish Museum, New York.

"Aye," they said, and nodded their heads. "The same moon that is in the sky is here in the borsht."

"Hand me the sack and the rope and the sealing wax!" Gimpel thundered. The others hastened to do his bidding.

Quickly Gimpel covered the tub with the sack, tied the sack tightly with the rope, made ten knots and sealed each knot with wax.

"Now," said Gimpel, triumphantly, "the moon is ours! We'll hide it in the Synagogue. And on the first dark night, when there is no moon in the sky, we'll be the masters!"

A couple of weeks passed. One dark night towards the end of the month, Gimpel announced:

"Helmites, this is the night we take out the moon." Whereupon, twelve foremost citizens were given the honor of bringing the tub from the Synagogue to the square. There, Gimpel and the Mayor examined the treasure together and made sure that no one had tampered with it—the cords were knotted and the seals untouched.

All around were assembled the people of Helm. Everyone wanted to see the moon taken out of the tub. They planned to carry it to the well, rinse it carefully in the clear water, and then hang it up again in the sky.

Gimpel went to work. He broke the wax seals and with a sharp knife, cut the knots. The ropes fell away. Quickly he snatched the sack off the tub and shouted:

"Let there be light! Let there be light!"

The people opened their mouths, all ready to shout with joy—but the night remained pitch black.

Gimpel thought that the moon must have gotten stuck on a nail. He overturned the tub of red borsht. It flowed all over the square, but the night still remained dark and black. Only the sweet smell of beet soup hung over the disappointed multitude.

In the silence, from way at the back of the crowd, someone was heard to mutter, "I'll bet *my* way would have worked." However, since Gimpel had failed to bring forth the moon, it was too dark to recognize Berel the Beadle.

It took a great deal of Gimpel's eloquence to explain to the Helmites that due to their negligence in failing to use preservatives, the moon had melted in the beet soup. For hours thereafter and late into the night, one could notice numbers of Helmites wandering around the square, peering at the cobblestones and actually seeing spots of light from bits of melted moon.

There was another little incident which occurred a few weeks later in connection with the moon event which shouldn't be left untold. One night Berel happened to run into Gimpel coming home from the Synagogue. Berel pointed to the orange moon riding low in the heavens and righteously remarked, "I don't like to criticize you, brother Gimpel, but was it right telling us the moon melted when it really escaped?"

Gimpel replied with the greatest tolerance, "This is *not* the same moon as the one we captured, brother Beadle. Every month there is a new moon."

Moses Mendelssohn
FROM JERUSALEM

Moses Mendelssohn (1729–1786) was a noted German Jewish philosopher and grandfather of composer Felix Mendelssohn. His writings were influential in the German Enlightenment. In Jerusalem, *he set forth his understanding of how Jews could confront modernity and still retain their Jewish heritage.*

It is true, *I acknowledge no other eternal truths but those, which are not only comprehensible to human reason, but which can likewise be proved and confirmed by human powers.* But he is still deceived by an incorrect appreciation of Judaism, if he believes that I cannot maintain this, without deviating from the religion of my fathers. On the contrary, I hold this for an essential point of the Jewish religion, and believe, that this doctrine constitutes a characteristic difference between it and the Christian religion. To express my meaning with one word: I believe that Judaism knows of no revealed religion, in the sense this is understood by Christians. The Israelites have divine *legislation*, laws, commandments, precepts, rules of life, instruction of the will of God, how they have to conduct themselves, in order to attain temporary and everlasting happiness; statutes and prescriptions of this kind were revealed unto them through Moses, in a wonderful and preternatural manner; but no doctrinal opinions, no saving truths, no universal dogmas. These the eternal Lord always reveals to us, as to all the rest of mankind, through *nature* and outward objects, but never through *word* and *writing*. . . .

Those positions are called *eternal* truths, which are not subject to time, and remain the same to all eternity. These are either *necessary*, in themselves *unchangeable*, or *accidental;* that is to say, their permanence is either founded on their *essence*,—they can therefore not be otherwise by any possibility, because they are *conceivable* in no other manner, or they are based on their *reality;* they are therefore universally true, therefore to be taken as they are, and not otherwise, because they have become *real,* in the manner we meet with them, and not otherwise, because they are, among all possible ones of their kind, the *best* as they are, and not otherwise. In other words: the necessary, no less than the accidental truths, emanate from a common source, out of the Source of all truths; the first from the *intellect* (reason), the last out of the *will of God*. . . .

Besides these eternal truths, there are yet *temporary, historical truths;* things which did occur at a certain period, and perhaps may never come again; positions which have become true through a concurrence of causes and effects at one point of time and space, and can therefore be conceived as true, in reference alone to this very point of time and space. Of this kind are all truths of history, in their widest extent, including the events of times past, which have once occurred and are told to us, which we ourselves, however, can never have the opportunity to observe.

In the same manner as these classes of positions and truths are differing in their nature, they differ likewise in respect to their means of producing conviction, or in the manner and process by which men can convince themselves and others of their reality. The doctrines of the first species, or the necessary truths, are based upon *reason*,—i. e. upon the unchangeable concatenation and essential connexion between the ideas, according to which they presuppose or exclude each other. Of this kind are all mathematical and logical demonstrations. . . .

To comprehend the truths of the second class, *observation* is required, in addition to reason. If we wish to know what laws the Creator has prescribed for his creation, according to what general rules the changes in the same take place, we must experience, observe, and test the individual cases,—i.e. we should in the first instance, make use of the evidence of our senses, and afterward deduct, by means of reason, out of several particular cases, that which they have in common. . . . But historical truths, the passages, so to say, which occur only once in the book of nature, must be elucidated through themselves, or they will remain unintelligible, i.e., they could have been perceived through means of the senses by those only who were present at the time and place when they occurred in the course of nature. By every other person they must be received upon authority and testimony. . . . Hence the respectability and the trustworthiness of the narrator constitute the sole evidence in historical matters. Without testimony, we cannot be convinced of any historical truth. Without authority, the truth of history vanishes with the occurrence itself.

★　　★　　★

I therefore do not believe, that the powers of human reason are not sufficient to convince mankind of the eternal truths, which are indispensable to human happiness, and that it was necessary for God to reveal the same to them in a preternatural manner. They, who maintain this, derogate, on the one side, from the omnipotence or the goodness of God, what they mean to attribute to his goodness on the other. He was, according to their opinion, good enough to reveal unto men those truths on which their happiness depends; but not potent enough, or not good enough, to endow them with the ability to discover the same themselves. Besides this, the necessity of a preternatural revelation is rendered, by this assertion, more universal than the revelation itself. If, therefore, the human race must, of necessity, be corrupt and miserable without a revelation, why has the far greater part of the same lived at all times without a *true revelation?* or why are both the Indies compelled to wait, till it pleases the Europeans to send them a few comforters, who are to bring them a message (gospel), without which, according to this opinion, they can neither live virtuously nor happy? to bring them a message which, from their circumstances and the state of their knowledge, they can neither understand correctly nor use properly?

According to the ideas of real Judaism, all the inhabitants of the earth are destined to felicity, and the means thereto are so extensively spread abroad as mankind itself; and are so bountifully scattered abroad as the means to ward off hunger and the other wants of nature; both when they are left under the control of rude nature, which perceives inwardly its power, and makes use thereof, without being able to express itself in words and speech, except in the most defective manner, and, so to say, stammeringly; and when they are upheld by sciences and arts, resplendent through words, images, and metaphors, by which means the perceptions of the inward spirit are transformed into an intelligible series of written signs, and are perpetuated by the same.

★　　★　　★

I now revert to my preceding remarks. Judaism boasts of no *exclusive* revelation of eternal truths which are indispensable to salvation; of no revealed religion, in the sense in which this word is generally used. A revealed *religion* is one thing, a revealed *legislation* something very different. The Voice, which caused itself to be heard on Sinai on that great day, did not proclaim, "I am the Everlasting One, thy God! the necessary self-existent Being, who is almighty and all-knowing, who recompenses men in a future life according to their doings." This is the universal *religion of mankind*, not Judaism; and this universal religion of mankind, without which men can neither become virtuous nor happy, was not intended to be revealed here; in truth it could not; for whom should the rolling thunder and the sounding cornet convince of those eternal saving doctrines? . . .

No! all this was presupposed, was perhaps taught in the preparatory days, explained and placed beyond doubt by human reasoning; and when the people stood before Sinai, the Divine Voice proclaimed, "I am the Everlasting One, thy God, who have brought thee out of the land of Egypt, from the house of slavery," &c., reciting an historical truth upon which the legislation of *this* people was to be based; and it was laws that should be revealed in this place, commandments and ordinances; no eternal religious truths. The whole legislation seems to say, "I am the Lord thy God, who have made a covenant with thy fathers, Abraham, Isaac, and Jacob, and sworn unto them to raise unto myself a people from their seed. The period has at length arrived when this promise is to be accomplished. I have for this purpose redeemed you from the servitude of the Egyptians, and redeemed you with unheard of miracles and signs. I am your Saviour, your Chief, and your King; I now make a covenant with you also, and give you laws according to which you are to live in the land which I will give unto you for a possession, whereby you can become a happy people." All these are historical truths, which, from their nature, rest upon historical evidence, *must* be verified by authority, and *can* be fortified through miracles.

Wonders and extraordinary signs are, in accordance with Judaism, no proof for or against eternal truths recognisable by reason. We are, therefore, ordered in Scripture itself, not to listen to a prophet, if he should teach or advise things which are contrary to established truths, though he were to fortify his mission by miracles; nay, to condemn to death the performer of the miracle if he endeavours to mislead us to idolatry. Because wonders can only verify testimonies, support authority, and strengthen the credibility of witnesses and messengers; but all evidences and authorities are not able to overthrow any settled truth demonstrable by reason, or to place the doubtful idea beyond the reach of doubt and uncertainty.

Although now this divine book, which we have received through Moses, should, properly speaking, be a book of laws and contain ordinances, rules of life, and prescriptions: it does, nevertheless, include, likewise, as is well known, an inexhaustible treasure of truths which are founded on reason, and of religious doctrines, which are so intimately connected with the law, that they constitute with it but one and the same religion. All laws refer to, or are based upon the just-named everlasting truths, or remind us of and awaken reflections concerning the same; so that our Rabbis say, justly, "That laws and doctrines are related to each other, as body and soul." . . . But all these excellent doctrines are offered to our power of understanding, laid before our reflection, without being forced upon our belief. Among all the prescriptions and ordinances of the Mosaic law, not one is in the words, "*Thou shalt believe, or not believe,*" but all say, "*Thou shalt do, or not do.*" No injunction is laid upon the belief, for it can receive no other commandments than those that come to it in the way of conviction. All the commandments of the divine law are directed to the will, to the acting power of men. . . . Command and prohibition, reward and punishment, are only suited for acts, for doing and omission, which things are under a man's control, and can be influenced by ideas of good and evil, and therefore by hope and fear likewise. Belief and doubt, assent and dissent, however, are not governed by our capacity of expecting to possess certain things, not according to our wish and desire, not by fear and hope, but by our own perception of truth and untruth.

Ancient Judaism, therefore, has no symbolic books, no *articles of faith*. No one was permitted to swear to symbols; no one was called upon to take an oath that he believed certain articles of faith; nay, we have no conception of what are called test-oaths, and must consider them as inadmissible according to the spirit of pure Judaism. *Maimonides*

DANIEL CHODOWIECKI. *Moses Mendelssohn.*
Late 18th century. Colored drawing.
Kunstsammlung der Jüdischen Gemeinde,
Berlin. Max. A. Polster Archive.

was the first to conceive the idea to condense the religion of his fathers into a certain number of principles; in order that, as he gives us to understand, religion, like all other sciences, might have its fundamental ideas, from which all the others are deduced. From this merely accidental thought have originated the *Thirteen Articles* of the Jewish catechism, to which we owe the hymn *Yigdal*, and some good writings by *Chisdai, Albo,* and *Abarbanell.* These, however, are, at the same time, all the consequences which they have produced hitherto. They have not yet, thank God! been forged into fetters in matters of belief. . . .

In truth, everything depends here also upon the difference between *believing* and *knowing* religious doctrines and religious commandments. We will admit that all human knowledge admits of being confined to a few fundamental ideas, which may be taken as the basis. The fewer these are, the firmer will the superstructure stand. But laws can admit of no abridgment. In them everything is fundamental, and in this respect we can say with reason: "That to us all the word of Scripture, all the positive and negative precepts of God, are fundamental." If you wish now to have the quintessence therefrom, then listen to what one of the very greatest teachers of our nation, *Hillel, the elder,* who lived before the destruction of the second temple, considered as such. A heathen said to him one day: "Rabbi, teach me the whole law, whilst I stand on one foot!" Shamai, to whom he had addressed previously the same intimation, had ordered him away with contempt; but Hillel, famed for his unconquerable calmness and mildness of temper, spoke to him: "My son, *love thy neighbour like thyself;* this is the text of the law; all the rest is but commentary. Now go and learn it!"

Napoleon Bonaparte
PROCLAMATION TO THE JEWISH NATION

The citizenship and equal rights won by French Jews in 1791 helped bring about monumental changes in Jewish life everywhere. This proclamation, issued by Napoleon, sought the assistance of the Jewish people in Napoleon's campaign in Palestine by promising a restoration of Jewish rights to political existence as a nation.

General Headquarters, Jerusalem
1st Floréal in the year 7 of the
French Republic (April 20, 1799)

Bonaparte, Commander-in-Chief of the Armies of the French Republic in Africa and Asia, to the Rightful Heirs of Palestine.

Israelites, unique nation, whom, in thousands of years, lust of conquest and tyranny were able to deprive of the ancestral lands only, but not of name and national existence!

Attentive and impartial observers of the destinies of nations, even though not endowed with the gifts of seers like Isaiah and Joel, have also felt long since what these, with beautiful and uplifting faith, foretold when they saw the approaching destruction of their kingdom and fatherland: that the ransomed of the Lord shall return, and come with singing unto Zion, and the enjoyment of henceforth undisturbed possession of their heritage will send an everlasting joy upon their heads (Isaiah 35:10).

Arise then, with gladness, ye exiled! A war unexampled in the annals of history, waged in self-defense by a nation whose hereditary lands were regarded by her enemies as plunder to be divided, arbitrarily and at their convenience, by a stroke of the pen of Cabinets, avenges her own shame and the shame of the remotest nations, long forgotten under the yoke of slavery, and, too, the almost two-thousand-year-old ignominy put upon you; and while time and circumstances would seem to be least favorable to a restatement of your claims or even to their expression, and indeed to be compelling their complete abandonment, she (France) offers to you at this very time, and contrary to all expectations, Israel's patrimony!

The undefiled army with which Providence has sent me hither, led by justice and accompanied by victory, has made Jerusalem my headquarters, and will, within a few days, transfer them to Damascus, a proximity which is no longer terrifying to David's city.

Rightful Heirs of Palestine!

The great nation which does not trade in men and countries as did those who sold your ancestors unto all peoples (Joel 4:6) hereby calls on you not indeed to conquer your patrimony, nay, only to take over that which has been conquered and, with that nation's warranty and support, to maintain it against all comers.

Arise! Show that the once overwhelming might of your oppressors has not repressed the courage of the descendants of those heroes whose brotherly alliance did honor to Sparta and Rome (Macc. 12:15), but that all the two thousand years of slavish treatment have not succeeded in stifling it.

Hasten! Now is the moment which may not return for thousands of years, to claim the restoration of your rights among the population of the universe which had been shamefully withheld from you for thousands of years, your political existence as a nation among the nations, and the unlimited natural right to worship Yehovah in accordance with your faith, publicly and in likelihood for ever (Joel 4:20).

Pauline Wengeroff
FROM MEMOIRS OF A GRANDMOTHER

Pauline Wengeroff (1833–1916) was born in Belorussia in 1833. Her memoirs describe the life of a wealthy Jewish family prior to the Jewish Enlightenment; they also recount the subsequent turmoil and ultimate disintegration of all aspects of Jewish society that occurred as people left the Jewish ghettos to pursue modern life. The conversion of the writer's son to Christianity underscores the effects that the Enlightenment and assimilation had upon her personal life.

Born at the beginning of the 1830's in Bobruysk and brought up by strictly observant parents, I was in a position to see the transformation which European education wrought on Jewish family life. I can see how easy it was for our parents to educate us and how hard it was for us, the second generation, to bring up our children. Though we became acquainted with German and Polish literature, we eagerly studied Pentateuch and Prophets, for they gave us pride in our religion and its traditions and bound us to our people. Biblical poetry stamped itself on the untouched childish mind and provided for the days to come chastity and purity, buoyancy and inspiration.

But how hard for us was that great transition period in the sixties and seventies. We had achieved a degree of European education, but we knew of the wide gaps in our knowledge. We did our utmost so that our children would not lack what we had missed. But we overlooked the wisdom of observing moderation. So we have only ourselves to blame for the abyss between us and our children.

We must now obey our children and submit completely to their will, just as once obedience to our parents was inviolable. As once with our parents, so now with our children, we must hold our tongues, and it is harder now than then. When our parents talked, we listened respectfully, as now we listen, in pride and joy, as our children talk about themselves and their ideals. Our submissiveness and admiration make them tyrannize us. This is the reverse side of the coin, the negative impact of European culture on the Jews of Russia. No group but the Jews so swiftly and irrevocably abandoned everything for West European culture, discarded its religion, and divested itself of its historical past and its traditions.

My parents were God-fearing, deeply pious, and respectable people. This was the prevalent type among the Jews then, whose aim in life was above all the love of God and of family. Most of the day was spent in the study of Talmud, and only appointed hours were set aside for business. Nevertheless, my father's business affairs often involved hundreds of thousands of rubles. Like my grandfather, my father was a contractor, an occupation which in the first half of the nineteenth century played a great economic role, enabling the Russian government to erect fortifications, build roads and canals, and thus supply the army.

A marriage was arranged between me and Hanan Wengeroff, and at eighteen I became the bride of a man I loved deeply but knew not at all. Konotop, where my husband's parents lived, was to be my new home. A small town of ten thousand inhabitants, it yet looked like a village. The inhabitants were mostly Christians; the few Jews were grain merchants and tavern keepers. My father-in-law, the richest man in town, held the government's wine and liquor concession. I remember the way the house was furnished—the large rooms, expensive furniture, beautiful silver, carriages and horses, servants, frequent guests.

Most Konotop Jews, including the Wengeroffs, were hasidim. A daughter of mitnagdim, I saw and heard much that was new.

I read a lot in Konotop, especially Russian. First I read the German books I had brought from home—Schiller, Zschokke, Kotzebue, Bulwer. Then I started on the Russian books which stood on the shelves of the Wengeroff library. I read *Moskauer Nachrichten* and taught my husband, eager to learn, German. But his chief study was Talmud. Every Monday and Thursday he spent the night with his rabbi, hunched over great tomes.

Since our betrothal, my husband experienced mystical religious moods and devoted himself to the sacred mysteries of the Kabbala. Then, this fervent young man yearned to make a pilgrimage to Lubavich, the seat of the head of the Lithuanian hasidim. The rabbi would surely have the complete answers to all disturbing questions and enigmas. Yet barely two years before, my husband had advocated modern ideas which led to conflicts with his parents.

One morning while I was busy at household tasks, my husband came into the kitchen and told me, elatedly, excitedly, that his father had permitted him and his elder brother to go to Lubavich in the company of their rabbi.

What happened there I do not know, for my husband never spoke of this tragic experience. All I know was that this young man, hopeful and inspired, made a pilgrimage to the rabbi, hoping he would unveil the great mystery, but returned sobered. He continued his religious observances and studied with the rabbi, but the magic and ecstasy had gone. Thereafter, little by little, he began to neglect his religious observances. Then he decided to cut his beard. We had our first quarrel. I begged him not to yield to vanity and let his beard grow. He would not hear of it. He reminded me that he was the man of the house and demanded my obedience and submission.

Four years later we left Konotop and the patriarchal way of life we had led. My husband had obtained the liquor concession in Lubny, where we were to start our own independent life. Now, without having to worry about his parents, my husband organized his life as he desired. Daily prayers, in prayer shawl and phylacteries, ceased, though he continued to study the Talmud. He used to discuss it at length with the town rabbi, who was our frequent guest, but his interest was just scholarly.

In 1859, my husband's father, grandfather, and another partner obtained the leasehold on liquor for the province of Kovno. My husband was put at the head of the office. We liquidated our business in Lubny, packed our possessions, and moved.

But before I go on about myself, I want to say something about 1855, which marked a new era in Russia, especially for Jews. It was the year Alexander II ascended the throne. He liberated sixty million peasants from bondage and the Jews from their chains. He opened the gates of his main cities into which swarms of Jewish youth thronged to quench their thirst for European education in the universities.

In this brilliant period of intellectual flowering, the Jews took part in the ferment in the whole country, the rise of the fine arts, the development of the sciences. The effects of the reforms in the forties were apparent now: a succession of Jewish professors, doctors, engineers, writers, musicians, and sculptors had won recognition abroad and brought fame to their country.

This made it possible also for the Jews to attain an unexpected influence in commerce and industry. Never before or after did the Jews in St. Petersburg live in such wealth and distinction as then, when a good part of the financial affairs of the capital city were in their hands. Jewish banking houses were founded. Corporations headed by Jews were organized. The stock exchange and the banks grew to immense proportions.

My wise mother once said: "Two things I know for certain. I and my generation will surely live and die as Jews. Our grandchildren will surely live and die not as Jews. But what our children will be I cannot foresee." The first two parts of this prophecy came true. The third is now coming true, for our generation is some kind of hybrid. Other peoples and other nations have drawn from modern, alien currents and ideas only what is congenial to their own character and thus have preserved their own individuality and uniqueness. But the course that befell the Jews was that they could not acquire the new, the alien, without renouncing the old and repudiating their unique individuality, and their most precious possessions. How chaotically these modern ideas whirled through minds of young Russian Jews! Traditional family ideals disappeared, but new ones did not arise in their stead. These young Jewish men had no sense of moderation nor did they want it. In this transitional period, the woman, the mother, was cruelly brushed aside, for clinging to tradition; she wanted to impart to her children the ethics of Judaism, the traditions of its faith, the sanctity of the Sabbath and the Holy Days, Hebrew, Bible study. She wanted to transmit this great treasure along with the enlightenment, with the new currents of West European culture. But the husbands had the same answer to all pleas: "The children need no religion." In their experience, they wanted to take the dangerous leap from the lowest level of education to the highest, without any intermediate step. They demanded not only assent from their wives, but also submission. They preached freedom, equality, fraternity in public, but at home they were despots.

Kovno was a pretty, provincial town when we settled there. Near the Prussian border, it was natural that a German style of life influenced the whole town. Though the Jewish tradition remained intact in the small Lithuanian towns, in Kovno the enlightenment was in full swing. In progressive Jewish homes, mostly among wealthy families whose fathers and sons were engaged in commerce with Germany and who frequently travelled across the border, the deviation from Jewish tradition was great. About the only thing that remained unchanged was the kosher kitchen.

The Sabbath was no longer kept holy, nor did it disturb the passion for business. The wife, clinging tenaciously to the traditions, used to light the Sabbath candles, but her enlightened husband lit his cigarette. He invited his friends for cards. The *kiddush* cup filled with wine stood on the table, but no one touched it; it had become a symbol. Only the peppered stuffed fish remained. Apostasy did not go so far as to banish that from the Friday evening meal. Instead of Sabbath songs, there were jokes and anecdotes.

A few years later we moved to St. Petersburg. I was going toward a future which would, in transforming the past, surpass all my expectations. The society we became part of consisted of distinguished and cultivated people, most of whom lived a carefree existence in wealth and luxury.

The St. Petersburg Jewish community had a magnificent synagogue and even two rabbis—one modern and seminary-trained, the other Orthodox. But the Jewish community had abandoned many Jewish customs and traditions. The more fashionable even celebrated Christmas. Only Yom Kippur and Passover were observed, but in an up-to-date way. Some Jews drove to the synagogue in their carriages and ate in the intervals between the Yom Kippur service. Passover was kept, even among the most progressive. It remained a festival of remembrance, joyful because it recalled not the Exodus from Egypt, but one's own childhood in the *shtetl*. The *seder* was observed, in a highly abbreviated form. Even baptized Jews kept the *seder*. Though they did not themselves make the holiday feast, they welcomed invitations from their not-yet baptized friends.

These were the customs of the upper stratum of Jewish Petersburg. To live in this milieu and remain impervious to it required a strong character and religious fidelity which my husband lacked. Yet here in Petersburg, I often witnessed the strong feeling of solidarity among these Jews who had given up traditional Judaism. Jews in trouble with the authorities anywhere in Russia used to turn to the Petersburg Jewish community for help. Petersburg Jews spared neither money nor time. They appealed to the highest authorities on behalf of the oppressed Jews. Their concern was natural and understandable. This Jewish solidarity became proverbial all over the world. Even the baptized Jews were not immune to it.

In our family, the struggle to keep the Jewish tradition went on in much the same way as in so many other families. First my husband requested, and then demanded, that his wishes be fulfilled. It was not enough for him to have complete freedom over all matters outside our home: I had to "reform" myself and my home. It began with small tings, intimate things, dear to me.

As soon as we settled in Petersburg I had to discard the peruke which pious Jewish women wore. It was here in Petersburg, after a violent struggle, that I ceased to keep a kosher kitchen. Little by little, I had to drive each cherished custom from our home. "Drive" is not the right word, for I accompanied each to the door with tears and sobs. I loved my husband intensely and as faithfully as in the first days of our marriage, yet I could not submit without resistance. I wanted to preserve this cherished tradition for myself and my children, and I fought a battle of life and death.

In Petersburg, a thousand different experiences always seemed to converge on the one problem of Judaism. What a time of heartbreak when my son attended the *gymnasium!* Simon was a fourth-year student. The students were taken to the chapel for religious services. All but Simon kneeled before the icons. When the teacher ordered him to kneel, he refused: "I am a Jew. My religion forbids me to kneel to an image." After the service, the enraged teacher told Simon he was expelled. I went to the school superintendent, imploring and weeping. I wanted to tell him my son had not willfully been disobedient; he wanted only to remain loyal to his own upbringing and religion. I could not speak; my throat was tight and the tears flowed. I foresaw that my son's whole life would be destroyed. The school superintendent reflected. The boy was dismissed from this gymnasium, but he would arrange to have Simon admitted to another. I was relieved and also proud. Simon was the flesh of my flesh. But ought I to expect that my children, growing up under alien influences, would follow the ways of their mother? They understood, in their way, what was happening and often took their father's side. I felt alone and abandoned by my husband and society. I submitted. But no one suspected the tragedy I experienced that day. Only a few yellowed pages to which thirty-eight years ago in an hour of despair I confided my unhappiness are the silent witness of my suffering. These words, which I first wrote April 15, 1871, I have set down again for they seem to express the woe and despair which so many wives and mothers suffered in that transitional era in Jewish life.

It was a piece of good luck for us when my husband was offered the position of vice-director of the Commerce Bank in Minsk. We did not ponder long, but packed our things and moved. That was at the end of 1871 and the end of our financial worries. In a short time, my husband became director of the bank and we once again led a comfortable and prosperous life.

The third generation came, fearing neither God nor the devil. They paid highest homage to their own will, raised altars to it, and shamelessly offered the most sacred sacrifices to it. This was the generation that grew up without tradition, without the memories of Judaism. The laments of the Ninth of Ab were foreign to them; foreign, too, the thrice-daily-repeated longing for Zion in the prayers; alien the cycle of the Jewish festivals in which a solemn one was succeeded by a gay one. This generation were atheists.

In time, the fathers who had raised their children in a manner of modern enlightened Europeans came to see their fateful mistake. Though they themselves had cast off Judaism and its traditions, they still remained Jews in their hearts, good Jews in a national sense, proud of their past. But their children no longer had memories of a Jewish past.

One partial remedy would have been the study of religion in the government schools. Able teachers might easily have interested their pupils in the Jewish past, introduced them to ancient Hebrew poetry, guided them through Jewish history, and so awakened their pride in belonging to a people whose culture and history were ancient, meaningful and impressive. These young Jews might, then, perhaps not have felt the humiliation at every reminder of their Jewish origin, nor would they have turned from their own people in rage, putting their abilities in the service of others.

COLORPLATE 62
Circumcision Set. Holland, 1827 and 1866. *Box:* silver: filigree, cast and hammered; inlaid with semi-precious stones. *Utensils:* silver: cast, filigree and hammered; mother-of-pearl, carved. *Box:* 9½ × 7⅜ × 4⅛″ (24.1 × 18.7 × 10.5 cm). The Jewish Museum, New York. The H. Ephraim and Mordecai Benguiat Family Collection.

COLORPLATE 63
Wimpel of Gershon Son of Abraham Seltz (detail). Germany, 1834. Undyed linen, polychrome pigments. 132 × 6½″ (335.2 × 12.5 cm). From the collection of Hebrew Union College Skirball Museum, Los Angeles.

COLORPLATE 64
Decorated Tabletop, Depicting Rabbi Nathan Marcus Adler. England, c. 1850. Papier maché with applied mother-of-pearl and painted. Diameter: 31⅝" (80.3 cm). Israel Museum, Jerusalem. Gift of the Goldyne Family, San Francisco, in memory of Dr. Alfred J. Goldyne.

COLORPLATE 68

Artist unknown. *Banner of the Fraternal Organization (Kesher shel Barzel). Last third of the 19th century. Oil on canvas windowshade. 60 × 36″ (152.4 × 91.5 cm). Buccleuch Mansion Museum, Jersey Blue Chapter D.A.R., New Brunswick, New Jersey. On loan to the Jewish Historical Society of Central Jersey, New Brunswick. The Kesher shel Barzel was an American Jewish fraternal organization that existed from 1860 until 1903.*

COLORPLATE 69

EDWARD C. MOORE, Tiffany and Company, New York. *Lewis May Presentation Vase.* 1888. Silver, embossed, chased, engraved; cutout appliqué work. Height 19″ (48.2 cm). Collection, Congregation Emanu-El of the City of New York. Gift of Winston Lewis, May, 1931. *The central cartouche of this presentation vase features a view of Temple Emanu-El, on the corner of Fifth Avenue and Forty-third street, in New York City. The two tablets with Roman numerals representing the Ten Commandments directly above, flank a ner tamid, a hanging light that is perpetually lit before the ark in the sanctuary.*

COLORPLATE 67 *(opposite)*

ZEMEH DAVIDSON. *Ketubbah.* Utica, New York, 1863. Watercolor and ink on paper. 12¹³⁄₁₆ × 9¹³⁄₁₆″ (32 × 24.5 cm). Courtesy of the Library of the Jewish Theological Seminary of America, New York. *In addition to the texts traditionally calligraphed on a ketubbah, this American example includes an abbreviation of "Mazel Tov"—good luck—written in the ovals above the clock faces.*

COLORPLATE 70
Beaker from the Burial Society, Prague. 1783–1784. Glass Enamel. 7⁷⁄₁₆ × 5½" (19 × 14 cm). State Jewish Museum, Prague. *A Hevra Kaddisha (Burial Society) was a communal organization whose main purpose was to provide a ritually proper burial for anyone in the Jewish community. Traditionally, on the anniversary of the death of Moses, following a day of fasting, Burial Societies held a banquet at which new members and officers were elected. During these ceremonies, it was customary to drink wine from a beaker, made from porcelain, glass, or silver, and decorated and inscribed, owned by the Society. The Hebrew inscription on this beaker reads: "Cup of Benediction for feasting and rejoicing, for drinking our fill of love, Lovers of friends, elders signed on the form of the H[oly] (Burial) S[ociety of] B[enefactors] and the new visitors and friends for the care of the sick; for the gathering of the scattered and the dispersed: Beauty and Bands, shall be in his hand to unite them. [in the] year [5]544" (1783/4).*

COLORPLATE 71
Burial Society Pitcher. Mikulov, Moravia, 1836. Painted and gilt pottery. 15⁵⁄₁₆ × 10¼" (39 × 26 cm). State Jewish Museum, Prague. *The central register of this pitcher shows a funeral procession. The Hebrew inscription reads: "Righteousness saves from death (Proverbs 10:2; 11:4). This jug belongs to the Holy Society of Benevolence and was made by the Treasurers Mendel Yedles, Abraham Isaac Pöhm, Moses Leib Bisentz [and] Ezekiel Mas 1836 in the year [5]696" (1836).*

St. Petersburg Choral Synagogue. 1975. Photograph.

In the sixties the government had begun its policy of russifying the Jews. After the Polish uprising of 1863, Russian was made compulsory in the Jewish schools in Poland and Lithuania. Then, the subject matter began to be regulated. Gradually, Jewish studies were shortened to make more time for the general curriculum. But the government's policy articulated the unspoken wish among the young generation, and especially their Jewish teachers, that general education be given priority. No wonder, then, that in the cold, dark and stormy eighties and nineties, our children in their frail boats, tossed on the raging waves of life, wanted to bring their little boats to safety. A safe harbor to them was baptism.

So this terrible word comes like a plague. The word has rarely crossed my lips for it was too close, piercing a mother's bleeding heart. After the terrible events, I never spoke of them, and confided only to my diary, damp with tears, and preserved them deep, deep in my memory—until today.

In those transitional seventies, all sorts of high-flown words become current: nihilism, materialism, assimilation, antisemitism, decadence. "Nihilism" made its appearance in Turgenev's *Fathers and Sons*. Our young people responded enthusiastically to the book and its hero, with whom they identified. Conflict between parents and their children became more embittered, and the young people became more alienated from their parents, often ashamed of them. They viewed in their parents only a purse which enabled them to satisfy their desires. But there was no respect. After all, one could only respect a person of high culture. If the relations between parents and children in the forties and fifties were tragicomic, these relations in the eighties and nineties were pure tragedy.

Jewish youth abandoned itself to total assimilation. Then came March 1, 1881, and the sun which had risen on Jewish life in the fifties suddenly set. Alexander II was killed by a bomb on the bank of the Catherine Canal in St. Petersburg. The hand that had freed sixty million serfs was stilled. The lips which had pronounced the great word of liberation were forever silenced.

The City Council of Minsk sent two delegates to St. Petersburg to place a wreath on his fresh grave. The mayor Minsk and my husband were chosen. It was the first time in Russian history that Jews had participated in a demonstration of mourning.

But different times came. The reptiles that had shunned the light emerged. Antisemitism erupted; the Jews were forced back into the ghetto. Without ceremony, the gateways to education were closed. The jubilation of the fifties and sixties turned into lamentation.

The few rights Jews had enjoyed were withdrawn. Disabilities began to pile up. Rights of residence for Jews in the cities became ever more restricted. An academic education became more and more difficult for Jews to attain, for only a very small Jewish quota was admitted to the gymnasium and even fewer were admitted to the universities.

Pogrom was a new word, coined in the eightites. The Jews of Kiev, Romny, Konotop were among the first to experience the savage assault of the local mobs.

That was the beginning.

In the eighties, with antisemitism raging all over Russia, a Jew had two choices. He could, in the name of Judaism, renounce everything that had become indispensable to him, or he could choose freedom with its offers of education and career—through baptism. Hundreds of enlightened Jews chose the latter. These apostates were not converts out of conviction, nor were they like the Marranos of an earlier age. These apostates disbelieved in all religions: they were nihilists.

My children went the way of so many others. The first to leave us was Simon. Upon learning this, my husband wrote him: "It is not becoming to abandon the camp of the besieged."

Volodya, my favorite child, no longer among the living, followed Simon's example. After completing the gymnasium in Minsk with a brilliant record, he applied to the university at St. Petersburg. He submitted his papers. The admissions clerk rejected them. "These are not your papers. You must have stolen them. You are a Jew, but these papers refer to someone with a Russian name—Vladimir." Several times more he applied to the university, with the same results. Then he took the fateful step, and was immediately accepted.

The baptism of my children was the hardest blow of my life. But the loving heart of a mother can bear a great deal. I forgave them; the blame was on us parents. My sorrow gradually lost its personal meaning, but evermore took on the character of a national misfortune. I mourn it not only as a mother, but as a Jewess mourning for the Jewish people that has lost so many of its noblest sons.

David Frishman
THREE WHO ATE

David Frishman (1859–1922) published his first sonnet at age 15. A versatile writer, he continued his renowned career as a poet, essayist, critic, translator, journalist, and editor, as well as author of short stories. Although Frishman is considered among the first important modern Hebrew authors, he also wrote works in Yiddish and German. This story poignantly illustrates that the sanctity of life takes precedence over all interpretations of the law.

This is the story of three who ate. Not on an ordinary day did these three eat, but on the Day of Atonement; not hidden where no one could see them, but openly, in the great synagogue, before the entire congregation did they eat. Nor were they strangers whom no one knew and nobody cared about, but the most honored citizens of the community: the *Rav* and his two *dayanim*. And yet they remained, even after having eaten in public on the Day of Atonement, the most honored citizens of the community. That Day of Atonement I shall not forget!

I was but a child then, understanding little of the significance of the thing they did, yet I vaguely realized that a stirring event had taken place in those bitter days.

Yes, those were bitter days! A great calamity had befallen us from Heaven—cholera! From far away, from the depths of Asia, it had come to our little town. It spread pestilence in the streets; and in the houses it heaped up horror hundredfold. Silent through the nights and invisible through the days it reaped its harvest. Who could enumerate the names of all who died during those days? Who could count the fresh mounds of earth of the graves?

And the worst of its grim work the plague did in the Jewish ghetto. Like flies people fell, young and old. There was no house but had its dead.

Above us, on the second floor, nine had died in one day; below us, in the cellar, a mother and her four children. In the house opposite, we heard, one night, the loud lamentations of the sick, but in the morning there was not a sound.

They who buried the dead grew weary. The corpses lay upon the ground, body against body, yet people no longer cared.

Thus the summer passed. And there came the Holy Days. And the holiest of all—the Day of Atonement. That day I shall not forget!

Evening in the synagogue. Before the Ark stood, not the cantor and two honored citizens, as is the custom, but the *Rav* and his two *dayanim*. Around and around immense wax candles burned. The worshippers stood facing the east wall, wrapped in their white prayer-shawls, swaying to and fro in silence. And the shadows on the walls swayed with them. Were they really shadows? Or were they the shadows of the dead swaying to and fro upon the walls? Shadows of the dead, who finding no peace in their graves, had come to hear *Kol Nidre*?

Silence! The *Rav*'s voice rose suddenly, accompanied by his two *dayanim*, with a great sigh that penetrated the congregation. And then the words were heard:

"With the grace of God and the forbearance of the assembled, we permit you to pray together with the transgressors."

I listened. . . . What did the *Rav* mean? Who were now the sinners? And did he not fear that Satan might overhear him now, in such a time, such a bitter time?

A looming dark fear swooped down upon me, and it seemed to me that the same fear fell upon the entire congregation, young and old.

Then I saw the *Rav* mounting the almemar. Did he mean to deliver a sermon to console the mourners and strengthen their faith?

But the *Rav* did not begin a sermon. Despite custom and ritual, he intoned a prayer for the recent dead. How long the list of names! The minutes passed one after another, and there seemed to be no end to his enumeration of the victims of the plague.

Those prayers will ever be vivid in my memory. They were not prayers but a painful moan—a long moan that rose from the hearts of the congregation to pierce the heavy skies. And when the prayers were over no one left the synagogue.

I stood there through the night and felt as if a fog rested on my eyes. I heard the men chanting: "And the angels flutter through the air, and fear and trembling embraces all." Fear and trembling! It seemed to me I could see the clouds through the fog, and the angels fluttering up and down, up and down. And amongst them I discerned in the darkness the Black Angel with his multitudinous eyes—from head to foot eyes—everywhere eyes— and what eyes!

No one left the synagogue that night, yet in the morning two were gone. Two who died in their prayer-shawls—ready to be taken from the House of Prayer to the House of

Sounding the Shofar.
Amsterdam, 1723.
Woodcut. Sir Isaac and
Lady Wolfson
Museum, Hechal
Shlomo, Jerusalem.
*The sounding of the
Shofar is an important
part of the High Holy
Day service. This
woodcut is from an 18th-
century Dutch book of
customs.*

the Dead. From the streets reports filtered in. But no one spoke of them or asked questions, so afraid were they to know what might be in their homes. That *Yom Kippur* eve I shall not forget.

And yet even more frightful was the day that followed. Even now, if I close my eyes for a second, I can see that scene!

Noon of the Day of Atonement. On the almemar stood the *Rav* with his head high and proud. The *Rav* was old, eighty or more years old, his beard was white with a silver whiteness, and the hair on his head was as newly-fallen snow. His face, too, was white; but his eyes, unlike the eyes of old men, were black and glowing. I had known the *Rav* from my earliest childhood. I knew him as a holy man whose wisdom was respected afar, and whose word and judgment was as the word of Moses. I stood in my corner looking at him, at the glowing black eyes that shone from his white face with its white hair. The congregation was silent, waiting for their leader to speak.

At first his voice was low and weak, but it gradually gained in strength and volume. He spoke of the holiness of *Yom-Tov,* and what the Giver of the Torah had meant to convey thereby; he spoke of living and of dying, of the living and the dead. He spoke then of the dreadful plague, of the horror of its pains and of the trail of woe it left behind it. And worst of all—he said—no end to its devatations seemed in sight. His voice rose. The pale cheeks flushed, and the blue lips turned red. Then I heard him say: "And when a man sees that great sorrows have befallen him, then it is that he should search his deeds in his relation to his God, but also in his relation to himself, his own body, his very flesh, his daily needs."

I was but a child then, but I remember that I suddenly turned cold.

And then the *Rav* spoke of the cleanliness that keeps us alive, and the uncleanliness that bereaves us of life; of thirst and of hunger; branding thirst and hunger as evil powers that come, in time of a plague, to kill and to destroy mercilessly. Then I heard him say: "In the holy *Gemara* it is said: 'And he shall live by his virtues and not die through them.' And again the Wise Men said: 'There comes a time when it is considered a virtue to trespass a law of the Torah. There is even a time when it is better that a man destroy all of the Torah if thereby he saves a life for the world!"

What did the *Rav* mean? At what did his words aim? Of what did he want to persuade his congregation on that day of days?

Then I saw that the *Rav* was weeping. And, as I stood there in my corner, I too began to cry, the tears running to the corners of my mouth.

Even now, as I close my eyes, I can see the *Rav* stretch out his hand and beckon to his *dayanim*. They approach and rise on the almemar. Now the three are standing there, the *Rav,* the tallest of them, in the center, with one *dayan* to the right of him and one *dayan* to the left of him. What does he whisper in their ears that they suddenly turn pale? Why do they lower their heads? A sigh passes through the congregation and is hushed by the voices of the three on the almemar chanting in unison:

"With the grace of God and the forbearance of the assembled, that you may not grow faint in this time of plague—we permit—you—to eat—and to drink—today!"

A deadly silence settled on the synagogue. No one stirred. I remained in my corner and heard my heart beating: one, one-two, one . . . And an inexpicable dark fear seized me. Shadows swam about the walls and among them I seemed to recognize the recent dead—passing in endless procession. Like a rushing tide the realization of what the *Rav* asked of us swept over me. He wanted us to eat! He wanted Jews to eat on the Day of Atonement! Because of the plague! The plague!

I began to cry loudly, but I was not heard. For I was not alone. Many wept. And the three on the almemar wept, too. And the tallest of the three wept like a child. And like a small child he pleaded: "Eat! Go and eat! The time is such! There comes a time when it is a virtue to trespass a law of the Torah! We must live by them, our virtues, and not die on account of them! Go! Go and eat!"

But no one in the synagogue stirred. He stood there pleading, assuring them that he would take upon himself their sin of eating and drinking on this fearful day; that they would appear innocent before God.

No one stirred.

Suddenly the *Rav's* voice changed. He no longer pleaded, but commanded: "I order you to eat! I! I! I!" His words darted forth like arrow.

The congregation listened with bent heads.

Again the *Rav* pleads tearfully: "Why have you all united against me? Must you drive me to the last extremity? Have I not suffered enough this day of days?"

And the *dayanim* plead with him. But no one moves.

The *Rav* pauses. His face turns ash white, his head sinks upon his breast, and a heart-rending sigh escapes his throat. "It is the will of God!" he murmurs. And with a dry, submissive voice he adds: "Eighty-two years have I lived and not been brought to such a trial. It seems God's will that I should not die before I have fulfilled this too!"

The silence of a graveyard!

And the *Rav* calls: *"Shammas!"*

The beadle approaches. The *Rav* whispers something in his ear and the beadle leaves the synagogue. Then the *Rav* turns to his *dayanim,* whispers to them, and they nod their heads in assent. In a little while the beadle returns from the *Rav's* home with wine and cake.

The scene will remain with me to my dying day! The scene of the three who ate, of the three heroic holy men who ate in the synagogue on the Day of Atonement before the entire congregation.

For heroes they were. Who can measure the struggle that must have torn their hearts? Who can weigh their pain and suffering?

"You wanted me to do it—and I did it!" The *Rav* now spoke with a firm clear voice, then added: "Blessed be the name of the Lord!"

And the congregation ate—ate and wept. . . .

Sholom Aleichem
ON ACCOUNT OF A HAT

Shalom Rabinovitz (1859–1916) took the pseudonym Sholom Aleichem in 1883, with the publication of his second Yiddish story in the St. Petersburg Yiddish Weekly. *(Prior to that he wrote primarily in Hebrew.) He is most familiar to American audiences as the author of the "Tevya" stories, the tales on which* The Fiddler on the Roof *was based. Even though he is now considered one of the greatest Yiddish authors, his works did not win wide critical acclaim during his lifetime.*

"Did I hear you say absent-minded? Now, in our town, that is, in Kasrilevke, we've really got someone for you—do you hear what I say? His name is Sholem Shachnah, but we call him Sholem Shachnah Rattlebrain, and is he absent-minded, is this a distracted creature, Lord have mercy on us! The stories they tell abut him, about this Sholem Shachnah—bushels and baskets of stories—I tell you, whole crates full of stories and anecdotes! It's too bad you're in such a hurry on account of the Passover, because what I could tell you, Mr. Sholom Aleichem—do you hear what I say?—you could go on writing it down forever. But if you can spare a moment I'll tell you a story about what happened to Sholem Shachnah on a Passover eve—a story about a hat, a true story, I should live so, even if it does sound like someone made it up."

These were the words of a Kasrilevke merchant, a dealer in stationery, that is to say, snips of paper. He smoothed out his beard, folded it down over his neck, and went on smoking his thin little cigarettes, one after the other.

I must confess that this true story, which he related to me, does indeed sound like a concocted one, and for a long time I couldn't make up my mind whether or not I should pass it on to you. But I thought it over and decided that if a respectable merchant and dignitary of Kasrilevke, who deals in stationery and is surely no *litterateur*—if he vouches for a story, it must be true. What would he be doing with fiction? Here it is in his own words. I had nothing to do with it.

This Sholem Shachnah I'm telling you about, whom we call Sholem Shachnah Rattlebrain, is a real-estate broker—you hear what I say? He's always with landowners, negotiating transactions. Transactions? Well, at least he hangs around the landowners. So what's the point? I'll tell you. Since he hangs around the landed gentry, naturally some of their manner has rubbed off on him, and he always has a mouth full of farms, homesteads, plots, acreage, soil, threshing machines, renovations, woods, timber, and other such terms having to do with estates.

One day God took pity on Sholem Shachnah, and for the first time in his career as a real-estate broker—are you listening?—he actually worked out a deal. That is to say, the work itself, as you can imagine, was done by others, and when the time came to collect the fee, the big rattler turned out to be not Sholem Shachnah Rattlebrain, but Drobkin, a Jew from Minsk province, a great big fearsome rattler, a real-estate broker from way back—he and his two brothers, also brokers and also big rattlers. So you can take my word for it, there was quite a to-do. A Jew has contrived and connived and has finally, with God's help, managed to cut himself in—so what do they do but come along and cut him out! Where's Justice? Sholem Shachnah wouldn't stand for it—are you listening to me? He set up such a holler and an outcry—"Look what they've done to me!"—that at last they gave in to shut him up, and good riddance it was too.

When he got his few cents Sholem Shachnah sent the greater part of it home to his wife, so she could pay off some debts, shoo the wolf from the door, fix up new outfits for the children, and make ready for the Passover holidays. And as for himself, he also needed a few things, and besides he had to buy presents for his family, as was the custom.

Meanwhile the time flew by, and before he knew it, it was almost Passover. So Sholem Shachnah—now listen to this—ran to the telegraph office and sent home a wire: *Arriving home Passover without fail.* It's easy to say "arriving" and "without fail" at that. But you just try it! Just try riding out our way on the new train and see how fast you'll arrive. Ah, what a pleasure! Did they do us a favor! I tell you, Mr. Sholom Aleichem, for a taste of Paradise such as this you'd gladly forsake your own grandchildren! You see how it is: until you get to Zlodievka there isn't much you can do about it, so you just lean back and ride. But at Zlodievka the fun begins, because that's where you have to change, to get onto the new train, which they did us such a favor by running out to Kasrilevke. But not so fast. First, there's the little matter of several hours' wait, exactly as announced in the schedule—provided, of course, that you don't pull in after the Kasrilevke train has left. And at what time of night may you look forward to this treat? The very middle, thank you, when you're dead tired and disgusted, without a friend in the world except sleep—and there's not one single place in the whole station where you can lay your head, not one. When the wise men of Kasrilevke quote the passage from the Holy Book, *"Tov shem meshemon tov,"* they know what they're doing. I'll translate it for you: We were better off without the train.

To make a long story short, when our Sholem Shachnah arrived in Zlodievka with his carpetbag he was half dead; he had already spent two nights without sleep. But that was nothing at all to what was facing him—he still had to spend the whole night waiting in the station. What shall he do? Naturally he looked around for a place to sit down. Whoever heard of such a thing? Nowhere. Nothing. No place to sit. The walls of the station were covered with soot, the floor was covered with spit. It was dark, it was terrible. He finally discovered one miserable spot on a bench where he had just room enough to squeeze in, and no more than that, because the bench was occupied by an official of some sort in a uniform full of buttons, who was lying there all stretched out and snoring away to beat the band. Who this Buttons was, whether he was coming or going, he hadn't the vaguest idea, Sholem Shachnah, that is. But he could tell that Buttons was no dime-a-dozen official. This was plain by his cap, a military cap with a red band and a visor. He could have been an officer or a police official. Who knows? But surely he had drawn up to the station with ringing of bells, had staggered in, full to the ears with meat and drink, laid himself out on the bench, as in his father's vineyard, and worked up a glorious snoring.

It's not such a bad life to be a gentile, and an official one at that, with buttons, thinks he, Sholem Shachnah, that is, and he wonders, dare he sit next to this Buttons, or hadn't he better keep his distance? Nowadays you never can tell whom you're sitting next to. If he's no more than a plain inspector, that's still all right. But what if he turns out to be a district inspector? Or a provincial commander? Or even higher than that? And supposing this is even Purishkevitch himself, the famous anti-Semite, may his name perish? Let someone else deal with him and Sholem Shachnah turns cold at the mere thought of falling into such a fellow's hands. But then he says to himself—now listen to this—Buttons, he says, who the hell is Buttons? And who gives a hang for Purishkevitch? Don't I pay my fare the same as Purishkevitch? So why should he have all the comforts of life and I none? If Buttons is entitled to a delicious night's sleep, then doesn't he, Sholem Shachnah that is, at least have a nap coming? After all, he's human too, and besides, he's already gone two nights without a wink. And so he sits down, on a corner of the bench, and leans his head back, not, God forbid, to sleep, but just like that, to snooze. But all of a sudden he remembers—he's supposed to be home for Passover, and tomorrow is Passover eve! What if, God have mercy, he should fall asleep and miss his train? But that's why he's got a Jewish head on his shoulders—are you listening to me or not?—so he figures out the answer to that one too, Sholem Shachnah, that is, and goes looking for the porter, a certain Yeremei, he knows him well, to make a deal with him. Whereas he, Sholem Shachnah, is already on his third sleepless night and is afraid, God forbid, that he may miss his train, therefore let him, Yeremei, that is, in God's name, be sure to wake him, Sholem Shachnah, because tomorrow night is a holiday, Passover. "Easter," he says to him in Russian and lays a coin in Yeremei's mitt. "Easter, Yeremei, do you understand, *goyisher kop?* Our Easter." The peasant pockets the coin, no doubt about that, and promises to wake him at the first sign of the train—he can sleep soundly and put his mind at rest. So Sholem Shachnah sits down in is corner of the bench, gingerly, pressed up against the wall, with his carpetbag curled around him so that no one should steal it. Little by little he sinks back, makes himself comfortable, and half shuts his eyes—no more than forty winks, you understand. But before long he's got one foot propped up on the bench and then the other; he stretches out and drifts off to sleep. Sleep? I'll say sleep, like God commanded us: with his head thrown back and his hat rolling away on the floor, Sholem Shachnah is snoring like an eight-day wonder. After all, a human being, up two nights in a row—what would you have him do?

He had a strange dream. He tells this himself, that is, Sholem Shachnah does. He dreamed that he was riding home for Passover—are you listening to me?—but not on the train, in a wagon, driven by a thievish peasant, Ivan Zlodi we call him. The horses were terribly slow, they barely dragged along. Sholem Shachnah was impatient, and he poked the peasant between the shoulders and cried, "May you only drop dead, Ivan darling! Hurry up, you lout! Passover is coming, our Jewish Easter!" Once he called out to him, twice, three times. The thief paid him no mind. But all of a sudden he whipped his horses to a gallop and they went whirling away, up hill and down, like demons. Sholem Shachnah lost his hat. Another minute of this and he would have lost God knows what. "Whoa, there, Ivan old boy! Where's the fire? Not so fast!" cried Sholem Shachnah. He covered his head with his hands—he was worried, you see, over his lost hat. How can he drive into town bareheaded? But for all the good it did him, he could have been hollering at a post. Ivan the Thief was racing the horses as if forty devils were after him. All of a sudden—tppprrru!—they came to a dead stop, right in the middle of the field—you hear me?—a dead stop. What's the matter? Nothing. "Get up," said Ivan, "time to get up."

Time? What time? Sholem Shachnah is all confused. He wakes up, rubs his eyes, and is all set to step out of the wagon when he realizes he has lost his hat. Is he dreaming or not? And what's he doing here? Sholem Shachnah finally comes to his senses and recognizes the peasant—this isn't Ivan Zlodi at all but Yeremei the porter. So he concludes that he isn't on the high road after all, but in the station at Zlodievka, on the way home for Passover, and that if he means to get there he'd better run to the window for a ticket, but fast. Now what? No hat. The carpetbag is right where he left it, but his hat? He pokes around under the bench, reaching all over, until he comes up with a hat—not his own, to be sure, but the official's, with the red band and the visor. But Sholem Shachnah has no time for details and he rushes off to buy a ticket. The ticket window is jammed, everybody and his cousins are crowding in. Sholem Shachnah thinks he won't get to the window in time, perish the thought, and he starts pushing forward, carpetbag and all. The people see the red band and the visor and they make way for him. "Where to, Your Excellency?" asks the ticket agent. What's this Excellency, all of a sudden? wonders Sholem Shachnah, and he rather resents it. Some joke, a gentile poking fun at a Jew. All the same he says, Sholem Shachnah, that is, "Kasrilevke." "Which class, Your Excellency?" The ticket agent is looking straight at the red band and the visor. Sholem Shachnah is angrier than ever. I'll give him an Excellency, so he'll know how to make fun of a poor Jew! But then he thinks, Oh, well, we Jews are in Diaspora—do you hear what I say?—let it pass. And he asks for a ticket third class. "Which class?" The agent blinks at

ILYA SCHOR. *Portrait of a Jewish Man in His Room.* c. 1950. Paint on cardboard. 13¼ × 9″ (33.7 × 22.9 cm). Jewish Museum, New York. Gift of Dr. Harry G. Friedman.

him, very much surprised. This time Sholem Shachnah gets good and sore and he really tells him off. "Third!" says he. All right, thinks the agent, third is third.

In short, Sholem Shachnah buys his ticket, takes up his carpetbag, runs out onto the platform, plunges into the crowd of Jews and gentiles, no comparison intended, and goes looking for the third-class carriage. Again the red band and the visor work like a charm, everyone makes way for the official. Sholem Shachnah is wondering, What goes on here? But he runs along the platform till he meets a conductor carrying a lantern, "Is this third class?" asks Sholem Shachnah, putting one foot on the stairs and shoving his bag into the door of the compartment. "Yes, Your Excellency," says the conductor, but he holds him back. "If you please, sir, it's packed full, as tight as your fist. You couldn't squeeze a needle into that crowd." And he takes Sholem Shachnah's carpetbag—you hear what I'm saying?—and sings out, "Right this way, Your Excellency, I'll find you a seat." "What the Devil!" cries Sholem Shachnah. "Your Excellency and Your Excellency!" But he hasn't much time for the fine points; he's worried about his carpetbag. He's afraid, you see, that with all these Excellencies he'll be swindled out of his belongings. So he runs after the conductor with the lantern, who leads him into a second-class carriage. This is also packed to the rafters, no room even to yawn in there. "This way please, Your Excellency!" And again the conductor grabs the bag and Sholem Shachnah lights out after him. "Where in blazes is he taking me?" Sholem Shachnah is racking his brains over this Excellency business, but meanwhile he keeps his eye on the main thing—the carpetbag. They enter the first-class carriage, the conductor sets down the bag, salutes, and backs away, bowing. Sholem Shachnah bows right back. And there he is, alone at last.

Left alone in the carriage, Sholem Shachnah looks around to get his bearings—you hear what I say? He has no idea why all these honors have suddenly been heaped on him—first class, salutes, Your Excellency. Can it be on account of the real-estate deal he just closed? That's it! But wait a minute. If his own people, Jews, that is, honored him for this, it would be understandable. But gentiles! The conductor! The ticket agent! What's it to them? Maybe he's dreaming. Sholem Shachnah rubs his forehead, and while passing down the corridor glances into the mirror on the wall. It nearly knocks him over! He sees not himself but the official with the red band. That's who it is! "All my bad dreams on Yeremei's head and on his hands and feet, that lug! Twenty times I tell him to wake me and I even give him a tip, and what does he do, that dumb ox, may he catch cholera in his face, but wake the official instead. And me he leaves asleep on the bench! Tough luck, Sholem Shachnah old boy, but this year you'll spend Passover in Zlodievka, not at home."

Now get a load of this. Sholem Shachnah scoops up his carpetbag and rushes off once more, right back to the station where he is sleeping on the bench. He's going to wake himself up before the locomotive, God forbid, lets out a blast and blasts his Passover to pieces. And so it was. No sooner had Sholem Shachnah leaped out of the carriage with his carpetbag than the locomotive did let go with a blast—do you hear me?—one followed by another, and then, good night!

The paper dealer smiled as he lit a fresh cigarette, thin as a straw. "And would you like to hear the rest of the story? The rest isn't so nice. On account of being such a rattlebrain, our dizzy Sholem Shachnah had a miserable Passover, spending both Seders among strangers in the house of a Jew in Zlodievka. But this was nothing—listen to what happened afterward. First of all, he has a wife, Sholem Shachnah, that is, and his wife—how shall I describe her to you? *I* have a wife, *you* have a wife, we all have wives, we've had a taste of Paradise, we know what it means to be married. All I can say about Sholem Shachnah's wife is that she's A Number One. And did she give him a royal welcome! Did she lay into him! Mind you, she didn't complain about his spending the holiday away from home, and she said nothing about the red band and the visor. She let that stand for the time being; she'd take it up with him later. The only thing she complained about was—the telegram! And not so much the telegram—you hear what I say?—as the one short phrase, *without fail*. What possessed him to put that into the wire: *Arriving home Passover without fail*. Was he trying to make the telegraph company rich? And besides, how dare a human being say 'without fail' in the first place? It did him no good to answer and explain. She buried him alive. Oh, well, that's what wives are for. And not that she was altogether wrong—after all, she had been waiting so anxiously. But this was nothing compared with what he caught from the town, Kasrilevke, that is. Even before he returned the whole town—you hear what I say?—knew all about Yeremei and the official and the red band and the visor and the conductor's Your Excellency—the whole show.

He himself, Sholem Shachnah, that is, denied everything and swore up and down that the Kasrilevke smart-alecks had invented the entire story for lack of anything better to do. It was all very simple—the reason he came home late, after the holidays, was that he had made a special trip to inspect a wooded estate. Woods? Estate? Not a chance—no one bought *that!* They pointed him out in the streets and held their sides, laughing. And everybody asked him, "How does it feel, Reb Sholem Shachnah, to wear a cap with a red band and a visor?" 'And tell us,' said others, 'what's it like to travel first class?' As for the children, this was made to order for them—you hear what I say? Wherever he went they trooped after him, shouting, 'Your Excellency! Your excellent Excellency! Your most excellent Excellency!'

"You think it's so easy to put one over on Kasrilevke?"

Alfred Dreyfus

FROM FIVE YEARS OF MY LIFE: 1894–1899

Alfred Dreyfus (1859–1935), was a French army officer, convicted of treason and sentenced to life imprisonment on Devil's Island in 1894. Believing Dreyfus to be a victim of anti-Semitic sentiment his many supporters worked to have the verdict overturned. In 1899 a second trial took place and his sentence was reduced to ten years, five of which had already been served. In 1906 an appeals court reexamined the case and Dreyfus was finally exonerated.

I was born at Mulhouse, in Alsace, October 9, 1859. My childhood passed happily amid the gentle influences of mother and sisters, a kind father devoted to his children, and the companionship of older brothers.

My first sorrow was the Franco-Prussian War. It has never faded from my memory. When peace was concluded my father chose the French nationality, and we had to leave Alsace. I went to Paris to continue my studies.

In 1878 I was received at the Ecole Polytechnique, which in the usual order of things I left in 1880, to enter, as cadet of artillery, the Ecole d'Application of Fontainebleau, where I spent the regulation two years. After graduating, on the 1st of October, 1882, I was breveted lieutenant in the Thirty-first Regiment of Artillery in the garrison at Le Mans. At the end of the year 1883, I was transferred to the Horse Batteries of the First Independent Cavalry Division, at Paris. On the 12th of September, 1889, I received my commission of captain in the Twenty-first Regiment of Artillery, and was appointed on special service at the Ecole Centrale de Pyrotechnie Militaire at Bourges. It was in the course of the following winter that I became engaged to Mlle. Lucie Hadamard, my devoted and heroic wife.

During my engagement I prepared myself for the Ecole Supérieure de Guerre (School for Staff Officers), where I was received the 20th of April, 1890; the next day, April 21, I was married. I left the Ecole Supérieure de Guerre in 1892 with the degree "very good," and the brevet of Staff Officer. My rank number on leaving the Ecole entitled me to be detailed as *stagiaire* (probationer) on the General Staff of the army. I took service in the Second Bureau of the General Staff (The Intelligence Bureau) on the 1st of January, 1893.

A brilliant and easy career was open to me; the future appeared under the most promising auspices. . . . Everything in life seemed to smile on me.

The year 1894 was to be the last of my service in the Second Bureau of the General

Staff of the army. During the last quarter of the year I was named for the regulation term of service in an infantry regiment stationed in Paris.

I began my term on the 1st of October. Saturday, the 13th of October 1894, I received a service-note directing me to go the following Monday, at nine o'clock in the morning, to the Ministry of War for the general inspection. It was expressly stated that I should be in *tenue bourgeoise* (civilian dress). The hour seemed to me very early for the general inspection, which is usually passed late in the day; the mention of civilian dress surprised me as well. Still, after making these remarks while reading the note, I soon forgot them, as the matter appeared unimportant. . . .

On Monday morning I left my family. . . . The morning was bright and cool, the rising sun driving away the thin mist; everything foretold a beautiful day. As I was a little ahead of time, I walked back and forth before the Ministry Building for a few minutes, then went upstairs. On entering the office I was received by Commandant Picquart, who seemed to be waiting for me, and who took me at once into his room. I was somewhat surprised at finding none of my comrades, as officers are always called in groups to the general inspection. After a few minutes of commonplace conversation Commandant Picquart conducted me to the private office of the Chief of General Staff. I was greatly amazed to find myself received, not by the Chief of General Staff, but by Commandant du Paty de Clam, who was in uniform. Three persons in civilian dress, who were utterly unknown to me, were also there. These three persons were M. Cochefert, *Chef de la Sûreté* (the head of the secret police), his secretary, and the Keeper of the Records, M. Gribelin.

Commandant du Paty de Clam came directly toward me and said in a choking voice: "The General is coming. While waiting, I have a letter to write, and as my finger is sore, will you write it for me?" Strange as the request was under the circumstances, I at once complied. I sat down at a little table, while Commandant du Paty placed himself at my side and very near me, following my hand with his eye. After first requiring me to fill

V. C. Burckhardt, Printer and Publisher, Weissenberg. *Captain Dreyfus before the Military Court in Rennes.* 1899. Colored engraving. 15 × 12″ (34.3 × 44 cm). Courtesy of the Leo Baeck Institute, New York.

up an inspection form, he dictated to me a letter of which certain passages recalled the accusing letter that I knew afterward, and which was called the *bordereau*. In the course of his dictation the Commandant interrupted me sharply, saying: "You tremble." (I was not trembling. At the Court Martial of 1894, he explained his brusque interruption by saying that he had perceived I was not trembling under the dictation; believing therefore that he had to do with one who was simulating, he had tried in this way to shake my assurance.) This vehement remark surprised me greatly, as did the hostile attitude of Commandant du Paty. But as all suspicion was far from my mind, I thought only that he was displeased at my writing it badly. My fingers were cold, for the temperature outside was chilly, and I had been only a few minutes in the warm room. So I answered, "My fingers are cold."

As I continued writing without any sign of perturbation, Commandant du Paty tried a new interruption and said violently: "Pay attention; it is a grave matter." Whatever may have been my surprise at a procedure as rude as it was uncommon, I said nothing and simply applied myself to writing more carefully. Thereupon Commandant du Paty, as he explained to the Court Martial of 1894, concluded that, my self-possession being unshakable, it was useless to push the experiment further. The scene of the dictation had been prepared in every detail; but it had not answered the expectations of those who had arranged it.

As soon as the dictation was over, Commandant du Paty arose and, placing his hand on my shoulder, cried out in a loud voice: "In the name of the law, I arrest you; you are accused of the crime of high treason." A thunderbolt falling at my feet would not have produced in me a more violent emotion; I blurted out disconnected sentences, protesting against so infamous an accusation, which nothing in my life could have given rise to.

Next, M. Cochefert and his secretary threw themselves on me and searched me. I did not offer the slightest resistance, but cried to them: "Take my keys, open everything in my house; I am innocent." Then I added, "Show me at least the proofs of the infamous act you pretend I have committed." They answered that the accusations were overwhelming, but refused to state what they were or who had made them.

I was then taken to the military prison . . .

During the seventeen days which followed, I was subjected to frequent cross-examination by Commandant du Paty, who acted as officer of judicial police. He always came in very late in the evening, accompanied by Gribelin, who was acting as his clerk. He dictated to me bits of sentences taken from the incriminating letter, or passed rapidly under my eyes, in the light, words or fragments of words taken from the same letter, asking me whether or not I recognized the handwriting. Besides all that has been recorded of these examinations, he made all sorts of veiled, mysterious allusions to facts unknown to me, and would finally go away theatrically, leaving my brain bewildered by the tangle of insoluble riddles. During all this time I was ignorant of the basis of the accusation, and in spite of most urgent demands I could obtain no light on the monstrous charge brought against me. I was fighting the empty air.

That my brain did not give way during these endless days and nights, was not the fault of Commandant du Paty. I had neither paper nor ink with which to fix my ideas; I was every moment turning over in my head fragments of sentences which I had drawn from him and which only led me further astray. But no matter what my tortures may have been, my conscience was awake and unerringly dictated my duty to me. "If you die," it said to me, "they will believe you guilty; whatever happens, you must live to cry aloud your innocence in the face of the world."

It was only on the fifteenth day after my arrest that Commandant du Paty showed me a photograph of the accusing letter since called the *bordereau*.

I did not write this letter, NOR WAS I IN ANY WAY RESPONSIBLE FOR IT.

Vladimir Medem

CEDARS OF LEBANON: YOUTH OF A BUNDIST

A Jewish Labor Leader Recalls His Beginnings

Vladimir Medem (1879–1923) was a prominent member of the Bund (Jewish Socialist Labor Party), the organization founded in 1897 that greatly influenced the lives of Jews in Czarist Russia and adjacent territories. Although his parents baptized him into the Orthodox church, as a young adult he fervently began to explore his Jewish identity. This selection comes from his autobiography, Fun Mein Leben.

My mother sits in the dining room. Before her stands a little old woman. I remember her name was Leyeh or, as she was called in our house, Leykeh. My mother sits, Leykeh stands, and they don't stop talking for a moment. I don't remember what they talked about, but I do remember that they spoke Yiddish.

I, a child of six or seven, hover near my mother. I hear Leykeh calling her "dear Madame," I hear my mother replying in "jargon" [Yiddish], and I am beside myself with anger. Who ever heard of such a thing: an intelligent, educated woman, the wife of a Russian general, speaking "jargon"? I can hardly wait for my father to come home. Such goings-on aren't allowed in his presence. And indeed, when my father is heard coming, Leykeh disappears hastily into the kitchen. I breathe more freely. Our home is once again truly Russian. . . .

Both my parents were Jews by birth, real honest-to-goodness Jews. I think that my father was even a *kohen.* He came from Shavli (Kovno region) and had settled in Minsk; my mother came from Vilna. I never met my paternal grandparents, but I know that my father's generation was stricken by conversion, as was my mother's family. Practically all my uncles and aunts were Christians and some of their children did not even know of their Jewish origin.

To understand this, we must remember that this epidemic of conversion began much earlier. My father, for example, was born in 1836. As a boy he studied in a Russian Gymnasium and later attended the St. Petersburg military medical academy. When he was graduated he became an army doctor and established himself in a Russian environment. He had left traditional Jewishness very early, if he had ever known it. Insofar as he had any contact with Jewish life, it was permeated with assimilationist leanings. In the 60's, the springtide of Alexander II's regime, the attitude toward Jews was liberal, and the Jewish community responded ardently in its desire to fuse with the Russian people.

Then came a shift in events. The political honeymoon ended and was replaced by years of reaction, pogroms, and anti-Semitism, especially when Alexander III ascended the throne. With political persecution also went social rejection of the Jews. The situation had changed. No matter how hard one had tried to forget one's former Jewishness, the outside world refused to allow it. "You are a Jew" became an insult, a detraction. And the Jew then began to feel ashamed of his Jewishness.

This shame about Jewishness and the desire to conceal one's Jewish origin was typical for our milieu. . . . My Jewish origin was a burden. It was a shame, a degradation, a sort of secret disease about which no one should know. And if people did know, then, if they were kind and friendly, they took no notice of it, just as one ignores the deformity of a hunchback so as not to hurt him.

This is why I used to become upset when my mother spoke Yiddish to old Leykeh. Every word reminded me of the ugly disease: you are a Jew, a cripple. I did not want to be a Jew, I did not consider myself a Jew, and I used to prattle in imitation of the grownups: we are Russians.

This was the atmosphere of our circle and it led to conversion as the final and drastic cure for the secret disease. Actually, conversion was no more than a formality, the last rung of the ladder. My parents did not take this step until quite late. My father became converted at the age of fifty-six, a few months before his death. He was one of the most distinguished citizens of our city, a division doctor, a *statski sovetnik,* a rank between colonel and general. He could not become a full general because he was a Jew. But that was not why he became converted. As I understood it (I was about thirteen years old then), new restrictions against Jewish officials had been introduced, and my father's position was endangered. Since he had no private practice, was old and sick, and could not possibly dream of beginning his career anew, he decided to join the Lutheran Church.

My mother became a Christian a short while later, soon after my father's death. She was very sick, and we children convinced her that her conversion had been our father's desire. She gave in unwillingly and with considerable distress.

At that time, all the children were Christians. My sister had become converted together with my father in order to marry a Russian. My oldest brother had long been an army officer and, necessarily, a Christian. Two other brothers had been converted, but it was spoken of so little that I don't even remember when. Oddly enough, all became Lutherans, as did most Jews who joined the Christian church. I believe it was because conversion to Protestantism involved less ceremonial and fewer technical difficulties than Orthodoxy. Thus, our whole family gradually became Lutherans. Only I was an exception—I belonged to the Greek Orthodox Church.

I was the first Christian in our family, even though I was the youngest. When I was born (July 1879), my parents decided: we have suffered enough because of our Jewishness; let our youngest not know such sufferings. And I was baptized in a Greek Orthodox church just as if I had been born into an Orthodox family, while they themselves remained Jews for a long time.

Thus, I was a Greek Orthodox child, reared in a Jewish, later a half-Lutheran, and finally a wholly Lutheran family. I never felt any inconsistency between my Orthodoxy and the Jewishness around me. Actually, I was for a long time convinced that my father had become converted much earlier than he had in fact. In our home all the Russian church holidays were observed. On official festivals my father even used to go to church, so that I never felt any barrier to the full and free development of my religious feeling.

I was about five when I first went to church. It made a great impression on me: the dark gold holy pictures, the glowing lights and candles, the somber mien of the priests in their extraordinarily beautiful vestments, the mysterious ceremonies, the vibrant bass of the proto-deacon, the singing of the choir. It is indeed hard to describe the full beauty of Russian church music with its earnest and sublime harmony.

But as I grew older, my religious emotions, based on externals rather than conscious religious awareness, began to dissipate, and when I reached my second year in Gymnasium, I began to develop critical attitudes. During my last years in Gymnasium, my circle gradually and imperceptibly turned Jewish. . . .

Yet even though I made friends with more and more Jews, I cannot definitely say that I began to consider myself a Jew. The question of my own Jewishness was not yet posed.

In 1897, I enrolled in the University of Kiev. During this year, I learned about Karl Marx and his *Capital* from Yasha Kaplan. I used to consider socialists a group of dreamers who with fantastic plans and bombs and riots sought to change the order of the world. Now I learned there was another kind of socialism, not a fantasy nor a dream, but a logical and necessary product of human development. The next year I began to study political economy, and a little later I met real live Marxists and learned the name of the Bund.

Besides studying Marx, I decided to learn Hebrew. But my interest in Hebrew was literary rather than Jewish. I wanted to read the Bible in the original. I did not consider the Bible a Jewish book, for, after all, it had been part of the Christian religious teaching I had had as a child. At home during the summer vacation, I did not have to search far for a teacher. Mitche, the older of the two boys who lived in our yard, agreed to teach me in exchange for Russian lessons. . . . I never did learn Hebrew, but I did accomplish something: I learned the alphabet, gaining the key to the Yiddish language. I read very poorly at that time, but the first step had been made.

When I returned to the university, I became active in the student movement. My political work increased my homesickness for Jewishness. Even though no distinction as to Jew or Christian was made among the students, there was one specifically Jewish institution among them—the Jewish student kitchen. Actually, I don't recall that I had ever been there. It was not merely an eating place; it was an intellectual gathering place, a kind of club for the Jewish students. At first I had paid no attention to it, but getting back from a visit home, I felt something akin to envy. I saw that my Jewish friends had their own group from which I was excluded. It was as though I stood before a closed door that shut me out from warmth and hominess. I felt homeless, and longed for a home. This home was Jewish life. This feeling of envy was a sign that I was still on the wrong side of the door, that I still did not consider myself Jewish. But also it was an expression of an awakening desire to become one of those to whom I was drawn.

In various ways and for various reasons, I began to turn to Jewishness. Here I should mention my friendship with Isaac Teumin, a man considerably older than I, who had read and seen much, been to America, Switzerland, seen the world, been imprisoned, and was associated with the Jewish labor movement. Teumin was a person with strong Jewish feeling. He came from a traditional Jewish family, knew Jewish life intimately, and loved it. This love communicated itself to me.

I was in Minsk during the summer and early fall of 1899. On Yom Kippur, Teumin took me to the synagogue. . . .

First we went to the large synagogue and immediately I felt the presence of a new, hitherto unknown atmosphere in all its uniqueness and magic. It was different from the Russian church. There, the large mass of people stood quiet, grave, and silent, and only the priest and the choir spoke and sang on behalf of the congregation, spoke and sang in lovely, carefully harmonic measured tones. But here, it was as though I had fallen among torrential waves. Hundreds upon hundreds of worshipers—each one taking his own case to God, each in a loud voice with passionate eagerness. Hundreds of voices ascended to the heavens, each for himself, without concord, without harmony, yet all joining together in one tremendous clamorous sound. No matter how strange to the Western ear, it makes a deep impression and has a great beauty derived from the passion of mass feeling.

Afterwards, we went to a small synagogue; it may have been a Hasidic prayer-room. There too, I was carried away by the passionate stream of hundreds of voices. Above the vast mass rumbling there rose a sharp and high-pitched voice, the voice of the old gray-bearded *baal-tefila*. This was no singing or preaching. It was a lament, a true lament in which you could feel the scorching tears of an anguished heart. There was none of the solemnity or measured harmony of a Christian prayer. It was the true Oriental passion of a suffering soul, a voice from the gray past which wept and beseeched its old age-gray God. In it lay a great beauty.

In the fall of 1899, Yasha Kaplan and I were expelled from the University of Kiev for our political activity among the student body and ordered by the police to return to Minsk. It was a foregone conclusion that we would sooner or later join the "movement," the Bund. We had enjoyed the taste of political work and it was clear that our place was in the local movement in Minsk. Even though I had some doubts as to whether the Russian workers were at a stage of readiness to accept socialist doctrines, I was well enough acquainted with the Jewish labor movement to know that its existence was an accom-

COLORPLATE 72
VALENTIN SCHULER. *Sabbath Lamp*. Late 17th century. Silver. 16 × 14″ (40.6 × 35.5 cm).
From the collection of Hebrew Union College Skirball Museum, Los Angeles.

COLORPLATE 73

Mizrach. Poland, 19th century, Papercut with ink and tempera. 17¼ × 13⅝″ (43 × 34 cm). Israel Museum, Jerusalem. Feuchtwanger Collection. *A mizrach (meaning "east") is hung on the eastern wall of Jewish homes in countries west of Israel, to indicate the location to direct one's prayers. The decoration and design of mizrachs vary among cultures, incorporating traditional Jewish iconography as well as individualistic decorations.*

COLORPLATE 74
JOEL FEUERSDORF.
Mizrach. Metz (?),
1799. Watercolor,
gouache, and ink on
paper. 13½ × 14¾″
(34.3 × 37.5 cm).
The Jewish Museum,
New York. Gift of
Dr. Harry G.
Friedman. *The artist
of this unusual
18th-century mizrach
combined forms, words,
and Jewish symbols to
create a powerful graphic
composition. The king
on the playing card at
the lower right has
become the biblical King
David; and the French*
citoyen *(citizen),
hidden to the left of the
central mizrach
rectangle, probably refers
to the rights, newly
granted, for the Jews of
France.*

COLORPLATE 75
Mizrach. Morocco,
19th century.
Papercut Mizrach on
colored foil with
six-branched menorah
in the form of hands,
surmounted by verses
from Psalms. 16 ×
20″ (40 × 50 cm). Sir
Isaac and Lady Edith
Wolfson Museum,
Hechal Shlomo,
Jerusalem.

195

COLORPLATE 76

MOSES GANBASH. *Shiviti Plaque (Map of the Holy Places)*. Istanbul, 1838–1839. Paper, paint, ink, paper-cut sections. 34¼ × 42⅜" (87 × 107.2 cm). The Jewish Museum, New York. Gift of Dr. Harry G. Friedman. *A shiviti is a plaque or paper that takes its name from the beginning of the Hebrew text of Psalm 16:8, "I am ever mindful of the Lord's presence." Central to a shiviti is the tetragrammaton, the four letters that comprise the name of God. This unusual and well-executed example from Istanbul contains the traditional quotation and a map of the holy sites in Israel, showing the Dead Sea at the top right and a Turkish steamship in the foreground. Maps of the sites of the Holy Land were popular during the 19th century, when many travelers made a "Grand Tour" of the Middle East.*

COLORPLATE 77

Shiviti. Prussia, 1804. Brass, repoussé and gilt; ink on parchment. 29¼ × 30⅛" (74.5 × 76.5 cm).
The Jewish Museum, New York. Gift of the Danzig Jewish Community. *This brass shiviti was from
the Great Synagogue in Danzig, which was destroyed in 1939.*

COLORPLATE 78

JOHANAN OF MOGILEV. *Reader's Desk Cover for Sabbath and Festivals.* Mogilev, Belorussia, 1870–1871.
Velvet embroidered with polychrome silk and metallic. 42⅛ × 55⅞″ (107 × 142 cm), exclusive of
fringe. The Jewish Museum, New York. Gift of Mrs. Rudnick, through Rabbi Louis Epstein, 1946.
The desk cloth covers the desk upon which the Torah is placed to be read. Like other beautiful objects
associated with the reading of the Torah, the cloth serves to separate the sacred Torah from the profane.

COLORPLATE 79
Sabbath Cloth. Persia, 18th–19th century. Undyed cotton embroidered with polychrome silk; polychrome silk and wool patchwork border. Diameter, 34⅝″ (88 cm). The Jewish Museum, New York. Gift of Dr. Harry G. Friedman.

COLORPLATE 80

Cushion Cover. Istanbul, late 17th–early 18th century. Silk embroidered with metallic threads, metallic braid. 19 × 21¾" (48.2 × 55.2 cm). The Jewish Museum, New York. Gift of Dr. Harry G. Friedman. *Sephardic Jews, escaping expulsions from Spain and Portugal in the 15th century, settled in Istanbul and established a position of prominence within the Ottoman Empire. Jewish ceremonial objects and art made there combined the art of the Ottoman culture with traditional Jewish iconography; thus, this example reflects Ottoman motifs, overlaid with Jewish symbols. A Star of David and a menorah adorn the cushion at the top.*

Bund Group. Warsaw, 1918. Photograph. *A portrait of Vladimir Medem hangs behind the young Bund members.*

plished fact, and that there could be no doubt about its survival. In the winter of 1899-1900, I became a member of the Bund.

At that time, I don't believe I understood the concept of the Bund as a Jewish organization, and its proper role in Jewish life. But, looking back, I realize that Bundist thought on this subject had not yet been clarified; Bundism as an ideology with its own concept of Jewish life and of the Jewish labor movement was still in the process of crystallization. The first formulation of the Bund's Jewish national program was made at the Bund convention of April 1901, when I was in prison. At the time I began working for the party in Minsk, we were still in a period of searching, groping in the dark. The national question was hardly ever discussed in Bundist literature, and what there was of such discussion was inaccessible to me, for I still could not read Yiddish.

I remember once Yasha's coming to ask: "What do you think—are the Jews a nation?" I didn't know what to answer; I had never thought about it. But so far as the Jewish labor movement was concerned, we all recognized it then as a unique and independent movement. I remember a conversation concerning the uniqueness of the Jewish labor movement some time later, in 1901. We were in prison, together in one cell, and behind bars we held a discussion about the quality of our movement. I tried to summarize. Our movement, I said, has two major characteristics. Most of our people are employed in small or very tiny workshops belonging to artisans who themselves work. The second characteristic of our movement is that it consists of Jews, children of the Jewish people. Thus, there are two forces impelling the Jewish worker into our movement: his class feeling, the consciousness that he is a worker who is being exploited, that he wants to fight together with his brothers for a better life; and his Jewish feeling, the consciousness that he is a Jew.

What was my personal Jewishness at that time? My new friends, Jewish workers, used to call me the *goy,* and in externals I was really quite *goyish.* I still had lots of trouble with Yiddish. I could understand it (I had heard it around so much), and my knowledge of German came to my aid. But the Hebrew elements used in Yiddish were strange and presented many difficulties. Nevertheless, I was able to follow the general content of a Yiddish speech. In fact, I even remember that when I heard someone read Peretz's *Der Kranker Yingel,* I understood it very well. But I still could not speak Yiddish. Once I went to visit a worker who happened to be out. I asked his wife in Yiddish when he would come. They were just four simple words, but immediately she had the feeling that a *goy* was speaking and answered me in Russian.

The articles I then wrote in the *Minsker Arbeiter* were written in Russian and then translated into Yiddish. I had already developed some feeling for the Yiddish language and though I wrote in Russian, I used such expressions as readily lent themselves to Yiddish translation. I could not read Yiddish either at the time, but I was learning.

Certainly the Jewish labor milieu influenced me greatly. I cannot say exactly how this influence expressed itself, but the constant association with Jews and Jewish life Judaized me. An especially strong influence was my friendship with Teumin.

I remember one evening when we went walking together through the Jewish quarter, in the outlying poor little streets with their poor little houses. It was Friday night; the streets were quiet and empty; the Sabbath candles burned in the little houses. We were talking about Jewish things. I don't remember the subject, but I do recall that I was strongly impressed by that unique charm of the peaceful Friday nights and felt a romantic association with the Jewish past, a warm, intimate closeness that one has with one's own past. And this feeling for the past has always remained associated with the small houses and quite streets of a Lithuanian Jewish town. My sentiment for Jewry was always, as a Zionist might express it, a *galut* feeling. The palm trees and the vineyards of Palestine were alien to me. I think this is an indication that my Jewishness was really an ingrained living Jewishness, not a literary fancy.

As I have said, I cannot exactly determine how this "nationalizing" influence of the Jewish labor circles expressed itself. It was the quiet effect of day-to-day living. This life became dear and important to me. It was Jewish and it drew me into its environs. When did I clearly and definitely feel myself to be a Jew? I cannot say, but at the beginning of 1901, when I was arrested for clandestine political activity, the police gave me a form to fill in. In the column "Nationality," I wrote Jew."

I. L. Peretz
THE GOLEM

The legend of the Golem comes from the idea of an unfinished being—a body without a soul—that can be brought to life through the use of the name of God. This legend, which gained great popularity among German Jews sometime in the fifteenth century, has inspired many works of art including films and literature. Here the Yiddish and Hebrew author I. L. Peretz (1851–1915) tells one version of the legend.

Great men were once capable of great miracles.

When the ghetto of Prague was being attacked, and they were about to rape the women, roast the children, and slaughter the rest; when it seemed that the end had finally come, the great Rabbi Loeb put aside his *Gemarah,* went into the street, stopped before a heap of clay in front of the teacher's house, and molded a clay image. He blew into the nose of the *golem*—and it began to stir; then he whispered the Name into its ear, and our *golem* left the ghetto. The rabbi returned to the House of Prayer, and the *golem* fell upon our enemies, threshing them as with flails. Men fell on all sides.

Prague was filled with corpses. It lasted, so they say, through Wednesday and Thursday. Now it is already Friday, the clock strikes twelve, and the *golem* is still busy at its work.

"Rabbi," cries the head of the ghetto, "the *golem* is slaughtering all of Prague! There will not be a Gentile left to light the Sabbath fires or take down the Sabbath lamps."

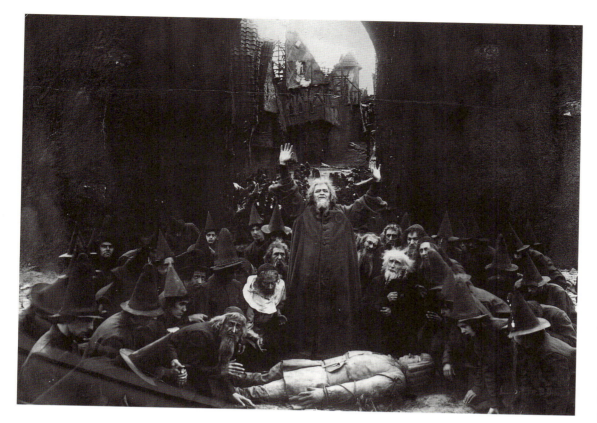

Movie still from *The Golem: How He Came into the World*. 1920.

Once again the rabbi left his study. He went to the altar and began singing the psalm "A song of the Sabbath."

The *golem* ceased its slaughter. It returned to the ghetto, entered the House of Prayer, and waited before the rabbi. And again the rabbi whispered into its ear. The eyes of the *golem* closed, the soul that had dwelt in it flew out, and it was once more a *golem* of clay.

To this day the *golem* lies hidden in the attic of the Prague synagogue, covered with cobwebs that extend from wall to wall. No living creature may look at it, particularly women in pregnancy. No one may touch the cobwebs, for whoever touches them dies. Even the oldest people no longer remember the *golem*, though the wise man Zvi, the grandson of the great Rabbi Loeb, ponders the problem: may such a *golem* be included in a congregation of worshippers or not?

The *golem*, you see, has not been forgotten. It is still here!

But the Name by which it could be called to life in a day of need, the Name has disappeared. And the cobwebs grow and grow, and no one may touch them.

What are we to do?

Isaac Bashevis Singer
THE LAST DEMON

Isaac Bashevis Singer (1904–1991) immigrated to the United States from his native Poland in 1935. Although he wrote in Yiddish, his books have been translated into many languages throughout the world. Singer's work has universal appeal. The European Jewish experience and Jewish folk tradition permeate his stories, which have mystical, poetic overtones. In 1978 Singer was awarded the Nobel Prize for literature.

I, a demon, bear witness that there are no more demons left. Why demons, when man himself is a demon? Why persuade to evil someone who is already convinced? I am the last of the persuaders. I board in an attic in Tishevitz and draw my sustenance from a Yiddish storybook, a leftover from the days before the great catastrophe. The stories in the book are pablum and duck milk, but the Hebrew letters have a weight of their own. I don't have to tell you that I am a Jew. What else, a Gentile? I've heard that there are Gentile demons, but I don't know any, nor do I wish to know them. Jacob and Esau don't become in-laws.

I came here from Lublin. Tishevitz is a God-forsaken place; Adam didn't even stop to pee there. It's so small that a wagon goes through town and the horse is in the market place just as the rear wheels reach the toll gate. There is mud in Tishevitz from Sukkot until Tisha b'Av. The goats of the town don't need to lift their beards to chew at the thatched roofs of the cottages. Hens roost in the middle of the streets. Birds build nests in the women's bonnets. In the tailor's synagogue a billy goat is the tenth in the quorum.

Don't ask me how I managed to get to this smallest letter in the smallest of all prayer books. But when Asmodeus bids you go, you go. After Lublin the road is familiar as far as Zamosc. From there on you are on your own. I was told to look for an iron weathercock with a crow perched upon its comb on the roof of the study house. Once upon a time the cock turned in the wind, but for years now it hasn't moved, not even in thunder and lightning. In Tishevitz even iron weathercocks die.

I speak in the present tense as for me time stands still. I arrive. I look around. For the life of me I can't find a single one of our men. The cemetery is empty. There is no outhouse. I go to the ritual bathhouse, but I don't hear a sound. I sit down on the highest bench, look down on the stone on which the buckets of water are poured each Friday, and wonder. Why am I needed here? If a little demon is wanted, is it necessary to import one all the way from Lublin? Aren't there enough devils in Zamosc? Outside the sun is shining—it's close to the summer solstice—but inside the bathhouse it's gloomy and cold. Above me is a spider web, and within the web a spider wiggling its legs, seeming to spin but drawing no thread. There's no sign of a fly, not even the shell of a fly. "What does the creature eat?" I ask myself. "It own insides?" Suddenly I hear it chanting in a Talmudic singsong: "A lion isn't satisfied by a morsel and a ditch isn't filled up with dirt from its own walls."

I burst out laughing.

"Is that so? Why have you disguised yourself as a spider?"

"I've already been a worm, a flea, a frog. I've been sitting here for two hundred years without a stitch of work to do. But you need a permit to leave."

"They don't sin here?"

"Petty men, petty sins. Today someone covets another man's broom; tomorrow he fasts and puts peas in the shoes. Ever since Abraham Zalman was under the illusion that he was Messiah, the son of Joseph, the blood of the people has congealed in their veins. If I were Satan, I wouldn't even send one of our firstgraders here."

"How much does it cost him?"

"What's new in the world?" he asks me.

"It's not been so good for our crowd."

"What's happened? The Holy Spirit grows stronger?"

"Stronger? Only in Tishevitz is he powerful. No one's heard of him in the large cities. Even in Lublin he's out of style."

"Well, that should be fine."

"But it isn't," I say. " 'All guilty is worse for us than All innocent.' It has reached a point where people want to sin beyond their capacities. They martyr themselves for the most trivial of sins. If that's the way it is, what are we needed for? A short while ago I was flying over Levertov Street, and I saw a man dressed in a skunk's coat. He had a black beard and wavy sidelocks; an amber cigar holder was clamped between his lips.

Across the street from him an official's wife was walking, so it occurs to me to say, "That's quite a bargain, don't you think, Uncle?" All I expected from him was a thought. I had my handkerchief ready if he should spit on me. So what does the man do? 'Why waste your breath on me?' he calls out angrily. 'I'm willing. Start working on her.' "

"What sort of a misfortune is this?"

"Enlightenment! In the two hundred years you've been sitting on your tail here, Satan has cooked up a new dish of kasha. The Jews have now developed writers. Yiddish ones, Hebrew ones, and they have taken over our trade. We grow hoarse talking to every adolescent, but they print their *kitsch* by the thousands and distribute it to Jews everywhere. They know all our tricks—mockery, piety. They have a hundred reasons why a rat must be kosher. All that they want to do is to redeem the world. Why, if you could corrupt nothing, have you been left here for two hundred years? And if you could do nothing in two hundred years, what do they expect from me in two weeks?"

"You know the proverb, 'A guest for a while sees a mile.' "

"What's there to see?"

"A young rabbi has moved here from Modly Bozyc. He's not yet thirty, but he's absolutely stuffed with knowledge, knows the thirty-six tractates of the Talmud by heart. He's the greatest Kabbalist in Poland, fasts every Monday and Thursday, and bathes in the ritual bath when the water is ice cold. He won't permit any of us to talk to him. What's more he has a handsome wife, and that's bread in the basket. What do we have to tempt him with? You might as well try to break through an iron wall. If I were asked my opinion, I'd say that Tishevitz should be removed from our files. All I ask is that you get me out of here before I go mad."

"No, first I must have a talk with this rabbi. How do you think I should start?"

"You tell me. He'll start pouring salt on your tail before you open your mouth."

"I'm from Lublin. I'm not so easily frightened."

II

On the way to the rabbi, I ask the imp, "what have you tried so far?"

"What haven't I tried?" he answers.

"A woman?"

"Won't look at one."

"Heresy?"

"He knows all the answers."

"Money?"

"Doesn't know what a coin look like."

"Reputation?"

"He runs from it."

"Doesn't he look backwards?"

"Doesn't even move his head."

"He's got to have some angle."

"Where's it hidden?"

The window of the rabbi's study is open, and in we fly. There's the usual paraphernalia around: an ark with the Holy Scroll, bookshelves, a mezuzah in a wooden case. The rabbi, a young man with a blond beard, blue eyes, yellow sidelocks, a high forehead, and a deep widow's peak sits on the rabbinical chair peering in the Gemara. He's fully equipped: *yarmulka*, sash, and fringed garment with each of the fringes braided eight times. I listen to his skull: pure thoughts! He sways and chants in Hebrew, *"Raḥel t'unah vegazezah,"* and then translates, "a wooly sheep fleeced."

"In Hebrew Rachel is both a sheep and a girl's name," I say.

"So?"

"A sheep has wool and a girl has hair."

"Therefore?"

"If she's not androgynous, a girl has pubic hair."

"Stop babbling and let me study," the rabbi says in anger.

"Wait a second," I say, "Torah won't get cold. It's true that Jacob loved Rachel, but when he was given Leah instead, she wasn't poison. And when Rachel gave him Bilhah as a concubine, what did Leah do to spite her sister? She put Zilpah into his bed.

"That was before the giving of Torah."

"What about King David?"

"That happened before the excommunication by Rabbi Gershom."

"Before or after Rabbi Gershom, a male is a male."

"Rascal. *Shaddai kra'Satan,*" the rabbi exclaims. Grabbing both of his sidelocks, he begins to tremble as if assaulted by a bad dream. "What nonsense am I thinking?" He takes his ear lobes and closes his ears. I keep on talking but he doesn't listen; he becomes absorbed in a difficult passage and there's no longer anyone to speak to. The little imp from Tishevitz says, "He's a hard one to hook, isn't he? Tomorrow he'll fast and roll in a bed of thistles. He'll give away his last penny to charity."

"Such a believer nowadays?"

"Strong as a rock."

"And his wife?"

"A sacrificial lamb."

"What of the children?"

"Still infants."

"Perhaps he has a mother-in-law?"

"She's already in the other world."

"Any quarrels?"

"Not even half an enemy."

"Where do you find such a jewel?"

"Once in a while something like that turns up among the Jews."

"This one I've got to get. This is my first job around here. I've been promised that if I succeed, I'll be transferred to Odessa."

"What's so good about that?"

"It's as near paradise as our kind gets. You can sleep twenty-four hours a day. The population sins and you don't lift a finger."

"So what do you do all day?"

"We play with our women."

"Here there's not a single one of your girls." The imp sighs. "There was one old bitch but she expired."

"So what's left?"

"What Onan did."

"That doesn't lead anywhere. Help me and I swear by Asmodeus' beard that I'll get you out of here. We have an opening for a mixer of bitter herbs. You only work Passovers."

"I hope it works out, but don't count your chickens."

"We've taken care of tougher than he."

III

A week goes by and our business has not moved forward; I find myself in a dirty mood. A week in Tishevitz is equal to a year in Lublin. The Tishevitz imp is all right, but when you sit two hundred years in such a hole, you become a yokel. He cracks jokes that didn't amuse Enoch and convulses with laughter; he drops names from the Haggadah. Every one of his stories wears a long beard. I'd like to get the hell out of here, but it doesn't take a magician to return home with nothing. I have enemies among my colleagues and I must beware of intrigue. Perhaps I was sent here just to break my neck. When devils stop warring with people, they start tripping each other.

Experience has taught that of all the snares we use, there are three that work unfailingly—lust, pride, and avarice. No one can evade all three, not even Rabbi Tsots himself.

Of the three, pride has the strongest meshes. According to the Talmud a scholar is permitted the eighth part of an eighth part of vanity. But a learned man generally exceeds his quota. When I see that the days are passing and that the rabbi of Tishevitz remains stubborn, I concentrate on vanity.

"Rabbi of Tishevitz," I say, "I wasn't born yesterday. I come from Lublin where the streets are paved with exegeses of the Talmud. We use manuscripts to heat our ovens. The floors of our attics sag under the weight of Kabbalah. But not even in Lublin have I met a man of your eminence. How does it happen," I ask, "that no one's heard of you? True saints should hide themselves, perhaps, but silence will not bring redemption. You should be the leader of this generation, and not merely the rabbi of this community, holy thought it is. The time has come for you to reveal yourself. Heaven and earth are waiting for you. Messiah himself sits in the Bird Nest looking down in search of an unblemished saint like you. But what are you doing about it? You sit on your rabbinical chair laying down the law on which pots and which pans are kosher. Forgive me the comparison, but it is as if an elephant were put to work hauling a straw."

"Who are you and what do you want?" the rabbi asks in terror. "Why don't you let me study?"

"There is a time when the service of God requires the neglect of Torah," I scream. "Any student can study the Gemara."

"Who sent you here?"

"I was sent; I am here. Do you think they don't know about you up there? The higher-ups are annoyed with you. Broad shoulders must bear their share of the load. To put it in rhyme: the humble can stumble. Hearken to this: Abraham Zalman was Messiah, son of Joseph, and you are ordained to prepare the way for Messiah, son of David, but stop sleeping. Get ready for battle. The world sinks to the forty-ninth gate of uncleanliness, but you have broken through to the seventh firmament. Only one cry is heard in the mansions, the man from Tishevitz. The angel in charge of Edom has marshalled a class of demons against you. Satan lies in wait also. Asmodeus is undermining you. Lilith and Namah hover at your bedside. You don't see them, but Shabriri and Briri are treading at your heels. If the Angels were not defending you, that unholy crowd would pound you to dust and ashes. But you do not stand alone, Rabbi of Tishevitz. Lord Sandalphon guards your every step. Metratron watches over you from his luminescent sphere. Everything hangs in the balance, man of Tishevitz; you can tip the scales."

"What should I do?"

"Mark well all that I tell you. Even if I command you to break the law, do as I bid."

"Who are you? What is your name?"

"Elijah the Tishbite. I have the ram's horn of the Messiah ready. Whether the redemption comes, or we wander in the darkness of Egypt another 2,689 years is up to you."

The rabbi of Tishevitz remains silent for a long time. His face becomes as white as the slips of paper on which he writes his commentaries.

"How do I know you're speaking the truth?" he asks in a trembling voice. "Forgive me, Holy angel, but I require a sign."

"You are right. I will give you a sign."

And I raise such a wind in the rabbi's study that the slip of paper on which he is writing rises from the table and starts flying like a pigeon. The pages of the Gemara turn by themselves. The curtain of the Holy Scroll billows. The rabbi's *yarmulka* jumps from his head, soars to the ceiling, and drops back onto his skull.

"Is that how Nature behaves?" I ask.

"No."

"Do you believe me now?"

The rabbi of Tishevitz hesitates.

"What do you want me to do?"

"The leader of his generation must be famous."

"How do you become famous?"

"Go and travel in the world."

"What do I do in the world?"

"Preach and collect money."

"For what do I collect?"

"First of all collect. Later on I'll tell you what to do with the money."

"Who will contribute?"

"When I order, Jews give."

"How will I support myself?"

"A rabbinical emissary is entitled to a part of what he collects."

"And my family?"

"You will get enough for all."

"What am I supposed to do right now?"

"Shut the Gemara."

"Ah, but my soul yearns for Torah," the rabbi of Tishevitz groans. Nevertheless he lifts the cover of the book, ready to shut it. If he had done that, he would have been through. What did Joseph do? Just hand Samael a pinch of snuff. I am already laughing to myself, "Rabbi of Tishevitz, I have you all wrapped up." The little bathhouse imp, standing in a corner, cocks an ear and turns green with envy. True, I have promised to do him a favor, but the jealousy of our kind is stronger than anything. Suddenly the rabbi says, "Forgive me, my Lord, but I require another sign."

"What do you want me to do? Stop the sun?"

"Just show me your feet."

The moment the rabbi of Tishevitz speaks these words, I know everything is lost. We can disguise all the parts of our body but the feet. From the smallest imp right up to Ketev Meriri we all have the claws of geese. The little imp in the corner bursts out laughing. For the first time in a thousand years I, the master of speech, lose my tongue.

"I don't show my feet," I call out in rage.

"That means you're a devil. *Pik,* get out of here," the rabbi cries. He races to his bookcase, pulls out the *Book of Creation* and waves it menacingly over me. What devil can withstand the *Book of Creation?* I run from the rabbi's study with my spirit in pieces.

To make a long story short, I remain stuck in Tishevitz. No more Lublin, no more Odessa. In one second all my stratagems turn to ashes. An order comes from Asmodeus himself, "Stay in Tishevitz and fry. Don't go further than a man is allowed to walk on the Sabbath."

How long am I here? Eternity plus a Wednesday. I've seen it all, the destruction of Tishevitz, the destruction of Poland. There are no more Jews, no more demons. The women don't pour out water any longer on the night of the winter solstice. They don't avoid giving things in even numbers. They no longer knock at dawn at the antechamber of the synagogue. They don't warn us before emptying the slops. The rabbi was martyred on a Friday in the month of Nisan. The community was slaughtered, the holy books burned, the cemetery desecrated. The *Book of Creation* has been returned to the Creator. Gentiles wash themselves in the ritual bath. Abraham Zalman's chapel has been turned into a pig sty. There is no longer an Angel of Good nor an Angel of Evil. No more sins, no more temptations! The generation is already guilty seven times over, but Messiah does not come. To whom should he come? Messiah did not come for the Jews, so the Jews went to Messiah. There is no further need for demons. We have also been annihilated. I am the last, a refugee. I can go anywhere I please, but where should a demon like me go? To the murderers?

I found a Yiddish storybook between two broken barrels in the house which once belonged to Velvel the Barrelmaker. I sit there, the last of the demons. I eat dust. I sleep on a feather duster. I keep on reading gibberish. The style of the book is in our manner: Sabbath pudding cooked in pig's fat: blasphemy rolled in piety. The moral of the book is: neither judge, nor judgment. But nevertheless the letters are Jewish. The alphabet they could not squander. I suck on the letters and feed myself. I count the words, make rhymes, and tortuously interpret and reinterpret each dot.

Aleph, the abyss, what else waited?
Bet, the blow, long since fated.
Gimel, God, pretending he knew,
Dalet, death, its shadow grew.
Hei, the hangman, he stood prepared;
Wov, wisdom, ignorance bared.
Zayeen, the zodiac, signs distantly loomed;
Het, the child, prenatally doomed.
Tet, the thinker, an imprisoned lord;
Yod, the judge, the verdict a fraud.

Yes, as long as a single volume remains, I have something to sustain me. As long as the moths have not destroyed the last page, there is something to play with. What will happen when the last letter is no more, I'd rather not bring to my lips.

When the last letter is gone,
The last of the demons is done.

Sigmund Freud

FROM MOSES AND MONOTHEISM
Hatred of the Jews

In Moses and Monotheism, *Sigmund Freud (1856–1939) theorizes that monotheism was an invention of the Egyptian pharaoh Ikhnaton, and that Moses (in reality an Egyptian prince) was eventually murdered by his followers, the Israelites. This negative picture of Jews notwithstanding, Freud's brief analysis of the causes of anti-Semitism is forceful for its introduction of the unconscious roots of anti-Semitism.*

The poor Jewish people, who with its usual stiff-necked obduracy continued to deny the murder of their "father," has dearly expiated this in the course of centuries. Over and over again they heard the reproach: "You killed our God." And this reproach is true, if rightly interpreted. It says, in reference to the history of religion: "You won't *admit* that you murdered God" (the archetype of God, the primeval Father, and his reincarnations). Something should be added—namely: "It is true, we did the same thing, but we *admitted* it, and since then we have been purified." Not all accusations with which antisemitism pursues the descendants of the Jewish people are based on such good foundations.

There must, of course, be more than one reason for a phenomenon of such intensity and lasting strength as the popular hatred of Jews. A whole series of reasons can be divined; some of them, which need no interpretation, arise from obvious considerations; others lie deeper and spring from secret sources, which one would regard as the specific motives.

In the first group the most fallacious is the reproach of their being foreigners, since in many places nowadays under the sway of antisemitism the Jews were the oldest constituents of the population or arrived even before the present inhabitants. This is so, for example, in the town of Cologne, where Jews came with the Romans, before it was colonised by Germanic tribes.

Other grounds for antisemitism are stronger, as, for example, the circumstance that Jews mostly live as a minority among other peoples, since the feeling of solidarity of the

masses, in order to be complete, has need of an animosity against an outside minority, and the numerical weakness of the minority invites suppression.

Two other peculiarities that the Jews possess, however, are quite unpardonable. The first is that in many respects they are different from their "hosts." Not fundamentally so, since they are not a foreign Asiatic race, as their enemies maintain, but mostly consist of the remnants of Mediterranean peoples and inherit their culture. Yet they are different—although sometimes it is hard to define in what respects—especially from the Nordic peoples, and racial intolerance finds stronger expression, strange to say, in regard to small differences than to fundamental ones.

The second peculiarity has an even more pronounced effect. It is that they defy oppression, that even the most cruel persecutions have not succeeded in exterminating them. On the contrary, they show a capacity for holding their own in practical life and, where they are admitted, they make valuable contributions to the surrounding civilisation.

The deeper motives of antisemitism have their roots in times long past; they come from the unconscious, and I am quite prepared to hear that what I am going to say will at first appear incredible. I venture to assert that the jealousy which the Jews evoked in other peoples by maintaining that they were the first-born, favourite child of God the Father has not yet been overcome by those others, just as if the latter had given credence to the assumption.

Furthermore, among the customs through which the Jews marked off their aloof position, that of circumcision made a disagreeable, uncanny impression on others. The explanation probably is that it reminds them of the dreaded castration idea and of things in their primeval past which they would fain forget.

Then there is lastly the most recent motive of the series. We must not forget that all the peoples who now excel in the practise of antisemitism became Christians only in relatively recent times, sometimes forced to it by bloody compulsion. One might say they all are "badly christened"; under the thin veneer of Christianity they have remained what their ancestors were, barbarically polytheistic. They have not yet overcome their grudge against the new religion which was forced on them, and they have projected it on to the source from which Christianity came to them. The fact that the Gospels tell a story which is enacted among Jews, and in truth treats only of Jews, has facilitated such a projection.

The hatred for Judaism is at bottom hatred for Christianity, and it is not surprising that in the German National Socialist revolution this close connection of the two monotheistic religions finds such clear expression in the hostile treatment of both.

Hayyim Nahman Bialik
MAKING THE CROOKED STRAIGHT

Hayyim Nahman Bialik (1873–1934) was born in Southern Russia where he received a traditional Jewish education. Even though he became a writer instead of a rabbi, his knowledge of Jewish classics permeates his work. His verses are deeply rooted in the European Jewish experience, but they easily adapt to the changing modern world and the challenges that face all Jews.

It was evening, and three of us were standing on the front platform of the street-car; on one end an elderly Jew, tall and gaunt; I, on the other end, facing him, and between us a fledgling lieutenant—about whose person everything cried, "new!"

At first I paid no attention to the old man. He was leaning, cane in hand, against the wire-meshed grill, keeping himself far in the shadow, where the faint light of the outer lamp hardly reached him. The young officer, who stood between us, shut him off from my view, so that I could see little of him beyond his gray hair fluttering with every jolt of the tram. But when, quite casually, I happened to look in his direction, he turned his head slightly to a side and nodded—and instantly I recognized him. He was the old gentleman that I was always running into on the street, and who always nodded to me so politely.

Somewhere I must once have been introduced to him, but when and where I could not remember; nor could I recall ever having exchanged words with him; I knew neither his name nor occupation. Occasionally I would come upon him standing, he and his cane, on some street corner, or sauntering along, pausing to look at posters or the show-windows—and seeing me, he would nod.

His clothes would be threadbare, but fairly clean; his shoes patched in places, but polished. Every morning, it was obvious, the brush had worked assiduously over his clothes, seeking to remedy today what yesterday had spoiled. But never, apparently, with complete success; for whenever he became sensitive to some detecting gaze, the palm of his hand would move quickly to cover a patch or a stain. Sometimes I met him carrying a book or bundle, but his walk would be no more hurried than usual. Passing me, he would nod his head in silence, fix me for a moment with his soft, melancholy eyes, and plod quietly on his way. . . .

Yes, I said to myself, this man is one of those unfortunates who, having no permanent employment, wander all day long, from the time they arise in the morning to the time they retire at night, in a dead emptiness—lose themselves in it and wander about lost, like a tiny cloud in infinite sky. Or, more unhappily, they manage to attach themselves somewhere: through someone's pity, say, or through some casual introduction, they succeed—after numerous rebuffs and refusals—in gaining access to the homes of the well-to-do people. From whom, after being sent away repeatedly with a "come back tomorrow," they eventually obtain some sort of pay. They cannot help but see, poor souls! that the work given them—whether it be cataloguing the house library or arranging the family records (already done for the tenth time), or copying manuscripts (copied already eleven times), or tutoring a youthful gymnast through his bar-mizvah exercises—is neither essential nor suited to their abilities: is given to them, in fact, out of charity. They can make no terms, they must accept what is offered. Entering the rich man's house, they steal in through the back door like trespassers. And when they receive their pay, they lower their eyes, their faces flush, and all self-possession leaves them. They mutter an abrupt good-by, and suddenly find themselves out in the street, without knowing how they got there or through which door they came.

Some, as this man here appears to be, are men of breeding, with refined and gentle souls. Some are hypersensitive and sick with hopeless pride. But all of them suffer from the same sense of inferiority, the same self-consciousness, which conquers their spirit during the day, and gnaws at their bowels in the night. It is not so much poverty that humiliates them, but its outward signs: every patch in their clothing conceals a smarting wound, every stain scorches the flesh underneath it. . . .

ISAAC LICHTENSTEIN. *Portrait: Head of a Jewish Man.* c. 1940. Tempera and wash on paper. 12¼ × 9¼" (31.1 × 23.5 cm). Jewish Museum, New York.

So, I thought, one who pities men such as these, who does not wish to aggravate their torture, does well not to look at them any longer than formality requires. And that is how I was careful to act towards my elderly gentlemen. I returned his nod with a slight nod and fixed my eyes on the front of the car.

The car stopped. Two more passengers, an older army officer and his wife, mounted the platform. The young officer drew to attention smartly and saluted. They diverted my attention, and I forgot all about the old man.

A few minutes later, however, I saw the young officer suddenly turn to the old man with a polite bow and a genteel wave of his gloved hand, at the same time saying softly:

"Sir, I beg your pardon."

This excessive politeness, like the new uniform he wore, betrayed the tyro. Here was a product of the military academy so recently graduated as to be still punctilious about the rules for a gentleman and an officer that he had learned in school, just as a bar-mizvah boy is careful with his tefillin the first few days he puts them on. How glad he must have been for the opportunity to display his academy manners in the presence of a senior officer!

What had made him beg the old man's pardon? Probably he had unwittingly jostled against him, or elbowed him by accident, or stepped on his toe. Whatever it was, the old man had not been aware of it. Taken aback, therefore, by the junker's unexpectedly courteous attention, he inclined his ear forward, and asked timidly and respectfully:

"What did you say, sir?"

"I humbly beg your pardon, sir," the junker repeated with even more exaggerated politeness than before.

"What? What?" the old man asked in amazement, refusing to believe his ears, and he bent forward even further, until his head was quite close to the young officer's.

Even then the junker did not quite lose his patience, and only his raised voice betrayed his irritation. He repeated his request for a pardon a third time, stressing each word by itself:

"I do ask your pardon, sir, very . . . very . . . much."

Now the old man grasped the matter. This handsome, elegant, young officer was begging pardon; not only that, but had been forced twice to repeat himself. And all on account of him. The old man was terribly embarrassed. Meeting, at this moment, the puzzled stare of the young officer, he was like one who is caught in some shameful act of weakness. With his lips he made a strange sound—pfff—accompanying it with a three-fold gesture: shrugging his shoulders, spreading out his arms, and twisting his mouth in an odd fashion, all at the same time. It was hard to tell what he meant to convey, whether amazement, or apology, or humiliation, or disdain. Maybe the gesture included them all, and each of the four witnesses—the officer, his wife, the junker and myself—was privileged to the interpretation he liked best.

The old man stood there pitiably restless and ill at ease. That he had brought so much attention upon himself, that so many eyes were looking at him, seemed to hurt him beyond measure. He seemed to feel that all eyes were examining him from head to foot, that he was revealed before everyone in all of his shabbiness and inferiority. It was as if all the humiliating poverty of his life, all the wounds on his soul, and all the wounds on his honor, had suddenly opened mouths and cried out in one bitter voice: Why not? Is it so unusual that a young officer should ask pardon of a man like me? Do I not deserve, for once in my life, some measure of courteous attention? Can I never hope, not even for once in my life, to experience the feelings of a complete man, without patch or stain?

The old man's eyes moved about incessantly, in tortured embarrassment. The palm of his hand moved nervously over his thread-worn clothes. It was obvious that he suffered excruciating pain. Yes, every patch had under it a deep sore, and each stain burned the brand of shame into his raw flesh.

He made hasty and furtive efforts to tidy himself. He resorted, all at one time, to all the devices he had ever employed. He hurriedly drew himself straight, smoothed his beard with a hasty gesture, straightened his hat on his head. Then he managed with the same quick motions to button his coat, covering thereby a yellow stain on his trousers. He moved his feet close together, concealing, in the one act, two large patches on his shoes. All these actions he performed hastily, almost all at one time, and, as it seemed to him, secretly, so as to attract no attention from his observers.

And at last he suddenly drew out a handkerchief, not overclean, from his pocket, and blew his nose upon it so violently that all the bystanders were shocked, particularly the polite and elegant young officer.

Poor man! In one moment he wanted to straighten out what so many years had made crooked!

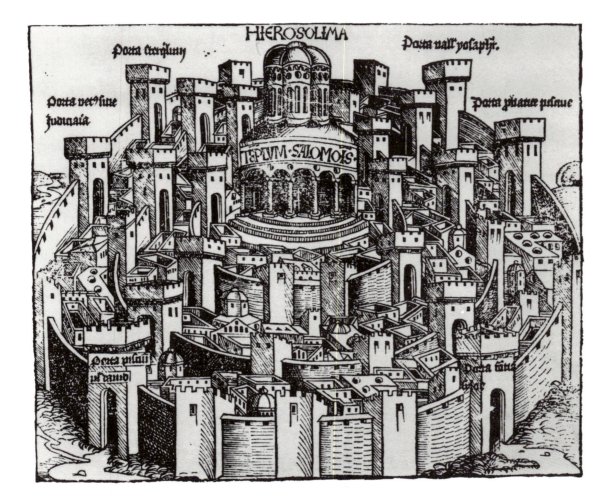

HARTMAN SCHEDEL, from *Liber Chronicarrum. Jerusalem in Circular Form.* Nuremberg, 1493. Woodcut. 7⁷⁄₁₆ × 8⁷⁄₈″ (19 × 22.5 cm). Israel Museum, Jerusalem. *This view of Jerusalem by Schedel, a German scholar, although completely unrealistic, portrays the city in a typically medieval circular form. Solomon's Temple stands at the center.*

Saul Tchernichovsky
THEY SAY THERE IS A LAND

Saul Tchernichovsky (1875–1943) was a major Hebrew poet whose subjects were not restricted to the European Jewish community. As a child he attended a modern Hebrew school and later a Russian school. After studying medicine at Heidelberg and Lausanne, he settled in Israel in 1931. Tchernichovsky often turned to the pagan world for inspiration for his poems. In this piece, translated by Rabbi Morrison David Bial, the author expresses his ardent love for the land of Israel.

They say there is a land,
    a land flooded with sun,

Where can that land be,
    where, o where, that sun?
They say there is a land,
    with seven pillars of story,
Seven stars are shining
    on every hill in glory.
A land where all is fulfilled,
    that ever heart held sweet.
Where anyone may enter,
    and there Akiva meet.
Shalom to you, Akiva,
    my Rabbi, peace to thee.
Where are they, the holy ones,
    where the Maccabee?
And Akiva answers,
    the rabbi answers true.
"All of Israel is holy,
    and the Maccabee is you."

Marc Chagall
WHAT IS A JEWISH ARTIST?

Marc Chagall (1887–1985) was born into a Hasidic family named Segal in Vitebsk, where he received a traditional education in ḥeder. His Jewish roots permeate his artistic works, which are filled with allusions to his heritage and rely on Jewish folktales for subject matter. In addition to his paintings, Chagall also designed sets and costumes, murals and stained glass windows.

And still you insist that I write and speak about Jewish art. I will, for the last time.

What sort of thing is it? Only yesterday Jewish artistic circles fought for this so-called Jewish art. Out of the tumult and the heat emerged a group of Jewish artists and among them also Marc Chagall. This misfortune occurred when I was still in Vitebsk. Just returned from Paris, I smiled in my heart.

Then I was busy with something else. On one hand, the new world, Jews, my hometown's narrow streets, hunchbacked herring residents, green Jews, uncles, aunts with their questions, "You have, thank God, grown up."

And I kept painting them. . . .

On the other hand, I was a hundred years younger then and I loved them, just loved them. . . .

This engrossed me more, this captivated me more than the idea that I was anointed a Jewish artist.

Once, still in Paris, in my room on La Ruche, where I worked, across the partition I heard Jewish emigrant voices quarreling: "What do you think, was Antokolsky not a Jewish artist, after all, nor Israels, nor Liebermann?"

When the lamp burned so dark and lit up my painting, standing upside down (that's how I work—laugh!), and finally when at dawn the Parisian sky began to grow light, I gayly scoffed at the idle thoughts of my neighbors about the fate of Jewish art: "So be it, you talk—and I will work."

Representatives from all countries and peoples—to you my appeal. Confess: when

Marc Chagall. 1927. Photograph. *The young artist is shown here in his Paris studio with his wife Bella and daughter Ida.*

Lenin sits in the Kremlin, there is not a stick of wood, the stove smokes, your wife is not well, do you have national art now?

You, wise B., and you others who preach international art, the best Frenchmen, and (if they are still living) you will answer me: "Chagall, you are right."

Jews, if they have a feeling for it (I happen to), may weep at the passing of the decorators of the wooden shtetl synagogues (why am I not in the grave with you?) and of the carvers of the wooden synagogue clackers (saw them in Ansky's collection, was amazed). But what really is the difference between my crippled great-grandfather Segal, who decorated the Mohilev synagogue, and me, who painted murals in the Jewish theater (at good theater) in Moscow?

Besides, I am sure that if I let my beard grow, you would see his exact likeness. . . .

By the way, my father.

Believe me, I put in no small effort. And we both expended no less love (and what love). The difference was only that he took orders also for signs and I studied in Paris, about which he also knew something.

And yet, both I and he and others as well (there are such), taken together, are still not Jewish art.

And why not tell the truth? Where should I get it from? God forbid, if it should have to come from an order! Because Efros writes an article or M. will give me an academic ration!

There is Japanese art, Egyptian, Persian, Greek, but from the Renaissance on, national arts began to decline. The distinctive traits disappear. Artists—individuals arise, subjects of one or another country, born here or there (may you be blessed, my Vitebsk) and a good identity card or even a Jewish passport expert is needed so that all artists can be precisely and fully nationalized.

Were I not a Jew (with the content that I put in the word), I would not be an artist at all, or I would be someone else altogether.

There is nothing new in that.

As for myself, I know quite well what this small people can accomplish.

Unfortunately, I am modest and cannot tell what it can accomplish.

Something to conjure with, what this small people has done!

When it wished, it brought forth Christ and Christianity. When it wanted, it produced Marx and socialism.

Can it be then that it would not show the world some sort of art?

Kill me, if not.

COLORPLATE 81
Wine Decanter and Goblet. Decanter: Meir Austerlitz Levy. Austria, 1740.
Glass: Bohemia, early 19th century. (Glass engraved "Elijah's Cup.")

COLORPLATE 82
Woman's Red Kiddush Glass. Possibly Bohemia,
late 19th century. Red glass, painted and
engraved. 5¼ × 4⅞″ (13.3 × 12.4 cm).
Collection, Congregation Emanu-El of the City
of New York. *The Sabbath is sanctified by reciting
the Kiddush, a prayer of sanctification, over the wine,
at the Sabbath table. The Kiddush cup is intended to
beautify the appearance of the Sabbath table, and aside
from being clean, unbroken, and of a mimimum size,
can be elaborately decorated with liturgical quotations
or beautiful designs. Various materials have been used
in their manufacture. Often, the most elaborate
examples were donated to the synagogue for the
Sabbath celebration.*

COLORPLATE 83
Kiddush Cup. Israel, 20th century.
Silver, engraved "Yom Tov."

COLORPLATE 84 *(opposite)*
POSEN. *Kiddush Cup.* Frankfurt, c. 1900. Silver. Height: 5″ (12.7 cm).
Courtesy Moriah Antique Judaica, New York.

COLORPLATE 85

Various Spiceboxes. European, 18th–20th century. Silver. Collection, Israel Museum, Jerusalem. *A spicebox is used during the Havdalah ceremony that ushers out the Sabbath and greets in the new week. When the blessing is recited commemorating God as the creator of all types of spices, the spicebox is shaken and the fragrant spices that symbolize the Sabbath*

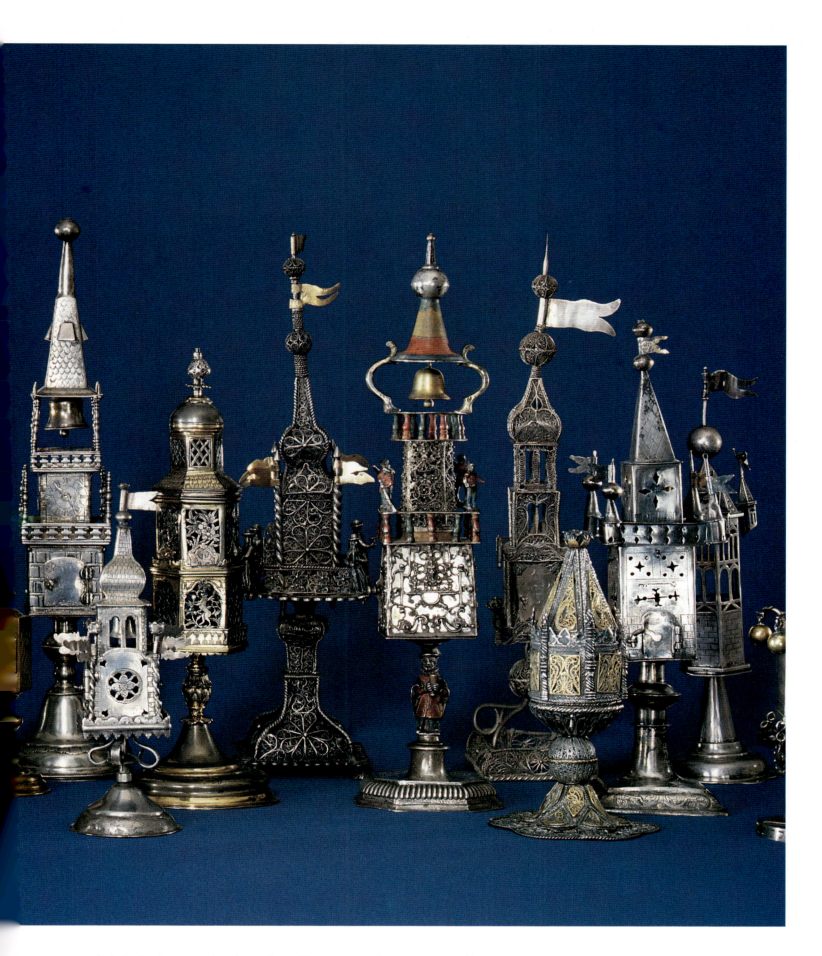

are inhaled. As the examples shown here illustrate, spiceboxes were usually engraved or filigreed silver and, from the Middle Ages on, often took the form of towers or church steeples. Spiceboxes sometimes replicated actual buildings in the town of their manufacture, replete with banners, pennants, and clocks that could be set to mark the hour the Sabbath ends.

COLORPLATE 86
Cover for the Reader's Desk. Italy, 1700. Red silk embroidered with polychrome silk and metallic thread. 19⁵⁄₁₆ × 25⁹⁄₁₆″ (49 × 65 cm). The Jewish Museum, New York. Gift of Dr. Harry G. Friedman, 1956.

COLORPLATE 87
Tallit, Tallit Bag. Tefillin Bag. China, 1904. Silk with silk embroidery. *Tallit:* 84 × 29½″ (213.3 × 74.9 cm). *Bag:* 7 × 8¾ × 2″ (17.7 × 22.2 × 5 cm). From the collection of Hebrew Union College Skirball Museum, Los Angeles.

COLORPLATE 88
Hallah Cover. Eretz Israel, 20th century. Silk, batik, braid trim. 19½″ (39.5 cm) square.
From the collection of Hebrew Union College Skirball Museum, Los Angeles.

NEW WORLDS

Jews of Amsterdam
PETITION TO THE DUTCH WEST INDIA COMPANY

This petition, requesting permission for Jews to both trade and live in New Netherlands, was written in Amsterdam in 1655. The directors of the Dutch West India Company permitted the Jews to live and trade there despite the objections of the director general of New Netherlands, Peter Stuyvesant. It remains one of the most important documents relating to Jewish settlement, not only in New York, but in the entire United States.

1655, January Petition of the Jewish Nation.

To the Honorable Lords, Directors of the Chartered West India Company, Chamber of the City of Amsterdam.

The merchants of the Portuguese Nation residing in this City respectfully remonstrate to your Honors that it has come to their knowledge that your Honors raise obstacles to the giving of permits or passports to the Portuguese Jews to travel and to go to reside in New Netherland, which if persisted in will result to the great disadvantage of the Jewish nation. It also can be of no advantage to the general Company but rather damaging.

Granted that they may reside and traffic, provided they shall not become a charge upon the deaconry or the Company.

There are many of the nation who have lost their possessions at Pernambuco and have arrived from there in great poverty, and part of them have been dispersed here and there. So that your petitioners had to expend large sums of money for their necessaries of life, and through lack of opportunity all cannot remain here to live. And as they cannot go to Spain or Portugal because of the Inquisition, a great part of the aforesaid people must in time be obliged to depart for other territories of their High Mightinesses the States-General and their Companies, in order there, through their labor and efforts, to be able to exist under the protection of the administrators of your Honorable Directors, observing and obeying your Honors' orders and commands.

It is well known to your Honors that the Jewish nation in Brazil have at all times been faithful and have striven to guard and maintain that place, risking for that purpose, their possessions and their blood.

Yonder land is extensive and spacious. The more of loyal people that go to live there, the better it is in regard to the population of the country as in regard to the payment of various excises and taxes which may be imposed there, and in regard to the increase of trade, and also to the importation of all the necessaries that may be sent there.

Your Honors should also consider that the Honorable Lords, the Burgomasters of the City and the Honorable High Illustrious Mighty Lords, the States-General, have in political matters always protected and considered the Jewish nations as upon the same footing as all the inhabitants and burghers. Also it is conditioned in the treaty of perpetual peace with the King of Spain that the Jewish nation shall also enjoy the same liberty as all other inhabitants of these lands.

Your Honors should also please consider that many of the Jewish nation are principal shareholders in the Company. They having always striven their best for the Company, and many of their nation have lost immense and great capital in its shares and obligations.

The Company has by a general resolution consented that those who wish to populate the Colony shall enjoy certain districts of land gratis. Why should now certain subjects of this State not be allowed to travel thither and live there? The French consent that the Portuguese Jews may traffic and live in Martinique, Christopher and others of their territories, whither also some have gone from here, as your Honors know. The English also consent at the present time that the Portuguese and Jewish nation may go from London and settle at Barbados, whither also some have gone.

As foreign nations consent that the Jewish nation may go to live and trade in their territories, how can your Honors forbid the same and refuse transportation to this Portuguese nation who reside here and have been settled here well on to about sixty years, many also being born here and confirmed burghers, and this to a land that needs people for its increase?

Therefore the petitioners request, for the reasons given above (as also others which they omit to avoid prolixity), that your Honors be pleased not to exclude but to grant the Jewish nation passage to and residence in that country; otherwise this would result in a great prejudice to their reputation. Also that by an Apostille and Act the Jewish nation be permitted, together with other inhabitants, to travel, live and traffic there, and with them enjoy liberty on condition of contributing like others, &c. Which doing, &c.

Benjamin Rush

LETTER TO HIS WIFE

The noted physician Benjamin Rush wrote this letter to his wife describing the details of a Jewish wedding he attended in 1787. The child of this union, Uriah P. Levy, won fame as an officer in the U.S. Navy; he helped abolish the naval policy of flogging and later rose to the rank of commodore.

My dear Julia,

Being called a few days ago to attend in the family of Jonas Phillips, I was honored this morning with an invitation to attend the marriage of his daughter to a young man of the name of Levy from Virginia. I accepted the invitation with great pleasure, for you know I love to be in the way of adding to my stock of ideas upon all subjects.

At one o'clock the company, consisting of sixty or forty men, assembled in Mr. Phillips' common parlor, which was accommodated with benches for the purpose. The ceremony began with prayers in the Hebrew language, which were chaunted by an old rabbi and in which he was followed by the whole company. As I did not understand a word except now and then an Amen or Hallelujah, my attention was directed to the haste with which they covered their heads with their hats as soon as the prayers began, and to the freedom with which some of them conversed with each other during the whole time of this part of their worship. As soon as these prayers were ended, which took up about twenty minutes, a small piece of parchment was produced, written in Hebrew, which contained a deed of settlement and which the groom subscribed in the presence of four witnesses. In this deed he conveyed a part of his fortune to his bride, by which she was provided for after his death in case she survived him.

This ceremony was followed by the erection of a beautiful canopy composed of white and red silk in the middle of the floor. It was supported by four young men (by means of four poles), who put on white gloves for the purpose. As soon as this canopy was fixed, the bride, accompanied with her mother, sister, and a long train of female relations, came downstairs. Her face was covered with a veil which reached halfways down her body. She was handsome at all times, but the occasion and her dress rendered her in a peculiar manner a most lovely and affecting object. I gazed with delight upon her. Innocence, modesty, fear, respect, and devotion appeared all at once in her countenance. She was led by her two bridesmaids under the canopy. Two young men led the bridegroom after her and placed him, not by her side, but directly opposite to her. The priest now began again to chaunt an Hebrew prayer, in which he was followed by part of the company. After this he gave to the groom and bride a glass full of wine, from which they each sipped about a teaspoonful. Another prayer followed this act, after which he took a ring and directed the groom to place it upon the finger of his bride in the same manner as is practised in the marriage service of the Church of England.

This ceremony was followed by handing the wine to the father of the bride and then a second time to the bride and groom. The groom after sipping the wine took the glass in his hand and threw it upon a large pewter dish which was suddenly placed at his feet. Upon its breaking into a number of small pieces, there was a general shout of joy and a declaration that the ceremony was over. The groom now saluted his bridge, and kisses and congratulations became general through the room. I asked the meaning, after the ceremony was over, of the canopy and of the drinking of the wine and breaking of the glass. I was told by one of the company that in Europe they generally marry in the open air, and that the canopy was introduced to defend the bride and groom from the action of the sun and from rain. Their mutually partaking of the same glass of wine was intended to denote the mutuality of their goods, and the breaking of the glass at the conclusion of the business was designed to teach them the brittleness and uncertainty of human life and the certainty of death, and thereby to temper and moderate their present joys.

Mr. Phillips pressed me to stay and dine with the company, but business . . . forbade it. I stayed, however, to eat some wedding cake and to drink a glass of wine with the guests. Upon going into one of the rooms upstairs to ask how Mrs. Phillips did, who had fainted downstairs under the pressure of the heat (for she was weak from a previous indisposition), I discovered the the bride and groom supping a bowl of broth together. Mrs. Phillips apologized for them by telling me they had eaten nothing (agreeably to the custom prescribed by their religion) since the night before.

Upon my taking leave of the company, Mrs. Phillips put a large piece of cake into my pocket for you, which she begged I would present to you with her best compliments. She says you are an old New York acquaintance of hers.

During the whole of this new and curious scene my mind was not idle. I was carried back to the ancient world and was led to contemplate the passovers, the sacrifices, the jubilees, and other ceremonies of the Jewish Church. After this, I was led forward into futurity and anticipated the time foretold by the prophets when this once-beloved race of men shall again be restored to the divine favor and when they shall unite with Christians with one heart and one voice in celebrating the prasies of a common and universal Saviour. . . .

Adieu. With love to your mama, sisters, and brothers, and to our dear children, I am your affectionate husband,

B. Rush. . . .

Newport Hebrew Congregation and George Washington CORRESPONDENCE

Moses Seixas, one of the organizers of the Bank of Rhode Island, was president of the Newport Hebrew Congregation in 1790 when the newly elected president, George Washington, visited the state. Both his letter and the response by President Washington stress that the newly founded government will not tolerate either bigotry or persecution.

―――――――

ADDRESS OF THE NEWPORT CONGREGATION TO THE
PRESIDENT OF THE UNITED STATES OF AMERICA.

"*Sir:*—Permit the children of the stock of Abraham to approach you with the most cordial affection and esteem for your person and merit, and to join with our fellow-citizens in welcoming you to Newport.

With pleasure we reflect on those days of difficulty and danger when the God of Israel, who delivered David from the peril of the sword, shielded your head in the day of battle; and we rejoice to think that the same spirit which rested in the bosom of the greatly beloved Daniel, enabling him to preside over the provinces of the Babylonian Empire, rests and ever will rest upon you, enabling you to discharge the arduous duties of the Chief Magistrate of these States.

Deprived as we hitherto have been of the invaluable rights of free citizens, we now—with a deep sense of gratitude to the Almighty Disposer of all events—behold a government erected by the majesty of the people—a government which to bigotry gives no sanction, to persecution no assistance, but generously affording to all liberty of conscience and immunities of citizenship, deeming every one of whatever nation, tongue or language, equal parts of the great governmental machine.

This so ample and extensive Federal Union, whose base is philanthropy, mutual confidence and public virtue, we cannot but acknowledge to be the work of the great God who rules in the armies of the heavens and among the inhabitants of the earth, doing whatever seemeth to Him good.

For all the blessings of civil and religious liberty which we enjoy under an equal and benign administration, we desire to send up our thanks to the Ancient of days, the great Preserver of men, beseeching Him that the angels who conducted our forefathers through the wilderness into the promised land may graciously conduct you through all the diffi-

LORADO TAFT.
*Memorial to Haym
Salomon in Chicago.*
1936. Bronze. Height:
19′4″ (589.3 cm).

culties and dangers of this mortal life; and when, like Joshua, full of days and full of honors, you are gathered to your fathers, may you be admitted into the heavenly paradise to partake of the water of life and the tree of immortality.

Done and signed by order of the Hebrew Congregation in Newport, Rhode Island.

MOSES SEIXAS, *Warden.*

NEWPORT, *August 17, 1790.*"

WASHINGTON'S REPLY TO THE HEBREW CONGREGATION IN NEWPORT, RHODE ISLAND.

"*Gentlemen:*—While I received with much satisfaction your address replete with expressions of esteem, I rejoice in the opportunity of assuring you that I shall always retain grateful remembrance of the cordial welcome I experienced on my visit to Newport from all classes of citizens.

The reflection of the days of difficulty and danger which are past is rendered the more sweet from a consciousness that they are succeeded by days of uncommon prosperity and security.

If we have wisdom to make the best use of the advantages with which we are now favored, we cannot fail, under the just administration of a good government, to become a great and happy people.

The citizens of the United States of America have a right to applaud themselves for having given to mankind examples of an enlarged and liberal policy—a policy worthy of imitation. All possess alike liberty of conscience and immunities of citizenship.

It is now no more that toleration is spoken of as if it were the indulgence of one class of people that another enjoyed the exercise of their inherent natural rights, for, happily, the Government of the United States, which gives to bigotry no factions, to persecution no assistance, requires only that they who live under its protection should demean themselves as good citizens in giving it on all occasions their effectual support.

It would be inconsistent with the frankness of my character not to avow that I am pleased with your favorable opinion of my administration and fervent wishes for my felicity.

May the children of the stock of Abraham who dwell in this land continue to merit and enjoy the good will of the other inhabitants—while every one shall sit in safety under his own vine and fig tree and there shall be none to make him afraid.

May the father of all mercies scattered light, and not darkness, upon our paths, and make us all in our several vocations useful here, and in His own due time and way everlastingly happy.

G. WASHINGTON."

Rebecca Samuel
LETTER TO HER PARENTS

In this letter to her parents in Germany, Mrs. Samuel complains of the religious hardships faced by her family in late 18th-century Virginia. She also tells how she greatly anticipates her imminent move to the much larger Jewish community of Charleston, South Carolina.

Dear Parents:

I hope my letter will ease your mind. You can now be reassured and send me one of the family to Charleston, South Carolina. This is the place to which, with God's help, we will go after Passover. The whole reason why we are leaving this place is because of [its lack of] Yehudishkeit [Jewishness].

Dear parents, I know quite well you will not want me to bring up my children like Gentiles. Here they cannot become anything else. Jewishness is pushed aside here. There are here [in Petersburg] ten or twelve Jews, and they are not worthy of being called Jews. We have a shohet here who goes to market and buys terefah [nonkosher] meat and then brings it home. On Rosh Ha-Shanah [New Year] and on Yom Kippur [the Day of Atonement] the people worshipped here without one sefer torah [Scroll of the Law], and not one of them wore the tallit [a large prayer shawl worn in the synagogue] or the arba kanfot [the small set of fringes, worn on the body], except Hyman and my Sammy's godfather. The latter is an old man of sixty, a man from Holland. He has been in America for thirty years already, for twenty years he was in Charleston, and he has been living here for four years. He does not want to remain here any longer, and will go with us to Charleston. In that place there is a blessed community of three hundred Jews.

You can believe me that I crave to see a synagogue to which I can go. The way we live now is no life at all. We do not know what the Sabbath and the holidays are. On the Sabbath all the Jewish shops are open, and they do business on that day as they do throughout the whole week. But ours we do not allow to open. With us there is still some Sabbath. You must believe me that in our house we all live as Jews as much as we can.

As for the Gentiles, we have nothing to complain about. For the sake of a livelihood we do not have to leave here. Nor do we have to leave because of debts. I believe ever since Hyman has grown up that he has not had it so good. You cannot know what a wonderful country this is for the common man. One can live here peacefully. Hyman made a clock that goes very accurately, just like the one in the Buchenstrasse in Hamburg. Now you can imagine what honors Hyman has been getting here. In all Virginia there

Evening Service

OF

ROSHASHANAH,

AND

KIPPUR.

OR

The BEGINNING of the YEAR,

AND

The DAY of ATONEMENT.

NEW-YORK:

Printed by *W. Weyman*, in *Broad-Street*, MDCCLXI.

§ S .

Title Page of the First Prayer Book for Jewish Holidays Published in New York. 1761. Courtesy, American Jewish Historical Society, Waltham, Massachusetts.

is no clock [like this one], and Virginia is the greatest province in the whole of America, and America is the largest section of the world. Now you know what sort of a country this is. It is not too long since Virginia was discovered. It is a young country. And it is amazing to see the business they do in this little Petersburg. At times as many as a thousand hogsheads of tobacco arrive at one time, and each hogshead contains 1,000 and sometimes 1,200 pounds of tobacco. The tobacco is shipped from here to the whole world.

When Judah . . . comes here, he can become a watchmaker and a goldsmith, if he so desires. Here it is not like Germany where a watchmaker is not permitted to sell silverware. [The contrary is true in this country.] They do not know otherwise here. They expect a watchmaker to be a silversmith here. Hyman has more to do in making silverware than with watchmaking. He has a journeyman, a silversmith, a very good artisan, and he, Hyman, takes care of the watches. This work is well paid here, but in Charleston, it pays even better.

All the people who hear that we are leaving give us their blessings. They say that it is sinful that such blessed children should be brought up here in Petersburg. My children cannot learn anything here, nothing Jewish, nothing of general culture. My Schoene [my daughter], God bless her, is already three years old, I think it is time that she should learn something, and she has a good head to learn. I have tuaght her the bedtime prayers and grace after meals in just two lessons. I believe that no one among the Jews here can do as well as she. And my Sammy [born in 1790], God bless him, is already beginning to talk.

I could write more. However, I do not have any more paper.

I remain, your devoted daughter and servant,

Rebecca, the wife of Hayyim, the son of Samuel the Levite

Stephen Birmingham
FROM OUR CROWD
"Mount Seligman"

In Our Crowd, *Stephen Birmingham (b. 1932) chronicles the saga of the German Jews who immigrated to America and ultimately became some of New York's wealthiest and most powerful families. This selection chronicles the small-town life of 19th-century Baiersdorf, Germany, where the Seligman family lived and worked.*

In the late summer of 1964 a small item in the obituary page of the *New York Times* carried the news that "James Seligman, Stockbroker" had died at the age of seventy-four in his Park Avenue apartment, following a heart attack. A few perfunctory details followed. Mr. Seligman had been born in New York City, had graduated from Princeton, maintained an office downtown in Broad Street, and was survived by his wife and an elderly sister. No mention was made of the once great eminence of his family in financial circles, nor of the Seligmans' still considerable prestige. No note was taken that Mr. Seligman's grandfather, the first James Seligman, had been one of eight remarkable brothers who had composed J. & W. Seligman & Company, once an international banking house of vast importance and power. Nor was it noted that Mr. Seligman's great-uncle, Joseph Seligman, the firm's founder, had been a personification of the American success story. In slightly more than twenty years' time, he had risen from an immigrant foot peddler to a financial adviser to the President of the United States.

The news item, however, contained one note that may have struck readers who knew the Seligman story as ironic. The Seligmans had once been known as the leading Jewish family in America. They had been called "the American Rothschilds." The deceased's grandfather for many years had been president of the board of trustees of New York's Temple Emanu-El. (The office was supposed to be an annual one, but every year the first James Seligman got to his feet and said, "Nominations for vice president are now in order.") Yet the obituary advised that funeral services would be held at Christ Church, Methodist.

The Seligmans may not have started everything, exactly, but they certainly started something. They also started early—proverbially an auspicious time. Few great American fortunes, furthermore—and few banking houses—have started from such unpromising beginnings. The base of Mount Seligman was humble indeed.

Baiersdorf is so small that it does not appear on most maps of Germany. It lies on the banks of the Regnitz River some twenty kilometers north of Nürnberg, near the edge of the Bohemian Forest. Old David Seligman was the village weaver. He was not technically "old," but at twenty-nine he seemed so. A small, stooped, dour man, he was given to complaining about his lot.

There had been Seligmans in Baiersdorf for over a century. Theirs had been a family name long before Napoleon had decreed that Germany's Jews no longer needed to be known as "sons" of their fathers' names—Moses ben Israel, and so on. Seventeenth- and eighteenth-century tombstones in Baiersdorf's Jewish cemetery recorded the upright virtues of many of David's ancestors, all named Seligman ("Blessed man" in German). To later generations in New York, this would become a fact of some importance. Families such as the Seligmans did not just "come" from Bavaria. They had been established there for many, many years.

None of the Baiersdorf Seligmans had been wealthy, but David seemed the poorest, most discouraged of the lot. He enjoyed poor health, made frequent trips to the cemetery, and from the words on headstones of departed Seligmans drew a kind of solitary comfort. He particularly admired one inscription from 1775:

HERE LIES BURIED

ABRAHAM SELIGMAN

IN RIPE OLD AGE, AN UPRIGHT MAN

HE WALKED THE WAY OF THE DOERS OF GOOD
JUST AND UPRIGHT HE ATTACHED HIS SOUL TO
RIGHTEOUSNESS
AND BUSIED HIMSELF WITH THE TEACHINGS OF GOD
AND WITH WORKS OF CHARITY
NIGHT AND DAY, FOREMOST AMONG MEN WHO
ARE BENEFACTORS

Such words did not apply to David. He was lonely and withdrawn. His boyhood friends were married and raising families, but David seemed resigned to bachelorhood. His little house in Baiersdorf's *Judengasse,* or "Jew Street," had begun to sag and leaned disconsolately against the next building. Business was terrible. Nevertheless, one morning in 1818, David returned from the neighboring village of Sulzbach with a plump, young girl named Fanny Steinhardt as his wife.

It was whispered on the *Judengasse* that David Seligman was incapable of fathering children. Fanny's condition during the next few months was watched with more than usual interest. One year after the marriage, Fanny bore David a son, Joseph. Over the next twenty years Fanny presented David with seven more sons and three daughters: William, James, Jesse, Henry, Leopold, Abraham, Isaac, Babette, Rosalie, and Sarah.

Joseph Seligman as a Young Man. 19th century. Photograph. Bass Business History Collection; University of Oklahoma Library, Norman/J. and W. Seligman and Co. Archive.

Child-bearing took its toll. Two years after the birth of her last child, at the age of forty-two, Fanny died. She had done her duty to the world. She had created the foundation of an international banking house.

But Fanny had given David more than eleven children. As her dowry, she had brought from Sulzbach a stock of dry goods—laces, ribbons, two feather beds, two dozen sheets, twenty pillowcases, and ten bolts of homespun cloth. These, she had cannily suspected, might appeal to the women of Baiersdorf. She had set up shop on the ground floor of David's house, and soon David, the weaver, had been able to call himself by the grander title of "woolen merchant," and had started a small side line selling sealing wax.

Joseph, her first-born, was Fanny's favorite child. As soon as he could see over the counter, he became his mother's assistant in her little shop. In the 1820's there was no German national monetary system. Coinage varied from region to region, and eight-year-old Joseph, at the cash drawer, was quick to notice this. As an accommodation to travelers passing through Baiersdorf, Joseph became a moneychanger—accepting out-of-town coins in exchange for local currency, and selling out-of-town money to men planning trips outside Bavaria. He made a small profit on each transaction. At the age of twelve he operated a miniature American Express Company. Foreign currency, including an occasional American dollar, passed through his hands. He was learning economics, arithmetic, and a bit of geography, his mother pointed out and patted him on the head approvingly.

Fanny was ambitious for all her children, but she focused her dreams on Joseph. At night mother and son would sit opposite each other at the wooden table in the sputtering light of a kitchen candle while she, bent over her mending, talked and the boy listened. Joseph remembered his mother's small, plump hands, and a gesture she had—placing her hand flat out on the table when she made a point. She told him of places better than Baiersdorf, and David reproved her for filling the boy's head with "grandiose ideas." He wanted Joseph for the woolen business.

But a Bavarian woolen business faced, in 1833, a gloomy future. Baiersdorf was a small town, and growing smaller. The Industrial Revolution was under way. Peasants, David's customers, were being forced from the land into industrial cities. Jobs and money in Baiersdorf were growing scarcer. The poor were faced with two choices, both involving further hardship: to move or struggle on where they were.

If the young German poor found themselves with little to look forward to, the outlook for young Jews was even more dismal. Jews were restricted on three sides—politically, economically, and socially. Forced to be peddlers, small shopkeepers, moneylenders— barred by law from dealing with goods that could not be carried with them—they were sequestered in the cramped *Judengassen* and trapped in a tightening strait jacket of regulations based on their religion. In the quarters where German laws forced them to live, they were permitted to own no property beyond the squares of land where their houses stood, and their right to even that much land was precarious. In Bavaria, where attitudes toward Jews were particularly reactionary, the number of Jewish marriages was limited by law in an attempt to keep the number of Jewish families constant. They were surrounded by a heavy network of special taxes, were obliged to pay the humiliating "Jew toll" whenever they traveled beyond the borders of the ghetto, were forced to pay a special fee for the privilege of not serving in the army—though it was an army that would not have accepted them had they tried to volunteer, because they were Jewish. Periodically, Jews were threatened with expulsion from their homes—and often were expelled— unless they paid an added tax for the privilege of remaining.

Three distinct currents of Jewish migration had begun in Europe. There was a migration from German villages in the south and east to northern cities, where Jews often found conditions somewhat worse than those they had faced before. (In 1816 the seven largest cities in Germany held only 7 percent of the Jewish population. A hundred years later over 50 percent of Germany's Jews lived in these seven cities.) There was a general east-to-west movement—out of Germany into England, Holland, and France. At the same time, there was a migratory wave *into* Germany from the east—from Czarist Russia and Poland. Some of these foreign Jews merely passed through Germany on their way to other lands, others stopped for a while, to rest. These latter had a further disruptive effect on the already shaky structure of Jewish communities. Some of these families paused long enough to pick up the German language and to take German names. (In future generations, in New York, it would become a matter of some importance whether such and such a Jewish family, with a German-sounding name, had been a true *native* German family, like the Seligmans, or a stranger from the east, passing through.) Swelled by immigrants from the east, the Jewish population in Western Europe more than tripled during the nineteenth century.

The final migratory move was also westward—across the Atlantic to the land of freedom and enlightenment, the land, moreover, of land and money. In 1819, the year Joseph Seligman was born, the American paddle-wheeler *Savannah* had been the first steam-driven vessel to cross the ocean. It made America seem wonderfully convenient. America fever swept through German villages, particularly in hard-pressed Bavaria. Already, from Baiersdorf, several bands of young men had taken off and were writing home of the wonders of the New World. Fanny Seligman wanted to get her children out of Germany, and she wanted Joseph to go armed with an education. She decided he would do something no Seligman had ever done. He would go to the university at Erlangen. He was just fourteen.

Interior of Temple Emanu-El, Fifth Avenue and Forty-Third Street, New York, 1868. Engraving from Harper's Weekly, November 14, 1868. The Temple's congregation included many immigrant Jews who had established themselves as prominent New York families. This illustration appeared in an article about the dedication of the Temple on September 11. The Temple's architects were Leopold Eidlitz and Henry Fernbach. This structure was demolished in 1927.

Abraham Kohn

FROM HIS DIARY

September 3–29, 1842

Abraham Kohn (1819–1871) left Bavaria in 1842 to establish a new life for himself in the New World. In only twenty short years, he became an elected city official in Chicago who supported the election of Abraham Lincoln. The excerpt from this mid-19th-century diary acknowledges the hardships confronted by the author and other German Jewish immigrants who attempted to make their living in America.

---

3.   At 8 o'clock on Saturday morning we saw the American coast. The rich green colors, the trees we have missed for so long, the beautiful buildings along the shore, the many busy freighters and boats and coastal steamers which passed us—all of these impressed us in a way which I cannot describe.

At nine we saw from afar the city of New York, and at eleven we anchored some two hours' distance from the city, where we were kept in quarantine. I was allowed to go by boat to the islands which extend in front of New York, but only after I had been examined by a doctor and found well. From there we took a steamboat to the city itself. I enjoyed my frist sight of the city immensely, but, as I proceeded through the crowded streets on my way to see my brother, I felt somewhat uncomfortable. The frantic hurry of the people, the hundreds of cabs, wagons, and carts—the noise is indescribable. Even one who has seen Germany's largest cities can hardly believe his eyes and ears. Feeling quite dizzy, I passed through Grand Street where, to my great joy, I met my old friend Friedmann, who has changed greatly since he left Fürth. He was taking a walk with his sister and guided me immediately to my brother's residence. The latter was out looking for me, having heard of the arrival of our ship. He soon returned home to embrace me, and at that moment I wished only that my mother could have been present. It is impossible to describe our feelings. It is enough to say that, with the Lord's help, we were together and happy.

Brother Moses was still on board ship, planning to enter the city on Monday night.

4.   Sunday, New Year's Day. On the eve of the New Year I found myself with a new career before me. What kind of career? "I don't know"—the American's customary reply to every difficult question.

At night, in the Attorney St. Synagogue, I prayed to the Almighty, thanking Him for the voyage happily finished and asking good and abiding health for my dear mother and brothers and sisters. I prayed then for my own good health and asked for all of us good fortune.

May the Almighty hear my prayer! May He bless and bestow upon us His infinite mercy and charity! Amen.

5 and 6.   These were the two New Year's holidays. I spent the morning in the synagogue, and in the afternoon I walked around a bit. However, both Moses—who had now joined me—and I felt so tired after this little exercise that we went to bed immediately. The long voyage and lack of exercise had left us weak.

7–29.   During this period I was in New York, trying in vain to find a job as clerk in a store. But business was too slow, and I had to do as all the others; with a bundle on my back I had to go out into the country, peddling various articles. This, then, is the vaunted luck of the immigrants from Bavaria! O misguided fools, led astray by avarice and cupidity! You have left your friends and acquaintances, your relatives and your parents, your home and your fatherland, your language and your customs, your faith and your religion—only to sell your wares in the wild places of America, in isolated farmhouses and tiny hamlets.

Only rarely do you succeed, and then only in the smallest way. Is this fate worth the losses you have suffered, the dangers you have met on land and sea? Is this an equal exchange for the parents and kinsmen you have given up? Is this the celebrated freedom of America's soil? Is it liberty of thought and action when, in order to do business in a

Steerage Deck, S.S.
Pennland of the Red Star
Line. 1893.
Photograph. Museum
of the City of New
York. The Byron
Collection.

single state, one has to buy a license for a hundred dollars? When one must profane the holy Sabbath, observing Sunday instead? In such matters are life and thought more or less confined than in the fatherland? True, one does hear the name "Jew," but only because one does not utter it. Can a man, in fact, be said to be "living" as he plods through the vast, remote country, uncertain even as to which farmer will provide him shelter for the coming night?

In such an existence the single man gets along far better than the father of a family. Such fools as are married not only suffer themselves, but bring suffering to their women. How must an educated woman feel when, after a brief stay at home, her supporter and shelterer leaves with his pack on his back, not knowing where he will find lodging on the next night or the night after? On how many winter evenings must such a woman sit forlornly with her children at the fireplace, like a widow, wondering where this night finds the head of her family, which homestead in the forests of Ohio will offer him a poor night's shelter? O, that I had never seen this land, but had remained in Germany, apprenticed to a humble country craftsman! Though oppressed by taxes and discriminated against as a Jew, I should still be happier than in the great capital of America, free from royal taxes and every man's religious equal though I am! . . .

There is woe—threefold woe—in this fortune which appears so glamorous to those in Europe. Dreaming of such a fortune leads a man to depart from his home. But when he awakens from his dreams, he finds himself in the cold and icy night, treading his lonely way in America. . . .

No, son of Israel, despair not; they God liveth. He is the one Eternal Being. He it was who led thine ancestors from the land of Egypt into Canaan. . . . Let us, therefore, look upon this wonderful land of America as a new Canaan. And lacking a leader such as Moses or Joshua, may we still look to Him, the Eternal, as our Guide, as the Guardian of our Destiny!

But to follow God sincerely we must observe His holy Scriptures, the sacred law given from Mount Sinai.

But leading such a life, none of us is able to observe the smallest commandment. Thousands of peddlers wander about America; young, strong men, they waste their strength by carrying heavy loads in the summer's heat; they lose their health in the icy cold of winter. And thus they forget completely their Creator. They no longer put on the phylacteries; they pray neither on working day nor on the Sabbath. In truth, they have given up their religion for the pack which is on their backs. Is such a life not slavery rather than liberty? Is this condition not misery rather than happiness?

"Hear me, brethren," our rabbis used to say: "Never forget what you are and to what you owe allegiance. Read your morning prayer and your evening prayer, but whenever you worship, conduct yourselves with fervor and with devotion to the Creator of the universe. No one of you is wise enough to live without prayer; for wisdom begins with the fear of God."

So long as one lives as we do here his thoughts cannot be with his Creator, his religion cannot be observed, his life cannot be virtuous or even happy. Yet it is not indolence or

W. A. ROGERS
(1854–1931). *Boston Jewish Quarters at the turn of the century*. 1900. Drawing.

weakness which pushes one to this way of life. Each of us works and pursues his calling, but only ten out of a thousand find any true happiness.

It is the inherent instinct for trade which leads one to this way of living. Could not this instinct be suppressed and our strength employed in other and better ways? Could not each of us, instead of carrying a burden on his back, cultivate the soil of Mother Nature? Would not such labor be more profitable? Why would it not be possible to form a society, based on the good will of its members, which would purchase a large tract of land for tillage and for the foundation of a Jewish colony? Here is a worthy project for honest German men of the Jewish faith. Here thousands and thousands of people could enjoy in happiness the profits of the soil they tilled themselves. Among us there are many craftsmen who could employ their skills in such a venture instead of carrying burdens on their backs. Such a truly great project could be carried out in a few years if the young among us could found such a society, supported by an annual contribution of a few dollars from everyone. With a few thousand dollars a large area of ground could be purchased in some well situated state. And, in a short time, there would be laid out a fine town, a new Jerusalem. To such a place thousands of our countrymen would come from Germany with bright prospects, to be welcomed by us. . . .

These were my thoughts on the first Sunday I spent in Dorchester, a village near Boston. These were the doubts I felt, O dear, good mother, feelings you cannot share with your son, who wanders through America with his bundle on his back. . . .

Major Raphael Moses
LETTER TO W. O. TUGGLE *(1878)*

Raphael J. Moses (1812–1893) was a South Carolina native who eventually settled in Georgia. A secessionist, he enlisted in the confederate army at the start of the Civil War, quickly attaining the rank of major. He served as Confederate Commissary for the State of Georgia and was elected to the first postwar Georgia state legislature. In 1878 he campaigned unsuccessfully for the U.S. Congress. During this campaign his opponent, W. O. Tuggle, criticized him for being a Jew. Major Moses's response, "An Open Letter to the Hon. W. O. Tuggle," was first published in the Columbus Daily Times *in August of that same year.*

I have taken time to authenticate a report which I heard for the first time on the evening of the last day of the convention. At West Point [Georgia], during your congressional campaign, and in my absence, you sought for me a term of reproach, and from your well-filled vocabulary selected the epithet of Jew.

Had I served you to the extent of my ability in your recent political aspirations, and your overburdened heart had sought relief in some exhibition of unmeasured gratitude, had you a wealth of gifts and selected from your abundance your richest offering to lay at my feet, you could not have honored me more highly, nor distinguished me more gratefully than by proclaiming me a Jew. I am proud of my lineage and my race; in your severest censure you can not name an act of my life which dishonors either, or which would mar the character of a Christian gentleman.

I feel it an honor to be one of a race whom persecution can not crush; whom prejudice has in vain endeavored to subdue; who, despite the powers of man and the antagonism of the combined governments of the world, protected by the hand of Deity, have burst the temporal bonds with which prejudice would have bound them, and after nineteen centuries of persecution still survive as a nation, and assert their manhood and intelligence,

COLORPLATE 89

Shofar. Germany, mid–19th century. Mahogany case by Marcus Jonas, United States. Late 19th century. 13 × 6 × 2″ (33 × 15.2 × 5 cm); 16½ × 7 × 3½″ (41.9 × 17.7 × 8.8 cm). From the collection of Hebrew Union Skirball Museum, Los Angeles.

COLORPLATE 92
Sukkah (Detail). Germany, early 19th century. Painted Wood. Collection, Israel Museum, Jerusalem. *This detail from the wall painting of the sukkah depicts* hakafot *(circuits) in the synagogue with* lulav and etrog.

COLORPLATE 90 *(opposite, above)*
New Year's Card Depicting Family at Holiday Table. Germany, early 20th century. Paper. 3⅝ × 3⅞ × 1½" (9.1 × 9.8 × 3.8 cm). The Jewish Museum, New York. Gift of Dr. Harry G. Friedman.

COLORPLATE 91 *(opposite, below)*
Yom Kippur Buckle. Central Europe, 20th century. Silver: repoussé. 4⅛ × 5⅝ × ¼" (10.4 × 14.2 × .6 cm). From the collection of Hebrew Union College Skirball Museum, Los Angeles.

COLORPLATE 93
Sukkah. Germany, early 19th century. Painted Wood. Collection, Israel Museum, Jerusalem. *Succoth, the Feast of Booths, is one of the three pilgrimage festivals of the Jewish liturgical year. This fall harvest festival of thanksgiving commemorates the Israelites' wanderings in the desert. On the walls of the 19th-century sukkah shown here, decorative painting depicts the village of Fischach, Germany, and visionary Jerusalem.*

COLORPLATE 94

Renaissance Hanukkah Lamp. Italy, late 16th century. Bronze: cast, natural dark patina. 10 × 10¼ × 1¾″ (25.4 × 26 × 4.4 cm). Collection, Congregation Emanu-El of the City of New York. *The eight-day festival of Hanukkah, a joyous celebration of religious freedom, celebrates the Maccabees' victorious revolt, c. 165 B.C.E., against the Graeco-Syrian conquerors of the Jews, and the subsequent rededication of the Temple. Lights are burned during the festival, beginning with one on the first night and an additional one on each of the following seven nights. Hanukkah lamps vary in decorative style and material according to the time and place in which they are made, often incorporating architectural elements, flowers, and animals as decorative motifs. The Renaissance Hanukkah menorah here depicts, in relief, a scene from the Apocryphal Book of Judith (Judith holds a sword in one hand, and the decapitated head of Holofernes in the other). The mask above this central scene is the shamash, the lamp that is used to kindle the other eight lights throughout Hanukkah. Although the story of Judith is not related to Hanukkah, her bravery and victory were associated with the story of Judah Maccabeus.*

COLORPLATE 95
Hanukkah Lamp. Augsburg, 18th century. Silver, partly gilt. Israel Museum, Jerusalem. *Menorah with prayers and chants for lighting Hanukkah lights*.

COLORPLATE 96
Sabbath or Festival Lamp. North Africa, 19th century. Ceramic. 17¾ × 13⅜ × 3⅜" (45 × 34 × 8.5 cm). Eretz Israel Museum, Department of Ethnography and Folklore Pavilion, Tel Aviv. *This is an unusual ceramic oil lamp, possibly used by the Jews who lived in caves in Libya or Morocco.*

COLORPLATE 97
Hanukkah Lamp. Damascus, 19th century. Sir Isaac and Lady Edith Wolfson Museum, Hechal Schlomo, Jerusalem.

Major Raphael J. Moses.
American Jewish
Archives, Hebrew
Union College—
Jewish Institute of
Religion, Cincinnati.

and give proof of "the divinity that stirs within them" by having become a great factor in the government of mankind.

Would you honor me? Call me a Jew. Would you place in unenviable prominence your own un-Christian prejudices and narrow-minded bigotry? Call me a Jew. Would you offer a living example of a man into whose educated mind toleration can not enter—on whose heart the spirit of liberty and the progress of American principles has made no impression? You can find it illustrated in yourself. Your narrow and benighted mind, pandering to the prejudices of your auditory, has attempted to taunt me by calling me a Jew—one of that peculiar people at whose altars, according to teachings of your theological masters, God chose that his son should worship.

Strike out the nationality of Judea, and you would seek in vain for Christ and his apostles. Strike out of sacred history the teachings of the Jews, and you would be as ignorant of God and the soul's immortal mission as you are of the duties and amenities of social life.

I am not angered, but while I thank you for the opportunity which you have given me to rebuke a prejudice confined to a limited number, distinguished for their bigotry and sectarian feelings, of which you are a fit exemplar, I pity you for having been cast in a mould impervious to the manly and liberal sentiments which distinguish the nineteenth century.

You are not created without a purpose; nature exhibits her beauties by the contrast of light and shade; humanity illustrates its brightest and noblest examples by placing its most perfect models in juxtaposition with the meanest specimens of mankind, so that you have the consolation of knowing that your mind has been thus deformed in the wisdom of the great architect, that you might serve as a shadow to bring forth in bold relief the brighter tints of that beautiful picture of religious toleration engrafted in the Constitution of the United States by the wisdom of our fathers.

I have the honor to remain, sir, your most obedient servant,

Raphael J. Moses

Emma Lazarus
THE BANNER OF THE JEW

Emma Lazarus (1849–1887) is remembered most for her sonnet "The New Colossus," which is engraved on a plaque on the pedestal of the Statue of Liberty. Lazarus was born in New York into a family of Sephardic descent and devoted much, but by no means all, of her career to Jewish topics. "The Banner of the Jews" is one of her better known Zionist works.

Wake, Israel, wake! Recall today
The glorious Maccabean rage,
The sire heroic, hoary-gray,
His five-fold lion-lineage:
The Wise, the Elect, the Help-of-God,
The Burst-of-Spring, the Avenging Rod.

From Mizpeh's mountain-side they saw
Jerusalem's empty streets, her shrine
Laid waste where Greeks profaned the Law,
With idol and with pagan sign.
Mourners in tattered black were there,
With ashes sprinkled on their hair.

Then from the stony peak there rang
A blast to ope the graves: down poured
The Maccabean clan, who sang
Their battle-anthem to the Lord.
Five heroes lead, and following, see,
Ten thousand rush to victory!

Oh, for Jerusalem's trumpet now,
To blow a blast of shattering power,
To wake the sleepers high and low,
And rouse them to the urgent hour!
No band for vengeance—but to save,
A million naked swords should wave.

Oh, deem not dead that martial fire,
Say not the mystic flame is spent!
With Moses' law and David's lyre,
Your ancient strength remains unbent.

Let but an Ezra rise anew,
To lift the Banner of the Jew!

A rag, a mock at first—ere long,
When men have bled and women wept,
To guard its precious folds from wrong,
Even they who shrunk, even they who slept,
Shall leap to bless it and to save.
Strike! for the brave revere the brave!

Irving Howe
FROM WORLD OF OUR FATHERS
"The Yiddish Theatre"

The Yiddish theatre offered comic relief to audiences of the poverty-stricken immigrant Jewish community. With its genesis in Manhattan's Lower East Side, Yiddish theatre was clearly entertainment for the Jewish masses. Many of the performers, however, went on to achieve national acclaim.

In the Yiddish theatre as it began to appear during the early 1880's the East Side found its first major outlet for communal emotion. This was a theatre of vivid trash and raw talent, innocent of art, skipping rapidly past the problems of immigrant life, and appealing to rich new appetites for spectacle, declamation, and high gesture. To the gray fatigue of Jewish life it brought the gaudy colors of Yiddish melodrama. It was a theatre superbly alive and full of claptrap, close to the nerve of folk sentiment and outrageous in its pretensions to serious culture.

The writers and actors of this early Yiddish theatre understood instinctively that their audiences, seemingly lost forever in the darkness of the sweatshop, wanted most of all the consolations of glamour. They wanted spectacles of Jewish heroism, tableaux of ancient and eloquent kings, prophets, and warriors; music, song, dance, foolery (*a bisl freylakhs*, a bit of fun) evoking memories of old-country ways; actors of a majesty and actresses of a fieriness beyond their own reach. In exploiting these desires, the writers and actors betrayed a mixture of shrewdness and innocence that would often characterize Yiddish theatre in its later, more imposing days. Contempt for "Moshe," the ill-lettered immigrant, soon began to be heard around the Yiddish theatres, and actors who were themselves greenhorns with little theatrical or any other culture started to assume aristocratic poses. Yet in spirit and mind they were stil very close to "Moshe"—that was a good part of their strength as performers.

In the opening years of the Yiddish theatre, hardly a glimmer of serious realism could break through. Realism seldom attracts uncultivated audiences: it is a sophisticated genre resting on the idea that a controlled exposure to a drab reality will yield pleasure. To the masses of early Jewish immigrants, most of whom had never before seen a professional stage production, realism seemed dry, redundant, without savor. What stirred their hearts was a glimpse of something that might transcend the wretchedness of the week: a theatre bringing a touch of the Sabbath, even if a debased or vulgarized Sabbath.

In the experience of the east European Jews, Yiddish theatre had deep roots but only a brief history. Among the Jews in the Diaspora theatricality had long been suspect as a

Poster for *Day and Night*. 1925. Lithograph. 42 × 28" (106.7 × 71.1 cm). Museum of the City of New York. The Theater Collection's Bella Bellarina Collection, Gift of Henry Rubinlicht. *"Day and Night" was a Yiddish drama in three acts, produced at the Unser Theater in the Bronx. It was written by S. Ansky (who also wrote "The Dybbuk"), music was by Lazar Weiner, while the sets and costumes were by Boris Aronson.*

threat to social discipline, yet it had all sorts of oblique ways of creeping into their culture: through "the high-church impressiveness of the reading of the Torah," the virtuoso performances of cantors and preachers, "the protocol of the Passover feasts, with the theatricality of suspense in the opening of the door for the invisible prophet Elijah." During the Purim festival, when moral constraints were relaxed and drinking and practical jokes tolerated, it became customary for comic-heroic performances to be improvised. By the early nineteenth century the *purim-shpil,* composed in homely Yiddish, was a regular feature of that holiday. But there were really no professional Yiddish actors until the middle of the nineteenth century, when groups of minstrels, acrobats, and singers began to wander from *shtetl* to *shtetl,* half-welcomed and half-scorned as ragamuffins of the culture. One such group, the popular Broder Zinger (folk singers from Brody, a Galician town), introduced a few strands of dialogue as continuity between songs. They were then persuaded by Abraham Goldfaden, a writer of Yiddish songs, to do a simple performance of a play he had composed; this performance, which took place in 1876 at Jassy, Romania, in a wine cellar, marks a formative point in the history of Yiddish theatre.

Goldfaden wrote a good many other plays rich in folk motifs and enlivened with charming songs, some of which like "Rozhinkes mit mandlen" ("Raisins and Almonds"), became in effect folk songs. A few theatrical troupes, harassed by czarist officials and disdained by the rabbinate, were formed, soon forced to break up, and sometimes formed again; but in truth, the birth of Yiddish theatre occurred almost simultaneously in eastern Europe and the United States, with many of the more ambitious actors opting for the freedom and supposed riches of the new world.

The first Yiddish stage production in New York was held on August 12, 1882, at Turn Hall on East Fourth Street between Second and Third avenues. A troupe of six men and two women, supported by local musicians and a choir from a nearby synagogue, put on Goldfaden's *The Sorceress,* "an operetta in 5 acts and 9 tableaux." Since no one in New York had a text of the play, it was patched together, like the choreography of a ballet, from the performers' memories of a European production. One of the actors, a plump sixteen-year-old named Boris Thomashefsky, would soon become a matinee idol, and in the memoirs he wrote many years later he tells a vivid story about hordes of Orthodox Jews angrily protesting the very idea of a stage production; the prima donna, Madame Sarah Krantzfeld, being pressured to drop out entirely; and he, Thomashefsky, racing to her apartment a few minutes before the show was to start and beginning her to appear: "We will starve, they'll lynch us." The prima donna's husband, according to Thomashefsky, then explained: "They promised me a candy store and even a few hundred dollars if my wife leaves the play." Who "they" were is not clear: apparently German Jews or Orthodox east European Jews grouped around the newspaper the *Yidishe Gazetn.* An even greater bribe, continues Thomashefsky, persuaded Madame to come to Turn Hall. But by then it was quite late, the musicians had left, Madame refused to sing without them, and the audience hissed. A few weeks later Thomashefsky had to lead his fellow artists to employment in a cigarette factory.

The historian of Yiddish theatre, B. Gorin, concluded some time later that Thomashefsky's account had been exaggerated: there were neither crowds nor riots nor intimidations, and as for Madame Krantzfeld, she had simply been inconvenienced by a cold. Yet Thomashefsky's version, if weak on facts, touched a certain truth. For there was opposition from Orthodox Jews, who looked upon theatre as a shameful trifling, and from German Jews, who feared that the coarse downtown brethren might embarrass them. One of the early Yiddish companies, reports Gorin, "behaved badly behind the scenes," becoming known as a "hangout for loose women," so that "respectable people kept away from the threatre as if it were a plague."

They could not keep away for long. From start to finish, the theatre would be their great cultural passion. In a few months a regular Yiddish company began to perform on weekends at the Bowery Garden, with the puffy young Thomashefsky delighting audiences through renditions of women's parts. (Actresses were still scarce: respectable fathers forbade their daughters to go on stage.) The repertory of this little company consisted mainly of comedies by Goldfaden, the most popular Yiddish playwright in eastern Europe but never, once in America, able to adapt himself to the rough conditions of New York theatre. Battening on the whole of European drama and opera, taking his tunes impartially from Offenbach and synagogue chants, Goldfaden wrote genre pieces that shrewdly sketched the major east European Jewish character types. Among his plays of these early years were *The Capricious Bride, The Fanatic, The Sorceress,* and, a particular success, *Shmendrik,* an amusing folk comedy featuring a hapless ninny who would become a stock presence in Yiddish farce. Soon there were two, sometimes three, competing companies at the Bowery Garden and the National and Thalia theatres. Most of the actors shuttled between shop and stage, according to where they could earn their bread.

In May 1884 there arrived in New York the Russian-Jewish Opera Company, led by Max Karp and Morris Silberman, the first more or less professional group to perform in Yiddish; its nine members had had some training with Goldfaden in Russia and among them was a "company dramatist," Joseph Lateiner, who had an acquaintance with European languages and a facility for twisting European plots to Jewish ends. The actors took themselves with a certain seriousness, announcing that Madame Sonya Heine would play feminine leads, Madame Esther Silberman supporting "soubrettes," Lateiner "serious youths to old men," and that Morris Heine would be "chief comic." The East Side was captivated, and even the stodgy *Yidishe Gazetn* acknowledged some delight.

Molly Picon
FROM SO LAUGH A LITTLE
"The Marvels of Rezshishtchov"

Molly Picon (1898–1992) was born in New York City to an immigrant family and began her professional career on the Yiddish stage at the age of 6. In this excerpt from her family biography, Picon explores how perceptions differ between the new and the old world.

I think one of my earliest memories is looking down the street where we lived in the south part of Philadelphia and seeing a stretch of row houses all connected, porch to porch to porch to porch, but separated into units of individuality by small wooden fence partitions between each porch. If you looked out on a Friday morning, it was as though someone had pressed a button and popped every housewife out of the house simultaneously. No matter how sloppy or careless a housekeeper a woman might be all week, when Friday came she became a beaver of energetic activity. She was, after all, preparing for the Sabbath. All the porches had wooden floors. All the women came out carrying pails and brushes and rags. The woman didn't live who would dare come out with a mop. She would have been scorned right out of the neighborhood.

There was a right way and a wrong way to scrub a floor. Many times my grandmother would cry out in anguish, "Molly, dolly. What are you *doing*?" Somehow I never learned the niceties of handling the scrubbing brush properly, not to my grandmother's satisfaction, at any rate. She used to despair that anyone would ever want to marry me if I didn't learn a *little* something about cleaning.

Before the porches were scrubbed, the doorknobs had to be polished. Every house had a brass doorknob and a knocker. Inside the house you might fall over children and clutter and general disorganized turmoil. But outside you had to be able to see your face reflected in brass. Each woman wore a cloth draped around her head, and a voluminous apron around her body. My grandmother carefully wore her apron wrong side out when she was cleaning. That way, she used to explain the facts of life to me earnestly, if someone should "fall in," she could whip her apron on right side out, and thus face the world with a clean apron. My grandmother spent years trying to convince me to wear an apron in the first place, and on the occasions when I yielded, to wear it wrong side out and save the good side for company.

At the end of the day when the Sabbath candles were lit, and the Sabbath meal was on the table—if you starved the rest of the week, it was not important; but the Sabbath meal had to be produced somehow—I would look around with satisfaction and say, "Doesn't everything look nice, Bubba?"

This would always set up a chain reaction in my grandmother. "You think this is nice?" And off my grandmother would sail, in a sea of recollection. "If you think this is nice, you should have seen the meals we used to prepare in Rezshishtchov."

Since the Sabbath meal consisted ritually and regularly of chopped fish, chicken soup

Poster of Molly Picon. 1935. American Jewish Historical Society, Waltham, Massachusetts. This poster was used to advertise a performance by Yiddish actress Molly Picon in Buenos Aires, Argentina. Some Yiddish performers achieved great international fame.

with noodles, roast chicken, potato pudding, a dish known as tzimmes, made up of a strange combination of prunes and carrots and on occasion raisins, sauerkraut and pickles, plenty of rye bread and a white twisted bread called challah, which my grandmother baked herself every Friday morning, fresh baked honey cake or sponge cake or nut cake, and generous amounts of tea, it was hard to believe this meal could be surpassed. But apparently it could be, in Rezshishtchov.

Every time my grandmother remembered how it used to be, the meals seemed to get better, the house got bigger, the town got grander.

Even my grandfather wasn't much better. He agreed vigorously with every word my grandmother said. "As true as I'm sitting here in this chair," I used to aid and abet her. "In Rezshishtchov . . ."

In Rezshishtchov, when you went to the synagogue, you wore a gold chain around your neck at the end of which there dangled a gold watch. I'm sure that it was only my grandmother who wore such a chain and such a watch, having received it as a wedding present. But as the story was repeated, after a while it was every woman in the village who wore a gold chain and gold watch to synagogue.

I recall how one day my grandmother came into the house in a state of great agitation. My uncle Daniel was visiting, with his wife Goldie, and my grandmother was taking them to her synagogue. At the last moment, she realized that this was absolutely impossible. She left them standing on the porch and came rushing back in to wail, in utter anguish. "Malkele. I don't know what to do. How can I take Goldie in with me? It's out of the question."

"What did she do?" I asked, quite surprised. She had looked fine to me when she had walked out the door.

"What did she do? She didn't do anything."

"Then why can't she go?"

"Why? I'll tell you a good reason why. She doesn't have a gold watch and a gold chain, that's why!"

"But, Bubba," I protested. "She has a beautiful diamond watch. I saw it with my own eyes. Uncle Daniel gave it to Aunt Goldie for their wedding anniversary. She wears it on her wrist all the time."

My grandmother shook her head at me.

"Children," she sighed. "What do they understand? Who sees a wristwatch?"

As the years passed, I began to feel as though America was in competition with Rezshishtchov, and always coming out a poor second. Nothing I could show Grandma really impressed her. If she was impressed, she felt the need to disclaim it. After all, her family had lived in Rezshishtchov for hundreds of years, for all she knew maybe before there even was an America, and she had an unswerving loyalty to the town of her birth.

It got to be a kind of challenge for me. Somewhere, somehow, there had to be something I could top Rezshishtchov with! But it took me years to do it. I had been married for seven years by then, and when I disclosed my plan to Yonkel, he was very amused that even as a young woman, I should still feel the need to meet this challenge.

"Why don't you let it go?" he asked me, reasonably. "If it gives her some pleasure, and it's such a a harmless pleasure, let it go."

"I can't, Yonkel," I said, stubbornly. "All my life I've been hearing about the marvels of Rezshishtchov. You'd think maybe it was the eighth wonder of the world."

"There's always room for one more wonder," Yonkel answered, grinning at me. But I had made up my mind. After all, I could be just as determined as my grandmother. I was appearing at the Second Avenue Theatre then, in a play called *Little Devil*. I was very busy, but not too busy to pick up my grandmother at the apartment and say, "Bubba, I want you to leave everything and come someplace with me."

"Where should I go with you in the middle of the day just like that without a reason?" she objected. "At least you could tell me where we are going so I'll know what to put on."

"You're fine the way you are," I insisted. "Just come with me. I want to show you something."

I didn't utter another word until we reached our destination. I had headed for the New York Paramount Theatre, newly built this year of 1926, and the most magnificent theatre on Broadway. I took my grandmother into the lobby. I walked her around slowly so she could drink in her luxurious surroundings. Then I pointed to the ceiling where the newly installed chandeliers glittered in all their splendor.

"Now what do you say, Bubba?" I asked in triumph.

My grandmother gazed in awe at the chandeliers. She drew in a deep breath, and expelled it in an even deeper sigh. I was sure that never, in all her years had she seen anything to equal those suspended lights.

"Well, Bubba?" I repeated. "What do you say now? Do they have chandeliers like this in Rezshishtchov?"

My grandmother admitted defeat. She shook her head in wonder.

"No," she said. "I can't tell a lie. This is one thing that they didn't have in Rezshishtchov."

I smiled broadly. I had finally done it, after all these years. I had laid low Rezshishtchov. And I finally topped my grandmother! But I crowed too soon.

My grandmother put her hand on my arm and said kindly, "I'll be the first to admit it, Malkele. Chandeliers like this they never even heard of in Rezshishtchov. But," she added firmly, putting me totally and forever in my place, "believe me, in King Solomon's Temple they were nicer."

Abraham Cahan

FROM THE RISE OF DAVID LEVINSKY
"I Discover America"

Abraham Cahan (1860–1951) received a traditional Jewish education in his native Russia before emigrating to the United States in 1882. A journalist, Cahan helped found and run the Jewish Daily Forward, *the legendary Yiddish language newspaper for immigrants living in America. His descriptions of the immigrant experience in* The Rise of David Levinsky *have made this semiautobiographical work a classic.*

The immigrant's arrival in his new home is like a second birth to him. Imagine a newborn babe in possession of a fully developed intellect. Would it ever forget its entry into the world? Neither does the immigrant ever forget his entry into a country which is, to him, a new world in the profoundest sense of the term and in which he expects to pass the rest of his life. I conjure up the gorgeousness of the spectacle as it appeared to me on that clear June morning: the magnificent verdure of Staten Island, the tender blue of sea and sky, the dignified bustle of passing craft—above all, those floating, squatting, multitudinously windowed palaces which I subsequently learned to call ferries. It was all so utterly unlike anything I had ever seen or dreamed of before. It unfolded itself like a divine revelation. I was in a trance or in something closely resembling one.

"This, then, is America!" I exclaimed, mutely. The notion of something enchanted which the name had always evoked in me now seemed fully borne out.

In my ecstasy I could not help thinking of Psalm 104, and, opening my little prayer-book, I glanced over those of its verses that speak of hills and rocks, of grass and trees and birds.

My transport of admiration, however, only added to my sense of helplessness and awe. Here, on shipboard, I was sure of my shelter and food, at least. How was I going to procure my sustenance on those magic shores? I wished the remaining hour could be prolonged indefinitely.

Psalm 104 spoke reassuringly to me. It reminded me of the way God took care of man and beast: "Thou openest thine hand and they are filled with good." But then the very next verse warned me that: "Thou hidest thy face, they are troubled: thou takest away their breath, they die." So I was praying God not to hide His face from me, but to open His hand to me; to remember that my mother had been murdered by Gentiles and that I was going to a strange land. When I reached the words, "I will sing unto the Lord as long as I live: I will sing praise to my God while I have my being," I uttered them in a fervent whisper.

*Two Continents.
c. 1909. Postcard
Print. Collection,
Jewish Historical
Museum, Amsterdam.
In this postcard image
from the beginning of the
century, immigrants who
have prospered in
America extend their
arms to welcome new
arrivals.*

My unhappy love never ceased to harrow me. The stern image of Matilda blended with the hostile glamour of America.

One of my fellow-passengers was a young Yiddish-speaking tailor named Gitelson. He was about twenty-four years old, yet his forelock was gray, just his forelock, the rest of his hair being a fine, glossy brown. His own cap had been blown into the sea and the one he had obtained from the steerage steward was too small for him, so that gray tuft of his was always out like a plume. We had not been acquainted more than a few hours, in fact, for he had been seasick throughout the voyage and this was the first day he had been up and about. But then I had seen him on the day of our sailing and subsequently, many times, as he wretchedly lay in his berth. He was literally in tatters. He clung to me like a lover, but we spoke very little. Our hearts were too full for words.

As I thus stood at the railing, prayer-book in hand, he took a look at the page. The most ignorant "man of the earth" among our people can read holy tongue (Hebrew), though he may not understand the meaning of the words. This was the case with Gitelson.

"Saying, 'Bless the Lord, O my soul'?" he asked, reverently. "Why this chapter of all others?"

"Because—Why, just listen." With which I took to translating the Hebrew text into Yiddish for him.

He listened with devout mien. I was not sure that he understood it even in his native tongue, but, whether he did or not, his beaming, wistful look and the deep sigh he emitted indicated that he was in a state similar to mine.

When I say that my first view of New York Bay struck me as something not of this earth it is not a mere figure of speech. I vividly recall the feeling, for example, with which I greeted the first cat I saw on American soil. I was on the Hoboken pier, while the steerage passengers were being marched to the ferry. A large, black, well-fed feline stood in a corner, eyeing the crowd of newcomers. The sight of it gave me a thrill of joy. "Look! There is a cat!" I said to Gitelson. And in my heart I added, "Just like those at home!" For the moment the little animal made America real to me. At the same time it seemed unreal itself. I was tempted to feel its fur to ascertain whether it was actually the kind of creature I took it for.

We were ferried over to Castle Garden. One of the things that caught my eye as I entered the vast rotunda was an iron staircase rising diagonally against one of the inner walls. A uniformed man, with some papers in his hands, ascended it with brisk, resounding step till he disappeared through a door not many inches from the ceiling. It may seem odd, but I can never think of my arrival in this country without hearing the ringing footfalls of this official and beholding the yellow eyes of the black cat which stared at us at the Hoboken pier.

The harsh manner of the immigration officers was a grievous surprise to me. As contrasted with the officials of my despotic country, those of a republic had been portrayed in my mind as paragons of refinement and cordiality. My anticipations were rudely belied. "They are not a bit better than Cossacks," I remarked to Gitelson. But they neither looked nor spoke like Cossacks, so their gruff voices were part of the uncanny scheme of things that surrounded me. These unfriendly voices flavored all America with a spirit of icy inhospitality that sent a chill through my very soul.

The stringent immigration laws that were passed some years later had not yet come into existence. We had no difficulty in being admitted to the United States, and when I was I was loath to leave the Garden.

Many of the other immigrants were met by relatives, friends. There were cries of joy, tears, embraces, kisses. All of which intensified my sense of loneliness and dread of the New World. The agencies which two Jewish charity organizations now maintain at the Immigrant Station had not yet been established. Gitelson, who like myself had no friends in New York, never left my side. He was even more timid than I. It seemed as though he were holding on to me for dear life. This had the effect of putting me on my mettle.

"Cheer up, old man!" I said, with bravado. "America is not the place to be a ninny in. Come, pull yourself together."

In truth, I addressed these exhortations as much to myself as to him; and so far, at least, as I was concerned, my words had the desired effect.

I led the way out of the big Immigrant Station. As we reached the park outside we were pounced down upon by two evil-looking men, representatives of boarding-houses for immigrants. They pulled us so roughly and their general appearance and manner were so uninviting that we struggled and protested until they let us go—not without some parting curses. Then I led the way across Battery Park and under the Elevated railway to State Street. A train hurtling and panting along overhead produced a bewildering, a daunting effect on me. The active life of the great strange city made me feel like one abandoned in the midst of a jungle. Where were we to go? What were we to do? But the presence of Gitelson continued to act as a spur on me. I mustered courage to approach a policeman, something I should never have been bold enough to do at home. As a matter of fact, I scarcely had an idea what his function was. To me he looked like some uniformed nobleman—an impression that in itself was enough to intimidate me. With his coat of blue cloth, starched linen collar, and white gloves, he reminded me of anything but the policemen of my town. I addressed him in Yiddish, making it as near an approach to German as I knew how, but my efforts were lost on him. He shook his head. With a witheringly dignified grimace he then pointed his club in the direction of Broadway and strutted off majestically.

"He's not better than a Cossack, either," was my verdict.

At this moment a voice hailed us in Yiddish. Facing about, we beheld a middle-aged man with huge, round, perpendicular nostrils and a huge, round, deep dimple in his chin that looked like a third nostril. Prosperity was written all over his smooth-shaven face and broad-shouldered, stocky figure. He was literally aglow with diamonds and self-satisfaction. But he was unmistakably one of our people. It was like coming across a human being in the jungle. Moreover, his very diamonds somehow told a tale of former want, of a time when he had landed, an impecunious immigrant like myself; and this made him a living source of encouragement to me.

"God Himself has sent you to us," I began, acting as the spokesman; but he gave no heed to me. His eyes were eagerly fixed on Gitelson and his tatters.

"You're a tailor, aren't you?" he questioned him.

My steerage companion nodded. "I'm a ladies' tailor, but I have worked on men's clothing, too," he said.

"A ladies' tailor?" the well-dressed stranger echoes, with ill-concealed delight. "Very well, come along. I have work for you."

That he should have been able to read Gitelson's trade in his face and figure scarcely surprised me. In my native place it seemed to be a matter of course that one could tell a tailor by his general appearance and walk. Besides, had I not divined the occupation of my fellow-passenger the moment I saw him on deck?

As I learned subsequently, the man who accosted us on State Street was a cloak contractor, and his presence in the neighborhood of Casstle Garden was anything but a matter of chance. He came there quite often, in fact, his purpose being to angle for cheap labor among the newly arrived immigrants.

We paused near Bowling Green. The contractor and my fellow-passenger were absorbed in a conversation full of sartorial technicalities which were Greek to me, but which brought a gleam of joy into Gitelson's eye. My former companion seemed to have become oblivious of my existence.

As we resumed our walk up Broadway the bejeweled man turned to me.

"And what was your occupation? You have no trade, have you?"

"I read Talmud," I said, confusedly.

"I see, but that's no business in America," he declared. "Any relatives here?"

"No."

"Well, don't worry. You will be all right. If a fellow isn't lazy nor a fool he has no reason to be sorry he came to America. It'll be all right."

"All right," he said in English, and I conjectured what it meant from the context. In the course of the minute or two which he bestowed upon me he uttered it so many times that the phrase engraved itself upon my memory. It was the first bit of English I ever acquired.

The well-dressed, trim-looking crowds of lower Broadway impressed me as a multitude of counts, barons, princes. I was puzzled by their preoccupied faces and hurried step. It seemed to comport ill with their baronial dress and general high-born appearance.

In a vague way all this helped to confirm my conception of America as a unique country, unlike the rest of the world.

When we reached the General Post-Office, at the end of the Third Avenue surface line, our guide bade us stop.

"Walk straight ahead," he said to me, waving his hand toward Park Row. "Just keep walking until you see a lot of Jewish people. It isn't far from here." With which he slipped a silver quarter into my hand and made Gitelson bid me good-by.

The two then boarded a big red horse-car.

I was left with a sickening sense of having been tricked, cast off, and abandoned. I stood watching the receding public vehicle, as though its scarlet hue were my last gleam of hope in the world. When it finally disappeared from view my heart sank within me. I may safely say that the half-hour that followed is one of the worst I experienced in all the thirty-odd years of my life in this country.

The big, round nostrils of the contractor and the gray forelock of my young steerage-fellow haunted my brain as hideous symbols of treachery.

With twenty-nine cents in my pocket (four cents was all that was left of the sum I had received from Matilda and her mother) I set forth in the direction of East Broadway.

Harry Golden

FROM ESS ESS MEIN KINDT

"Jewish Names"

Harry Golden (1902–1981), born Herschel Goldhurst on New York's Lower East Side, drew on his intimate knowledge of the immigrant Jewish experience for much of his literary work. As a young man in the 1920s, Golden served a five-year prison term for running a gambling establishment. He won fame as a journalist and is primarily remembered for his great wit and liberal political views.

To the immigrant Jew, the most English of all names was Shirley. Sheldon ran it a close second. Today, every novelist who wants to write about a Jewish girl calls her Shirley. When the Jews adopted Shirley and Sheldon en masse, the Gentiles dropped these two names like hot potoates. Now the Jews are dropping them and Shelly is gaining popularity along with Robin and Penny.

Down in the South, names like Hershel and Mendel persevere among the Presbyterians and the Baptists but the Jews are going to Jonathan and Scott.

The surname Schwartz was as Germanic as the surname Bismarck. The Russian Jews who came to America with the surname Chornee met with immigration officers who couldn't spell it.

"What does it mean?" asked the inspectors.

"Chornee means *schwartz* [black]," was the answer, naturally.

So the immigration officers did the Jews a favor. They translated black into Yiddish— Schwartz.

Among the rigorously Orthodox Jews, the Cohanim are the priestly caste. To the immigration officials, Cohen was as good and easy a Jewish name as any, so many the Litvak who welcomed the immigration shorthand which transformed him immediately into a man of the highest standing in the synagogue.

Judge Samuel Leibowitz tells the story about his name being Leibow and a neighbor advising the family to Americanize it into Leibowitz. At Baltimore, the immigration inspector ran out of names one morning and the last Jewish family that day was hurriedly catalogued as "Baltimore." The family of Joseph Baltimore eventually became prominent in Maryland.

The attempt to shed every vestige of Jewish life extended to the language. Some of the folks stopped talking Yiddish. My uncle was one of these. When my mother talked to him at a time when at best he knew but eighty English words he still pretended he didn't understand her Yiddish. He would turn to one of us and ask, "Vot did she sed?" and we always translated for him.

One lady lost a suit in court because she would not surrender her pride and speak Yiddish. She had brought a suit against a storekeeper who had refused to repair the sidewalk in front of his place of business. She fell, sustained painful and costly injuries.

During the trial, the lawyer asked "Where did you fall?"

She replied, "Offn sidewalk," which in Yiddish means "On the sidewalk," but translated was "off the sidewalk."

The lawyer repeated the question.

Again she answered, "Offn sidewalk." She wouldn't budge.

She lost.

Only in America.

Sam Levenson

FOODS

Sam Levenson (1911–1980), the consummate humorist, first made his living as a teacher and guidance counselor. In this selection he reminisces about Jewish culinary "delicacies."

———————

Purim and *Homentaschen* brought this on.

As I was picking the savory poppy seeds from my teeth, I remembered other flavors and odors that were part of our traditional Jewish past; the taste sensations that were part of Momma's household, and I feel like Pavlov's dog as my mouth recalls:

Matzohs gently coated in chicken fat over which a good healthy *tsibbeleh* had been rubbed. This rubbing the half-onion over the matzoh became in itself an experience in ecstatic anticipation. I've never sampled marijuana but I can't imagine that it would produce a more glowing sensation than golden chicken fat on hemstitched boards. But this voluptuous experience must have been a sin, because, just as you were reaching the climax of sense experience, the matzoh would snap, and the reality of a dimly lighted slum kitchen would burst in upon this little piece of heaven.

The dietitians have definitely outlawed some specific delights of Jewish children. At the age of three, I had already experienced an exquisite heartburn from a red-skinned *Retach*. Let the dietitians eat pablum and skins of baked potatoes! For me, life was just a bowl of *Retach*. And I had a better complexion than the dietitian.

The child was ushered into the world with an array of herring. A *Briss* meant HERRING. For months before the great day our house was inhabited by pickled herrings. Jars, big ones, little ones, glass and clay ones. Eyes, herring eyes, staring at you through windows, in clothing closets, in kitchen closets, on fire escapes—the phosphorescent glow of herrings swinging on onion-hoops. (Notes from a psychiatrist's casebook.)

What better lunch for a school child than cold *koogle* from the previous night with a crust that looked like the scales of a prehistoric mammal, with a side dish of yesterdays *tsimmes* and a seeded roll oozing *hock-flaish* in all directions. For dessert, a penny for a "twist" and back to school raring to go—to sleep. You can imagine the enthusiasm of forty-two such well-oiled scholars for the remainder of the afternoon. What with the noon sun pouring through the windows and the teacher's sweet and gentle voice, the odds were 30 to 1 against arithmetic; and the unceasing parade to the watertrough and other places.

During a holiday, there were special delicacies.

Momma's home-baked *choleh* which was so arranged that you didn't have to slice it. There were bulges all around which you just pulled out of their sockets with ease and *toonked* into nice, oily soup with big eyes that looked up at you from the plate. The sought-after prize in the soup, like the trinket in the cracker-jack box, was a small un-hatched egg which Momma had found in the chicken. There was one egg and eight children. What a strain on Momma's impartiality to choose the deserving child. The *ayeleh* usually went to the girls because of some folk-theory about fertility.

Soup could offer a variety of surprises—*kreplach* (meat balls with sport jackets), ex-quisitely shaped by the sculptural genius of a *balabusteh,* who always planned the structure of the *kreple* so that a tempting bit of the buried treasure should show through, just enough to make the mouth water.

Or soup might contain *lokshen,* which hung like weeping willows over the *flaishigeh leffel.* The excess lokshen could either be sucked into the mouth or bitten into.

What better contribution to *fressen* have we given the world than the incomparable *kishkeh* (sections of fire hose)? They tell me my *zadeh* stuffed his own kishkeh with cow's kishkeh to the age of 94. He carried around a permanent heartburn which kept his body warm and protected him from the severe Russian winters.

FROM A BINTEL BRIEF

Letters

A Bintel Brief *was the advice column of the Yiddish newspaper the* Jewish Daily Forward. *The questions asked and the advice given afford intimate glimpses of the daily experience of immigrant life.*

———————————

1906

Dear Editor,

I am a girl from Galicia and in the shop where I work I sit near a Russian Jew with whom I was always on good terms. Why should one worker resent another?

But once, in a short debate, he stated that all Galicians were no good. When I asked him to repeat it, he answered that he wouldn't retract a word, and that he wished all Galician Jews dead.

I was naturally not silent in the face of such a nasty expression. He maintained that only Russian Jews are fine and intelligent. According to him, the *Galitzianer* are inhuman savages, and he had the right to speak of them so badly.

Dear Editor, does he really have a right to say this? Have the Galician Jews not sent enough money for the unfortunate sufferers of the pogroms in Russia? When a Gentile speaks badly of Jews, it's immediately printed in the newspapers and discussed hotly everywhere. But that a Jew should express himself so about his own brothers is nothing? Does he have a right? Are Galicians really so bad? And does he, the Russian, remain fine and intelligent in spite of such expressions?

As a reader of your worthy newspaper, I hope you will print my letter and give your opinion.

> With thanks in advance,
> B.M.

ANSWER:
The Galician Jews are just as good and bad as people from other lands. If the Galicians must be ashamed of the foolish and evil ones among them, then the Russians, too, must hide their heads in shame because among them there is such an idiot as the acquaintance of our letter writer.

1943

Worthy Editor,

I write to you here about a vital question and wait impatiently for your opinion.

I came to America as a young girl, thirty-three years ago. My uncle, who brought me over, took me into the shop where he worked. And there I met a boy, also a "green-horn." We fell in love and were married four months later.

I worked along with my husband till I was well along in my pregnancy. I gave birth to a boy. Three years later I had another boy, and then in another three, a girl. We cared for our children and strove to give them the best of everything. In time my husband took over a small store and I, as well as the children when they grew up, helped him. We worked hard to make a living, and we were happy with our children, who were studious and obedient. Even when they went to college they helped us in the store.

COLORPLATE 98 *(above)*
Hanukkah Lamp. Galicia, late 18th–early 19th
century. Silver, gilt, fabricated, cast, repoussé. 26 ×
22″ (66 × 55.8 cm). From the collection of Hebrew
Union College Skirball Museum, Los Angeles.
*During the 19th century, artisans working in various
materials often imitated plant forms. One such fanciful
example is this "Oak Tree" Hanukkah lamp,
commissioned by a Polish family.*

COLORPLATE 99
Hanukkah Lamp. Morocco, 20th century. Silver:
pierced and engraved with basin for drippings. 12³⁄₁₆
× 7½ × 1¹³⁄₁₆″ (31 × 19 × 4.5 cm). The Sir Isaac
and Lady Edith Wolfson Museum, Hechal Schlomo,
Jerusalem. *Delicate foliate and animal motifs characterize
this 20th-century lamp from Morocco.*

COLORPLATE 100 *(above)*
MOSHE ZABARI. *Hanukkah Lamp*. U.S., late 1960s. Silver. 5½ × 10″ (13.9 × 25.4 cm). From the collection of Hebrew Union College Skirball Museum, Los Angeles.

COLORPLATE 101
Hanukkah Lamp. Eastern Europe, 19th century. Bronze: cast. 29¾ × 26½ × 13¾″ (75.5 × 67.3 × 34.9 cm). The Jewish Museum, New York. The Rose and Benjamin Mintz Collection.

COLORPLATE 102 *(opposite)*
JOSEPH ZVI GEIGER. *Scenes from the "Esther" Story*. 1893. Oil painting on glass. 21 × 12¹³⁄₁₆″ (52.5 × 32 cm). Israel Museum, Jerusalem. Feuchtwanger Collection, purchased and donated to the Israel Museum by Baruch and Ruth Rappaport of Geneva.

אסתר המלכה · כתר מלכות · ארור המן אשר בקש לאבדי · ברוך מרדכי היהודי ·

הרצים יצאו דחופים בדבר המלך והדת נתנה בשושן הבירה ·

עשרת בני המן ימח שמם וזכרם

נעשה בשנת תרנ"ג לפ"ק פה עיה"ק צפת תובב אמן ·

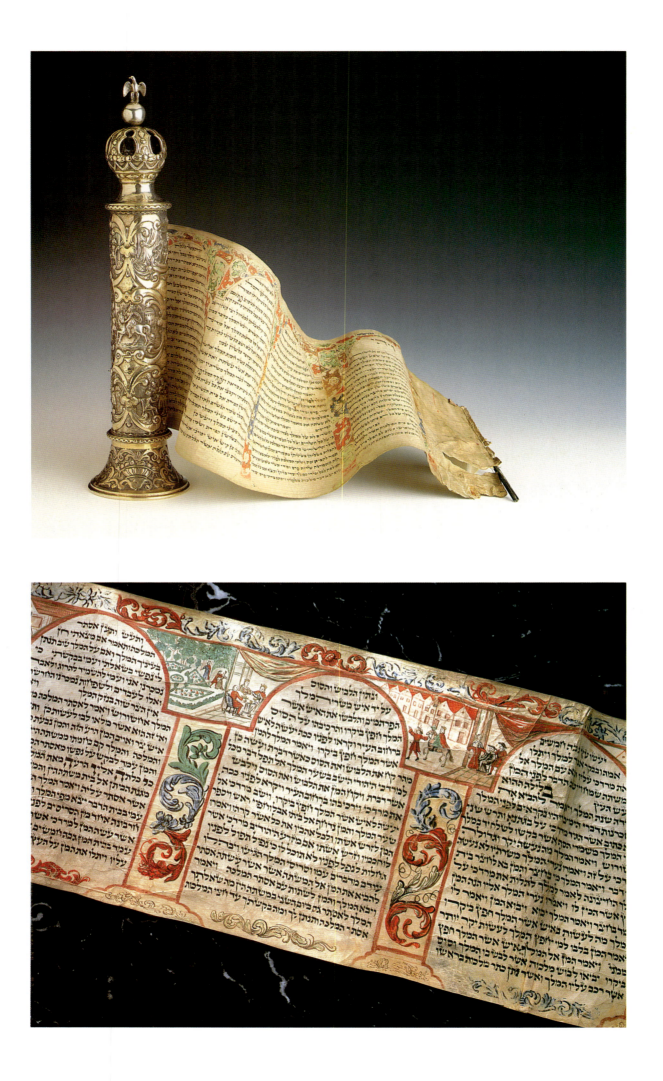

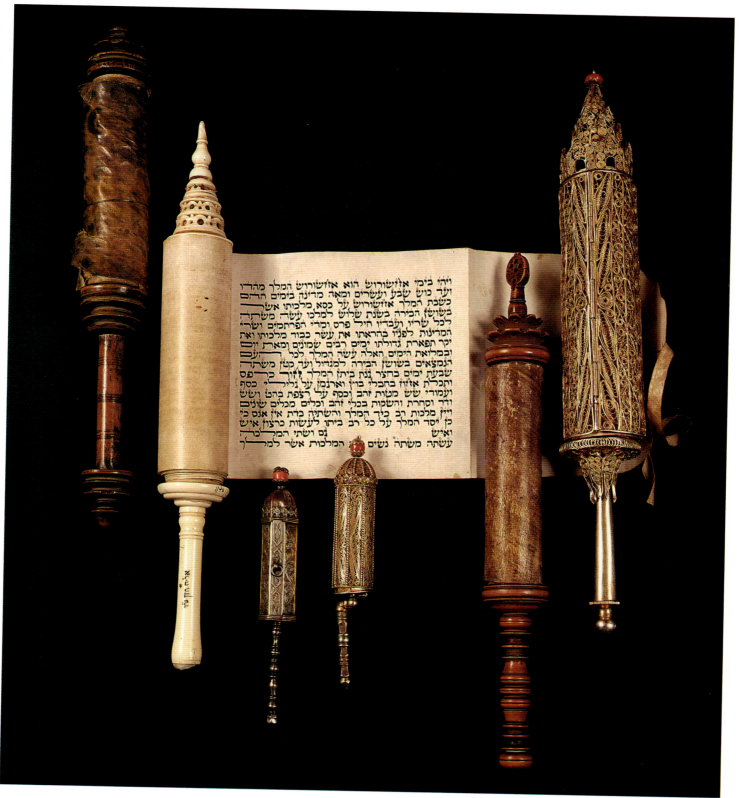

COLORPLATE 105
Various Esther Scroll Cases. Yemen, Turkey, Persia, and Morocco, 18th–19th centuries. Sir Isaac and Lady Edith Wolfson Museum, Hechal Shlomo, Jerusalem.

COLORPLATE 103 *(opposite, above)*
Esther Scroll. Eastern Europe, early 19th century. Silver: Embossed, partly gilt. 2 × 73″ (5.1 × 185.4 cm) long. From the collection of Hebrew Union College Skirball Museum, Los Angeles. *Esther Scrolls contain the biblical Book of Esther, often illustrated with scenes from the story and decorative motifs. Prior to reading from the scroll on Purim, it is fully unrolled; the reader then chants the text.*

COLORPLATE 104 *(opposite, below)*
Scroll of Esther. Germany, c. 1700. Parchment, ink, tempera. 11 × 177½″ (27.9 × 450.8 cm). From the collection of Hebrew Union College Skirball Museum, Los Angeles.

COLORPLATE 106
Seder Plate. Spain, c. 1470.
Glazed clay. Diameter: 22½"
(57 cm). Israel Museum,
Jerusalem. *As part of the
celebration of Passover, a Seder
plate is set in the cener of the
table at the Passover Seder, or
meal. Although the material and
decoration of the Seder plate may
vary, it traditionally is designed
to hold at least five of the
Passover symbols: Zeroa (a
roasted shank bone, symbol of
the pascal lamb); a roasted egg
(symbol of the Festival offering
made by pilgrims to Jerusalem
when the Temple still stood);
maror (bitter herbs that
symbolize the bitterness of the
enslavement); charoset (a
mixture of fruits and wine that
symbolize the mortar used for
bricks); and karpas (a spring
green to be dipped in salt water).
This example from 15th-century
Spain is characterized by the
Hispano-Moresque decorations,
colors, and techniques typical of
pottery of the era. The plate is
interesting because the word
"matzah" is misspelled.*

COLORPLATE 107
Seder Plate. Jerusalem, late
19th century. Copper.
Michael Kaniel Judaica
Collection.

COLORPLATE 108

Ewer and Basin Used on Passover. Istanbul, 1840–1850. The Jewish Museum, New York. The H. Ephraim and Mordecai Benguiat Family Collection. *A ewer and basin, such as the Ottoman set shown here, were used to pour water over the hands for the ritual washing at the Seder table. The design and metalwork of this ewer and basin display the skill and artistic creativity of metalsmiths from the Ottoman Empire. Typical of ceremonial objects, its beauty symbolizes the desire to embellish all aspects of the performance of ritual acts.*

COLORPLATE 109

EL LISSITZKY. Illustration from *Had Gadya Suite (Tale of a Goat)*. 1919. Colored lithograph on paper. 10¾ × 10″ (27.3 × 25.4 cm). The Jewish Museum, New York. Promised gift of Leonard and Phyllis Greenberg. *El (Eleazer) Lissitzky, well known as a Russian Constructivist painter, was one of a group of Jewish artists in Russia who looked to cultural idioms and traditions of Jewish life as a source of inspiration for their work. His illustrations from Had Gadya are unusual because they do not directly follow the text of the poem.*

WILLIAM GROPPER.
Newspaper Clipper.
1936. Oil on canvas.
27 × 34″ (68.6 × 86.4
cm). Courtesy of Gene
Gropper. *Jewish
immigrants, unfamiliar
with the language and
mores of American
culture relied upon the
Yiddish newspaper* The
Daily Forward *to keep
abreast of the news.
Despite their desire to
assimilate, many also
clung to the paper to keep
in touch with the
immigrant cultures they
left behind.*

You can't imagine our joy when our eldest son graduated as a doctor. By that time our second son was already going to college and our daughter attending high school. Our son, the doctor, could have married a girl with a large dowry. Instead he married a fine girl, also a college graduate, whose parents are not wealthy, but decent people. The couple is very much in love, they have a darling little son, and have lived happily.

When Hitler began the war, our eldest son decided to volunteer for the army. Our children were always interested in world affairs and were concerned with the Jewish problems. I tried to talk him out of it, and told my husband to discourage him but my husband told me that our son knew what he was doing.

I ran to my daughter-in-law, because I thought she, too, didn't want him to leave her alone with the child, and to give up the practice he had worked up. Yet she began to console me and held back her tears. In short, my doctor went.

Then we, that is, America, declared war and our second son also enlisted in the army. That time I didn't raise a fuss, because I knew they would draft him anyway.

My heart is breaking, but I know I am not the only mother whose sons went to war. I know they must fight now for our dear country and we must make sacrifices to destroy our enemies. If it were not enough that our sons went away, now our daughter wants to join the WACs. When she told me this, it was as if I were struck on the head with a club.

I worry about her. She is not yet married. All the young men are in the army and now she wants to enlist in the army like her brothers. Instead of discouraging her, my husband says that if he were younger he wouldn't stay home either.

I am a simple woman. I understand clearly that a terrible wrath is being poured out on our world, and that we Jews should be more interested than all others in overcoming the bitter enemy. But must I, with my two sons in the war, also give up my daughter?

Many times I read the "Bintel Brief" to my daughter. She thinks highly of your wise answers, and agrees to wait until you print my letter and state your opinion.

With thanks,
An Unhappy Mother

We understand fully how you feel. The fact is that we are all patriotic and loyal to our country, and we simply cannot talk your daughter out of serving in the women's military corps. She will get along well there, and when she comes back home you will very likely be pleased that she will have learned a great deal from her experience.

Naturally, a mother hopes for a good future for her daughter. But it is possible that the good future can come from her service in the WACs.

Kadia Molodowsky
THE LOST SHABES

Kadia Molodowsky (1894–1975) is known as the "First Lady of Yiddish Poetry," and is by far the best known of all Yiddish female authors. She was born in Lithuania and taught Yiddish in Warsaw before immigrating to the United States. Her subjects include modern Jewish history and Zionism, as well as American Jewish life. "The Lost Shabes" deals with the issue of assimilation.

Mrs. Haynes drops in on her neighbor Sore Shapiro at least twice a day. She does it out of the goodness of her heart. She is teaching Sore Shapiro, who is all of two years in the country (dragged herself through Siberia, Japan, and finally reached New York)—she is teaching her how to be a homemaker in America while keeping in mind the role of *vaytaminz*. She sticks her head in the door (she is wearing the red bow which she never

ISIDOR KAUFMANN.
Friday Evening.
c. 1920. Oil on canvas.
28½ × 35½" (72.4 × 90.2 cm). Jewish Museum, New York. Gift of Mr. and Mrs. M. R. Schweitzer.

removes from her hair) and without any preliminaries begins talking about *vaytaminz*. She speaks with gusto, with heart, as if she were keeping Sore Shapiro alive.

The little red bow in Mrs. Haynes' hair looks alive as if it had swallowed all the vitamins at one time and had become fiery hot.

Mrs. Haynes comes in with her six-year-old daughter Teresa Filipine. While her mother is busy with the theory of vitamins, Teresa Filipine hangs around the kitchen testing the faucets to see if water pours out when they are turned. Every so often Mrs. Haynes calls the child to her.

—Teresa Filipine!—And seeing the child is wet, adds—You good-for-nothing.

—Why call such a small child by such a long name, Mrs. Haynes?

—What's to be done? My mother's name was Toybe Faygl. And it's forbidden to give only half a name. If you do, they say the ghost is disappointed.

Sore Shapiro calls the child by her Yiddish name Toybe Faygele, gives her a prune to eat and teaches her a rhyme:

—Toybe Faygl a girl like a bagel.

The little one repeats the rhyme, nibbles on the prune and laughs.

Teresa Filipine's grandfather calls her Toybe Faygele. He visits them every Friday night and brings her a lollipop, and Teresa Filipine understands that her grandfather and the neighbor Mrs. Shapiro have some connection to Friday night and to her Yiddish name Toybe Faygele.

Sometimes the little one drops in on Mrs. Shapiro by herself without her mother. She knocks on her door, and before anyone asks who's there, she gives her Yiddish name: Toybe Faygele. Sore Shapiro gives her a piece of bread with butter and talks to her in Yiddish, just like her grandfather:

—Eat, Toybe Faygele! Eat! A trifle, all they feed her constantly are *vaytaminz*.

Teresa Filipine sits on a stool and eats simply and with great pleasure. The piece of bread with butter which she eats at Mrs. Shapiro's has also something to do with her Yiddish name, with her grandfather and with Friday nights when her grandfather brings her a lollipop. Teresa Filipine eats obediently and seriously with childlike self-importance.

When her mother looks around and sees that the child has disappeared, she calls out through the open window down into the street:

—Teresa Filipine! *Kam hir!* Where are you, you good-for nothing?

Teresa Filipine hears "good-for-nothing" and knows that her mother is angry. With a sly smile, she places the piece of bread with butter on the table, stops being Toybe Faygele and immediately begins speaking English:

—*Am hir!*—and her small steps click rapidly through the stone corridor.

Mrs. Haynes asks Sore Shapiro with a friendly reproach:

—*Pliz*, don't give Teresa Filipine bread and butter. What does she get from it? A little bit of *startsh*? The child needs protein.

But Teresa Filipine doesn't know what she needs. When her mother leaves her neighbor's house, the little one slips inside, in an instant reverts to being Toybe Faygele again and finishes eating the piece of bread and butter which she had left on the table. She eats with obedient earnestness down to the very last crumb, as if she were finishing praying.

Friday night Teresa Filipine's mother lights four candles. She puts on velvet slacks, sticks a red handkerchief in the pocket of her white blouse; in the light of the candles the red bow in her hair becomes a flaming yellow. Teresa Filipine stands, looks at her mother's fingers as she lights the candles. Soon her grandfather will come, will give her a lollipop, will call her Toybe Faygele—and that's *shabes*.

One Friday evening after her mother put on her velvet slacks and lit the candles, she told Teresa Filipine that her grandfather was not coming. He is sick and is in the hospital. Teresa Filipine became lonely: without her grandfather, without her grandfather's lollipop, and without her Yiddish name Toybe Faygele, she was left with half a *shabes*. She remembered their neighbor Mrs. Shapiro. She left and knocked on her door looking for the second half of *shabes*.

—Toybe Faygele—she announced even before anyone asked who was knocking.

There were no candles on Mrs. Shapiro's table. She herself was dressed in a housecoat and not in velvet pants: it was like any other day.

—Oh, Toybe Faygele! Come in, Toybe Faygele!

Teresa Filipine stood in the middle of the room and looked around. She walked slowly into the kitchen, took a look at the table, turned around, and feeling dejected, walked towards the door.

What are you looking for, Toybe Faygele?—the neighbor asked her and followed her.

—*Nottink*—Teresa Filipine answered in English.

—So why did you come?

The child didn't answer, moved slowly closer to the exit.

From the other apartment Mrs. Haynes' voice echoed in the summer air:

—Teresa Filipine! *Ver ar u?*—and angrily threw the words good-for-nothing.

It was all like any other weekday.

This time Teresa Filipine did not run to her mother. Her small steps clicked slowly on the stone floor of the corridor. She went down to the floor below, sat down on a stone step and cried.

Louis D. Brandeis
A CALL TO THE EDUCATED JEW

Louis Brandeis (1856–1941), the youngest of four siblings, was born in Louisville, Kentucky, to two immigrant parents from Prague. He graduated from Harvard Law school before he was 21, with an academic record unequaled in the history of the school. Brandeis was appointed to the Supreme Court in 1916, and served as the first Jewish member of the Court until his resignation in 1939. In this selection, the author eloquently enumerates the qualities to which every Jew should aspire.

[T]hree men were found who volunteered to give him instruction. None of them was a teacher by profession. One was a newspaper man; another was a chemist; the third, I believe, was a tradesman; all were educated men. And throughout five long years these three men took from their leisure the time necessary to give a stranger an education.

The three men of Bialystok realized that education was not a thing of one's own to do with as one pleases—not a personal privilege to be merely enjoyed by the possessor— but a precious treasure transmitted upon a sacred trust to be held, used and enjoyed, and if possible strengthened—then passed on to others upon the same trust. Yet the treasure which these three men held and the boy received in trust was much more than an education. It included that combination of qualities which enabled and impelled these three men to give and the boy to seek and to acquire an education. These qualities embrace: first, *intellectual capacity;* second, *an appreciation of the value of education;* third, *indomitable will;* fourth, *capacity for hard work.* It was these qualities which enabled the lad not only to acquire but to so utilize an education that, coming to America, ignorant of our language and of our institutions, he attained in comparatively few years the important office he has so honorably filled.

Now whence comes this combination of qualities of mind, body and character? . . . they were developed by three thousand years of civilization, and nearly two thousand years of persecution; developed through our religion and spiritual life; through our traditions; and through the social and political conditions under which our ancestors lived. They are, in short, the product of Jewish life.

Portrait of Louis Dembitz Brandeis, Justice of the Supreme Court. 1934. Photograph.

★   ★   ★

But our inheritance comprises far more than this combination of qualities making for effectiveness. These are but means by which man may earn a living or achieve other success. Our Jewish trust comprises also that which makes the living worthy and success of value. It brings us that body of moral and intellectual perceptions, the point of view and the ideals, which are expressed in the term Jewish spirit; and therein lies our richest inheritance.

THE KINSHIP OF JEWISH AND AMERICAN IDEALS

Is it not a striking fact that a people coming from Russia, the most autocratic of countries, to America, the most democratic of countries, comes here, not as to a strange land, but as to a home? The ability of the Russian Jew to adjust himself to America's essentially democratic conditions is not to be explained by Jewish adaptability. The explanation lies mainly in the fact that the twentieth century ideals of America have been the ideals of the Jew for more than twenty centuries. We have inherited these ideals of democracy and of social justice as we have the qualities of mind, body and character to which I referred. . . .

Among the Jews democracy was not an ideal merely. It was a practice—a practice made possible by the existence among them of certain conditions essential to successful democracy, namely:

First: *An all-pervading sense of the duty in the citizen.* . . .
Second: *Relatively high intellectual attainments.* . . .
Third: *Submission to leadership as distinguished from authority.* . . .
Fourth: *A developed community sense.* . . .

THE TWO-FOLD COMMAND OF NOBLESSE OBLIGE

Such is our inheritance; such the estate which we hold in trust. And what are the terms of that trust; what the obligations imposed? The short answer is *noblesse oblige;* and its command is two-fold. It imposes duties upon us in respect to our own conduct as individuals; it imposes no less important duties upon us as part of the Jewish community or race. Self-respect demands that each of us lead individually a life worthy of our great inheritance and of the glorious traditions of the race. But this is demanded also by respect for the rights of others. . . .

And yet, though the Jew make his individual life the loftiest, that alone will not fulfill the obligations of his trust. We are bound not only to use worthily our great inheritance, but to preserve and, if possible, augment it; and then transmit it to coming generations. The fruit of three thousand years of civilization and a hundred generations of suffering may not be sacrificed by us. It will be sacrificed if dissipated. Assimilation is national suicide. And assimilation can be prevented only by preserving national characteristics and life as other peoples, large and small, are preserving and developing their national life. Shall we with our inheritance do less than the Irish, the Servians, or the Bulgars? And must we not, like them, have a land where the Jewish life may be naturally led, the Jewish language spoken, and the Jewish spirit prevail? Surely we must, and that land is our fathers' land: it is Palestine.

A LAND WHERE THE JEWISH SPIRIT MAY PREVAIL

The undying longing for Zion is a fact of deepest significance—a manifestation in the struggle for existence. Zionism is, of course, not a movement to remove all the Jews of the world compulsorily to Palestine. In the first place, there are in the world about 14,000,000 Jews, and Palestine would not accommodate more than one-fifth of that number. In the second place, this is not a movement to compel anyone to go to Palestine. It is essentially a movement to give to the Jew more, not less, freedom—a movement to enable the Jews to exercise the same right now exercised by practically every other people in the world—to live at their option either in the land of their fathers or in some other country; a right which members of small nations as well as of large—which Irish, Greek, Bulgarian, Servian or Belgian, as well as German or English—may now exercise.

Furthermore, Zionism is not a movement to wrest from the Turk the sovereignty of Palestine. Zionism seeks merely to establish in Palestine for such Jews as choose to go and remain there, and for their descendants, a legally secured home, where they may live together and lead a Jewish life: where they may expect ultimately to constitute a majority of the population, and may look forward to what we should call home rule.

The establishment of the legally secured Jewish home is no longer a dream. For more than a generation brave pioneers have been building the foundations of our new old home. It remains for us to build the superstructure.

MOLLY SIMON. *The Baking of Hallah for the Sabbath*. Oil on canvas. 12 × 16″ (30.5 × 40.6 cm). 1966. The Jewish Museum, New York. Gift of the Artist.

Alfred Kazin

FROM A WALKER IN THE CITY

"The Kitchen"

A Walker in the City, the autobiography of Alfred Kazin (b. 1915) is a sensitive chronicle of first-generation American life in the twentieth century. The first volume of his three-volume work focuses on his desire to physically and psychologically move beyond the confines of his native Brooklyn. In this excerpt, the writer recalls his hardworking immigrant mother and the warmth of her Jewish kitchen.

In Brownsville tenements the kitchen is always the largest room and the center of the household. As a child I felt that we lived in a kitchen to which four other rooms were annexed. My mother, a "home" dressmaker, had her workshop in the kitchen. She told me once that she had begun dressmaking in Poland at thirteen; as far back as I can remember, she was always making dresses for the local women. She had an innate sense of design, a quick eye for all the subtleties in the latest fashions, even when she despised them, and great goldness. For three or four dollars she would study the fashion magazines with a customer, go with the customer to the remnants store on Belmont Avenue to pick out the material, argue the owner down—all remnants stores, for some reason, were supposed to be shady, as if the owners dealt in stolen goods—and then for days would patiently fit and baste and sew and fit again. Our apartment was always full of women in their housedresses sitting around the kitchen table waiting for a fitting. My little bedroom next to the kitchen was the fitting room. The sewing machine, an old nut-brown Singer with golden scrolls painted along the black arm and engraved along the two tiers of little drawers massed with needles and thread on each side of the treadle, stood next to the window and the great coal-black stove which up to my last year in college was our main source of heat. By December the two outer bedrooms were closed off, and used to chill bottles of milk and cream, cold borscht and jellied calves' feet.

The kitchen held our lives together. My mother worked in it all day long, we ate in it almost all meals except the Passover *seder,* I did my homework and first writing at the kitchen table, and in winter I often had a bed made up for me on three kitchen chairs near the stove. On the wall just over the table hung a long horizontal mirror that sloped to a ship's prow at each end and was lined in cherry wood. It took up the whole wall, and drew every object in the kitchen to itself. The walls were a fiercely stippled whitewash, so often rewhitened by my father in slack seasons that the paint looked as if it had been squeezed and cracked into the walls. A large electric bulb hung down the center of the kitchen at the end of a chain that had been hooked into the ceiling; the old gas ring and key still jutted out of the wall like antlers. In the corner next to the toilet was the sink at which we washed, and the square tub in which my mother did our clothes. Above it, tacked to the shelf on which were pleasantly ranged square, blue-bordered white sugar and spice jars, hung calendars from the Public National Bank on Pitkin Avenue and the Minsker Progressive Branch of the Workman's Circle; receipts for the payment of insurance premiums, and household bills on a spindle; two little boxes engraved with Hebrew letters. One of these was for the poor, the other to buy back the Land of Israel. Each spring a bearded little man would suddenly appear in our kitchen, salute us with a hurried Hebrew blessing, empty the boxes (sometimes with a sidelong look of disdain if they were not full), hurriedly bless us again for remembering our less fortunate Jewish brothers and sisters, and so take his departure until the next spring, after vainly trying to persuade my mother to take still another box. We did occasionally remember to drop coins in the boxes, but this was usually only on the dreaded morning of "mid-terms" and final examinations, because my mother thought it would bring me luck. She was extremely superstitious, but embarrassed about it, and always laughed at herself whenever, on the morning of an examination, she counseled me to leave the house on my right foot. "I know it's silly," her smile seemed to say, "but what harm can it do? It may calm God down."

The kitchen gave a special character to our lives; my mother's character. All my memories of that kitchen are dominated by the nearness of my mother sitting all day long at her sewing machine, by the clacking of the treadle against the linoleum floor, by the patient twist of her right shoulder as she automatically pushed at the wheel with one hand or lifted the foot to free the needle where it had got stuck in a thick piece of material. The kitchen was her life. Year by year, as I began to take in her fantastic capacity for labor and her anxious zeal, I realized it was ourselves she kept stitched together. I can never remember a time when she was not working. She worked because the law of her life was work, work and anxiety; she worked because she would have found life meaningless without work. She read almost no English; she could read the Yiddish paper, but never felt she had time to. We were always talking of a time when I would teach her how to read, but somehow there was never time. When I awoke in the morning she was already at her machine, or in the great morning crowd of housewives at the grocery getting fresh rolls for breakfast. When I returned from school she was at her machine, or conferring over *McCall's* with some neighborhood woman who had come in pointing hopefully to an illustration—"Mrs. Kazin! Mrs. Kazin! Make me a dress like it shows here in the picture!" When my father came home from work she had somehow mysteriously interrupted herself to make supper for us, and the dishes cleared and washed, was back at her machine. When I went to bed at night, often she was still there, pounding away at the treadle, hunched over the wheel, her hands steering a piece of gauze under the needle with a finesse that always contrasted sharply with her swollen hands and broken nails. Her left hand had been pierced through when as a girl she had worked in the infamous Triangle Shirtwaist Factory on the East Side. A needle had gone straight through the palm, severing a large vein. They had sewn it up for her so clumsily that a tuft of flesh always lay folded over the palm.

The kitchen was the great machine that set our lives running; it whirred down a little only on Saturdays and holy days. From my mother's kitchen I gained my first picture of life as a white, overheated, starkly lit workshop redolent with Jewish cooking, crowded with women in housedresses, strewn with fashion magazines, patterns, dress materials, spools of thread—and at whose center, so lashed to her machine that bolts of energy seemed to dance out of her hands and feet as she worked, my mother stamped the treadle hard against the floor, hard, hard, and silently, grimly at war, beat out the first rhythm of the world for me.

Every sound from the street roared and trembled at our windows—a mother feeding her child on the doorstep, the screech of the trolley cars on Rockaway Avenue, the eternal smash of a handball against the wall of our house, the clatter of "*der Italyéner*"'s cart packed with watermelons, the sing-song of the old-clothes men walking Chester Street, the cries "*Árbes! Árbes! Kinder! Kinder! Heyse gute árbes!*" All day long people streamed into our apartment as a matter of course—"customers," upstairs neighbors, downstairs neighbors, women who would stop in for a half-hour's talk, salesmen, relatives, insurance agents. Usually they came in without ringing the bell—everyone knew my mother was always at home. I would hear the front door opening, the wind whistling through our front hall, and then some familiar face would appear in our kitchen with the same bland, matter-of-fact inquiring look: no need to stand on ceremony: my mother and her kitchen were available to everyone all day long.

New York's Lower East Side. c. 1900. *Photograph.*

281

At night the kitchen contracted around the blaze of light on the cloth, the patterns, the ironing board where the iron had burned a black border around the tear in the muslin cover; the finished dresses looked so frilly as they jostled on their wire hangers after all the work my mother had put into them. And then I would get that strangely ominous smell of tension from the dress fabrics and the burn in the cover of the ironing board— as if each piece of cloth and paper crushed with light under the naked bulb might suddenly go up in flames. Whenever I pass some small tailoring shop still lit up at night and see the owner hunched over his steam press; whenever in some poorer neighborhood of the city I see through a window some small crowded kitchen naked under the harsh light glittering in the ceiling, I still smell that fiery breath, that warning of imminent fire. I was always holding my breath. What I must have felt most about ourselves, I see now, was that we ourselves were like kindling—that all the hard-pressed pieces of ourselves and all the hard-used objects in that kitchen were like so many slivers of wood that might go up in flames if we came too near the white-blazing filaments in that naked bulb. Our tension itself was fire, we ourselves were forever burning—to live, to get down the foreboding in our souls, to make good.

Bernard Malamud
THE LOAN

Bernard Malamud (1914–1986) was a master storyteller in the best Jewish tradition. In the aftermath of the Holocaust he explored his own Jewishness through his writing. Malamud's works have won two National Book Awards as well as the Pulitzer Prize.

The sweet, the heady smell of Lieb's white bread drew customers in droves long before the loaves were baked. Alert behind the counter, Bessie, Lieb's second wife, discerned a stranger among them, a frail, gnarled man with a hard hat who hung, disjoined, at the edge of the crowd. Though the stranger looked harmless enough among the aggressive purchasers of baked goods, she was at once concerned. Her glance questioned him but he signaled with a deprecatory nod of his hatted head that he would wait—glad to (forever)—though his face glittered with misery. If suffering had marked him, he no longer sought to conceal the sign; the shining was his own—him—now. So he frightened Bessie.

She made quick hash of the customers, and when they, in response to her annihilating service, were gone, she returned to him her stare.

He tipped his hat. "Pardon me—Kobotsky. Is Lieb the baker here?"

"Who Kobotsky?"

"An old friend"—frightening her further.

"From where?"

"From long ago."

"What do you want to see him?"

The question insulted, so Kobotsky was reluctant to say.

As if drawn into the shop by the magic of a voice, the baker, shirtless, appeared from the rear. His pink, fleshy arms had been deep in dough. For a hat he wore jauntily a flour-covered, brown paper sack. His peering glasses were dusty with flour, and the inquisitive face white with it so that he resembled a paunchy ghost; but the ghost, through the glasses, was Kobotsky, not he.

"Kobotsky," the baker cried almost with a sob, for it was so many years gone

Kobotsky reminded him of, when they were both at least young, and circumstances were altered—ah, different. Unable, for sentimental reasons, to refrain from smarting tears, he jabbed them away with a thrust of the hand.

Kobotsky removed his hat—he had grown all but bald where Lieb was gray—and patted his flushed forehead with an immaculate handkerchief.

Lieb sprang forward with a stool. "Sit, Kobotsky."

"Not here," Bessie murmured.

"Customers," she explained to Kobotsky. "Soon comes the supper rush."

"Better in the back," nodded Kobotsky.

So that was where they went, happier for the privacy. But it happened that no customers came so Bessie went in to hear.

Kobotsky sat enthroned in a private corner of the room, stoop-shouldered, his black coat and hat on, the stiff, gray-veined hands drooping over thin thighs. Lieb, peering through full moons, eased his bones on a flour sack. Bessie lent an attentive ear but the visitor was dumb. Embarrassed, Lieb did the talking: ah, of old times. The world was new. We were, Kobotsky, young. Do you remember how both together, immigrants out of steerage, we registered in night school?

"Haben, hatte, gehabt." He cackled at the sound of it.

No word from the gaunt one on the tall stool. Bessie fluttered around an impatient duster. She shot a glance into the shop: empty.

Lieb, acting the life of the party, recited, to cheer his friend: " 'Come, said the wind to the trees one day, Come over the meadows with me and play.' Remember, Kobotsky?"

Bessie sniffed aloud. "Lieb, the bread!"

The baker bounced up, strode over to the gas oven and pulled one of the tiered doors down. Just in time he yanked out the trays of brown breads in hot pans, and set them on the tin-top worktable.

Bessie clucked at the narrow escape.

Lieb peered into the shop. "Customers," he said triumphantly. Flushed, she went in. Kobotsky, with wetted lips, watched her go. Lieb set to work molding the risen dough into two trays of pans. Soon the bread was baking, but Bessie was back.

The honey odor of the new loaves distracted Kobotsky. He deeply breathed the sweet fragrance, as if this were the first air he was tasting, and even beat his fist against his chest at the delicious smell.

"Oh, my God," he all but wept. "Wonderful."

"With tears," Lieb said humbly, pointing to the large pot of dough.

Kobotsky nodded.

For thirty years, the baker explained, he had been never with a penny to his name. One day, out of misery, he had wept into the dough and thereafter his bread was so sweet it brought customers in from everywhere.

"My cakes they don't like so much, but my bread and rolls they run miles to buy."

Kobotsky blew his nose, then peeked into the shop: three customers.

"Lieb"—a whisper.

Despite himself the baker stiffened.

The visitor's eyes swept back to Bessie out front, then, under raised brows, questioned the baker.

Lieb, however, remained mute.

Kobotsky coughed clear his throat. "Lieb, I need two hundred dollars." His voice broke.

Lieb slowly sank onto the sack. He knew—had known. From the minute of Kobotsky's appearance he had weighed in his thoughts this against the remembrance of the lost and bitter hundred, fifteen years ago. Kobotsky swore he had repaid it, Lieb said no. Afterwards a broken friendship. It took years to blot out of the system the memoried outrage.

Kobotsky bowed his head.

At least admit you were wrong, thought Lieb, waiting a cruelly long time.

Kobotsky stared at his crippled hands. Once a cutter of furs, driven by arthritis out of the business.

Lieb gazed too. He breathed with pain on the right side. The button of a truss bit into his belly. Both eyes were cloudy with cataracts. Though the doctor swore he would see after the operation, he feared otherwise. He sighed. The wrong was in the past. Forgiven: forgiven at the sight of him.

"For myself, positively, but she"—Lieb nodded shopwise—"is a second wife. Everything is in her name." He held up empty hands.

Kobotsky's eyes were shut.

"But I will ask her—" Lieb looked doubtful.

"My wife needs—"

The baker raised a palm. "Don't speak."

"Tell her—"

"Leave it to me."

He seized the broom and circled the room, raising clouds of white dust.

When Bessie, breathless, got back she threw one look at them, and with tightened lips, waited adamant.

Lieb hastily scoured the pots in the iron sink, stored the bread pans under the table and stacked the fragrant loaves. He put one eye to the slot of the oven: baking, all baking.

Facing Bessie, he broke into a sweat so hot it momentarily stunned him.

Kobotsky squirmed atop the stool.

"Bessie," said the baker at last, "this is my old friend."

She nodded gravely.

Kobotsky lifted his hat.

"His mother—God bless her—gave me many times a plate of hot soup. Also when I came to this country, for years I ate at his table. His wife is a very fine person—Dora—you will someday meet her—"

Kobotsky softly groaned.

"So why I didn't meet her yet?" Bessie said, still, after a dozen years, jealous of the first wife's prerogatives.

"You will."

"Why didn't I?"

"Lieb—" pleaded Kobotsky.

"Because I didn't see her myself fifteen years," Lieb admitted.

"Why not?" she pounced.

Lieb paused. "A mistake."

Kobotsky turned away.

"My fault," said Lieb.

"Because you never go anyplace," Bessie spat out. "Because you live always in the shop. Because it means nothing to you to have friends."

Lieb solemnly agreed.

"Now she is sick," he announced. "The doctor must operate. This will cost two hundred dollars. I promised Kobotsky—"

Bessie screamed.

Kobotsky got off the stool, hat in hand.

Pressing a palm to her bosom, Bessie lifted her arm to her eyes. She tottered. They both ran forward to catch her but she did not fall. Kobotsky retreated quickly to the stool and Lieb returned to the sink.

Bessie, her face like the inside of a loaf, quietly addressed the visitor. "I have pity for your wife but we can't help you. I am sorry, Mr. Kobotsky, we are poor people, we don't have the money."

"A mistake," Lieb cried, enraged.

Bessie strode over the shelf and tore out a bill box. She dumped its contents on the table, the papers flying everywhere.

"Bills," she shouted.

*Hester Street Bakery,
Lower East Side, New
York.* 1933. Photograph.

Kobotsky hunched his shoulders.

"Bessie, we have in the bank—"

"No—"

"I saw the bankbook."

"So what if you saw a few dollars, so have you got life insurance?"

He made no answer.

"Can you get?" she taunted.

The front door banged. It banged often. The shop was crowded with customers clamoring for bread. Bessie stomped out to wait on them.

In the rear the wounded stirred. Kobotsky, with bony fingers, buttoned his overcoat.

"Sit," sighed the baker.

"Lieb, I am sorry—"

"Sit."

Kobotsky sat, his face lit with sadness.

When Bessie finally got rid of the rush, Lieb stirred, went into the shop. He spoke to her quietly, almost in a whisper, and she answered as quietly, but it took only a minute to set them quarreling.

Kobotsky slipped off the stool. He went to the sink, wet half his handkerchief and held it to his dry eyes. Folding the handkerchief he put it away in his overcoat pocket then took out a small penknife and quickly pared his fingernails.

As he entered the shop, Lieb was pleading with Bessie, reciting the embittered hours of his toil, the enduring drudgery. And now that he had a cent to his name, what was there to live for if he could not share it with a dear friend? But Bessie had her back to him.

"Please," Kobotsky said, "don't fight. I go away now."

Lieb gazed at him in exasperation, Bessie stayed with head averted.

"Yes," Kobotsky sighed, "the money I wanted for Dora, but she is not sick, Lieb, she is dead."

"Ai," Lieb cried, wringing his hands.

Bessie faced the visitor, pallid.

"Not now," he spoke kindly, "five years ago."

"Lieb groaned.

"The money I need for a stone on her grave. She never had a stone. This Sunday is five years that she is dead and every year I promise her, Dora, this year I will give you a stone, and every year I give her nothing."

The grave, to his everlasting shame, lay uncovered before all eyes. He had long ago paid a fifty-dollar deposit for a headstone with her name on it in clearly chiseled letters but had never got the rest of the money. It there wasn't one thing to do with it there was always another: the first year an operation, the second he couldn't work, imprisoned again by arthritis, the third a widowed sister lost her only son and the little Kobotsky earned had to help support her, the fourth incapacitated by boils that made him ashamed to walk out into the street, this year he was at least working, but only for just enough to eat and sleep, so Dora still lay without a stone, and for aught he knew he would someday return to the cemetery and find her grave gone.

Tears sprang into the baker's eyes. One gaze at Bessie's face—at the odd looseness of neck and body—told him that she too was moved. Ah, he had won out. She would now say yes, give the money, and they would then all sit down at the table and eat supper together.

But Bessie, though weeping, shook her head, and before they could guess what, had blurted out the story of her afflictions: how the Bolsheviki came, when she was a little girl, and dragged her darling father into the snowy fields without his shoes on; the shots scattered the blackbirds in the trees and the snow oozed blood; how, when she was married a year, her husband, a sweet and gentle man, an educated accountant—rare in those days and that place—died of typhus in an epidemic in Warsaw; and how she, abandoned in her grief, years later found sanctuary in the home of an older brother in Germany, who sacrificed his own chances to send her, before the war, to America, and as a result, in all probability ended up with his wife and daughter and her two blessed children in Hitler's incinerators.

"So I came to America and met here a baker, a poor man—who was always in his life poor—without a penny and without enjoyment in his life, and I married him, God knows why, and with my both hands, working day and night, I fixed up for him his piece of business and we make now, after twelve years, a little living. But Lieb is a sick man, with weak lungs, and eyes that he needs an operation, and this is not yet everything. Suppose, God forbid, that he died, what will I do alone by myself? Where will I go, where, and who will take care of me if I have nobody?"

The baker, who had often heard this tale, munched, as he listened, chunks of soft white bread.

When she had finished he tossed the shell of the loaf away. Kobotsky, at the end, had held his hands over his ears.

With copious tears streaming from her eyes, Bessie raised her head and suspiciously sniffed the air. Screeching suddenly, she ran into the rear and with a cry wrenched open the oven door. A cloud of smoke billowed out at her. The loaves in the trays were blackened bricks—charred corpses.

Kobotsky and the baker embraced and sighed over their lost youth. They pressed mouths together and parted forever.

Chaim Potok

FROM THE CHOSEN

The Chosen, by Chaim Potok (b. 1929), presents a glimpse into the religious life of a Hasidic family living in Brooklyn after World War II. This story underlines the tension between that world and the non-Hasidic Jewish community, as expressed by the relationship of two boys who are friends; each represents a vastly different, albeit authentic, Jewish world. In this excerpt, each boy chooses an opposite path: one, the modern, scientific world; the other, a life of traditional studies and prayers.

Reb Saunders moved forward slightly in the chair and put his hands on the desk. Slowly, he closed the Talmud from which he and Danny had been studying. Then he sighed, a deep, trembling sigh that filled the silence of the room like a wind.

"Nu, Reuven," he said quietly, "finally, finally you come to see me." He spoke in Yiddish, his voice quavering a little as the words came out.

"I apologize," I said hesitantly, in English.

He nodded his head, and his right hand went up and stroked his gray beard. "You have become a man," he said quietly. "The first day you sat here, you were only a boy. Now you are a man."

Danny seemed suddenly to become conscious of the way he was twisting his earlock. He put his hand on his lap, clasped both hands tightly together and sat very still, staring at his father.

Reb Saunders looked at me and smiled feebly, nodding his head. "My son, my Daniel, has also become a man. It is a great joy for a father to see his son suddenly a man."

Danny stirred faintly in his chair, then was still.

"What will you do after your graduation?" Reb Saunders asked quietly.

"I have another year to study for smicha."

"And then what?"

"I'm going into the rabbinate."

He looked at me and blinked his eyes. I thought I saw him stiffen for a moment, as though in sudden pain. "You are going to become a rabbi," he murmured, speaking more to himself than to me. He was silent for a moment. "Yes. I remember. . . . Yes. . . ." He sighed again and shook his head slowly, the gray beard moving back and forth. "My Daniel will receive his smicha in June," he said quietly. Then he added, "In June. . . . Yes. . . . His smicha. . . . Yes. . . ." The words trailed off, aimless, disconnected and hung in the air for a long moment of tight silence.

Then, slowly, he moved his right hand across the closed Talmud, and his fingers caressed the Hebrew title of the tractate that was stamped into the spine of the binding. Then he clasped both hands together and rested them on top of the Talmud. His body followed the movements of his hands, and his gray earlocks moved along the sides of his aged face.

"Nu," he said, speaking softly, so softly I could barely hear him, "in June my Daniel and his good friend begin to go different ways. They are men, not children, and men go different ways. You will go one way, Reuven. And my son, my Daniel, he will—he will go another way."

I saw Danny's mouth fall open. His body gave a single convulsive shudder. Different ways, I thought. *Different* ways. Then he—

"I know," Reb Saunders murmured, as if he were reading my mind. "I have known it for a long time."

Danny let out a soft, half-choked, trembling moan. Reb Saunders did not look at him. He had not once looked at him. He was talking to Danny through me.

"Reuven, I want you to listen carefully to what I will tell you now." He had said: Reuven. His eyes had said: Danny. "You will not understand it. You may never understand it. And you may never stop hating me for what I have done. I know how you feel. I do not see it in your eyes? But I want you to listen.

"A man is born into this world with only a tiny spark of goodness in him. The spark is God, it is the soul; the rest is ugliness and evil, a shell. The spark must be guarded like a treasure, it must be nurtured, it must be fanned into flame. It must learn to seek out other sparks, it must dominate the shell. Anything can be a shell, Reuven. Anything. Indifference, laziness, brutality, and genius. Yes, even a great mind can be a shell and choke the spark.

"Reuven, the Master of the Universe blessed me with a brilliant son. And he cursed me with all the problems of raising him. Ah, what it is to have a brilliant son! Not a smart son, Reuven, but a brilliant son, a Daniel, a boy with a mind like a jewel. Ah, what a curse it is, what an anguish it is to have a Daniel, whose mind is like a pearl, like a sun. Reuven, when my Daniel was four years old, I saw him reading a story from a book. And I was frightened. He did not read the story, he swallowed it, as one swallows food or water. There was no soul in my four-year-old Daniel, there was only his mind. He was a mind in a body without a soul. It was a story in a Yiddish book about a poor Jew and his struggles to get to Eretz Yisroel before he died. Ah, how that man suffered! And my Daniel *enjoyed* the story, he *enjoyed* the last terrible page, because when he finished it he realized for the first time what a memory he had. He looked at me proudly and told me back the story from memory, and I cried inside my heart. I went away and cried to the Master of the Universe, 'What have you done to me? A mind like this I need for a son? A *heart* I need for a son, a *soul* I need for a son, *compassion* I want from my son, righteousness, mercy, strength to suffer and carry pain, *that* I want from my son, not a mind without a soul!' "

Reb Saunders paused and took a deep, trembling breath. I tried to swallow; my mouth was sand-dry. Danny sat with his right hand over his eyes, his glasses pushed up on his forehead. He was crying silently, his shoulders quivering. Reb Saunders did not look at him.

"My brother was like my Daniel," he went on quietly. "What a mind he had. What a mind. But he was also not like my Daniel. My Daniel, thank God, is healthy. But for many, many years my brother was ill. His mind burned with hunger for knowledge. But for many years his body was wasted with disease. And so my father did not raise him as he raised me. When he was well enough to go off to a yeshiva to study, it was too late.

"I was only a child when he left to study in Odessa, but I still remember what he was able to do with his mind. But it was a cold mind, Reuven, almost cruel, untouched by his soul. It was proud, haughty, impatient with less brilliant minds, grasping in its search for knowledge the way a conqueror grasps for power. It could not understand pain, it was indifferent to and impatient with suffering. It was even impatient with the illness of its own body. I never saw my brother again after he left for the yeshiva. He came under the influence of a Maskil in Odessa and went away to France where he became a great mathematician and taught in a university. He died in a gas chamber in Auschwitz. I learned of it four years ago. He was a Jew when he died, not an observer of the Commandments, but not a convert, thank God. I would like to believe that before he died he learned how much suffering there is in this world. I hope so. It will have redeemed his soul.

"Reuven, listen to what I am going to tell you now and remember it. You are a man, but it will be years before you understand my words. Perhaps you will never understand them. But hear me out, and have patience.

"When I was very young, my father, may he rest in peace, began to wake me in the middle of the night, just so I would cry. I was a child, but he would wake me and tell me stories of the destruction of Jerusalem and the sufferings of the people of Israel, and I would cry. For years he did this. Once he took me to visit a hospital—ah, what an experience that was!—and often he took me to visit the poor, the beggars, to listen to them talk. My father himself never talked to me, except when we studied together. He taught me with silence. He taught me to look into myself, to find my own strength, to walk around inside myself in company with my soul. When his people would ask him why he was so silent with his son, he would say to them that he did not like to talk, words are cruel, words play tricks, they disort what is in the heart, they conceal the heart, the heart speaks through silence. One learns of the pain of others by suffering one's own pain, he would say, by turning inside oneself, by finding one's own soul. And it is

COLORPLATE 110
Pouch for Afikoman. China, 19th
century. Cotton, satin, embroidery
thread, gold thread. 5¾″ (14.6 cm)
diameter. From the collection of
Hebrew Union College Skirball
Museum, Los Angeles.

COLORPLATE 111
Matzah Cover (Case). Hungary, 19th
century. Velvet, embroidered with
fish scales and gold thread. Sir Isaac
and Lady Edith Wolfson Museum,
Hechal Shlomo, Jerusalem. *This
matzah cover is noteworthy for its
skillful use of disparate materials, such as
fishscales.*

COLORPLATE 112
Tiered Seder Set. Poland, 18th–19th century. Brass: cast, cut-out, engraved. Wood: painted and stained. Ink on paper. Silk: embroidered. Linen. Cotton. 13¾ × 14" (35 × 35.5 cm). The Jewish Museum, New York. Gift of the Danzig Jewish Community. *This Seder set is unique among 19th-century tiered examples in its elaborate incorporation of sculptural figures and grillwork. The interior contains wooden trays to hold the matzahs, as well as wooden holders for the other Passover foods. The prayer in the cartouche between the lions' paws is for the blessing of the matzah.*

COLORPLATE 113 *(below)*
Passover Goblet (with inscription "Let my people go.") Germany, 18th century. Carved ivory. 3¹¹⁄₁₆ × 2⁵⁄₁₆" (9.5 × 6 cm) diameter. Sir Isaac and Lady Edith Wolfson Museum, Hechal Shlomo, Jerusalem. *This carved ivory goblet depicts Pharaoh seated on a raised throne, with Moses and Aaron before him.*

COLORPLATE 114 *(opposite)*
MAURICE MAYER. *Omer Calendar.* France, mid-19th century. Glass, silver, partly gilt, semiprecious stones, painted parchment. 13¾ × 10¼ × 3" (34.9 × 26 × 7.6 cm). From the collection of Hebrew Union College Skirball Museum, Los Angeles. *The period between the second day of Passover and the festival of Shavuot (the Feast of Weeks) commemorates the time when an omer (a measure) of the first of the barley was brought to the Temple in Jerusalem. The 49 days between Passover and Shavuot is the period of the omer, and each day is counted on an omer calendar. This French omer calendar is a particularly ornate example.*

COLORPLATE 115
MAX BECKMANN. *The Synagogue*. 1919. Oil on canvas. 35½ × 55⅛″ (90 × 140 cm). Städtische Galerie, in the Städelsches Kunstinstitut, Frankfurt. © 1992 ARS, New York/Bild-Kunst, Bonn.

The Frankfurt synagogue depicted here was a monumental structure, capped by an onion dome. Like most other synagogues in Germany, it was destroyed during Kristallnacht (November 9, 1938).

COLORPLATE 116
JOZEF ISRAELS. *A Jewish Wedding.* 1903. Oil on canvas. 53¹⁵⁄₁₆ × 58¼″ (137 × 148 cm). Rijksmuseum, Amsterdam.

COLORPLATE 117 *(opposite, above)*
ISSACHAR RYBACK. *The Old Synagogue.* 1917. Oil on canvas. 38¹³⁄₁₆ × 58⁷⁄₁₆″ (97 × 146 cm). Collection, Tel Aviv Museum of Art, Israel. *Ryback, along with El Lissitzky, was a member of the Jewish Ethnographic Society, whose expeditions explored the wooden synagogues along the Dnieper River in Russia. This painting, which depicts the Synagogue of Dobrovna, reflects Cubist influence, but draws its impact from the folk-art character of the wooden structures that so deeply influenced Ryback.*

COLORPLATE 118 *(opposite, below)*
JACOB KRAMER. *The Day of Atonement.* 1919. Oil on canvas. 39¼ × 48⅛″ (99.7 × 122.2 cm). Leeds City Art Galleries, England. *In this painting, the artist portrays the congregation in silent prayer during a Yom Kippur service.*

COLORPLATE 119
(opposite)
MARC CHAGALL.
Green Violinist. 1923–
1924. Oil on canvas.
78 × 42¾" (198 ×
108.6 cm). Solomon
R. Guggenheim
Museum, New York.
Gift of Solomon R.
Guggenheim, 1937.
© 1992 ARS, New
York/ADAGP, Paris.
*Born in Vitebsk of
Orthodox parents,
Chagall typically
incorporates memories of
his native Russia into
his paintings. The
Green Violinist is
characteristic of
Chagall's sense of
fantasy and whimsy and
includes images of shtetl
life, such as the wooden
buildings, villagers, and
music.*

important to know of pain, he said. It destroys our self-pride, our arrogance, our indifference toward others. It makes us aware of how frail and tiny we are and of how much we must depend upon the Master of the Universe. Only slowly, very slowly, did I begin to understand what he was saying. For years his silence bewildered and frightened me, though I always trusted him, I never hated him. And when I was old enough to understand, he told me that of all people a tzaddik especially must know of pain. A tzaddik must know how to suffer for his people, he said. He must take their pain from them and carry it on his own shoulders. He must carry it always. He must grow old before his years. He must cry, in his heart he must always cry. Even when he dances and sings, he must cry for the sufferings of his people.

"You do not understand this, Reuven. I see from your eyes that you do not understand this. But my Daniel understands it now. He understands it well.

"Reuven, I did not want my Daniel to become like my brother, may he rest in peace.

Better I should have had no son at all than to have a brilliant son who had no soul. I looked at my Daniel when he was four years old, and I said to myself, How will I teach this mind what it is to have a soul? How will I teach this mind to understand pain? How will I teach it to *want* to take on another person's suffering? How will I do this and not lose my son, my precious son whom I love as I love the Master of the Universe Himself? How will I do this and not cause my son, God forbid, to abandon the Master of the Universe and His Commandments? How could I teach my son the way I was taught by my father and not drive him away from Torah? Because this is America, Reuven. This is not Europe. It is an open world here. Here there are libraries and books and schools. Here there are great universities that do not concern themselves with how many Jewish students they have. I did not want to drive my son away from God, but I did not want him to grow up a mind without a soul. I knew already when he was a boy that I could not prevent his mind from going to the world for knowledge. I knew in my heart that it might prevent him from taking my place. But I had to prevent it from driving him away completely from the Master of the Universe. And I had to make certain his soul would be the soul of a tzaddik no matter what he did with his life."

He closed his eyes and seemed to shrink into himself. His hands trembled. He was silent for a long time. Tears rolled slowly down alongside the bridge of his nose and disappeared into his beard. A shuddering sigh filled the room. Then he opened his eyes and stared down at the closed Talmud on the desk. "Ah, what a price to pay. . . . The years when he was a child and I loved him and talked with him and held him under my tallis when I prayed. . . . 'Why do you cry, Father?" he asked me once under the tallis. 'Because people are suffering,' I told him. He could not understand. Ah, what it is to be a mind without a soul, what ugliness it is. . . . Those were the years he learned to trust me and love me. . . . And when he was older, the years I drew myself away from him. . . . 'Why have you stopped answering my questions, Father?' he asked me once. 'You are old enough to look into your own soul for the answers,' I told him. He laughed once and said, 'That man is such an ignoramus, Father.' I was angry. 'Look into his soul,' I said. 'Stand inside his soul and see the world through his eyes. You will know the pain he feels because of his ignorance, and you will not laugh.' He was bewildered and hurt. The nightmares he began to have. . . . But he learned to find answers for himself. He suffered and learned to listen to the suffering of others. In the silence between us, he began to hear the world crying."

He stopped. A sigh came from his lips, a long, trembling sigh like a moan. Then he looked at me, his eyes moist with his own suffering. "Reuven, you and your father were a blessing to me. The Master of the Universe sent you to my son. He sent you when my son was ready to rebel. He sent you to listen to my son's words. He sent you to be my closed eyes and my sealed ears. I looked at your soul, Reuven, not your mind. In your father's writings I looked at his soul, not his mind. If you had not found the gematriya mistake, Reuven, it would have made a difference? No. The gemitriya mistake only told me you had a good mind. But your soul I knew already. I knew it when my Daniel came home and told me he wanted to be your friend. Ah, you should have seen his eyes that day. You should have heard his voice. What an effort it was for him to talk to me. But he talked. I knew your soul, Reuven, before I knew your mind or your face. A thousand times I have thanked the Master of the Universe that He sent you and your father to my son.

"You think I was cruel? Yes, I see from your eyes that you think I was cruel to my Daniel. Perhaps. But he has learned. Let my Daniel become a psychologist. I know he wishes to become a psychologist. I do not see his books? I did not see the letters from the universities? I do not see his eyes? I do not hear his soul crying? Of course I know. For a long time I have known. Let my Daniel become a psychologist. I have no more fear now. All his life he will be a tzaddik. He will be a tzaddik for the world. And the world needs a tzaddik."

Reb Saunders stopped and looked slowly over at his son. Danny still sat with his hand over his eyes, his shoulders trembling. Reb Saunders looked at his son a long time. I had the feeling he was preparing himself for some gigantic effort, one that would completely drain what little strength he had left.

Then he spoke his son's name.

There was silence.

Reb Saunders spoke his son's name again. Danny took his hand away from his eyes and looked at his father.

"Daniel," Reb Saunders said, speaking almost in a whisper, "when you go away to study, you will shave off your beard and earlocks?"

Danny stared at his father. His eyes were wet. He nodded his head slowly.

Reb Saunders looked at him. "You will remain an observer of the Commandments?" he asked softly.

Danny nodded again.

Reb Saunders sat back slowly in his chair. And from his lips came a soft, tremulous sigh. He was silent for a moment, his eyes wide, dark, brooding, gazing upon his son. He nodded his head once, as if in final acknowledgment of his tortured victory.

Dan Jacobson
THE EXAMPLE OF LIPI LIPPMANN

Dan Jacobson (b. 1923) is a South African author who eventually settled in England. Jacobson's work often focuses on one of two themes: the struggle of Jewish identity in the modern world, and the moral problem of South African apartheid.

In Lyndhurst, if a Gentile spoke enviously to a Jew about how rich the Jews of Lyndhurst were, how clever they were, how well they did in business, the reply was often made, "Well, it's not really true about all the Jews. Just look at Lipi Lippmann!" No one, not even the biggest anti-Semite in the world, could say that Lipi Lippmann was rich or clever or did well in business.

Lipi Lippmann once said that the Jews of Lyndhurst should pay him to remain poor, his poverty was so useful in arguments. But the joke was received in silence; it was felt to be in bad taste. The Jews of Lyndhurst were ready to use Lipi Lippmann's poverty to propitiate an envious Gentile, but they were ashamed of him nevertheless; ashamed of his old Ford lorry, laden with fruit and vegetables, going from door to door; ashamed that Lipi was the only white man who bickered among the colored and Indian hawkers at dawn in the market place. Every other Jew in town was a licensed wholesaler or a licensed hotelkeeper, a licensed dentist or a licensed doctor; but Lipi Lippmann had remained nothing but a licensed hawker.

Lipi was a small man, with the head of a large one: his cheekbones were strong and prominent, his nose was bony and arched, his eyes were set wide apart. He was a widower, and lived by himself in a tiny single-storied house in one of the oldest suburbs of Lyndhurst. Around Lipi's house were houses as small and as shabby as his own with the same high *stoeps* in front, and the same iron roofs above. In the back yards behind the houses there lived troops of raucous African servants who, with their dirty bare feet and torn clothes, were as different from the trim, white-overalled servants in the wealthier suburbs as the employers in the one district were from those in the other. All Lipi's neighbors in the street were Afrikaner railwaymen or mine workers, and their children somtimes shouted *"Koelie-Jood"* after him—*Koelie* being an insulting term for an Indian, and thus being a disdainful way of referring to Lipi's trade. But the mothers of these children always waited for Lipi to return home at the end of the afternoon, when they bought from him at cut-prices the softened carrots and moulting cabbages he had been unable to sell elsewhere. Then the children also came round, and asked Lipi if he had any *ertjies* for them. And often enough Lipi would produce a handful of peapods which were no longer green, but gray and pale brown or white, and distribute them among the clamoring children. When they had dispersed, he would pack the empty crates neatly together in the back of the van, tie them down with rope, and go into his house.

Nobody followed him inside it. . . . Saturday was his busiest day, so he went to synagogue only on the high festivals; but he always went to the evening meetings of the local Zionist society. At these meetings he sat in the front row, listening intently and nodding his large head, almost like a man at prayer, to every word that was said.

That nod was Lipi's characteristic gesture; it seemed to be a gesture of profound acquiescence, of acceptance; yet it never brought to an end the debate he appeared to be having with himself. He nodded at Zionist meetings, he nodded when he drove his lorry, when he bargained with the housewives, when he sat alone on his *stoep*. And he nodded in the same way when he came home from work one day and found that while he had been away and the girl had been paying her regular afternoon visit to a friend in the back yard of a nearby house, someone had broken into his house and robbed him of everything that could be put into a trunk and carried out of the house. Almost all his clothes were gone, including his best *shul*-going suit; so was the money-box in which he kept the few pounds he earned one day and laid out for stock the next day. The thief or thieves had also taken the single bottle of whiskey Lipi kept hidden in his wardrobe; an old gold fobwatch and chain he had bought on the occasion of his marriage, and which he had not worn for years; two silver napkin-rings, with his own and his wife's initials engraved upon them; a couple of tablecloths. Someone, it was clear, had been unable to believe that Lipi was as poor as he had appeared to be; someone must have had the fantasy that Lipi was a miser, and had been hoarding money and valuables over the years. Whoever it was—a black man or a white one—was no doubt disillusioned now; and he had left the marks of what looked like rage in the splintered drawers thrown upon the floor, the razor-rents in the armchair in the front room and the mattress in the bedroom, the wanton destruction of the basin in the bathroom.

Because the basin was smashed, Lipi went into the kitchen and washed himself carefully at the sink, and then, in his shirtsleeves, came into the front room of the house. All day it had been hot; now, with the sun hanging low in the west, the heat seemed to have a settled, brooding quality, quite different in its intensity from the morning's direct glare, or the throb of noon. The windows of the room were wide open, but no breeze came in through them; it was as warm indoors as it was outside. Lipi stood in the middle of the room, staring at the drawers of the sideboard upside down on the floor, and the hideous lumps of blue and white stuffing protruding from the ripped armchair. A strange, cracked sound came from his breast; this sharp noise was followed by a sigh, as if something broken inside him sought to knit itself together again. He hunched his shoulders higher and went to the window. His shoulders shook, and again he uttered that abrupt sound, which was again followed by the faint complaining wheeze.

Lipi was laughing. When his girl came back she found him standing at the window, looking across the *stoep* and garden into the bit of street beyond. Seeing the wreckage in the room and the blood on Lipi's knuckles, she thought he had been in a fight with the intruders; and Lipi could not explain to her how he had laughed and bitten at his own knuckles, laughed and bitten at himself, like a madman, with the smashed room behind him.

It was the girl who went running to the neighbors with the news, and the neighbors who telephoned the police. The police found Lipi standing alone in the room. While one man in the police squad went around looking for fingerprints, the other, perturbed by the fixity of Lipi's expression and the sudden jerky nods of his head, tried to get him to sit down. But Lipi would not move; he did not seem to know what the man wanted of

HERMANN STRUCK. *Man Making Havdalah.* 1902. Etching. The Jewish Museum, New York. Given by Mrs. Peter Addelston in honor of the memory of Mrs. Tillie E. Hyman and Dr. and Mrs. Harold K. Addelston.

him. Readily enough, however, when the policemen asked him to make a statement, he began to detail what had been taken from him. There was his best suit, and the other clothes; his gold watch and the bottle of whiskey; there was his money-box.

"Money-box?" the policeman interrupted. "What kind of money-box? How much was in it? Where did you keep it?"

"How much was in it?" Lipi repeated. He laughed loudly, and his eyes stared forward without expression, looking beyond the policeman. "A fortune, what do you think? The work of a lifetime was in the money-box. Isn't that enough? Enough—enough—for what? What do I want? I want to go to *Eretz Yisroel* before I die. That's how much money there was in the money-box."

"Mr. Lippmann—"

"Yes," Lipi cried out, "put it down in your book, why not, put it down that there was money to go to *Eretz Yisroel* in the money-box, put it down. What difference does it make now?" Lipi laughed and shouted, he gnawed at his fists, he cried out that before he died he wanted to go to the Holy Land, and now he knew he never would be able to. He was a poor man, he had always been poor, but he had had one ambition, one hope;

now he saw what nonsense it had always been. . . . The amount of the loss was greatly exaggerated as the story went from one servant or housewife to the next, though no single exaggeration was greater than the one that the policeman, at Lipi's bidding, had written into his book.

The next morning the story was in the local paper. Lipi was described as "a well-known city fruiterer and green-grocer"; his loss was estimated at "several hundred pounds, which Mr. Lippmann had been saving to fulfill his lifelong ambition of visiting the Holy Land." The police, the report added, were continuing their inquiries.

A few days later another report appeared, in which it was stated that several leading members of the Lyndhurst Jewish community were offering a reward for information leading to the arrest of the thief or thieves; the report stated also that it had been decided that, should the money not be recovered, a fund would be established to make good Mr. Lippmann's loss, and thus enable him to fulfill his lifelong ambition of visiting the Holy Land.

For Lipi had become a hero, even something of a martyr in Lyndhurst, and especially so to the members of the Lyndhurst Jewish community. If they felt any embarrassment or shame in connection with him now, it was only because they had been ashamed of him and embarrassed by him in the past. His poverty now appeared to them noble; his ambition to visit Israel exemplary; his attempts to realize that ambition inspiring; his defeat pitiable. . . . And three months after the burglary had taken place, the paper published a photograph showing Lipi being presented with a return air ticket to Israel and a check large enough to cover his expenses during the visit. The presentation was made by half a dozen leading members of the Jewish community, among them an ex-Mayor of Lyndhurst, the local rabbi, and the chairman of the Zionist society. Many Gentiles, including some of Lipi's neighbors, it was said, had contributed to the fund.

Lipi dreamed that he was in Palestine. It was a dream he very often had, and the landscape was familiar to him, though it was unlike any he had ever seen. In front of him, pale ploughed fields stretched away to a group of white houses with red-tiled roofs, in the distance; behind the houses were hills, vaguely outlined. Nothing grew from the fields, yet they were not barren; there was no sun in the sky, but the scene was evenly filled with light; no one stirred about the houses, yet Lipi knew that there were people living in them. As he had done a hundred times before, Lipi began walking towards the houses.

As always, Lipi awoke before he reached the houses. And immediately he was fully awake, in the darkness, confronting once again, with the poignance of the dream still upon him, the enormity of his lie, his crime, and its consequences. Lipi had not anticipated anything of what had happened since he had told the policeman, in a frenzy of rage and self-hatred, that the thieves had stolen from him savings he had never had. Lipi could not even remember telling the lie to the policeman; if it had not been for the report in the newspaper the next morning he would never have believed that he had in fact done so. . . . What a lifetime of work had failed to bring him a single lie had made possible; and Lipi lay in his bed and marveled at the world, and especially, of all the world, at the city of lyndhurst. With a satisfaction that was sweeter than any he had felt since he had been a young man lying beside his wife, Lipi knew that at last, at last, he would be able to settle the problem that had for so long been a dear, familiar, secret riddle to him: he would be able to see if Israel really looked as it did to him in his dreams.

But later that same night, Lipi woke again. His own beating heart had shaken him out of sleep; his body was filled with a dread that his mind was still ignorant of. Baffled by the warm, thick darkness around him, hardly knowing who or where he was, Lipi again remembered, as when he had woken earlier, the journey he was about to make. But this time the recollection came slowly, painfully, and seemed to carry the dread with it. Was he afraid of the burglars? Did he fear that the police might find them, or that they might come forward themselves, and expose his fraud? But that was an anxiety that had visited him before, and that had never had the power to make him lose his own sense of himself. It was another fear that possessed him now, and it was as formless, impenetrable, and insistent as the darkness around him. And even when he had recognized it, the dread remained formless to Lipi, and as compelling as before. He could not believe that the landscape of his dreams would accept him, if he came to it as a liar and a fraud. It would reject him—he did not know how—it would thrust him from itself, it would disgorge him as unclean, a tainted thing.

In the morning Lipi rose and went to see the ex-Mayor, who had formally handed to him his travel tickets and money, on behalf of the Lyndhurst Jewish community. . . . He received Lipi with the benevolence of a man who knows he has done well by his visitor; but his benevolence had altogether disappeared by the time Lipi had finished his confession. However, the ex-Mayor was a man of decision; and he said nothing to Lipi of his rage at the deception Lipi had practiced upon the people of Lyndhurst, or of his own personal indignation at having been shown up as a sentimental fool, or even of his anxieties about the possible effects of Lipi's confession on "interfaith relations" in Lyndhurst. Instead, he told Lipi, "Look, I want you to leave for Johannesburg at once, and wait for your plane there. You can go on the train tonight. And I don't want you to say a word of this to anyone else, do you hear? Not a word. As far as I'm concerned, this conversation never took place. I haven't heard you, and no one else ever will. Now go, go on, go on, I'll send my car around to pick you up tonight. Do you understand? Just go!" Only at the very end did the ex-Mayor add, with sudden ferocity, "And I wish you'd never come back!"

Bewildered, Lipi allowed himself to be hustled out of the office; he found himself on the placid sunlit pavement, his hat in his hand. Around him the people of Lyndhurst went about their business, and Lipi joined them, though he had no business to attend to. In his ears there was a voice that shrieked that everyone, everything in the world was tainted; that he had nothing to fear, for Israel was tainted too. All day he wandered about the town; he was seen standing outside the shops in the commercial district and walking down the middle of streets in residential areas far from his own; he was even seen in the African locations around the town, where people stared in amazement at the spectacle of a white man, alone and on foot, making his way between the mud and iron huts laid down in rows upon the veld. At nightfall Lipi found himself in the railway shunting yards; and there, too late, he was glimpsed by a horrified engine driver, in front of whose slowly moving locomotive Lipi threw down his body. What the engine driver most vividly remembered, what he always mentioned when he subsequently told his tale to others, was how Lipi had brought his hands to his ears at the very moment he fell.

At the inquest it was declared that Lipi had committed suicide while the balance of his mind was disturbed. The coroner added that the death was all the more tragic in view of the efforts that had recently been made to restore to the deceased his own hopes for himself and his faith in the good will of the people around him. Lipi's funeral was enormous; and it was noted that the ex-Mayor of the town was among those who seemed most affected by grief at the graveside.

Mordecai Richler

FROM SOLOMON GURSKY WAS HERE

Mordecai Richler's (b. 1931) bizarre and outrageous sense of humor are evident in this selection from his novel. In this scene, a young "Arctic" Hasid visits New York City for the first time, where his thoughts stray far from his religious studies.

One Saturday morning in 1974 a flock of the Faithful gathered at Henry's house to celebrate the bar mitzvah of the great-great-grandson of Tulugaq. Nialie, who had learned to use local produce to temper recipes plucked from her Jenny Grossinger cookbook, served chopped chicken liver moistened with seal shmaltz. Though most of the knishes were filled with mashed potatoes, there were others that were stuffed with minced caribou. In the absence of candy, a platter of succulent seal's eyes was available for the children. Among Isaac's gifts, there was a book from his father, a collection of sermons by the Rebbe who reigned over 770 Eastern Parkway, illuminating eternal mysteries, deciphering the code hidden within the holy texts:

"We can hasten the arrival of the Moshiach by intensifying our simcha, or rejoicing. Simcha is obviously connected with the Moshiach or why do both words contain the Hebrew letters 'Shin,' 'Mem,' and 'Ches'? Similarily there is an inner link between Moses and Moshiach, as witness the verse 'And the scepter shall not depart from Judah, nor a lawgiver from between his feet, until Shiloh come . . . ,' which is clearly a concealed reference to the Moshiach, as the words 'yavo Shiloh' and 'Moshiach' are numerically equal. Also equal are the words 'Shiloh' and 'Moses,' proof postive that the coming of the Moshiach is related to Moses. Furthermore, 'yavo' is numerically equal to 'echad,' which means one; therefore we can deduce that the Moshiach = Moses + One."

When Isaac enrolled in the yeshiva a month later, an elated Henry flew down to New York with him. Father and son made directly for Crown Heights. They stopped for a Lubavitch beefburger at Marmelstein's, on Kingston Avenue, and then went out for a stroll.

"We're being stared at," Isaac said.

"It's your imagination."

They paused to look in Suri's window, filled with glamorous wigs for the wives of the faithful who had shaven their heads to render themselves unattractive to men other than their husbands. Reflected in the glass, Isaac saw men across the street pointing him out, whispering together.

Sleek black hair. Brown skin. "They're going to take me for some kind of freak of nature here," Isaac said.

"*Narishkeit*. We're among good people," Henry said, taking him by the hand and leading him into the Tzivos Hashem store.

Garishly colored portraits of the Rebbe, similar to the pictures of saints peddled at the kiosks outside provincial cathedrals in Europe, were on display everywhere, framed in plastic pressed and burnished to resemble pine. The Rebbe's graven image was also available in postcard and wallet-window size or embossed on canvas tote bags. Isaac overheard a bearded man say, "Don't look now, but it's the rich *meshuggeneh* from the northland."

"What can I buy for you?" Henry asked.

"Nothing," Isaac said, glaring right back at a couple of pimply boys f his own age. "Let's go."

Next Henry took Isaac to the yeshiva to sit in on a study session with one of the Rebbe's younger acolytes, who was swaying over his text.

"We look into the mirror," he asked the men gathered at the long table, "and what do we see? The self, of course. You see yourself, I see myself, and so forth and so on. If we have a clean face, we see a clean face in the mirror. If we have a dirty face, that is what the mirror reflects back on us. So when we see bad in another person, we know that we too have this bad.

"Now, looking up into the mirror, we see the face, but looking down, what? The feet. You see your feet. I see my feet, and so forth and so on. The Rebbe has pointed out to us that on Simchas Torah one does not dance with his head—he dances with his feet. From this our beloved teacher has deduced that a person's intellectual capacities make no difference on Simchas Torah and this is equally true for every Jew worldwide.

"Looking into the mirror you should also note that the higher is contained in the lower and the lower in the higher. But the reverse is also true. Chassidus teaches us that the lower is revealed in the higher and the higher in the lower."

Isaac yawned. He yearned to see Broadway. The Felt Forum. A hockey game in Madison Square Garden. The offices where *Screw* was published. The McTavish building on Fifth Avenue.

Anne Roiphe
TAKING DOWN THE CHRISTMAS TREE

In this response to criticism of an earlier article she wrote, author Anne Roiphe (b. 1935) discusses how the controversy sparked investigation of her Jewishness and the issues surrounding assimilation.

In December of 1978, the *New York Times* asked me to write a small piece on a Christmas theme for the home section of the paper. I dashed off an essay on being Jewish and having a Christmas tree. The *Times* published it the Thursday before the holiday. I had thought this a small, unimportant piece, a kind of family musing that would melt in the mind of the reader like a snowflake on the tongue. I have made misjudgments in my life but none so consequential for me as this one.

The phones rang at the *New York Times*—it seemed as if all the officers of all the major Jewish organizations were complaining to their personal friends at the *Times* about my piece. Housewives, rabbis, lawyers, doctors, businessmen, all but Indian chiefs phoned or wrote in, furious that the paper had published an article that advocated assimilation, displayed ignorance of Judaism, and seemed to express contempt for the Jewish way of life. At our house the phone calls began on Thursday at noon and lasted for weeks. . . .

What I wrote in the *New York Times* was this: every Christmas, my family bought a Christmas tree—and it seemed as if every Christmas we ran into the rabbi who lived across the street just as we were bringing the tree into our house. I always felt uncomfortable, embarrassed, and I didn't quite understand why. True, my family was Jewish, and all of us identified as such. But we had made a decision not to celebrate Chanukah—because we were secular Jews, because Chanukah had always seemed to me to be a holiday about an unacceptable miracle. God, I said, should have prevented the war in the first place, saved the lives of those who died in battle on both sides, instead of merely allowing a small can of oil an extended life. After the Holocaust, the miracle of the can of oil seemed pretty weak. At this point in my article, I made an embarrassing mistake. I confused the Romans with the Syrians and revealed to the readers of the *New York Times* that I had learned about Chanukah so many years before and had become so indifferent that even my grasp of Jewish history had grown weak. I aptly, if unconsciously, demonstrated the point that ignorance about Judaism is the ice on the slippery slope to total assimilation. In my essay, I concluded by stating that we celebrated Christmas because it was a way to come together as a family, to pause in our daily efforts, to be with each other, and to give something to each other. In honor or what? In honor of the family, I supposed.

The intense response to the piece made me realize that I had inadvertently offended many people. Rabbis were using the piece as the subject of their sermons, treating me as if I were a female Arafat. Every day, rabbis, scholars, and friends invited me to explore Judaism and see what it was that I had missed.

I accepted those invitations. . . .

My studies made me realize that I had not freely chosen to be less Jewish and more American. I hadn't known that assimilation was something that was happening to me and my family. I hadn't known that a tide of history had borne my family from Central

Europe to the shores of the Lower East Side and up to the portals of the best colleges in the land. I had not understood the force of the dominant culture playing against my fragile identity, telling me that I would be more beautiful if I looked like a non-Jew, with straight blond hair and a short nose. I hadn't understood that, growing up in the forties, I had absorbed the anti-Semitism of the culture, and that's why I thought that people who spoke with accents were peculiar, that Jews were outsiders. I wanted to be inside with the others. And where were the others at Christmas? They were gathered around their Christmas tree.

Before I began to learn about Judaism, I didn't realize that assimilation had a dark side. I thought assimilation was a process as natural and inevitable as breathing. That's not quite true. I didn't think about it at all. I now realize that assimilation can produce an identity that is shallow, materialistic, unrooted, and anxious. Assimilation can deprive a person of the pleasure of belonging and the vitality that comes from real knowledge about and interest in that person's own community. To be American and nothing else is to be bland like a McDonald's hamburger, to be flat like the highways that cross Kansas, to be dull like our nightly TV programs. Americans can spout platitudes about the Constitution and brotherly love and the wonder of Paul Revere riding through the night, but the American identity, if it is not grafted onto something firm, turns to vapor, a substance that cannot sustain or nourish.

My studies of Judaism made me understand the conflicts my parents and I had faced. I realized that the concepts of Diaspora and melting pot are directly opposed and that my parents had chosen the melting pot for reasons that were legitimate enough for them.

When I was growing up, Christmas was the only holiday of the solstice that was important. My mother found it hard to resist the twinkling lights, the fir trees, the reindeer, and the presents that were all around her. At that time, no one celebrated Chanukah in a way that could compete with the apparent joyousness of Christmas. This was no small matter, because the power of Christmas—the carols, the Mass, and the commercial hoopla—was very great and made the American mainstream Christian world seem more appealing than the Jewish one. The choices individuals and families make about Christmas are significant statements about assimilation, about how these individuals and families will live as Jews in America and where they will stand on the tightrope between being Jewish and being American. When Jews resist Christmas, we affirm our own separate identity. When Jews resist Christmas, we reduce the hypocrisy in our lives and increase our personal security by deepening our roots within our own traditions. We claim our right to participate as equals and not just as a barely tolerated minority when we insist on *not* going along with the dominant culture.

★　　★　　★

I now see Chanukah not as a celebration of the miracle of the oil. (I still think that God must make a grander miracle to earn our amazement.) I see Chanukah as a time when, as we light the candles, we pause in awe before the Jewish people whose survival through adversity brings light into the darkness of the human soul. This view makes me Jewish in a different way from the way in which I was Jewish before. It makes me a part of the continuity while allowing me still to be myself, a modern American Jew filled with all the doubts and dark thoughts that are common to my times. Christmas is not the innocent matter that I had once thought.

THE HOLOCAUST

André Schwartz-Bart

FROM THE LAST OF THE JUST

"The Marriage of Ernie Levy"

André Schwartz-Bart (b. 1928) was the sole member of his family to survive the Holocaust. As a framework for this book, he uses the traditional mystical belief that the continuation of the world depends on the perpetual presence of thirty-six righteous individuals. In this selection, Schwartz-Bart offers a glimpse of two Jewish teenagers seeking a moment of freedom during the Nazi occupation of Paris.

The promenade took place on a Sunday in August. All their tattered outdoor clothing bore a star over the left breast. Golda proposed that they go out in shirtsleeves—without stars. The weather was fine, finer than it would ever be again in their lives. Ernie and Golda went down to the bank of the Seine, and in the shadows under the arch of a bridge doffed their compromising jackets, which Golda stuffed into a shopping basket, covering it with a newspaper. Holding hands, they strolled along the Seine as far as the Pont-Neuf, where in a delicious anguish they mounted the stone stairs to the surface of the Christian world.

In those days Ernie walked erectly, once again with the solemn stride of his childhood,

Jewish Star. Cotton. 3" (8 cm). Collection, Jewish Historical Museum, Amsterdam. *This yellow star was decreed to be worn in occupied Holland on April 29, 1942.*

CHARLOTTE SALOMON. From the series *"Life? or Theater."* c. 1939. Gouache 12¾ × 9¹³/₁₆" (32.5 × 25 cm). Collection, Jewish Historical Museum, Amsterdam. *As a Jewish refugee living in France, Salomon documented her life with over one thousand colorful gouache drawings. She and her husband were arrested in 1943 when Nazi troops occupied Southern France; they died at Auschwitz. The script on this picture reads, "Out with the Jews/Just confiscated a first-rate fountain pen at Cohn's."*

and his long black curls—carefully combed by Golda—fell over either side of his forehead, screening the scars. His white shirt bright under the sun, his thin body straight and slim with the sinewy grace of a young cedar, he looked like any young man who loved life; like a casual leash, his fingers restrained the childish frisking of a red-haired animal with an equal claim on life. Golda seemed to dance. She glowed with a peasant beauty, her hair braided in a wreath and still glossy from the waters of the Seine, a trace of lipstick she caressed now and then with an amazed finger, and a blouse out of dream—a brilliant white, dazzlingly starched, that two weeks before had promoted her to the rank of "young lady," and that she had insisted on ironing herself, delicately and lovingly, the iron heated by her own heart, according to M. Engelbaum.

In mingled agony and delight, not daring to look at each other, they strolled peacefully, knowing each other there, like two birds who fly in perfect formation by instinct. Forgetting his promise, Ernie occasionally swayed slightly toward Golda, who brought him to order with a slight squeeze of the hand. They reached the Place Saint-Michel and lingered in front of a movie. Golda broke the silence suddenly. "I've never been to a movie. Have you?"

"Neither have I," Ernie realized in surprise. "But as long as we don't have our stars," he whispered gently in Yiddish, "we can go on in for once. I can't even imagine what it's like. Look, I have four, five, seven francs left."

"It's much too expensive," Golda said. "And anyway I like it better outside, where life is."

She made a sweeping, possessive gesture. Ordering her to stay where she was, Ernie came back with two ice-cream cones. She chose the green one, and twisting her neck to avoid spotting her blouse, she bit into the ice cream and choked, strangled, spit up the delicious surprise. Then she followed Ernie's learned example, and as she ran her tongue around the cone he thought that she was savoring herself in the ice cream, as she seemed to in all things, in her slightest word or gesture, even in the greedy glances she trained on the nearby stalls of a street, on the festive Boulevard Saint-Michel and on Ernie—who felt that his whole body was living a dream and that there was no longer the slightest trace of self-hate within him.

The ice cream devoured, they followed the Boulevard Saint-Michel and arrived before the lion in the Place Denfert-Rochereau, as majestic and dominant as the Lion of Judah, guardian of the Ark of the Holy of Holies. Tempted then by the neighborhood charm of an alleyway, they emerged at the Avenue du Maine and saw an enchanting little plaza, a true oasis surrounded by sunstruck buildings that, with all their shutters closed, seemed to have fallen into a final sleep. They took their time choosing a bench. Golda set down her basket, and in the immemorial attitude of lovers in Paris they watched—without seeing them—the children, housemaids and old ladies who were also soaking in the happiness of the Square Mouton-Duvernet.

"Imagine," Ernie said, "thousands of people have sat here before us. It's funny to think about it. . . ."

"Listen," Golda said, "I existed before Adam was created. I've always been one of two colors. Thousands of years have gone by and I haven't changed at all. What am I?"

Ernie said, "My father had little anecdotes for every occasion. Yours has riddles."

"I'm Time," Golda said dreamily, "and my colors are Day and Night."

The same thought drew them together while Time hurtled by around them with cruel speed, branding their happiness with a star.

"I wonder why they forbid us the public squares," Golda whispered. "It's nature, after all. . . ."

A cloud of pink silk crossed the sky of Paris just above the tall building outlined behind the foliage, on the other side of an empty Avenue du Maine, and in his imagination Ernie followed it all the way to Poland, where, under the same evanescent August sky, the Jewish people lay dying.

"Oh, Ernie," Golda said, "you know them. Tell me why, *why* do the Christians hate us the way they do? They seem so nice when I can look at them without my star."

Ernie put his arm around her shoulders solemnly. "It's very mysterious," he murmured in Yiddish. "They don't know exactly why themselves. I've been in their churches and I've read their gospel. Do you know who the Christ was? A simple Jew like your father. A kind of Hasid."

Golda smiled gently. "You're kidding me."

"No, no, believe me, and I'll bet they'd have got along fine, the two of them, because he was really a good Jew, you know, sort of like the Baal Shem Tov—a merciful man, and gentle. The Christians say they love him, but I think they hate him without knowing it. So they take the cross by the other end and make a sword out of it and strike us with it! You understand, Golda," he cried suddenly, strangely excited, *"they take the cross and they turn it around, they turn it around, my God . . ."*

"Sh, quiet," Golda said. "They'll hear you." And stroking the scars on Ernie's forehead, as she often liked to do, she smiled. "And you promised you wouldn't 'think' all afternoon. . . ."

Ernie kissed the hand that had caressed his forehead and went on stubbornly, "Poor Jesus, if he came back to earth and saw that the pagans had made a sword out of him and used it against his sisters and brothers, he'd be sad, he'd grieve forever. And maybe he does see it. They say that some of the Just Men remain outside the gates of Paradise, that they don't want to forget humanity, that they too await the Messiah. Yes, maybe he sees it. Who knows? You understand, Goldeleh, he was a little old-fashioned Jew, a real Just Man, you now, no more nor less than . . . all our Just Men. And it's true, he and your father would have got along together. I can see them *so* well together, you know. 'Now,' your father would say, 'now my good rabbi, doesn't it break your heart to see all that?' And the other would tug at his beard and say, 'But you know very well, my good Samuel, that the Jewish heart must break a thousand times for the greater good of all peoples. *That* is why we were chosen, didn't you know?' And your father would say, 'Oi, oi, didn't I know? Didn't I know? Oh, excellent rabbi, that's all I *do* know, alas. . . .' "

They laughed. Golda took her harmonica from the bottom of the basket, flashed sunlight off it into Ernie's eyes, and still smiling brought it to her lips and played a forbidden melody. It was Hatikvah, the ancient chant of hope, and as she inspected the Square Mouton-Duvernet with uneasy eyes, she tasted the sweetness of forbidden fruit. Ernie leaned down and plucked a tuft of slightly mildewed grass and planted the blades in Golda's still moist hair. As they got up to leave he tried to strip her of that poor garland, but she stopped his hand. "Too bad about the people who see. And too bad about the Germans too. Today I say too bad about everybody. Everybody . . ." she repeated, unexpectedly solemn.

Anne Frank

FROM ANNE FRANK: THE DIARY OF A YOUNG GIRL

Anne Frank (1929–1945) was born in Frankfurt, but her family fled to Holland and settled in Amsterdam in 1933. On July 9th, 1942, the Frank family went into hiding in the attic of a house in Amsterdam where they were betrayed and discovered by the German police on August 4th, 1944. Anne Frank died in a concentration camp, but her diary has given the world an intimate view of one family's life during the Holocaust.

Friday, 9 October 1942

Dear Kitty,

I've only got dismal and depressing news for you today. Our many Jewish friends are being taken away by the dozen. These people are treated by the Gestapo without a shred of decency, being loaded into cattle trucks and sent to Westerbork, the big Jewish camp in Drente. Westerbork sounds terrible: only one washing cubicle for a hundred people and not nearly enough lavatories. There is no separate accommodation. Men, women, and children all sleep together. One hears of frightful immorality because of this; and a lot of the women, and even girls, who stay there any length of time are expecting babies.

It is impossible to escape; most of the people in the camp are branded as inmates by their shaven heads and many also by their Jewish appearance.

If it is as bad as this in Holland whatever will it be like in the distant and barbarous regions they are sent to? We assume that most of them are murdered. The English radio speaks of their being gassed.

Perhaps that is the quickest way to die. I feel terribly upset. I couldn't tear myself away while Miep told these dreadful stories; and she herself was equally wound up for that matter. Just recently for instance, a poor old crippled Jewess was sitting on her doorstep; she had been told to wait there by the Gestapo, who had gone to fetch a car to take her away. The poor old thing was terrified by the guns that were shooting at English planes overhead, and by the glaring beams of the searchlights. But Miep did not dare take her in; no one would undergo such a risk. The Germans strike without the slightest mercy. Elli too is very quiet: her boy friend has got to go to Germany. She is afraid that the airmen who fly over our homes will drop their bombs, often weighing a million kilos, on Dirk's head. Jokes such as "he's not likely to get a million" and "it only takes one bomb" are in rather bad taste. Dirk is certainly not the only one who has to go: trainloads of boys leave daily. If they stop at a small station en route, sometimes some of them manage to get out unnoticed and escape; perhaps a few manage it. This, however, is not the end of my bad news. Have you ever heard of hostages? That's the latest thing in penalties for sabotage. Can you imagine anything so dreadful?

Prominent citizens—innocent people—are thrown into prison to await their fate. If the saboteur can't be traced, the Gestapo simply put about five hostages against the wall. Announcements of their deaths appear in the papers frequently. These outrages are described as "fatal accidents." Nice people, the Germans! To think that I was once one of them too! No, Hitler took away our nationality long ago. In fact, Germans and Jews are the greatest enemies in the world.

Yours, Anne

Children at Terezin
TWO POEMS

The Czechoslovakian town of Theresienstadt (Terezin) was operated by the German SS as a "model settlement," to camouflage the Nazi plan to exterminate the Jewish population. At first the internees of Theresienstadt believed that they would survive the ghetto, but early in 1942 deportations to the death camps began. By October 1942 all the transports from Theresienstadt were sent to the Auschwitz extermination camp.

HOMESICK

I've lived in the ghetto here more than a year,
In Terezin, in the black town now,
And when I remember my old home so dear,
I can love it more than I did, somehow.

Ah, home, home,
Why did they tear me away?
Here the weak die easy as a feather
And when they die, they die forever.

I'd like to go back home again,
It makes me think of sweet spring flowers.
Before, when I used to live at home,
It never seemed so dear and fair.

I remember now those golden days . . .
But maybe I'll be going there soon again.

People walk along the street,
You see at once on each you meet
That there's a ghetto here,
A place of evil and of fear.
There's little to eat and much to want,
Where bit by bit, it's horror to live.
But no one must give up!
The world turns and times change.

Yet we all hope the time will come
When we'll go home again.
Now I know how dear it is
And often I remember it.

                                        Anonymous
                                        1943

TEREZIN

The heaviest wheel rolls across our foreheads
To bury itself deep somewhere inside our memories.

We've suffered here more than enough,
Here in this clot of grief and shame,
Wanting a badge of blindness
To be a proof for their own children.

A fourth year of waiting, like standing above a swamp
From which any moment might gush forth a spring.

Meanwhile, the rivers flow another way,
Another way,
Not letting you die, not letting you live.

And the cannons don't scream and the guns don't bark
And you don't see blood here.

Nothing, only silent hunger.
Children steal the bread here and ask and ask and ask
And all would wish to sleep, keep silent and just to go to sleep again. . . .

The heaviest wheel rolls across our foreheads
To bury itself deep somewhere inside our memories.

                                        Mif
                                        1944

Elie Wiesel
FROM NIGHT

*Until he was a teenager, Elie Wiesel (b. 1928) lived in an orthodox and hasidic Jewish community
in his native Rumania. In 1944 the Nazis deported him along with the entire community. He spent*

COLORPLATE 120
YOSSEF ZARITSKY. *Safed.* 1924. Watercolor over black chalk. 25¼ × 24⁷⁄₁₆″ (63 × 61 cm). Collection, Israel Museum, Jerusalem.

COLORPLATE 121
THERESA BERNSTEIN, *Zionist Meeting, New York*. 1923. Oil on canvas. 34¼ × 44½" (87 × 113 cm).
Courtesy of the Jewish National Fund, New York.

COLORPLATE 122 *(opposite)*
MAX WEBER. *The Talmudists*. 1934. Oil on canvas. 50 × 33¾" (127 × 85.7 cm). The Jewish
Museum, New York. Gift of Mrs. Nathan Miller. *The American modernist Max Weber turned to
religious subjects in his art. This painting of Talmudic scholars conveys the scholars' involvement with the
texts and captures their lively gesturing as they debate and discuss the content.*

COLORPLATE 123

DAVID BOMBERG. *Ghetto Theatre*. 1920. Oil on canvas. 30 × 25″ (75 × 62.5 cm). Ben Uri Art Society, London. *The theater depicted here is probably based on the Pavilion Theatre at Whitechapel, where classic plays by writers such as Shakespeare and Chekhov were performed in Yiddish. Just as New York's Jewish immigrants did on the Lower East Side, London's Jewish immigrants thrived on the lively entertainment of the Yiddish theater.*

COLORPLATE 124

RAPHAEL SOYER. *Dancing Lesson.* 1926. Oil on canvas. 24 × 20″ (60.9 × 50 cm). Collection of Renee and Chaim Gross. *In this canvas, Soyer captures a family scene in their Bronx apartment. The artist's sister Debbie is teaching his twin brother Moses how to dance, while his younger brother plays the harmonica and the rest of the family looks on. The details in the canvas—the flowered rug, Yiddish newspaper, family portrait on the wall, and rubber plant—evoke the interior of a typical Jewish middle-class New York apartment of the period.*

COLORPLATE 125
Ezekiel David Kirszenbaum. *Jewish Villagers Greeting the Messiah*. 1937. Oil on cardboard.
23¼ × 27³⁄₁₆" (59 × 69 cm). Collection, Israel Museum, Jerusalem. *In this folk-inspired painting, the Messiah is pictured as a Hasid, seated on a white donkey to signify his role of authority. The lively atmosphere and bright colors infuse the painting with a festive atmosphere.*

COLORPLATE 126

RAPHAEL SOYER. *In a Jewish Cafe.* 1925. Watercolor and pencil on paper. 21¾ × 19⅜″
(55.3 × 49.1 cm). Hirshhorn Museum and Sculpture Garden, Smithsonian Institution, Washington,
D. C. Gift of Joseph H. Hirshhorn, 1966 (Acc. 66.4717).

COLORPLATE 127

ISRAEL LITWAK. *Family Gathering.* 1940. Crayon and pencil on board. 19¾ × 29¾″ (50.2 × 75.5 cm). The Jewish Museum, New York. Gift of Dr. Joseph Tucker.

time in the Auschwitz, Birkenau, Buchenwald, and Buna concentration camps. Wiesel survived the Nazi atrocities, but they continue to haunt his writings. Night, *his first novel, is autobiographical, recounting his experiences in the camps. In 1986 Wiesel won the Nobel Peace Prize in recognition of his writings against oppression and violence.*

Pressed up against the others in an effort to keep out the cold, head empty and heavy at the same time, brain a whirlpool of decaying memories. Indifference deadened the spirit. Here or elsewhere—what difference did it make? To die today or tomorrow, or later? The night was long and never ending.

When at last a gray glimmer of light appeared on the horizon, it revealed a tangle of human shapes, heads sunk upon shoulders, crouched, piled one on top of the other, like a field of dust-covered tombstones in the first light of the dawn. I tried to distinguish those who were still alive from those who had gone. But there was no difference. My gaze was held for a long time by one who lay with his eyes open, staring into the void. His livid face was covered with a layer of frost and snow.

My father was huddled near me, wrapped in his blanket, his shoulders covered with snow. And was he dead, too? I called him. No answer. I would have cried out if I could have done so. He did not move.

My mind was invaded suddenly by this realization—there was no more reason to live, no more reason to struggle.

The train stopped in the middle of a deserted field. The suddenness of the halt woke some of those who were asleep. They straightened themselves up, throwing startled looks around them.

Outside, the SS went by, shouting:

"Throw out all the dead! All corpses outside!"

The living rejoiced. There would be more room. Volunteers set to work. They felt those who were still crouching.

"Here's one! Take him!"

They undressed him, the survivors avidly sharing out his clothes, then two "grave diggers" took him, one by the head and one by the feet, and threw him out of the wagon like a sack of flour.

From all directions came cries:

"Come on! Here's one! This man next to me. He doesn't move."

Polish Jews. Warsaw, March, 1940. Photograph. *Flanked by Gestapo agents, this group is shown marching to the concentration camp.*

I woke from my apathy just at the moment when two men came up to my father. I threw myself on top of his body. He was cold. I slapped him. I rubbed his hands, crying:

"Father! Father! Wake up. They're trying to throw you out of the carriage. . . ."

His body remained inert.

The two gravediggers seized me by the collar.

"Leave him. You can see perfectly well that he's dead."

"No!" I cried. "He isn't dead! Not yet!"

I set to work to slap him as hard as I could. After a moment my father's eyelids moved slightly over his glazed eyes. He was breathing weakly.

"You see," I cried.

The two men moved away.

Twenty bodies were thrown out of our wagon. Then the train resumed its journey, leaving behind it a few hundred naked dead, deprived of burial, in the deep snow of a field in Poland.

We were given no food. We lived on snow; it took the place of bread. The days were like nights, and the nights left the dregs of their darkness in our souls. The train was traveling slowly, often stopping for several hours and then setting off again. It never ceased snowing. All through these days and nights we stayed crouching, one on top of the other, never speaking a word. We were no more than frozen bodies. Our eyes closed, we waited merely for the next stop, so that we could unload our dead.

Ten days, ten nights of traveling. Sometimes we would pass through German townships. Very early in the morning, usually. The workmen were going to work. They stopped and stared after us, but otherwise showed no surprise.

One day when we had stopped, a workman took a piece of bread out of his bag and threw it into a wagon. There was a stampede. Dozens of starving men fought each other to the death for a few crumbs. The German workmen took a lively interest in this spectacle.

Some years later, I watched the same kind of scene at Aden. The passengers on our boat were amusing themselves by throwing coins to the "natives," who were diving in to get them. An attractive, aristocratic Parisienne was deriving special pleasure from the game. I suddenly noticed that two children were engaged in a death sturggle, trying to strangle each other. I turned to the lady.

"Please," I begged, "don't throw any more money in!"

"Why not?" she said. "I like to give charity. . . ."

In the wagon where the bread had fallen, a real battle had broken out. Men threw themselves on top of each other, stamping on each other, tearing at each other, biting each other. Wild beasts of prey, with animal hatred in their eyes; an extraordinary vitality had seized them, sharpening their teeth and nails.

A crowd of workmen and curious spectators had collected along the train. They had probably never seen a train with such a cargo. Soon, nearly everywhere, pieces of bread were being dropped into the wagons. The audience stared at these skeletons of men, fighting one another to the death for a mouthful.

A piece fell into our wagon. I decided that I would not move. Anyway, I knew that I would never have the strength to fight with a dozen savage men! Not far away I noticed an old man dragging himself along on all fours. He was trying to disengage himself from the struggle. He held one hand to his heart. I thought at first he had received a blow in the chest. Then I understood; he had a bit of bread under his shirt. With remarkable speed he drew it out and put it to his mouth. His eyes gleamed; a smile, like a grimace, lit up his dead face. And was immediately extinguished. A shadow had just loomed up near him. The shadow threw itself upon him. Felled to the ground, stunned with blows, the old man cried:

"Meir. Meir, my boy! Don't you recognize me? I'm your father . . . you're hurting me . . . you're killing your father! I've got some bread . . . for you too . . . for you too. . . ."

He collapsed. His fist was still clenched around a small piece. He tried to carry it to his mouth. But the other one threw himself upon him and snatched it. The old man again whispered something, let out a rattle, and died amid the general indifference. His son searched him, took the bread, and began to devour it. He was not able to get very far. Two men had seen and hurled themselves upon him. Others joined in. When they withdrew, next to me were two corpses, side by side, the father and the son.

I was fifteen years old.

In our wagon, there was a friend of my father's called Meir Katz. He had worked as a gardener at Buna and used to bring us a few green vegetables occasionally. Being less undernourished than the rest of us, he had stood up to imprisonment better. Because he was relatively more vigorous, he had been put in charge of the wagon.

On the third night of our journey I woke up suddenly and felt two hands on my throat, trying to strangle me. I just had the time to shout, "Father!"

Nothing but this word. I felt myself suffocating. But my father had woken up and seized my attacker. Too weak to overcome him, he had the idea of calling Meir Katz.

"Come here! Come quickly! There's someone strangling my son."

A few moments later I was free. I still do not know why the man wanted to strangle me.

After a few days, Meir Katz spoke to my father:

"Chlomo, I'm getting weak. I'm losing my strength. I can't hold on. . . ."

"Don't let yourself go under," my father said, trying to encourage him. "You must resist. Don't lose faith in yourself."

But Meir Katz groaned heavily in reply.

"I can't go on any longer, Chlomo! What can I do? I can't carry on. . . ."

My father took his arm. And Meir Katz, the strong man, the most robust of us all, wept. His son had been taken from him at the time of the first selection, but it was now that he wept. It was now that he cracked up. He was finished, at the end of his tether.

On the last day of our journey a terrible wind arose; it snowed without ceasing. We felt that the end was near—the real end. We could never hold out in this icy wind, in these gusts.

Someone got up and shouted:

"We mustn't stay sitting down at a time like this. We shall freeze to death! Let's all get up and move a bit. . . ."

We all got up. We held our damp blankets more tightly around us. And we forced ourselves to move a few steps, to turn around where we were.

Suddenly a cry rose up from the wagon, the cry of a wounded animal. Someone had just died.

Others, feeling that they too were bout to die, imitated his cry. And their cries seemed to come from beyond the grave. Soon everyone was crying out. Wailing, groaning, cries of distress hurled into the wind and the snow.

The contagion spread to the other carriages. Hundreds of cries rose up simultaneously. Not knowing against whom we cried. Not knowing why. The death rattle of a whole convoy who felt the end upon them. We were all going to die here. All limits had been passed. No one had any strength left. And again the night would be long.

Meir Katz groaned:

"Why don't they shoot us all right away?"

That same evening, we reached our destination.

It was late at night. The guards came to unload us. The dead were abandoned in the train. Only those who could still stand were able to get out.

Meir Katz stayed in the train. The last day had been the most murderous. A hundred of us had got into the wagon. A dozen of us got out—among them, my father and I.

We had arrived at Buchenwald.

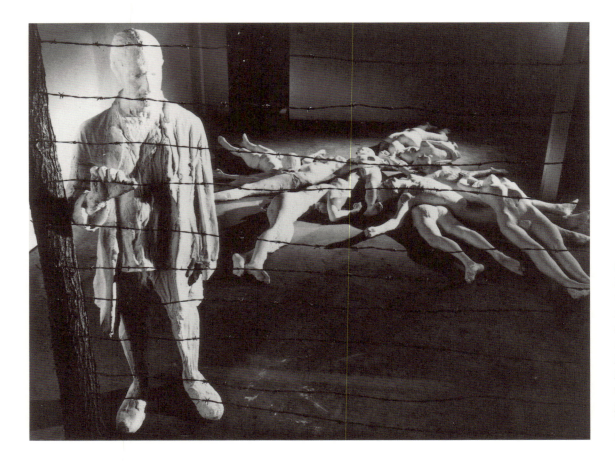

George Segal. *The Holocaust*. Plaster, wood, and wire. 10 × 20 × 20′ (304.8 × 609.6 × 609.6 cm). 1982. The Jewish Museum, New York. Museum purchase through an anonymous gift. © George Segal/ VAGA, New York, 1992.

Primo Levi

THE COMMANDER OF AUSCHWITZ

Primo Levi (1919–1987) became a writer only after the Holocaust. A trained chemist, he was considered an "economically useful Jew" and survived Auschwitz by working in the laboratory of a rubber factory. After he was liberated, Levi returned to his native Italy and began writing to bear witness to the horrors that he had survived.

Richard Baer, the SS major of whose arrest we have just heard, was the successor to Rudolf Höss in the position of commander of the Auschwitz concentration camp. I was his subject for almost a year, one of his hundred thousand slaves; together with another ten thousand I was in fact "rented out" by him to the I.G. Farbenindustrie, the mastodontic German chemical trust, which for each of us paid four to eight marks a day as salary for our work. Paid, but not to us: just as you don't pay a horse or an ox, so this money was handed to our masters, that is, to the SS ruling the camp.

I belonged to him, therefore: yet I would not even recognize his face. Unless it might coincide with that of the frowning, corpulent individual, his abdomen bristling with decorations, who every morning and every evening was in the habit of attending the interminable march of our squads in step with band music on the way to and from work. But they were all identical, those faces, those voices, those attitudes: all of them distorted by the same hate and the same anger, and by the lust of omnipotence. So their hierarchy was obscure to us—SS, Gestapo, Labor Services, Party, Factory, the whole enormous machine stood above us, and appeared to us flattened, without perspective: an imperium of night and fog whose structure we did not know.

Until today not much was known about Richard Baer. He is briefly mentioned in the memoirs of Höss, his predecessor, who described him in the terrifying weeks of Janaury 1945 as perplexed and uncertain as to what he should do: he is at Gross-Rosen, a *Lager* of ten to twelve thousand prisoners, and he is diligently concentrating on transferring there the forty thousand from Auschwitz, whom it is necessary to "salvage" in the face of the sudden Russian advance. Just think of what the relationship between these two figures signifies: just think about that other solution, which common sense and humanity and prudence all together suggested—that is, accepting the inevitable, leaving the throngs of half-dead to their destiny, opening the doors, and departing. Think about all this, and the sort of man we are dealing with will appear before us reasonably well defined.

He belongs to the century's most dangerous human type. If you look carefully, without him, without the Hösses, the Eichmanns, the Kesselrings, without thousands of other faithful and blind executors of orders, the great savage beasts, Hitler, Himmler, and Goebbels, would have been impotent and disarmed. Their names would not appear in history: they would have passed like grim meteors through Europe's dark sky. But the opposite happened: the seed sown by these black apostles, as history has shown, struck root in Germany with disconcerting speed and depth in all social classes and led to a proliferation of hatred that to his day poisons Europe and the world.

Resistance was timid and rare, and was immediately overwhelmed: the National Socialist message found an echo precisely in the Germans' traditional virtues, in their sense of discipline and national cohesion, their unquenched thirst for primacy, their propensity for slavish obedience.

This is why men like Baer are dangerous: men who are too loyal, too faithful, too docile. It must be taken as either heresy or sacrilege: in the spirit of the whole, upright man whom modern morality should point to as an example, there will always, despite everything, be a place for love of country and intelligent conscious obedience.

A question arises spontaneously: what should one say of the German people of today? How should one judge them? What should one expect from them?

It is difficult to auscultate the heartbeat of a people. Anyone who travels in Germany today finds the outward appearances that I found everywhere. A growing affluence, peaceful people, large and small intrigues, a moderate subversive atmosphere; on the stands, newspapers like ours, conversations like ours on trains and in trams; a few scandals that end like all scandals. And yet in the air you sense something that you do not sense elsewhere. Anyone who takes them to task for the dreadful events of recent history rarely finds repentance, or even critical consciousness: much more often he encounters an ambiguous response, in which are intertwined a feeling of guilt, a desire for vindication, and a deliberate and impudent ignorance.

Therefore, the so strangely slow and tortuous behavior of the German police and magistrature should not astonish. The picture is confused and rich in contradictions, but a substantially defined line of conduct seems to emerge from it: for its past actions, the slaughters and sufferings inflicted on Europe, Germany intends, so to speak, to be responsible civilly, not penally. It is known that the German government has publically shown itself ready to grant monetary indemnification to the victims of Nazism in all the countries previously occupied (but not in Italy), and the same has been done or is being done by a number of German industries that exploited slave labor during the war. But police and magistrature have proven much less ready to complete the purges initiated by the Allies: so we have reached today's disconcerting situation, in which it can happen that a commander of Auschwitz lives and works undisturbed in Germany for fifteen years, and that the executioner of millions of innocents is tracked down, not indeed by the German police but "illegally" by victims who slipped through his hands.

Leslie Epstein

FROM KING OF THE JEWS

King of the Jews, *by Leslie Epstein (b. 1938), is based upon the experience of the Jews of the Polish ghetto of Lodz during World War II. In this scene, Krystal is modeled upon the real-life photographer Mendel Grossman, whose photographs survived to document the atrocities of the Lodz ghetto.*

From the Astoria Café to the Orphanage Number 2 was not a long walk. For Trumpelman, however, there was a detour, since the old Council of Elders, arranged neatly head to toe, lay in what was the most direct path. When he saw this, the Lithuanian turned left instead of right. It is not difficult to imagine what his thoughts must have been, as he and Lipiczany walked through the windy street. Of course it was he, Trumpelman, who should have been lying there, with Blum's feet on his forehead and his own feet on Zweideneck's nose. It was as if God had put down His hand and, groping about on the darkened earth, specifically had forbidden this to happen. Perhaps that is why Trumpelman stopped and looked up at the nighttime sky. It was covered with stars, like a wizard's cloak.

At that instant, while they were standing there, an awful thing took place. Nisel was aware of it first. He pulled the Elder's arm and pointed to where a figure, half-naked and missing an ear, was running toward them out of an alley. This bleeding person threw his bare arms around Trumpelman's shoulders. It was Nomberg, the Italianate Synagogue rabbi.

"They missed! They shot at me but they missed! I fell down and when they weren't looking I ran away! I'm not a ghost! I'm alive!" The wounded man took Trumpelman's hand and kissed it. Tears dropped from his eyes. "I know why you were saved! You will be the new Moses! You will lead us out of the land of suffering. Happy am I! To have kissed the savior's hand!" Smiling, nodding, also weeping, Nomberg ran off, along a perpendicular side street.

The man and the boy—what choice had they?—continued. By the time they reached Krzyzanowsky, Nisel, from the danger, the excitement, was wheezing and gulping. He pushed the air like a pudding into his throat. Trumpelman grasped him under his arms, around his chest. He carried the boy into the Hatters' Asylum and up the dark stairs. What strength the Elder had! What power! For a man aged three score and ten!

Upstairs, at the center of the hallway, a light was on. At once Trumpelman put Nisel down. The light went out. Then, a moment later, weakly, without many watts, it shone again. The Director moved carefully forward. The beams were coming through the half-open door of a closet for brooms. Inside were Mann Lifshits and Krystal, each in his long sleeping gown. Lifshits had a stopwatch on one hand and the light cord in the other. Myer Krystal was holding a pane of glass, with paper stuck to it, right up to the unshaded bulb.

"Time," whispered Lifshits, the left-hander, pulling the cord.

In the blackness the boys fumbled their way to the deep double sink, which was supposed to be used for wringing out mops. The water ran there. For a time you could hear it swishing around. Then the boys groped through the darkness again.

"Ready?" asked Krystal.

"Ready," said Lifshits, and the yellow light, with a wire in it, started to glow.

Trumpelman ripped the door fully open. "What is this?" he demanded. His voice rang through the whole Asylum. "Sabotage? Saboteurs?"

The Lublin Ghetto.
Poland, early 20th
century. Photograph.

The boys stood petrified, wide-eyed, and silent. But Trumpelman did not give them a slap. And he no longer shouted. Instead he stared in amazement at the ceiling of the little room. There, with clothespins, on clotheslines, hung pieces of paper. These were snapshots, dozens and dozens of them, glossy, dripping, wet. The Director of the Asylum, with his neck craned, walked underneath. Here, a Jew in a top hat, wearing striped pants. There, the white horses. Photo after photo of the slick-haired, thin-faced, eagle-nosed man. Totenkopfers, with the skulls on their caps. Jews upside down. Jews, all blurry, running. Fiebig, in a fur coat, holding a match. A complete record, in short, of the events at the Central Square.

The orphans looked at Trumpelman. He stared back at the boys. At last he asked them, "Where did you get such a camera?"

Lifshits hopped to the corner and picked up an overturned pail. There was a black American Kodak, with a leather strap. Trumpelman took it, pushed at the bellows, and then pulled back his lips in a grin.

"Ha! Ha! It's Faulhaber's! From three years ago!"

It was indeed the American's camera, dropped by him on his visit to the Orphanage Number 2. Quick-witted Krystal had scooped it up and hidden it inside his bed.

"Ha! Ha! Ha!" It wasn't just Trumpelman, not just the boys, who laughed at this joke. Ten or twelve orphans were standing in the doorway, too.

"Hee, hee," they giggled. They put their hands over their mouths.

Trumpelman grew suddenly grim. "This is an illegal act! It could mean death and torture! You will be shot!"

Boldly, Krystal stepped forward. He took the camera from the Elder's hands. "No! We have to remember!"

Lifshits was holding the reflector for the photoflash. He cried out, "So people will know!"

Then, before the old man could touch it, the camera, with its metallic lamp, went off. The light in the room was blinding. It seemed to collect, to burn, in the strands of Trumpelman's hair. It was precisely this picture, with the face of the Elder part way to the side, his hair making a halo and with a star on his coat, that later appeared throughout the Baluty Suburb—in miniature on all of the Ghetto stamps, and blown up larger than life size on hundreds of buildings and hundreds of walls.

The flash lamp exploded again. The orphans who had gathered in the doorway—Gutta Blit, Rose Atlas, Szypper, Kipnis, young Flicker—took each other's hands or clutched their friends' nightgowns. Together they watched Trumpelman shining, melting, in the rainbows and spangles of light. Nisel Lipiczany shielded his eyes.

"Oh!" he cried. "He is the King of the Jews!"

Simon Wiesenthal

FROM THE MURDERERS AMONG US
"Two Candles"

Simon Wisenthal (b. 1908) was liberated from the Mauthausen concentration camp in May of 1945, and since that time he has devoted himself to the relentless pursuit of Nazi criminals. The two most infamous fugitives captured as a result of Wiesenthal's efforts were Adolf Eichmann and the Nazi official who deported the young Anne Frank to a concentration camp.

When I was a young student, I often spent a few weeks in the Polish mountain resort of Zakopane in the Carpathians. In summertime there were the woods, sunshine, peace. In winter there was good skiing. Today, Zakopane is again a popular place for skiers. Not far away is the small town of Rabka. And there once lived a little Jewish boy named Sammy Rosenbaum. I first heard of Sammy Rosenbaum one morning in September 1965, when a Mrs. Rawicz from Rabka came into my office in Vienna. I was looking for witnesses who might testify at a trial that was to be held in Germany in connection with Nazi crimes at Rabka.

Mrs. Rawicz had known Sammy Rosenbaum well. He had been "a frail boy, with a pale, thin face and big, dark eyes, who looked much older than his age—as so many children do who learned too early about life and never laughed much." Sammy was nine years old in 1939, when the Germans came to Rabka in the early days of the Polish campaign, and life became a nightmare for the Jews there. Until then life had been fairly normal—if it ever could be called normal for a poor Jew in Poland. Sammy's father was a tailor who worked long hours and made little money. People like the Rosenbaums were fair game for the authorities, and in Poland the hunting season lasted twelve months a year.

The family lived in two musty rooms and a tiny kitchen in an old, dark house. But they were happy, and very religious. Sammy learned to say his prayers. Every Friday night he would go with his father to the synagogue, after lighting the candles at home. Mother and Sammy's sister Paula, three years his senior, stayed at home and prepared dinner.

That sort of life became only a memory after the Germans occupied Poland. In 1940, the SS set up what it called a "police school" in former Polish Army barracks in the woods that surrounded Rabka. It was not an ordinary school; it was a training center for future cadres of SS killers. This was the early phase of extermination. Executions were carried out by platoons of SS men who shot their victims. Sometimes they had to shoot fifty, a hundred, perhaps a hundred fifty people a day. SS men at Rabka were being hardened so they would not break after a few weeks of duty. They had to become insensitive to the sight of blood, to the agonized shouts of women and children. The job must be done with a minimum of fuss and a maximum of efficiency. That was a *Führerbefehl*—the Führer's order.

SS *Untersturmführer* Wilhelm Rosenbaum from Hamburg was made school commander. Rosenbaum was a true SS type: cynical, brutal, convinced of his mission. He would walk around town with a riding crop. "When we saw him in the street we got so frightened that we would hide in the nearest house entrance," the woman from Rabka remembered. Early in 1942, SS man Rosenbaum ordered all Jews in Rabka to appear at the local school to "register." The Jews knew what that meant. The sick and the elderly would soon be sent away. Others would have to work for the SS, the *Wehrmacht,* wherever they were sent.

Toward the end of the registration, SS *Führer* Rosenbaum appeared in the schoolroom, accompanied by his two deputies, Hermann Oder and Walter Proch. (Both were among my first postwar "clients." I found Proch in 1947 in Blomberg-Mondsee, a village near Salzburg. He was sentenced to six years in prison. Oder, also an Austrian, was arrested in Linz in the big villa he had "requisitioned" from the former Jewish owner. He was later released by the Americans and is now a prosperous businessman in Linz. SS *Führer* Rosenbaum disappeared after the war but remained near the top of my private "Wanted" list.)

In the schoolroom in Rabka, SS *Führer* Rosenbaum looked through the list of names. "Suddenly he beat his riding crop hard on the table," the woman from Rabka told me. "Each of us winced as though we had been whipped. SS man Rosenbaum shouted: "What's that? Rosenbaum? Jews! How dare these *verdammte Juden* have my good German name? Well, I'm going to take care of it!' " Perhaps SS *Führer* Rosenbaum would be surprised to discover that his good German name is generally considered a Jewish one, though there are, of course, people called Rosenbaum who are not Jewish.

He threw the list back on the table and strode out. From that day on everybody in Rabka knew that the Rosenbaums would be killed; it was only a question of time. People in other places were known to have been arrested and executed because their name was Rosenberg, or because they were Jews and their first name happened to be Adolf or Hermann.

By that time, frightening rumors were being whispered in Rabka about the police school. Practice executions were said to be taking place in a clearing in the woods. Examinations were held, with the SS students shooting people while with clinical detachment SS *Führer* Rosenbaum and his deputies observed the students' reactions. The living targets for these examinations were Jews and Poles who had been rounded up by the Gestapo. If a student flenched, he would be taken out of the execution squad and sent to a front-line outfit.

Mrs. Rawicz knew what she was talking about. After the registration she'd been sent to the police school as a charwoman. "When the SS men came back from the clearing in the woods I had to clean their boots, which were always covered with blood."

It was a Friday morning in June 1942. The eye witnesses, two of whom now live in Israel, cannot remember the exact date, but they know it was a Friday. One of the witnesses had been working in the house across from the playground behind the school. He saw what happened. Two SS men escorted "the Jew Rosenbaum," his wife, and their fifteen-year-old daughter Paula. Behind them came SS *Führer* Rosenbaum.

"The woman and the girl were marched around the corner of the schoolhouse and then I heard some shots," the witness has said under oath. "I saw how SS man Rosenbaum began to beat our Rosenbaum with his riding crop. He shouted: 'You dirty Jew, I'll teach you a lesson for having my German name!' Then the SS man took his revolver and shot Rosenbaum the tailor. He shot him twice or three times. I couldn't count the shots; I was too horrified."

Earlier, the SS men had come for the Rosenbaums in a small truck. Rosenbaum, his wife, and their daughter were around the table in the front room having breakfast. Sammy was already at a large stone quarry in nearby Zakryty, where he'd been sent as a forced

Dachau Survivors Cheer American Liberators, May 1945. Photograph.

laborer after his twelfth birthday. All Jewish men had to work, and Sammy was now classified as a man. But he was weak and undernourished and couldn't do much except sort out the stones and put the smaller ones on a truck.

The SS sent an unarmed Jewish policeman to the quarry for Sammy. They often sent Jewish policemen to arrest other Jews when they were too busy with their curriculum at the police school. The Jewish policeman later told the Jewish charwoman at the school exactly what happened. He'd gone out to Zakryty in a small horsedrawn cart. He'd stopped the horse and waved at Sammy Rosenbaum. Everybody in the quarry stopped working and stared—the Jewish laborers and the two SS men who guarded them. Sammy put the big stone he held in his hands on the truck, and walked toward the cart. Sammy knew what was going to happen.

Sammy looked at the Jewish policeman. "Where are they?" he asked—"Father, Mother, and Paula. Where?"

The policeman just shook his head.

Sammy understood. "They're dead." His voice was low. "I've known for a long time that it was going to happen. Because our name is Rosenbaum."

The policeman swallowed, but Sammy didn't seem to notice.

"And now you've come for me." He spoke matter-of-factly. There was no emotion in his voice. He stepped up and sat down on the seat next to the Jewish policeman.

The policeman was unable to say a word. He had expected the boy to cry, perhaps to run away. All the while he was riding out to Zakryty the policeman had wondered how he could warn the boy, make him disappear in the woods, where the Polish underground might later help him. Now it was too late. The two SS guards were watching with guns in their hands.

The policeman told Sammy what had happened that morning. Sammy asked if they could stop for a moment at his house. When they got there, he stepped down and walked into the front room, leaving the door open. He looked over the table with the half-filled teacups left from breakfast. He looked at the clock. It was half past three. Father, Mother, and Paula were already buried, and no one had lit a candle for them. Slowly, methodically, Sammy cleaned off the table and put the candlesticks on it.

"I could see Sammy from the outside," the Jewish policeman later told Mrs. Rawicz. "He put on his skullcap, and started to light the candles. Two for his father, two for his

330

mother, two for his sister. And he prayed. I saw his lips moving. He said *Kaddish* for them."

Kaddish is the prayer for the dead. Father Rosenbaum had always said *Kaddish* for his dead parents, and Sammy had learned the prayer from his father. Now he was the only man left in his family. He stood quietly, looking at the six candles. The Jewish policeman outside saw Sammy slowly shaking his head, as though he'd suddenly remembered something. Then Sammy placed two more candles on the table, took a match and lit them, and prayed.

"The boy knew that he was already dead," the policeman said later. "He lit the candles and said *Kaddish* for himself."

Then Sammy came out, leaving the door open, and quietly sat down on the cart next to the policeman, who was crying. The boy didn't cry. The policeman wiped away the tears with the back of his hand and pulled the reins. But the tears kept coming. The boy didn't say a word. Gently he touched the older man's arm, as if he wanted to comfort him—to forgive him for taking him away. Then they rode out to the clearing in the woods. SS *Führer* Rosenbaum and his "students" were waiting for the little boy.

"About time!" said the SS man.

I told Mrs. Rawicz from Rabka that I had known about the SS police school since 1946. Several years earlier I had given the authorities in Hamburg all the facts and testimony in the case against SS man Wilhelm Rosenbaum. Now there would be testimony for an additional case.

"Where is SS man Rosenbaum now?" she asked.

"Wilhelm Rosenbaum was arrested in 1964 and is now in a prison in Hamburg awaiting trial."

She gave a sigh. "What's the use? They are all dead. And the murderer is alive." She signed the affidavit. "It makes no sense."

No tombstone bears Sammy Rosenbaum's name. No one might have remembered him if the woman from Rabka had not come into my office. But every year, one day in June, I light two candles for him and say *Kaddish*.

THE NEW NATION

Theodor Herzl
FROM THE JEWISH STATE

Theodor Herzl (1860–1904), founder of the World Zionist Organization, was born in Budapest and grew up believing that assimilation was not only inevitable, but desirable for the Jews. His confrontations with anti-Semitism, particularly the Dreyfus Affair, prompted Herzl to cry out for a Jewish national homeland.

PREFACE

The idea which I have developed in this pamphlet is a very old one: it is the restoration of the Jewish State.

The world resounds with outcries against the Jews, and these outcries have awakened the slumbering idea.

I wish it to be clearly understood from the outset that no portion of my argument is based on a new discovery. I have discovered neither the historic condition of the Jews nor the means to improve it. In fact, every man will see for himself that the materials of the structure I am designing are not only in existence, but actually already in hand. If, therefore, this attempt to solve the Jewish Question is to be designated by a single word, let it be said to be the result of an inescapable conclusion rather than that of a flighty imagination.

I must, in the first place, guard my scheme from being treated as Utopian by superficial critics who might commit this error of judgment if I did not warn them. I should obviously have done nothing to be ashamed of if I had described a Utopia on philanthropic lines; and I should also, in all probability, have obtained literary success more easily if I had set forth my plan in the irresponsible guise of a romantic tale. But this Utopia is far less attractive than any one of those portrayed by Sir Thomas More and his numerous forerunners and successors. And I believe that the situation of the Jews in many countries is grave enough to make such preliminary trifling superfluous.

★   ★   ★

The present scheme . . . includes the employment of an existent propelling force. In consideration of my own inadequacy, I shall content myself with indicating the cogs and wheels of the machine to be constructed, and I shall rely on more skilled mechanicians than myself to put them together.

Everything depends on our propelling force. And what is that force? The misery of the Jews.

Who would venture to deny its existence? We shall discuss it fully in the chapter on the causes of Anti-Semitism.

Everybody is familiar with the phenomenon of steampower, generated by boiling water, which lifts the kettle-lid. Such tea-kettle phenomena are the attempts of Zionist and kindred associations to check Anti-Semitism.

I believe that this power, if rightly employed, is powerful enough to propel a large engine and to move passengers and goods: the engine having whatever form men may choose to give it.

I am absolutely convinced that I am right, though I doubt whether I shall live to see myself proved to be so. Those who are the first to inaugurate this movement will scarcely live to see its glorious close. But the inauguration of it is enough to give them a feeling of pride and the joy of spiritual freedom.

★   ★   ★

I must guard against a danger in setting forth my idea. If I describe future circumstances with too much caution I shall appear to doubt their possibility. If, on the other hand, I announce their realization with too much assurance I shall appear to be describing a chimera.

I shall therefore clearly and emphatically state that I believe in the practical outcome of my scheme, though without professing to have discovered the shape it may ultimately take. The Jewish State is essential to the world; it will therefore be created.

The plan would, of course, seem absurd if a single individual attempted to do it; but if worked by a number of Jews in co-operation it would appear perfectly rational, and its accomplishment would present no difficulties worth mentioning. The idea depends only on the number of its supporters. Perhaps our ambitious young men, to whom every road of progress is now closed, seeing in this Jewish State a bright prospect of freedom, happiness and honors opening to them, will ensure the propagation of the idea.

I feel that with the publication of this pamphlet my task is done. I shall not again take

Theodor Herzl. 1895. Zionist Archives and Library, New York.

up the pen, unless the attacks of noteworthy antagonists drive me to do so, or it becomes necessary to meet unforeseen objections and to remove errors.

Am I stating what is not yet the case? Am I before my time? Are the sufferings of the Jews not yet grave enough? We shall see.

It depends on the Jews themselves whether this political pamphlet remains for the present a political romance. If the present generation is too dull to understand it rightly, a future, finer and a better generation will arise to understand it. The Jews who wish for a State shall have it, and they will deserve to have it.

★　　★　　★

CONCLUSION

I have tried to meet certain objections; but I know that many more will be made, based on high grounds and low.

To the first class of objections belongs the remark that the Jews are not the only people in the world who are in a condition of distress. Here I would reply that we may as well begin by removing a little of this misery, even if it should at first be no more than our own.

It might further be said that we ought not to create new distinctions between people;

we ought not to raise fresh barriers, we should rather make the old disappear. But men who think in this way are amiable visionaries; and the idea of a native land will still flourish when the dust of their bones will have vanished tracelessly in the winds. Universal brotherhood is not even a beautiful dream. Antagonism is essential to man's greatest efforts.

But the Jews, once settled in their own State, would probably have no more enemies. As for those who remain behind, since prosperity enfeebles and causes them to diminish, they would soon disappear altogether. I think the Jews will always have sufficient enemies, such as every nation has. But once fixed in their own land, it will no longer be possible for them to scatter all over the world. The diaspora cannot be reborn, unless the civilization of the whole earth should collapse; and such a consummation could be feared by none but foolish men. Our present civilization possesses weapons powerful enough for its self-defence.

Innumerable objections will be based on low grounds, for there are more low men than noble in this world. I have tried to remove some of these narrow-minded notions. . . .

Again, people will say that I am furnishing the Anti-Semites with weapons. Why so? Because I admit the truth? Because I do not maintain that there are none but excellent men amongst us?

Will not people say that I am showing our enemies the way to injure us? This I absolutely dispute. My proposal could only be carried out with the free consent of a majority of Jews. Action may be taken against individuals or even against groups of the most powerful Jews, but Governments will never take action against all Jews. The equal rights of the Jew before the law cannot be withdrawn where they have once been conceded; for the first attempt at withdrawal would immediately drive all Jews, rich and poor alike, into the ranks of revolutionary parties. The beginning of any official acts of injustice against the Jews invariably brings about economic crises. Therefore, no weapons can be effectually used against us, because these injure the hands that wield them. Meantime hatred grows apace. The rich do not feel it much, but our poor do. Let us ask our poor, who have been more severely proletarized since the last removal of Anti-Semitism than ever before.

Some of our prosperous men may say that the pressure is not yet severe enough to justify emigration, and that every forcible expulsion shows how unwilling our people are to depart. True, because they do not know where to go; because they only pass from one trouble into another. But we are showing them the way to the Promised Land; and the splendid force of enthusiasm must fight against the terrible force of habit.

Persecutions are no longer so malignant as they were in the Middle Ages? True, but our sensitiveness has increased, so that we feel no diminution in our sufferings; prolonged persecution has overstrained our nerves. . . .

Will some one say: Were it feasible it would have been done long ago?

It has never yet been possible; now it is possible. A hundred—or even fifty years ago it would have been nothing more than a dream. Today it may become a reality. . . .

Here it is, fellow Jews! Neither fable nor deception! . . . [I]f we only begin to carry out the plans, Anti-Semitism would stop at once and for ever. For it is the conclusion of peace.

The news of the formation of our Jewish Company will be carried in a single day to the remotest ends of the earth by the lightning speed of our telegraph wires.

And immediate relief will ensue. The intellects which we produce so superabundantly in our middle classes will find an outlet in our first organizations, as our first technicians, officers, professors, officials, lawyers, and doctors; and thus the movement will continue in swift but smooth progression.

Prayers will be offered up for the success of our work in temples and in churches also; for it will bring relief from an old burden, which all have suffered.

But we must first bring enlightenment to men's minds. The idea must make its way into the most distant, miserable holes where our people dwell. They will awaken from gloomy brooding, for into their lives will come a new significance. Every man need think only of himself, and the movement will assume vast proportions.

And what glory awaits those who fight unselfishly for the cause!

Therefore I believe that a wondrous generation of Jews will spring into existence. The Maccabeans will rise again.

Let me repeat once more my opening words: The Jews who wish for a State will have it.

We shall live at last as free men on our own soil, and die peacefully in our own homes.

The world will be freed by our liberty, enriched by our wealth, magnified by our greatness.

And whatever we attempt there to accomplish for our own welfare, will react powerfully and beneficially for the good of humanity.

Golda Meir

FIRST DAYS IN KIBBUTZ MERHAVIA
A Memoir

Golda Meir (1898–1978), who became the fourth Prime Minister of Israel in 1969, was born in Kiev, Russia, and emigrated to the United States with her family in 1906. Meir went to Palestine as a pioneer settler on a kibbutz in 1921. In this article she recounts what life was like during her three-year tenure at kibbutz Merhavia.

When I first left the United States, I came to Palestine; not simply to Palestine but to a kibbutz. It would be stretching a point to claim that in 1921 I knew much about kibbutzim, as the only Palestinians I had met at that time were Ben Gurion, Ben Zvi, Yaacov Zerubavel and Chashin—four people who had been expelled from Palestine by the Turks and had come to my town. I heard much from them about Palestine, but little about the kibbutz itself. I knew that Syrkin was thinking of establishing cooperatives in Palestine. I, therefore, cannot pride myself on having known very much about what went on here while I was in America; but I did know that I wanted to go to a kibbutz.

It took three meetings of the kibbutz Merhavia general assembly for them finally to agree to accept my husband and me as members, and this was mainly due to the ex-members of the Jewish Legion, most of whom had come from America, and thus naturally regarded themselves as experts on everything American, including the character of an American girl like myself. They were determined that we should not be accepted; not only because I was American, but also because we were a married couple. They were all bachelors and wanted only single girls. There were also objections from several veteran single girl members of the kibbutz, who had been in Palestine for close to eight years, and who had heard—most likely from those boys—all about American girls. . .

When we first came to Merhavia there were already houses there left over from the cooperative that had been set up before World War I. There was a kitchen in a shack, a very primitive kitchen, and a bakery. Baking bread was for me one of the profoundest mysteries of life. My mother used to bake her own *challa*. But bread! We were then 30–32 members in the kibbutz. We bought the flour in Nazareth and it was rarely well-sifted

Golda Meir. 1918.
Golda Meir Memorial
Association, Tel Aviv,
Israel.

so that the bread came out all purple and somewhat bitter. What nearly petrified me with fear was when the old timers in the bakery wanted to teach me to knead the dough when it was dry. When you put a lot of water into the dough, it's easier to knead it, but nothing much comes out of it; the trick lies in kneading it with very little water. When I finally learned how to do it, I was really proud of myself.

Another problem we had was with the oil. We used to buy that from the Arabs, too, and it was bitter. I thought it was silly to use it for baking and cooking for you couldn't eat a thing made with that oil.

When my turn came to work in the kichen I decided not to use the bitter oil, and I did all my cooking without it. The food was not too varied: we had *humus* (chickpeas) which we soaked in water for twenty-four hours and then cooked it with onions for soup; later the same concoction served as a cereal; and later still, in the evening, we ground it with onions as a salad.

★　　★　　★

In the winter it was very cold in Merhavia. When we came into the kitchen in the morning we first had some tea, usually unboiled, and then the comrades would come in to have breakfast. In Palestine after the war there were leftover canned goods; bully beef, and what was called "fresh herring"—fish perserved in tomato paste. That's what we served for breakfast. When we needed something hot I started to cook cereal, and they used to say: she'll have us eating cereal for breakfast, yet. But they soon learned to like it, and it was good.

★　　★　　★

336

COLORPLATE 128

JACK LEVINE. *Planning Solomon's Temple*. c. 1940. Oil on masonite. 10⅙ × 7¹⁵⁄₁₆″ (25.2 × 20.2 cm).
Israel Museum, Jerusalem. Gift of Rebecca Shulman, New York, 1955. © Jack Levine/VAGA,
New York 1992. *Jack Levine, who at one time was a W.P.A. artist, is known for his expressionistic
canvasses, with their themes of social criticism. In this painting, which supposedly relates to the death of his
father, Levine turns to the biblical subject of King Solomon's building of the First Temple.*

COLORPLATE 129

FELIX NUSSBAUM. *Self-Portrait with a Jewish Identity Card.* 1943. Oil on canvas. 22⁷⁄₁₆ × 19⁵⁄₈″ (56 × 49 cm). Kulturgeschichtliches Museum Osnabrück. © Auguste Moses–Nussbaum and Shulamit Jaari. *During the Holocaust, the artist went into hiding, moving from place to place in constant fear of discovery. This painting captures his grave anxiety. Nussbaum and his wife were, in fact, arrested in 1944, and both died in Auschwitz.*

COLORPLATE 130

BEN SHAHN. *1943 A.D.* c. 1943. Tempera on illustration board. 30¾ × 27¾″ (78.1 × 70.5 cm).
Courtesy of the Syracuse University Art Collection, New York. © Estate of Ben Shahn/VAGA,
New York 1992. *Ben Shahn's social realism is evident in the riveting portrait of a concentration camp inmate.*

COLORPLATE 131
MORRIS HIRSHFIELD.
Moses and Aaron.
1944. Oil on canvas.
28 × 40″ (71.1 ×
101.6 cm). Courtesy
of the Sidney Janis
Gallery, New York.
© Estate of Morris
Hirshfield/VAGA,
New York 1992. *In
this folk painting by
American artist Morris
Hirshfield, Moses stands
on the right holding the
tablets of the Ten
Commandments; his
brother, Aaron, the high
priest, is on the left
holding a censer.*

הלוים מנגנים בבית המקדש (שלום מושקוביץ הגלילי צפת)

COLORPLATE 132

SHALOM OF SAFED. *Levites Playing Music in the Holy Temple*. 1972. Acrylic on canvas. 24 × 24″ (61 × 61 cm). The Jewish Museum, New York. Gift of Louis Stein.

COLORPLATE 133

HARRY LEIBERMAN. *The Blessing of the Moon.* 1977. Acrylic on canvas. 20 × 16″ (50.8 × 40.6 cm).
Collection, H. Popkin. *In Judaism, each new moon and new month is ushered in with the recitation of
blessings and psalms. In this painting, contemporary folk artist Harry Leiberman celebrates that ritual.*

COLORPLATE 134

YOCHANAN SIMON. *Sabbath in a Kibbutz.* 1947. Oil on canvas. 26 × 22″ (65 × 55 cm). Collection, Tel Aviv Museum of Art, Israel. *After working and studying in Europe and America, Simon emigrated to Israel in 1936, where he spent 17 years as a member of a kibbutz. This painting captures the exuberance the artist felt toward kibbutz life.*

Saturday mornings we used to make coffee. Because we couldn't ship our milk to Haifa on this day, the Shabbat menu was all based on milk. We had coffee, and we made *leben* (cultured milk akin to yogurt) and lebeniya. The cookies were in charge of the girl who was on the Saturday morning kitchen shift, and she guarded them as if her life depended on it, because breakfast consisted of coffee and cookies. Friday nights, after supper, some of the fellows used to start hunting for the cookies, but girls on the Saturday morning shift usually took them with her to her room, and didn't leave her room all night. Nevertheless the fellows sometimes managed to lay their hands on the cookie and then Saturday morning would be a tragedy. When my turn came to work on Saturday morning I figured as follows: we have no oil, sugar or eggs (we started off with a few scrawny chickens who would lay a solitary egg now and again) so why should we care? Let's add more water and a little flour and make a lot of cookies, enough for Friday night and Saturday breakfast, too. . . .

We had other problems, too. We did our laundry communally but not the ironing. Everyone took his own laundry home and ironed it himself. At that time we used heavy irons heated by coal. All week long the girls would go out to work in the unironed dresses and headkerchiefs. When it came to that I, admittedly, was spoiled. I couldn't stand the thought of going out to work in unironed clothes. And they couldn't stand "that American girl" who went to work daily in an ironed dress and kerchief. I couldn't udnerstand what made them so mad. Why should they have cared. After all I did the ironing on my own time, in my own room. . . .

But one time I took my revenge. Merhavia, of course, had a water tower, but the flow of water was none too dependable. In summer we sometimes used to go into the communal shower all covered with dust, open the tap, and having nothing come out. When the water stopped running one had to climb up a tall ladder to the top of the tower to make some adjustment and the girls who were caught without water in the shower used to run around looking for the handyman to fix it. I didn't understand why we needed a man to fix it—and when I climbed up the ladder the first time, it was a shock, to the girls and the boys too.

The one thing which drove me wild, however, was the *barhash* (tiny flies which fill the air during the barely season). . . . Would there ever be an end to these pesky flies? In the summer we went out to work at four in the morning, for when the sun came up it was impossible to stay in the field for the *barhash* came out. I had a solution for all my other problems; but not for the *barhash*.

And then the babies started to come. My son Menahem was born in Jerusalem, but when he was four months old I went back to Merhavia with him. In the meantime two or three other babies were born in the kibbutz. At that time we had two-room houses— one big room and one small one. So we put all four babies in the big room and I slept in the small room for I told the comrades: Why should we have a girl stay up all night with each of the four babies? . . . And so I took care of all the babies at night and the kibbutz did without a night-watch girl for them. Everything worked out fine except for the fact that we had only one bathtub for all the children, and in time the word got around in the kibbutz that "Golda's babies drink alcohol." This was because I was adamant about sloshing alcohol around the bathtub after each baby's turn and "burning" the bathtub after every baby's bath.

A prevalent disease in the country at the time was *papetache* (a debilitating high-fever called sandfly fever). . . . It was as much a cause of despair as the *barhash:* fever, a terrible headache, loss of appetite—you couldn't even bear the thought of food. When I came down with *papetache* I was in charge of the chicken houses and of the incubator which we had just bought (a "giant" 500-egg incubator, which, I believe, was the first of its kind in the country). I remember that when I was in bed with fever, they forgot to water the ducks and when my fever went down and I could go out again I saw a few ducks which had died of thirst. My fever rose again and I had an attack of hallucinations in which I felt as if the entire room was filled with dead ducks. . . .

In those days only members recovering from bouts of malaria received potatoes, lemon and similar delicacies. But God was merciful. In the neighboring private village of Merhavia there was a grocer named Blumenfield, who came from Germany and soon after brought over his wife and daughter. They decided that the daughter had to learn English and sent her to me several times a week for English lessons which I gave her after work. In lieu of payment Blumenfield gave us a monthly credit of three pounds in his shop, and with this we bought all our "luxuries": potatoes for the sick, "kwoker" (the name being derived from the trade name Quaker Oats), salt, and sometimes even raisins for our wonderful cookies.

Our big shopping was done in the cooperative Hamashbir store in Haifa, which reminds me of the case of the cups. . . . We drank tea from cups. The cups from Hamashbir were of the enamelled metal sort. When they were new they were rather nice; but the enamel soon chipped off and the cups turned rusty. I decided that this could not go on: as long as Hamashbir did not stock different cups we would refuse to buy any. The result was, of course, that all of us had to take turns drinking tea. But I refused to give in.

We also had another madness. On Friday nights we spread white sheets on the tables in the dining hall (of course we had no table clothes) and decorated them with flowers. . . .

Since I had been accepted as a member of the Kibbutz with such reluctance, I took pains to prove that they had been wrong about me, and, like the other girls, I insisted on doing any job that the men did. There is a big stand of trees near the entrance to the kibbutz today and at the time it provided our main source of income. The Jewish National Fund paid us six Pounds per member to plant the trees. The plot was full of rocks and boulders and we had to loosen them with picks to get to some soil in which to plant the saplings. I will never forget the first days I worked at that job. When I returned to my room in the evening I couldn't as much as move a finger but I knew that if I didn't show up for supper they would jeer: what did we tell you? That's American girls for you: I would gladly have foregone supper, for the chickpea mush we ate wasn't worth the effort of lifting the fork to my mouth—but I went.

As I said, the food was poor and skimpy, so we used to prepare an extra two eggs and an onion for the night watchmen. And they, in turn, announced that anyone who would come to visit with them a bit, to break the monotony and boredom at one in the morning, would share in their feast. They used to fry the onion, and I couldn't tell you what else they added to the eggs. But at one in the morning I would turn up in the kitchen, and not simply for the food, believe me; and I was among the last to leave.

We used to pour our tea straight from the hot water heater but we hardly ever had the patience to wait for the water to boil, so we drank it hot but unboiled. When they heated water in the kitchen we had tea, but for every drop of it one had to trek to the kitchen. . . .

And one other thing before I finish.

There was of course no fruit at the time, either in Merhavia or in all of Emek Jezreel. Every now and then I would go to Tel Aviv to visit my sister. In those days, in order to get from Tel Aviv to Merhavia one had to go to Haifa first, stay overnight there, and then take the train to Afula. On one such visit at the height of the citrus season I wanted to bring back a sack of oranges, which cost all of two or three grush. The problem was how to lug the sack to the station, get it on the train and all the way to Afula and home. Of course, the idea of hiring a porter—that I should walk and someone else should carry the sack for me—would have been unthinkable for us at the time. When I finally did bring home a sack of oranges, there was great joy in Merhavia. Which reminds me of a "big scandal" we once had. Someone once brought a few lemons from town and one of the girls dared to take one . . . to wash her hair (there was no shampoo and the only soap we had was laundry soap, so that it was outright torture for any girl who insisted on growing long hair). I will never forget the outcry that arose around that filched lemon— for a lemon was not simply a piece of fruit but a medicine for those suffering from malaria and *papetache*.

And finally I would like to repeat something that I have said many times. The reason

I have felt good here in Israel—it's nearly 50 years already—is due to two things: I never felt I was making a sacrifice by being here; and it never occurred to me that I deserved praise for being here.

Permit me to end by expressing a hope: that I, together with all of Israel, will live to see the day when we know that no one is in danger; when every ring of the telephone and every arrival of my military aide is not a cause for anxiety; a day when we will feel confident that whatever peace we have is not fleeting or accidental, but that every day and every night will be peaceful. That day may yet come.

S. Y. Agnon
FABLE OF THE GOAT

In 1966, Shmuel Yosef Agnon (1888–1970), born Samuel Josef Czaczkes in Galicia, won the first Nobel Prize for literature granted to a Hebrew author. Agnon emigrated from Eastern Europe to Israel in 1907, yet many of his stories are set in the shtetl world he left behind.

The tale is told of an old man who groaned from his heart. The doctors were sent for, and they advised him to drink goat's milk. He went out and bought a she-goat and brought her into his home. Not many days passed before the goat disappeared. They went out to search for her but did not find her. She was not in the yard and not in the garden, not on the roof of the House of Study and not by the spring, not in the hills and not in the fields. She tarried several days and then returned by herself; and when she returned, her udder was full of a great deal of milk, the taste of which was as the taste of Eden. Not just once, but many times she disappeared from the house. They would go out in search for her and would not find her until she returned by herself with her udder full of milk that was sweeter than honey and whose taste was the taste of Eden.

One time the old man said to his son, "My son, I desire to know where she goes and whence she brings this milk which is sweet to my palate and a balm to all my bones."

His son said to him, "Father, I have a plan."

He said to him, "What is it?"

The son got up and brought a length of cord. He tied it to the goat's tail.

His father said to him, "What are you doing, my son?"

He said to him, "I am tying a cord to the goat's tail, so that when I feel a pull on it I will know that she has decided to leave, and I can catch the end of the cord and follow her on her way."

The old man nodded his head and said to him, "My son, if your heart is wise, my heart too will rejoice."

The youth tied the cord to the goat's tail and minded it carefully. When the goat set off, he held the cord in his hand and did not let it slacken until the goat was well on her way and he was following her. He was dragged along behind her until he came to a cave. The goat went into the cave, and the youth followed her, holding the cord. They walked thus for an hour or two, or maybe even a day or two. The goat wagged her tail and bleated, and the cave came to an end.

When they emerged from the cave, the youth saw lofty mountains, and hills full of the choicest fruit, and a fountain of living waters that flowed down from the mountains; and the wind wafted all manner of perfumes. The goat climbed up a tree by clutching at

ISSACHAR RYBACK. *Boy with a Goat.* 1930. Oil on canvas. 38⁹⁄₁₆ × 31⁷⁄₁₆″ (98 × 80 cm). Ryback Museum, Bat-Yam, Israel.

the ribbed leaves. Carob fruits full of honey dropped from the tree, and she ate of the carobs and drank of the garden's fountain.

The youth stood and called to the wayfarers: "I adjure you, good people, tell me where I am, and what is the name of this place?"

They answered him, "You are in the Land of Israel, and you are close by Safed."

The youth lifted up his eyes to the heavens and said, "Blessed be the Omnipresent, blessed be He who has brought me to the Land of Israel." He kissed the soil and sat down under the tree.

He said, "Until the day breathe and the shadows flee away, I shall sit on the hill under this tree. Then I shall go home and bring my father and mother to the Land of Israel." As he was sitting thus and feasting his eyes on the holiness of the Land of Israel, he heard a voice proclaiming:

"Come, let us go out to greet the Sabbath Queen."

And he saw men like angels, wrapped in white shawls, with boughs of myrtle in their hands, and all the houses were lit with a great many candles. He perceived that the eve of Sabbath would arrive with the darkening, and that he would not be able to return. He uprooted a reed and dipped it in gallnuts, from which the ink for the writing of Torah scrolls is made. He took a piece of paper and wrote a letter to his father:

"From the ends of the earth I lift up my voice in song to tell you that I have come in peace to the Land of Israel. Here I sit, close by Safed, the holy city, and I imbibe its sanctity. Do not inquire how I arrived here but hold onto this cord which is tied to the goat's tail and follow the footsteps of the goat; then your journey will be secure, and you will enter the Land of Israel."

The youth rolled up the note and placed it in the goat's ear. He said to himself: When she arrives at Father's house, Father will pat her on the head, an she will flick her ears. The note will fall out, Father will pick it up and read what is written on it. Then he will take up the cord and follow the goat to the Land of Israel.

The goat returned to the old man, but she did not flick her ears, and the note did not fall. When the old man saw that the goat had returned without his son, he clapped his hands to his head and began to cry and weep and wail, "My son, my son, where are you? My son, would that I might die in your stead, my son, my son!"

So he went, weeping and mourning over his son, for he said, "An evil beast has devoured him, my son is assuredly rent in pieces!"

And he refused to be comforted, saying, "I will go down to my grave in mourning for my son."

And whenever he saw the goat, he would say, "Woe to the father who banished his son, and woe to her who drove him from the world!"

The old man's mind would not be at peace until he sent for the butcher to slaughter the goat. The butcher came and slaughtered the goat. As they were skinning her, the note fell out of her ear. The old man picked up and the note and said, "My son's handwriting!"

When he had read all that his son had written, he clapped his hands to his head and cried, "*Vay! Vay!* Woe to the man who robs himself of his own good fortune, and woe to the man who requites good with evil!"

He mourned over the goat many days and refused to be comforted, saying, "Woe to me, for I could have gone up to the Land of Israel in one bound, and now I must suffer out my days in this exile!"

Since that time the mouth of the cave has been hidden from the eye, and there is no longer a short way. And that youth, if he has not died, shall bear fruit in his old age, full of sap and richness, calm and peaceful in the Land of the Living.

Benjamin Tammuz
AHAD HA'AM'S FUNERAL

Ahad Ha'Am (1856–1927), the celebrated Hebrew essayist, was born Asher Zvi Ginsberg in the Russian Ukraine. Ahad Ha'am stressed a slow systematic modernization of the Jewish people through a cultural revival. Although he never held an office in the Zionist movement, he was one of Chaim Weizmann's closest advisors during the negotiation for the issuance of the Balfour Declaration. As this story recounts, Ahad Ha'am was so important a man that when he lived in Tel Aviv, the street where he lived was closed to traffic during his afternoon rest.

Ahad Ha'am died when I was seven years old.

I had no idea who Ahad Ha'am was, but I heard from Molchadski the grocer, that

the police had closed the street where he lived, to horses and carts and buses, because he couldn't bear the noise. They would not allow the traffic to pass his house. This astonished me and I gathered that Ahad Ha'am was, perhaps, the most important man in town.

The whole business impressed me but also bothered me a little. I began to investigate. My parents knew nothing for they read nothing but *Poslediniyeh-Novosti,* the Russian newspaper which came from Paris. It never carried a word about Ahad Ha'am. But, eventually, they also heard from old Molchadski. He received a Warsaw newspaper called *Heint,* and there was the story of Ahad Ha'am, the police, the carts—the lot. That's how the neighbourhood got to know the story and began to talk about it. In those days we used to live in the APC district, named after the Anglo-Palestine Bank, which sold the building lots in the neighbourhood and APC stood for the Anglo-Palestine Company and all of this happened at the border with Manshiyeh where Arabs lived and they had never heard of Ahad Ha'am.

That's how we were the only ones in the neighbourhood to be in the know—especially me as I was anxious to see how it would end.

I didn't like old Molchadski but I was scared of him. If he gave you a sweet from his shop he would pinch your cheek as if he was going to tear out a lump of flesh. He always did things that way. He never gave anything away for nothing except words. Talking was his strong point and if I asked him anything he always answered. He always gave much more detailed answers than mother for she was always busy, and even than father, for he wasn't involved in anything much beyond his job. Unfortunately his job didn't interest me at all. I, for instance, was very much taken with this whole business of Ahad Ha'am and the police, whereas father said that it was nonsense. So I used to go to Molchadski and ask him what was the latest in *Heint*.

At first they wrote that things were so-so—Ahad Ha'am was sick, condition uncertain, but he was in need of complete quiet and this the police took care of. I have said this already. But later, they wrote that his condition was worsening and they began to reveal the whole truth. It became known that Ahad Ha'am was not Ahad Ha'am but was a Mr. Ginsberg. In Russia he used to write illegal things and, so that he wouldn't be caught, he disguised himself as Ahad Ha'am. In the end he was forced to run away and he fled to England and worked at selling tea and didn't do too badly out of it. Then, he came to Palestine and was given a house near the Herzliya Gymnasium. My parents used to say that if I managed to get through primary school with good marks they would send me to the Herzliya Gymnasium. That is why I knew its name before I had heard of Ahad Ha'am. That is why it was not news to me when I heard that Ahad Ha'am lived in the vicinity of the Herzliya Gymnasium.

Finally, they printed his picture in the paper and wrote that he had died. Old Molchadski let me look at the picture and I had the surprise of my life. I had always thought that a fellow who wrote, and, especially, a fellow who wrote illegal things, would have a lot of hair, a bushy beard and staring eyes; perhaps because so much writing wears the eyes out. But, Ahad Ha'am had a face—how can I describe it—like a triangle: at the top it was broad and bald and at the bottom it was narrow and sharp. Since seeing his picture I have changed my mind about scribblers for I understand that for them the brain is all-important and that is why their brain is developed and swollen whilst the rest of their face is a bit shrivelled, for the rest of the face is not as important as the brain. He also wore glasses like all men of his kind except that his didn't have a gold frame around the lenses and they didn't have the two oars which ride the ears. I know this kind. My father had the same. The lenses are connected by a spring and the spring grips the nose between the eyes and leaves red marks; that is why they don't fall off: not very comfortable but quite impressive, only one has always to take care that they don't fall and get broken.

I don't think that Ahad Ha'am was bothered with these problems. I could see from the picture that he had other worries. His face was very troubled. In fact Molchadski told me that Ahad Ha'am was always preoccupied with the fate of our nation and tried to solve all our problems. That is why he became so famous and that also explains the police's attitude towards him.

I asked Molchadski when the funeral was for I felt I had to be there. To start with, it was free of charge and then it could be interesting. Molchadski looked it up in the newspaper and said that it was on Tuesday at three o'clock in the afternoon starting from the house of the late lamented. The day he told me this was Monday—exactly at the last minute.

That evening I told my parents that I wanted to go to the funeral. Father said, don't talk nonsense and mother said, but first you have to do your homework. That's how, at about half-past two on Tuesday, I came to be at the Herzliya Gymnasium where I parked myself on the steps of the building where there was a bookshop and stationers, exactly opposite Ahad Ha'am's house and waited. It is better to be half an hour early than two hours late.

I waited patiently but was surprised that I was the only person there. Several hours later I decided to go straight to the cemetery in Trumpeldor Street.

There, I found the place to be reasonably peaceful except for some women who were weeping at various graves but not at Ahad Ha'am's. It was not nice to ask and, in any case, I did not speak to strangers. So, I decided to walk back along Allenby Street. The funeral procession would have to go that way and I hoped to catch up with it. Something must have happened and that was why there was such a hold-up.

I think that I was already dog-tired when I decided to return to the Herzliya Gymnasium. So I sat down on a bench in Allenby Street, exactly opposite Geula Street, to rest. From there I could see the stone building with the barber's shop where my father was shaved and had his hair cut. The barber had come to Eretz Israel on the same boat as my parents.

I sat on that bench and waited for the funeral procession to pass by so that I could join in and go down Pinsker Street with it to the cemetery. This was my plan and that is when I fell asleep.

I don't know how long I had been sleeping but, suddenly, I felt someone put a hand on my shoulder and in a very nice way, politely and without shouting, say to me, "Boy—get up, boy."

At first it was pitch black and a bit coolish, but not cold. Slowly, I was able to make out a fellow standing in front of me, not as old as Molchadski and not as young as me but somewhere in between, let us say sixteen. I only found out afterwards that he was twenty-three but at first I didn't know.

"Listen," he said to me, "I live opposite here and several hours ago I saw you sitting on this bench. Now it is night and I thought that maybe you had fallen asleep and they were worrying about you at home. So, come on and let me take you home. Where do you live?"

I got up and felt that my leg was numb. Nevertheless I stood up and looked at him. A nice fellow—makes a good impression and talks beautifully. I told him not to worry for I could go by myself. The truth was that it was not very pleasant to walk the whole length of Geula Street and then along Hayarkon Street to the Mosque of Hassan Beq. Not that I was afraid but at night one never knows because of the darkness. I hoped that he wouldn't let me go on my own and in fact he didn't. He spoke nicely to me, but with authority, so I accepted his offer and gave him my hand and we started walking down Geula Street.

All adults who see a child for the first time ask him his name. He also asked and I told him that my name was Elyakim. He said his name was Victor. I thought he was fibbing but later I believed him for I got to know him better and I learned who he was.

He asked me how old I was and I said seven and he said, twenty-three. Afterwards I told him that I went to the Geula primary school and he told me that he had finished his studies and was working in three languages, Hebrew, Arabic and French. At first, I thought that he was fibbing about this too; how could he know all those languages? But now I am certain that he wasn't fibbing.

We walked slowly because it was difficult to walk quickly in sand and one's sandals are always filling with sand. He saw that I had trouble with the sand so he told me a joke; how the children of Israel walked in the desert for forty years from Egypt to here; if they would have had sandals it would have taken them eighty years. We both laughed, for, while I knew the story already I couldn't tell it so funnily. As we passed my school I told him that this was where I studied and he asked me if I liked learning and I told him that it all depends.

Afterwards he asked me why I had fallen asleep on the bench and I told him about Ahad Ha'am and told him that I knew that his name was Ginsberg and the whole business about the tea shop and England and everything and that I had wanted to join the funeral procession.

At this, Victor stopped and looked at me for a while and then said, "What? Do you meant to tell me that you have been sleeping on that bench for twelve days?" Such a question can drive one crazy. Twelve days asleep on that bench and my parents not knowing what had happened to me—that's too much. Even when I don't show up at home for half a day they make an awful fuss about it. What would happen this time I had no idea. I said to Victor, "What's this twelve day business?" Victor said, "Because Ahad Ha'am died exactly twelve days ago and I saw his funeral from the window with my own eyes."

"So why did I think that it was today?" I asked Victor. "Who told you that it was today," said Victor. I told him that our grocer, Molchadski, had told me. "And where did he pick up such nonsense?" Victor answered. "From the newspaper," I said. "Which newspaper?" he asked. "From *Heint*," I told him. I also told him that my parents read *Posediniyeh-Novosti* and that they had said nothing, but *Heint* had it all the time and it was one hundred per cent reliable for it came from Warsaw. Then he started to laugh like mad and explained to me that foreign newspapers came by post and they sometimes took a fortnight to arrive and the paper in which I had seen Ahad Ha'am's picture was more or less two weeks old. And, if one reckons up carefully then two weeks and twelve days are more or less the same. Victor laughed but I didn't and when he saw that I wasn't laughing he said, "Don't worry and don't be sad, Elyakim. If it hadn't been for that mistake, how would we have become friends?"

I heard what he said but I didn't answer, feeling that I was happier than I had ever been before. And then Victor asked if I could hear the sound of the sea. I said yes, and he said that this was a sign that the sea was nearby and very soon we would turn left into Hayarkon Street. I told him that I wanted the sea to be far away because I wanted us to walk together for a long time. Victor said that time was not reckoned by the clock but by friendship and that the whole of our lives were in front of us so why should we care about time.

I don't think that I understood him then but I do understand now. But where is Victor now?

So we walked and Victor said, "Listen, I'll sing you a song." And he said, "All the boats have Sabbath lights lit," to the very end of the song. He asked me if I could sing something which I liked but I was shy. Then he sang me another song, "O night, O night, O fatherland." Then he told me that poets are the greatest men in the world. I asked him if they were even greater than Ahad Ha'am and he said that it was certain. I was very surprised but didn't argue.

Suddenly, I saw that we were nearly home for we were next to Molchadski's grocery and I felt that I wanted to cry even though it was out of happiness but it was all very strange and I was glad that it was dark. I struggled to control myself and I showed him where the grocery was and he told me to tell the grocer next morning that he should start reading a Hebrew newspaper. "Tell him," Victor said, "Hebrew, speak Hebrew."

He went up the steps with me and he knocked at the door himself. As we walked in, and before he could explain to them, my father boxed my ears and my mother burst out crying and hugged me. So Victor said goodbye and left.

I didn't mind the good hiding and the moment I emerged from my mother's arms I ran to the balcony, lifted my head above the parapet and saw Victor leaving our house and turning right. I yelled with all my might, "Victor—you are a good man—I love you." Immediately I dived under the parapet so that he wouldn't know who had called to him. As I bent down I hit myself so hard on the chin that I cut my lip and knew that I had drawn blood because of the taste in my mouth.

Mother was scared and so was my father. They began to nurse me and applied iodine and a bandage and all sorts of other medicines but I fell asleep in the middle. It wasn't that I was particularly tired but I wanted to be alone. I mean with Victor again.

That night, I didn't manage to dream about him. But, afterwards, I did. To this day.

Chaim Weizmann

OUR UNIQUE DESTINY

With the establishment of the State of Israel, Chaim Weizmann(1874–1952) was invited to become its first president, a position he held from 1949 until his death in 1952. Weizmann was trained as an organic chemist; his research for the British government during the World War I helped persuade Lord Balfour to issue the Balfour Declaration. As a Zionist, Weizmann never faltered in his fight for a Jewish homeland in Palestine, which, at times put him at odds with other Zionist leaders.

It is a moving experience for me to come before this committee of the United Nations for the purpose of summarizing the view and sentiments of the Jewish people at this turning point of its fortunes.

My mind goes back a quarter of a century to the previous assembly of nations which solemnly endorsed our program for the reconstitution in Palestine of our National Home.

I came from the council room in which the mandate was ratified with the feeling that the most cherished ideals of our own history had been sanctioned by the conscience of all mankind.

Our ancient civilization, which had enriched the thought and spirit of the world, was to be given a free abode in the very cradle of its birth. Our people were to find a home—not a refuge, not an asylum, not a mere shelter, but a home with which their past memory and future hope were inseparably bound up. The Jewish people was to fashion its own political and social institutions in the image of its own character and tradition, on a level of equality with all other nations in the human family.

I can testify here that the establishment of the Jews as a nation among the nations of the world was the real purpose and motive of that international covenant endorsed by the League of Nations.

It is no coincidence that the statesmen who developed the idea of organized international cooperation as well as the leaders in the creation of the United Nations found time, amid their universal preoccupations, to plan for the Jewish State.

Despite some of the things that have been said in this debate, I retain my belief in the prospect of Arab-Jewish cooperation once a solution based on finality and equality has received the sanction of international consent. The Jewish State in Palestine may become a pilot plant for processes and examples which may have a constructive message for its neighbors as well.

Albert Einstein

FROM OUT OF MY LATER YEARS
"The Jews of Israel"

Albert Einstein (1879–1955), a Nobel Prize winning physicist, was a great humanist and ardent Zionist. After the death of Chaim Weizmann, Einstein was urged by Ben-Gurion to run for the presidency of the State of Israel. He declined the offer, feeling he was unsuited for the position.

There is no problem of such overwhelming importance to us Jews as consolidating that which has been accomplished in Israel with amazing energy and an unequalled willingness for sacrifice. May the joy and admiration that fill us when we think of all that this small group of energetic and thoughtful people has achieved give us the strength to accept the great responsibility which the present situation has placed upon us.

When appraising the achievement, however, let us not lose sight of the cause to be served by this achievement: rescue of our endangered brethren, dispersed in many lands, by uniting them in Israel; creation of a community which conforms as closely as possible to the ethical ideals of our people as they have been formed in the course of a long history.

One of these ideals is peace, based on understanding and self-restraint, and not on violence. If we are imbued with this ideal, our joy becomes somewhat mingled with sadness, because our relations with the Arabs are far from this ideal at the present time. It may well be that we would have reached this ideal, had we been permitted to work out, undisturbed by others, our relations with our neighbors, for we *want* peace and we realize that our future development depends on peace.

It was much less our own fault or that of our neighbors than of the Mandatory Power, that we did not achieve an undivided Palestine in which Jews and Arabs would live as equals, free, in peace. If one nation dominates other nations, as was the case in the British Mandate over Palestine, she can hardly avoid following the notorious device of Divide et Impera. In plain language this means: create discord among the governed people so they will not unite in order to shake off the yoke imposed upon them. Well, the yoke has been removed, but the seed of dissension has borne fruit and may still do harm for some time to come—let us hope not for too long.

The Jews of Palestine did not fight for political independence for its own sake, but they fought to achieve free immigration for the Jews of many countries where their very existence was in danger; free immigration also for all those who were longing for a life among their own. It is no exaggeration to say that they fought to make possible a sacrifice perhaps unique in history.

I do not speak of the loss in lives and property fighting an opponent who was numerically far superior, nor do I mean the exhausting toil which is the pioneer's lot in a neglected arid country. I am thinking of the additional sacrifice that a population living under such conditions has to make in order to receive, in the course of eighteen months, an influx of immigrants which comprise more than one third of the total Jewish population of the country. In order to realize what this means you have only to visualize a comparable feat of the American Jews. Let us assume there were no laws limiting the immigration into the United States; imagine that the Jews of this country volunteered to receive more than one million Jews from other countries in the course of one year and a half, to take care of them, and to integrate them into the economy of this country. This would be a tremendous achievement, but still very far from the achievement of our brethren in Israel. For the United States is a big, fertile country, sparsely populated with a high living standard and a highly developed productive capacity, not to compare with small Jewish Palestine whose inhabitants, even without the additional burden of mass immigration, lead a hard and frugal life, still threatened by enemy attacks. Think of the privations and personal sacrifices which this voluntary act of brotherly love means for the Jews of Israel.

The economic means of the Jewish Community in Israel do not suffice to bring this tremendous enterprise to a successful end. For a hundred thousand out of more than three hundred thousand persons who immigrated to Israel since May 1948 no homes or work could be made available. They had to be concentrated in improvised camps under conditions which are a disgrace to all of us.

It must not happen that this magnificent work breaks down because the Jews of this country do not help sufficiently or quickly enough. Here, to my mind, is a precious gift with which all Jews have been presented: the opportunity to take an active part in this wonderful task.

David Ben-Gurion

FROM ISRAEL: A PERSONAL HISTORY
"The Six-Day War"

David Ben-Gurion (1886–1973) was the first Prime Minister and the first Defense Minister of the State of Israel. Raised in a Zionist household, Ben-Gurion inevitably became an ardent Zionist. He firmly believed that once the State of Israel was founded, no one could be a Zionist and remain in the Diaspora. In this selection, he records his impressions of the Six-Day War of 1967.

Wednesday, June 7, 1967, will be remembered as one of the great days in Jewish history: the day when the Old City of Jerusalem was liberated and the Temple Mount and Western Wall restored to Jewish hands.

Paratroopers in A-Tor under Mordekhai Gur that day carried out a decisive assault on the eastern ridge in order to complete the encirclement of the Old City. At 8:30 A.M. the Air Force, accompanied by a heavy artillery barrage, attacked Augusta Victoria and at the same time two paratroop battalions charged up the hill, one in the north in the direction of Mount Scopus and another in a frontal attack up the steep western slope. The third battalion advanced south along the wall from the area of the Rockefeller Museum.

In this concentrated assault, carried out with the support of tanks and infantry units equipped with recoilless guns, the entire Augusta Victoria ridge commanding the Old City was captured. The three battalions, the tanks, and the reconnaissance units were immediately diverted to the Lions Gate and the east wall of the Old City. An artillery barrage was leveled at the Moslem Quarter of the Old City near this gate and tanks kept the enemy's firing positions on the wall pinned down. One of the tanks knocked open the door of the Lions Gate with a shell.

The brigade commander quickly burst through the gate on his half-track and, hurrying through the city, turned left and reached the Temple Mount. He was followed by the three brigades that deployed from the Temple Square to mop up the entire Old City. The first paratroopers reached the Western Wall at 10 A.M. A short time after the brigade commander reached the Temple Square, the leader of the Arab City came up and declared there would be no violent resistance to the Israeli forces. Snipers continued firing for a few more hours but the paratroopers took good care of them. At the same time the Jerusalem Regional Brigade was operating in the southern part of the city. One of the Brigade's forces, attacking from Mount Zion eastward outside the southern wall, mopped up the entire area to the Pool of Shiloah and the Dung Gate. In the afternoon the brigade advanced southward, capturing the Legion positions at Mar Elias and continuing on southward.

The enemy collapsed. Advancing quickly against relatively light resistance, the Brigade conquered Bethlehem, liberated the Gush Etzion area and the city of Hebron, and from there sent out two armored units—one in the direction of Dahariyeh and the other to the area of Samua (Eshtamoah), where on Thursday, June 8, they joined up with the Southern Command forces from Beersheba. On Wednesday, June 7, Ben-Ari's armored brigade completed the conquest of the area between Jerusalem and Nablus. Two battalions, descending to Jericho, reached the Jordan Valley by two different routes. Jericho was taken in a rapid thrust of armored forces that passed back and forth through the city several times, breaking down the enemy's resistance. Following the conquest of the city, the Brigade forces set out to blow up the bridges on the Jordan and to link up with the forces of the Northern Command in the upper part of the Jordan Valley. The third battalion headed north from Ramallah to Nablus through a series of valleys and ravines. At its destination it made contact with Northern Command forces that had taken Nablus.

The northern section of Jordan had been opened on the second day of the fighting, Tuesday, with an assault on Jenin by an armored brigade of Peled's division. Jordanian tank reinforcements arrived, but Peled's Shermans succeeded in knocking out their Pattons. The force gained control of the hills southeast of Jenin. After the capture of the outposts resistance within Jenin itself, first by tanks and artillery and then by the local police, had to be overcome. When the police had been defeated, white flags appeared. Meanwhile, however, a Jordanian Patton battalion had reached the Kabatiyeh crossroads and was advancing on Jenin. The Israeli Air Force was called in and knocked out the enemy tanks.

While the fighting in Jenin and its environs was going on, Peled's division sent an additional armored brigade under Uri to the north of the Shomron Hills. On Wednesday this brigade began a night attack on the Jordanian armored force. It took Toubas without any resistance and continued to the junction of the road leading from Damya Bridge to

Nablus. A surprising sight met the eyes of our armored troops. Peace and quiet prevailed in the city. Inhabitants on both sides of the main road were waving gaily at our tank crews. Later it was learned that the Nablunites had been expecting Iraqi troops from the Damya Bridge direction. After a few minutes they realized their mistake, dispersed, and locked themselves in their houses. Sniping began. A force from the Golani Brigade helped nail down control of the city.

Continuing its advance, the armored brigade met a Jordanian armored force assigned to defend Nablus. The encounter occurred at 11:30 A.M. and a tank battle at very close quarters ensued. The Israel Air Force joined in and the Jordanian tanks were reduced. The battle was at an end. The conquest of the West Bank was complete.

The bitter struggle for the Golan Heights began on Friday, June 9, after fighting on the Egyptian and Jordanian fronts had ended. Within one day the Heights were conquered and the ceasefire went into effect on the Syrian front as well.

Next to the conquest of the Old City and surrounding areas, this operation was perhaps the most difficult. The terrain presented enormous obstacles. Our forces in the lowlands had to scale a mountain on which the Syrian Army was entrenched in a series of trenches and bunkers. The length of the Heights from the Banyas in the north to Tawafik in the south was sixty kilometers. From a width of fifteen kilometers at the foot of Mount Hermon the Heights widened to a breadth of twenty-five to thirty kilometers in the Boutmiyeh area, and farther south narrowed again, ending in a sharp point where the Yarmuk emptied into the Jordan River. On three sides—east, north, and south—the Golan Heights were practically impregnable. Only from the lowlands of the Galilee in the west, bounded by the Yarmuk in the south and Mount Hermon in the north, was the area at all accessible. This gave the Syrians an inestimable strategic advantage and they had spent the nineteen years since the War of Independence fortifying the Heights.

Though the border with Israel constituted less than 4 percent of Syria's land frontier, all of Syria's military efforts for nearly twenty years had been concentrated on this small sector. Here they had numerous military strongholds occupied permanently, summer and winter. Concrete bunkers were provided for housing, equipment, and ammunition. The bunkers and operational positions were connected by deep narrow trenches and every outpost was surrounded by broad barbed-wire fences and minefields. Three Syrian infantry brigades, each provided with an armored battalion, were permanently maintained here. At the start of the war three more infantry brigades were added. The Syrians also had a "shock force" consisting of two motorized and two armored brigades.

Documents found in Syrian Army headquarters after the victory attested to a plan to invade and conquer the northern part of Israel. They spoke of an invasion force of two divisions, each with an armored spearhead. One division was to have crossed the border in the Jordan Valley and advanced toward Tiberias; the second was to erect a bridgehead on the West Bank in the vicinity of Mishmar Hayarden and overrun the entire eastern Galilee up to the Gush Halav-Safad line on the first day with Haifa as the final objective. Practical preparations for the invasion included the equipment of units in the Mishmar Hayarden area with rubber boats.

When the war actually started, the Syrians had preferred to await the results in the southern and central zones. In the meantime they engaged in warlike activities that, in their view, involved little danger to themselves. Their artillery was directed at Israeli settlements on the border, and especially against Rosh Pina, on the assumption that it was situated on an important strategic crossroads. The Israelis in those settlements were forced to live in bunkers. There were places where settlers had to remain in bunkers for five straight days.

In the first stage of the war, before the Syrian airfields were attacked, Syrian planes struck at several Israeli settlements and airfields in the north. The IDF returned fire with aircraft and artillery. The Israeli artillery was in an inferior position, exposed to the Syrian fire. The exchange of fire continued during the second day of the war as well. Syrian infantry and an armored force of company strength made three attempts to advance in the direction of Tel Dan, and once in the direction of Sh'ar Yashuv. The attackers sustained

WERNER BRAUN. *The Wailing Wall Is Ours.* 1967. Photograph. *When the photographer was on duty as a soldier, he took this photograph on June 12, 1967, at the end of the Six-Day War.*

heavy losses when Israeli tanks and planes went into action against them. An additional attack on Ashmura was also repulsed. Syrian artillery fire and Israeli artillery and aircraft fire continued from Monday, June 5, until Friday, June 9. As it finished its work on other fronts the Israeli Air Force daily stepped up its attacks on airfields in southern Syria.

On Friday morning ground forces of Gen. David Elazar's Northern Command began the assault on the Golan Heights. Starting at 9:40 A.M., the Air Force increased its operations on this front—the only one that remained after Egypt and Jordan had agreed to the ceasefire ordered by the United Nations.

The spearhead of the breakthrough was an armored brigade commanded by Colonel Albert which set out at 11:30 A.M. on June 9 from Giv'at Haem, north of Kfar Szold in upper Galilee. It was preceded by men of the Engineering Corps who cleared mines, and by bulldozers that opened a way for the armored vehicles on the rocky slopes. On reaching its marshaling area at the foot of the Heights, Albert's brigade was subjected to a heavy artillery barrage. The path that had been cleared was very narrow and if any vehicle got stuck it would have obstructed the advance of the entire force. From time to time the Syrian fire was silenced by Israeli warplanes. But despite the bombardment, the forces pressed forward. The tank battalion had crossed the border and attacked the Syrian outpost of Na'amoush. At this position, as at those positions taken later in the breakthrough, no delays were encountered because after the Israeli tank unit had passed, the remaining Syrians stopped fighting, and if they had not managed to escape unarmed, they were taken prisoner.

From Na'amoush, despite heavy losses, the armored force continued to fight its way forward toward the village of Kala. On reaching the outskirts of the village, which was a military garrison, the force was met by and engaged a Syrian armored battalion. Again the Air Force moved in to support the tanks. Meanwhile the Brigade's main force advanced northeast along a parallel axis toward the village of Za'oura, which was taken without particular difficulty. From there it headed for the outposts above Za'oura, the conquest of which took several hours. The topmost positions were captured at 4:30 P.M. From there the force headed south and at nightfall joined the force fighting at Kala. This linkup meant that at the end of the first day's fighting a powerful Israeli armored force was entrenched on the Golan Heights.

Amos Oz
STRANGE CITY

In this essay, a noted Israeli author tells of his great love for his native Jerusalem. Oz reminisces about his childhood and the war and hostility that tore the city asunder in 1948. He then speaks of his feelings when, in June of 1967, he returned to Jerusalem three days after it was reunited during the Six-Day War.

I was born in Jerusalem and lived there throughout my childhood; when I was nine I lived through the days when Jerusalem was besieged and shelled. It was then that I first saw a dead man: a shell fired from the Arab Legion's gun batteries on Nebi Samuel hit a pious Jew and tore his stomach apart. I saw him lying in the street. He was a small man whose chin sprouted a meager beard. His face, as he lay there dead, was white and amazed. It was July, 1948. For many days afterwards I hated that man because he kept appearing in my dreams and frightening me. I knew that Jerusalem was surrounded by forces whose only desire was the city's death and mine, too.

Later I moved away from Jerusalem. I still loved her with a stubborn love as one might love a woman who holds aloof. Sometimes on my free days I would go to Jerusalem to pay court to her. Her alleyways knew me well though they affected not to.

I loved Jerusalem because she was journey's end, a city one arrived at but could never pass beyond; and also because she was never really a true part of the State of Israel; with the exception of a few roads Jerusalem has always held herself aloof, as if she had consciously chosen to turn her back on all the flat white commercial cities: Tel Aviv, Holon, Herzlia and Nethanya.

Jerusalem was different. She was the absolute negation of towns made up of cube-like blocks of flats, all painted white. She was different from the flat stretches of citrus groves, the gardens surrounded by hedges, the red roofs and irrigation pipes shining in the sun. Even the blue of her summer skies was different. Not for her the dusty white heavens of the coastal plain and the Sharon valley. An enclosed city. Wintry. Even in the summer it was always a wintry city. Rusty iron railings. Grey stone, sometimes imperceptibly shading into pale blue, sometimes into a reddish hue. Tumbledown fences. Rocky hillsides. Walled courtyards, closed in as if in anger.

And its citizens: a silent people, bitter as if for ever overcoming some inner fear. Observant Jews. Ashkenazi Jews in their fur *streimels* and old Sephardim in their striped robes. Soft-stepping scholars wandering through the streets, as if at a loss. Dreamy-eyed girls. Blind beggars, dumb or cursing. Madmen abroad with the divine spark in their eyes.

For twenty years Jerusalem turned her stubborn back on the stream of modern life.

COLORPLATE 135
JOE LASKER. *Memo*. 1954. Oil on canvas. 20 × 34″ (50.8 × 86.4 cm). Courtesy Kraushaar Galleries,
New York. *This painting centers on the Jewish rite of circumcision.*

COLORPLATE 137
NAHUM GUTHMAN. *Dilliganses, Jaffa*. Oil on canvas. Tel Aviv Museum, Israel.

COLORPLATE 136 *(opposite)*
R. B. KITAJ. *Study for the Jewish School (Joe Singer as a Boy)*. 1980. Pastel and charcoal on paper.
30½ × 22¼″ (77.5 × 56.5 cm). The Jewish Museum, New York. Purchase: Marlborough—Eileen
Dougherty.

COLORPLATE 138

MARC CHAGALL. *The Twelve Tribes of Israel*. Stained glass windows in Hadassah's Medical Center
Synagogue, Ein Karem, Israel. 1961. Each window: 133⅛ × 98⅞″ (338.1 × 251.1 cm). © 1992
ARS, New York/ADAGP, Paris. *Chagall's attachment to religious subject matter began with his Orthodox
childhood and grew stronger with the Holocaust. The twelve windows of the medical center represent the
twelve tribes of Israel. One shown here, on the left, represents the tribe of Dan, inspired by Jacob's prophecy
in Genesis (49:16): "Dan shall judge his people, as one of the tribes of Israel." That passage is inscribed on
the window.*

COLORPLATE 139
LARRY RIVERS. *History of Matzah, The Story of the Jews. (Part I–Before the Diaspora).* 1982. Acrylic on canvas. 116¾ × 166½″ (296.5 × 422.9 cm). Private Collection, New York. © Larry Rivers/VAGA, New York 1992.

(opposite, above)
LARRY RIVERS. *History of Matzah, The Story of the Jews. (Part II—European Jewry).* 1983. Acrylic on canvas. 116¾ × 168″ (296.5 × 426.7 cm). Private Collection, New York. © Larry Rivers/VAGA, New York 1992.

(opposite, below)
LARRY RIVERS. *History of Matzah, The Story of the Jews. (Part III—Immigration to America).* 1984. Acrylic on canvas. 116¼ × 180″ (292.3 × 822.9 cm). Private Collection, New York. © Larry Rivers/VAGA, New York 1992.

367

COLORPLATE 140
YAACOV AGAM. *Star of Love*. 1989. Gouache. 35⁷⁄₁₆ × 35⁷⁄₁₆″ (90 × 90 cm). Courtesy Artra.

This staged photograph shows men and women praying together at the Western Wall, as was the custom until the Ashkenazi influence changed the practice. For centuries Jews have been drawn to pray at the only surviving wall of the reconstructed Second Temple in Jerusalem.

A slow moving town in a country of feverish activity. An old, neglected mountainous suburb whose few flat stretches, crammed with buildings, burst at the seams with overflowing energy. The sad capital city of an exultant state. And the stranglehold.

There were mutilated streets descending to blocked alleys. Barricades of concrete and rusty barbed wire. A city which is all border. A city not of gold but of tin sheeting, bent and full of holes. A city surrounded at night by the sound of foreign bells, foreign odors, distant views. A ring of hostile villages surrounded the city on three sides: Sha'afat, Wadi Jos, Issawia, Silwan, Azaria, Tsur Bachr, Bet Tsafafa. It seemed as if they had only to clench their hand and Jerusalem would be crushed within their fist. On a winter night you could sense the evil intent that flowed from them toward the city.

There was fear too in Jerusalem. An inner fear that must never be expressed in words, never called by name. It grew, solidified and crystallized in the twisting alleyways and the desolate lanes.

The city fathers, the heads of government, the housing estates, the newly planted trees, the traffic lights, all tried to tempt Jerusalem into a union with the State of Israel; and she, with the exception of some few streets, refused that union. Twenty years. Jerusalem continued to preserve a faded obstinate. Mandatory character. She remained sad.

Not within the State of Israel, but alongside it; Jerusalem as opposed to Israel.

I loved this town, because I was born there and because people who stand aloof tend to love towns which hold aloof.

This was a love which was received without mercy: Jerusalem was often the background for nightmares and dreams of terror. I no longer live in Jerusalem, but in my dreams I am hers and she does not relinquish her hold on me. I would see us both surrounded by enemies. The enemy in my dreams came not only from east, north and south, but completely surrounded us. I saw Jerusalem falling into the hands of her enemies. Destroyed, pillaged and burned, as in the stories of my childhood, as in the Bible, as in the tales of the destruction of the Temple. And I too, with no way of escape, with no place to hide, was trapped in the Jerusalem of my dreams.

Many were the stories I was told as a child of Jerusalem under siege. Jewish children always died in these stories. They died heroically, or were slaughtered, but the stories always ended with the town burning and the children dying. Sennaccherib, Titus, the Crusaders. Riots, terrorists. Military rule. The High Commissioner, searches, curfew. Abdullah, the desert king. The guns of the Arab Legion. The convoy to Mount Scopus. The convoy to the Etzion bloc. An incited rabble. Inflamed mobs. Blood-thirsty ruffians. Brutal armed irregulars. All forever aimed at me. I always belonged to the minority, to the besieged, to those whose fate was sealed, who lived a life hovering on the brink of disaster.

So this time too, the city will be attacked. We shall die there like that little pious Jew who lay in the street, his face pale and amazed, as if he had suffered some grave insult. And more.

After the siege was lifted, a border was drawn through the heart of the city. All my childhood was passed in dead-end alleyways, facing streets one was forbidden to enter. The scar of destruction, no-man's land, mine fields, wasteland, ruined, blackened buildings. Twisted, despairing iron girders rising starkly out of the ruined houses. And ever opposite: the other Jerusalem. The city surrounding my city. Foreign sounds and smells emanated from it, pale lights flickered there by night, and the cry of the muezzin at dawn. Atlantis. The lost continent. A city which was forever the focus of one's most insubstantial visions. I had blurred memories dating from my earliest childhood, the memory of colorful alleyways in the Old City, the narrow arched street leading to the Wall, Mandatory Arab policemen, street-vendors' stalls, tamarind, a riot of color, an ever present sense of lurking danger.

From over there, from beyond the border, an angry threat has been directed at me throughout most of my life. I remember wandering down the streets of Musrara at dusk, to the edge of no-man's-land. A glimpse of Schneller Woods from afar. Forbidden views seen from the observation point at Abu Tor. The shattered square of Notre Dame. The towers of Bethlehem opposite the woods of Ramat Rachel. Desert hillsides falling away form the suburb of Talpiyot. The Dead Sea glittering in the distance like a mirage. Rocky valleys at dawn.

On Sunday, June 11, 1967, I went to see the Jerusalem that lay beyond the border. I came to places which with dreams and the years had become petrified symbols within my heart, and lo and behold—people lived here—houses, shops, stalls, signposts.

And I was thunderstruck, as if my whole inner world had collapsed. The dreams were a deception. The world of terrible tales became a mockery. The perpetual threat was nothing but a cruel twisted joke. Everything was burst asunder. Laid wide open. My Jerusalem, beloved and feared, was dead.

Now the town was different. Long-forgotten, neglected corners had come to life again. Bulldozers pushed new roads through heaps of rubble which I had imagined would be there for all eternity. Districts which had been utterly forgotten were filled with feverish activity. Hosts of pious Jews, soldiers in battledress, amazed tourists, smartly dressed women from Tel Aviv and Haifa, all streamed eastward. The tide flowed strongly to Jerusalem. The rest of the country poured into the open city. Everything within her orbit took an air of festivity. And I along with it.

These things cannot be expressed in words. Again I say that I loved Jerusalem in its entirety, but what does this mean? It is like a love affair, a contradictory, tortuous force: she is mine and yet strange to me, conquered but hostile, devoted yet inaccessible.

I could disregard all this. The skies are the same skies and the Jerusalem stone is the same throughout. Sheikh Jarrah is almost like Katamon.

But the city is inhabited. People live within her streets, and they are strangers, I do not understand their language, they are there—in their homes—and I am the stranger who comes from without. Courteous people, courteous to the point of offense, as if they have reached the very peak of happiness in having merited the honor of selling me post-cards or Jordanian stamps. Welcome, we are brothers, it is just for you alone that we have waited all these years, just so that we could embrace you. And their eyes hate me, wish me dead. The accursed stranger. It grieves me, but I cannot order my words in a rational way.

I was in East Jerusalem three days after the conquest of the city. I arrived there straight from El Arish, in Sinai, wearing uniform and carrying a sub-machine-gun. I was not born to sound the trumpet or liberate lands from foreign yokes. The lament of an enslaved people finds an echo in my ears, but I am deaf to the lament of "enslaved territory."

In my childhood dreams it was the Arabs who wore uniforms and carried machine-guns, Arabs who came to my street in Jerusalem to kill me. Twenty-two years ago, a slogan painted in red appeared on a courtyard wall not far from our house: "Judah fell in blood and fire; by blood and fire will Judah rise again." One of the underground had written these words at night in burning red. I don't know how to write about blood and fire. If I ever write anything about this war, it will be about pus, sweat and vomit and not about blood and fire. With all my soul, I desired to feel in Jerusalem as a man who has dispossessed his enemies and returned to the patrimony of his ancestors. The Bible came to life for me: The Prophets, the Kings, Temple Mount, Absolom's Pillar, the Mount of Olives. The Jerusalem of Abraham Mapu and Agnon. I wanted to be part of it all, I wanted to belong.

Were it not for the people. I saw enmity and rebelliousness, sycophancy, amazement, fear, insult and trickery. I passed through the streets of East Jerusalem like a man breaking into some forbidden place. Depression filled my soul.

City of my birth. City of my dreams. City of my ancestors' and my people's yearnings. And I was condemned to walk through its streets armed with a sub-machine-gun like one of the characters from my childhood nightmares. To be a stranger in a very strange city.

Bernard Isaacs
OR WAS IT A DREAM?

Born in Lithuania, Bernard Isaacs (1882–1975) came to the United States in 1904. His greatest contribution to the Jewish community was not as an author but as an educator. Because of his deep love of the Hebrew language, Isaacs was one of very few authors to write his stories in Hebrew, even while living in America. This story speaks of the great emotion evoked by a trip to Israel.

There were five of us in the taxi that took us from Jerusalem to Beersheba—the driver and four tourists from America. One was a slight woman of about fifty. She was short and slim, spry and quick of movement and she was loaded down with all kinds of tourist accessories. A camera was slung over one shoulder, dark sun-glasses protected her eyes and one hand clutched a parasol and an enormously capacious handbag. She never stopped her chatter. . . . "You told me that we'd covered all the points in the north and here I see Safed marked; it's a must! That means that if we haven't done Safed, we haven't seen anything! You understand? We must do Safed!"

Her dozing husband opened his eyes, smiled and said: "But, sweetheart, don't you remember the place where they served us cold, salty soup and you quarreled with the waiter and nearly had a fight with the owner? Remember? That was Safed."

His wife sighed with relief: "I'm so glad we covered it. I would never have forgiven myself if we had missed Safed!"

The driver, who was sitting bent over the steering-wheel seemingly concentrating on the road stretching out before him, burst into laughter when he heard the remarks about Safed having been covered after all. Even the fourth passenger in the taxi, a woman of about sixty, who sat in her corner, sighing deeply every now and then—even this apparently dejected women bestowed a smile on the group.

This tourist, with her reserved posture, her frequent sighs, and her sad, delicate face attracted me and I tried repeatedly to draw her out of her isolation, but in vain. To every question that I addressed to her, she responded with but a single word.

Our journey ended when we returned to Tel Aviv and I was glad to be rid of the talkative woman who had come to cover the whole country and of her sleepy husband. Only the silent woman had stirred my curiosity and she too was forgotten in the course of touring the beloved old-new land. How great then was my surprise when I met the same retiring woman on the ship that was taking me back to the United States! Her face was pale and worried as when I had seen her in the taxi but she welcomed me with a warm greeting, seemingly anxious to make up for her rather discourteous behavior on that trip. We met a number of times on the deck and chatted casually. But once, when I asked her about her impressions of Israel, she invited me to sit down beside her and told me her story:

"I am a widow. My husband died twelve years ago. The first year after his passing I was stunned, as if I had been struck by something blunt and heavy, but I did not lose my balance. I knew that I must not be idle, so I kept myself busy in the store and at home and prepared myself for a new life, for a lifeless life, and so did not feel too strongly the loneliness that was gnawing away at my heart. But after everything was arranged, I felt how solitary my life was. . . . As a result I came to a daring decision—to remarry.

"As soon as the members of my family heard this, they rose up against me as though I were going to profane the memory of my late husband. . . . When I saw how much they objected to my remarrying, I felt deeply offended and hurt. I came to the conclusion that actually they understood neither their father nor me; I did not alter my decision to marry. I had met a man of my age through my business contacts and we almost reached a mutual understanding. Once he visited me on a Saturday afternoon; he had brought his daughter along in order to prevent gossip. We sat drinking tea and chatting. Suddenly my two sons arrived. They burst in like policemen; evidently they had been spying and caught me red-handed, so to speak. They insulted him and his daughter. Since then we haven't seen each other. Incidents of this kind occurred several times. So the years passed, I grew old and I finally became reconciled to my lot.

"In the meantime, a remedy for my sickly loneliness came from an altogether different direction, from my activities in the Women's League for the Jewish National Fund. I had

An Open-Air Meeting Held in 1908 to Decide on the Founding of Tel-Aviv. 1908. Photograph. Yivo Institute for Jewish Research, New York.

always wanted to devote time to this work, but the pressure of our business and my responsibilities at home did not permit me to take on any additional task. However, when I suddenly found myself alone and free from my duties of the past, I dedicated myself to this work and found that it gave me, in return, both pleasure and interest and filled the vacuum that had been created by my husband's death. It filled my days with meaning and brought back my peace of mind. I don't know what I would have done had I not had this job that was sent to me like a blessing!

"My love for *Eretz Yisrael* I inherited from my father, the only inheritance I received. He was a *melamed* in our little town in Lithuania and taught only boys. During his teaching I was sent away to my mother, who was in the kitchen. But when he told them stories, he allowed me to come in and sit on a stool a little removed from the boys. He used to tell them about sages and scholars and he always finished off with something about the Holy Land and those blessed days when every man sat beneath 'his vine and his fig tree'. He also spoke of the approaching days of the Messiah and then he would exclaim joyously: 'We shall again live in our land that is flowing with milk and honey, on our soil which will give forth fresh new fruit every day. And the people will be good to each other, all the people, and there will be no pain and no illness, and the prophets will come to life again and walk the streets of Jerusalem prophesying!' Thus my father used to talk, in a sing-song, his eyes shut, the tears rolling down his furrowed cheeks onto the book lying open on the table; and all of us, the boys and I, used to weep with him. Then, all of a sudden, he would open his eyes and, his face alight and radiant, he would exclaim: 'All this will transpire soon, in our days!' And all of us said: 'Amen'.

"Those words of my father are etched deeply in my heart, but here in America, as I've already told you, I was always too busy to think of them. But when my husband died, and I was alone, this work on behalf of Eretz Yisrael came as a redeemer, as an angel from heaven and in it I found consolation and satisfaction.

"I remember a certain Zionist speaker who was invited to address our annual banquet; his words were a continuity of my father's and had the same fire and a similar ring. It seemed to me that he was the greatest speaker in the world. He spoke not in a sing-song but with his eyes shut like my father, may he rest in peace. He told us of his visits to the Holy Land and particularly to Mt. Carmel and I recall his saying: 'When I walk on Mount Carmel, I concentrate all my thoughts on one thing, on the vision of Elijah the Prophet, and then he, Elijah, appears before me and I behold his face, his long hair, the leather girdle tied about his loins and I hear his voice crying: The Lord He is God!' And then this speaker opened his eyes and asked us all to rise and sing with him the song *Eliyahu hanavi, Eliyahu hatishbi.* We women sang and our tears fell, and then he concluded: 'To build, to plant, to redeem our country, that is your sacred duty!' And then we all sang *Hatikvah.*

"After this banquet we all worked with great enthusiasm and energy and collected money to plant not only trees but whole forests and we redeemed many, many dunams of land. Now one of our main functions is the annual dinner that is followed by a dance. Last year, the first year after the State of Israel was established, we decided to award prizes to those of our members who would sell the largest number of tickets, and the first prize was a trip to Israel. I worked very hard but never dreamed that I might win the prize for never in my life have I won anything or gotten anything for nothing. But here, you see, my children without my knowledge, took an active part in this competition. Evidently they wished to make up for their offensive behavior. At the climax of the dinner-dance, the president got up and, calling my name, invited me to come up on the stage. I was so surprised that in my confusion I remained sitting on my chair. My friends began to urge me to go to the stage; I arose and went. The president embraced and kissed me and praised me to the skies and then she announced that I was the winner of the first prize. I wept with joy. At night, my father came to me in a dream and urged me to go to Israel and then that famous speaker entered my dream and gave me his encouragement as well. My joy knew no bounds.

"And so I came to Israel. I arrived full of joy and enthusiasm; but I return completely

disappointed. First of all, when I disembarked from the boat in Haifa, I faced some men who said they worked in the port and they cross-examined me rudely as though I were a thief and had come to steal; I stood there and wept. When they finally let me go, I went to the hotel on Mount Carmel where my travel agent had reserved a room for me. The realization that in a few minutes I would be standing on the holy mountain helped to erase the unhappy experience at the port from my mind. But when I reached the hotel, I was again disappointed; it was a hotel like all other hotels. I had imagined that here on this mountain I would find something different, something—I don't quite know how to express it—more fitting to this land and this mountain. Instead, I saw a hotel such as those one finds in New York or any other American city. But I put these thoughts aside for I was very happy to be in Israel at last. One evening, after I had rested a bit from the fatigue of the journey, I went out for a walk. I remembered very vividly the words of the speaker and I, too, tried to concentrate all my thoughts on the prophet Elijah. When

I felt a little tired from the walk, I sat down on a rock at the side of the road. I put my handbag down on one side of the rock and sat, concentrating my thoughts on Elijah. I heard soft footsteps as of someone walking on feathers and I thought: 'These are the footsteps of Elijah.' I listened attentively and sat for a long time, tense and excited. Then I opened my eyes: my handbag had disappeared!''

She finished talking and remained sitting quietly, pale, exhausted and drained of emotion. "I feel empty now, emptied of everything," she said. "Something has been taken from me. I am afraid, very much afraid of the solitude that awaits me. . . I feel dizzy now. I'll go and lie down a while." Two days passed and I did not see her. She was never on deck nor in the dining room. I was told that she was seasick, and had had to be moved to the infirmary where the ship's doctor was looking after her. When I inquired about her of the doctor, he said it was difficult to diagnose her illness. The ocean was certainly a factor but not the only one. "It may be a case of nerves. She talks a lot in her sleep and laughs, too. There must be something hidden in her subconscious mind that comes out in her dreams and nightmares; in that case, these outbursts will relieve her."

Several more days passed and then, walking on the deck one morning, I saw her sitting in the same place where we had had our previous talk. "She is waiting for me," flashed through my mind.

Her face, which had become much thinner, was suffused with joy and her whole appearance expressed great happiness. I sat down beside her and we chatted. I inquired about her ailment: "I wasn't sick; it was only dizziness and it's all gone now."

I asked whether the doctor had been helpful.

"Not the doctor; my father, of blessed memory. He came to help me. He grasped my hand and led me through the streets of Jerusalem. No, no, it was not a dream, positively not! I have dreamt a lot in my life and I know what a dream is. In a dream everything is nebulous, vague and when you wake up you don't remember anything. But this time everything was clear and bright and I remember every word, every gesture and movement that he made. We strolled on the streets of Jerusalem and he talked in the sing-song voice I know, his eyes closed. And when he finished, he said: 'Soon, soon, in our days,' and I said, 'Amen.' So I walked at his side and listened to his enthusiastic words; then, suddenly, he let go of my hand and walked away. When I looked to see where he had gone, I felt a light touch on my shoulder. I raised my eyes and saw the famous speaker beside me. He motioned me to follow him. We walked and walked until we reached Mount Carmel and then sat down on that same rock. We sat and listened. Suddenly we heard footsteps approaching. He whispered to me: 'Those are the footsteps of Elijah. Listen well, concentrate all your senses.' Then a powerful voice burst forth. I knew it was the voice of Elijah and I listened with all my being. The voice cried out: 'The Lord He Is God!' and then there was silence. The speaker turned to me and said: 'To build, to plant, to redeem the land, that is your duty!' When he finished these words he began to retreat. I stretched out my hand to hold him back and tell him of my visit to Israel, of my heartache and disappointment. But he had known all my thoughts and without turning to me said: "These are dreams, only dreams and nightmares. Go back to your work, work for the land of Israel."

"I jumped for joy and then I felt a warm, soft hand holding my arm and caressing it. I opened my eyes. The nurse was standing by my side. She stroked my hand and said that the doctor had told her I was well again and could leave my bed. Apparently he did not know that I had not been sick at all and had only suffered a light dizziness that was due to the movement of the ship.

"And now that I am going back to my work I won't be lonely or afraid. Blessed be the memories of my good father and of that fine speaker."

Edward Norden

"THE INGATHERING"

The "Law of Return" has made Israel a safe haven for any and all Jews, and many immigrants from the former Soviet Union have been arriving since the late 1980s. This colossal migration has created many problems for the new refugees, including difficulty finding professional jobs and ultimately assimilating into Israeli culture.

Ben-Gurion airport at the end of last year was comparable to Ellis Island in its glory. Every night, at least a thousand newcomers landed. They came from Ethiopia, black beauties as mild and disoriented as deer, but mainly they came from the fracturing Russian empire, pale little girls hugging Soviet-issue dolls, entire clans from Georgia and Uzbekistan. And the tempo was constantly accelerating—if in all of 1989, some 25,000 Jews moved to Israel, as many as that arrived last November alone, and no fewer than 37,000 in December, an all-time monthly record. Anxious, euphoric, relieved, exhausted, they were greeted, put through the first round of the bureaucratic mill, dispensed pocket money, let loose to discover their new country.

Night after night, this scene was reenacted, an emotional spectacle, a mundane business. The clerks processing the travelers, who work more gently than those at Ellis Island were said to do at the turn of the century, could be forgiven for forgetting the historical significance of it all. Simply enough, it was the Law of Return in action—any Jew or close relative of a Jew showing up was welcome, and unlike at Ellis Island, where if you had trachoma or an anarchist record you were turned back, here there was and is no check for TB or seropositivity, or for a Stalinist past.

The grand total for the year would be 200,000, of whom 185,000 came from the Soviet Union and 15,000 from Ethiopia, Argentina, and elsewhere. This was the most people to exit the Diaspora since 1951, and though Yuval Ne'eman, Minister of Science, cautioned that there was a war in the offing, those in the know said the flood could only swell. The majority predicted with delight and dread that this year the number of refugee-immigrants would double, would reach 400,000, casting in the shade any other year in Israel's interesting history.

★   ★   ★

A Zionist is the prey of joy and foreboding. For this Zionist dream come true, this biggest-ever ingathering of the exiles, has definite nightmarish aspects. The time-out for the Scuds afforded a breather from last year's frantic rate, when the absorption apparatus seemed about to be swamped. The list of relevant questions to which satisfactory answers are yet to be given is long. What about housing for all these arrivals? And schooling? And medical care? And water, in a region of the planet where it will soon be more expensive than oil? What about veteran Israelis, who have scrimped and hustled and cheated on their taxes for as long as they can remember and have already taken the first of the many cuts in their standard of living which will be required if the million or more people said to be on the way are to be accommodated? What are the better-off Jews of the Diaspora ready to do to help? In short, can the Jewish state digest such a feast?

No country except Israel itself in its heroic, lean, regimented first years has ever tried to do so. The numbers, the ratios, are staggering—this country is such a news factory that foreigners are liable to forget that at this writing there are barely four million Jews here to absorb another million. It is as if the U.S. for some reason decided to take in and

Soviet Immigrant Jews at Ben-Gurion Airport in Israel. 1991. Photograph.

resettle the entire population of Great Britain overnight, while at the same time having to keep an eye on its neighbors, suppress the Indians, and attend to the interests and feelings of old-timers whom the melting pot had disappointed.

This class or ethnic angle is touchy. Some Israelis originating in the Muslim countries, who had to live rough when they immigrated a generation ago, and too many of whom are still stuck around the poverty line, fret that the Soviet Jews, arriving with nothing but brains, education, discipline, high culture, ambition, and self-respect, are going to be blended into the national fabric at their expense. Already you hear grumbling. Some of it is brought on by the pinch of the government's economic policy, hastily revised last year to finance absorption, which meant higher taxes, higher prices for de-subsidized bread and milk and cigarettes, soaring rents, less welfare, fewer services. Some of it is inspired by old resentments, unhappy memories, wounded pride.

"Let them live in tents like we did," a night watchman born in Morocco said the other day. His deeper meaning was no less obvious for being coded. This *aliyah,* if it indeed comes to a million, will give the Ashkenazim a majority in Israel, bringing it in that respect back in line with the Diaspora, a prospect which would not be so displeasing to some Sephardim if they were not also hurt by the fuss being made over "the Russians," one they seem to remember was not made over them and their parents. What, were they less desirable? Were they really "human dust," as Ben-Gurion said? The Sephardim were idealists, Zionists, good Jews, so goes the counter-myth, while these Soviet Ashkenazim are atheists and materialists. "They expect to get everything on a platter—a car, an apartment, everything," a grocer whose father came from Iraq in 1951 complains in almost the same breath as he hails Saddam Hussein's comeuppance.

Not quite. All that most of the people from Moscow, Kiev, Baku, and Tashkent want is some kind of roof over their heads—a trailer will do for starters—food, and work. Sweeping the streets or washing dishes for starters is not beneath their dignity, and in some towns and restaurants they are already doing it, replacing Palestinians—for example, in the kitchen at Gilly's, which is Jersualem's answer to Elaine's, Marina and Masha have replaced Ahmed and Mustapha. Nor do all the newcomers arrive with such a terrific stock of adaptable inner strength. When the high of escaping from the Soviet Union wears off, when the wonderful supermarkets grow familiar, when the subsidy is spent, they all have to face themselves in a strange world, in a country no longer predominantly socialist nor yet truly capitalist, and not all can handle it to perfection.

The children generally take to Israel like ducks to water. The adults often have it harder. Bleakness follows euphoria, poverty aggravating culture shock. A number of recent arrivals are laboring as call girls in Tel Aviv to pay the rent. Several men and women have taken their own lives in the Promised Land. A pair of brothers who arrived in the record month of December have been charged by the Haifa district attorney with beating to death a real-estate agent, who, it seems, cheated them out of $2,200 of their immigrant subsidy. The Hebrew press and the blossoming local Russian-language press report such stories, heartbreaking and altogether predictable. They are reproduced every time masses move from continent to continent. Invariably, though this society has always been comparatively kind, the same thing happens each time the Zionist scenario plays itself out.

If you consult the Tel Aviv newspapers from 35 and 55 years ago, you will find that some of the new immigrants then from Poland, Bulgaria, and Morocco were in the same kind of trouble as some of the ex-Soviets today. There was crime. There were suicides. Unhappy stories, painful casualties, victims, and victimizers seem to be an unavoidable spinoff of great migrations. The movement of Jews from czarist Russia to New York's Lower East Side at the end of the last century and the beginning of this one, chronicled in its grace and squalor by Abraham Cahan and Samuel Ornitz and Henry Roth, was one such mass uprooting, adjusting the course of Jewish history. Another is the current move to Israel of the descendants of those Russian Jews who did not get out then.

They are fleeing an empire infected by anti-Semitism and veering toward chaos. Even though, now that there is Israel, they are not to be considered stateless, psychologically many are as much refugees as they are immigrants. They are refugees, besides, whose first choice of a haven was not Israel. Most, though they will not tell you so or even allow themselves to remember, would have preferred enormous, quiet, rich America. It takes a measure of callousness to say, quite rightly, that in the long run this makes little difference for Israel, since most of the Jews who have moved here in this century have done so for lack of another open door. That did not keep them, and especially their children, from nailing the Jewish state more firmly on the map. Subjectively, they were

Russian Immigrant Performing as a Street Musician in Israel. 1991. Photograph.

refugees, but objectively, as Marxists used to say, they could not have been better Zionists. More or less the same pattern is visible in this, the greatest *aliyah* of them all.

And probably the best-educated one also. The stereotype of the newcomer from the Soviet Union is of a biochemist who plays in a string quartet for relaxation. The statistics compiled by the Jewish Agency explain why this cliché has taken root. Of the 100,000 immigrants who came from the prison of nations in the first nine months of last year, more than 40,000 had graduated from a university. There were 14,000 engineers and architects, 7,000 scientists, 3,500 doctors and dentists, 2,500 nurses, 5,000 schoolteachers, 3,000 writers, musicians, and artists. In the short run, few of these men and women will be able to earn a living in their professions. In the long run, if Israel is unlucky, all these M.A.'s and Ph.D.'s and violinists will overwhelm it. But if it is as lucky and ingenious as it has been in the past, they and their children will be its salvation, somewhat in the way the German Jews were.

David Grossman
THE SPARK AND THE FLUTE

The massive aliyah *of the Ethiopian Jews was carried out by a well-orchestrated airlift; planes continuously landed and took off again until all the refugees safely arrived in Israel.*

Soon enough, the newcomers will be part of the Israeli potage, rising again to its surface in caustic newspaper accounts of the vagaries of absorption and in bitter reports of despair. But for a brief 24 hours, no mean amount of time to us, we knew a forgotten joy amid our cynical, cantankerous, rapacious existence.

The arrivals from Ethiopia proceeded down the ramp leading from the plane with slow, suspended steps. Their browned soles—bare, or shod in colorful sneakers—groped hesitantly for the metal stairs. A first glance was sent out, cautious, covert: not a gaze that claimed propriety over the new landscape. Nor a joy-filled glimmer. Just eyes that twinkled behind the dull mask of the refugee.

The silence and slow motion of the arrivals enveloped those who received them, too. Before our eyes an entire culture was uprooted from its life source and brought here, to be replanted. Everything melded together: the pain of being severed from a homeland, the physical sensation of roots rent, strands of life left hanging from these souls; and the joy of receiving these people. We Israelis are so trained in negation, callousness and restraint that given the chance to overflow, to make good, we gulp these rare drops thirstily.

And the flow was never-ending. Plane after plane landed around us: 14,000 refugees. Even underneath the veil of torpor their beauty was apparent. Apparent, too, was the majesty of these new Israelis: little Queens of Sheba; children of almond, of olive; adolescents without the arrogant glare of our teen-agers; old men and women angular and black as coal, only their eyes ember. A Judaism seared. A Judaism that strayed for 2,500 years through the thicket of history, that rose and fell, that was separated, yet survived.

Perhaps what survived is what we seek with our eternal question: who is a Jew? Perhaps, it is they in their remoteness, in their longing, who bring us the answer. Perhaps this is why we scrutinize them so closely—to see, in the blazing blue light, the photographic negative of our history.

Nearly 40 jets, coming and going, night and day. As if in a modern fable. Aboard one flight, Elazar Rahamim, an Ethiopian Jew who had been in Israel for 20 years and

Ethiopian Immigrants and Israeli Children at a Practice Seder in Israel. 1984. Photograph.

had been asked to accompany his countrymen on the airlift, spoke to the newcomers. A 2,500-year-old dream is coming true, he told them as the plane came over Jerusalem: It is for her we have longed and prayed, and now we have been granted the right to come to her—thanks to the Government of Israel and because, thank God, we have a State.

They descended from the plane carefully. Some in rags, some in Sabbath whites embroidered in a rainbow of colors. Their belongings were pitiably few: One plastic bag per family, a Styrofoam jerrycan, a goatskin canteen. And these, too: Young girls with patterns tattooed in blue on their faces and necks; talismans jangling from women's dresses; old people toting colorful parasols; venerable *kazes,* the high priests of the sect, fondling *chirah,* the horsehair symbol of their rank. They were wrapped in antique splendor that, like ancient frescos suddenly exposed to a dazzling light, faded there on the tarmac, before our know-it-all eyes.

It was difficult for those who received them not to be tempted by voyeurism: there, on the asphalt runway, the inner lining of life was exposed for all to see. But even the journalists and photographers, even the politicians who flocked there for you-know-what—even they slowed down a bit, showed reverence for the power of tenacity and passivity. They faced it, discomfited, as the West faces the barrenness of the third world. Most of all, and with that silence that is the end of words, they faced the thing itself: the bareness of another fate.

The Ethiopians passed between those who stared at them. A trying test of their natural shyness, their dignity. It seemed as if their souls closed a bit. Not in fear, in caution. Even the adults among them became children in the face of the genial, knowing bustle of those who received them.

But then a boy burst through the doorway of the plane, a boy of 5 or 6, shaved head, very black, a large wooden flute in his hand. Standing at the head of the ramp, he began to play. For a moment, all activity stopped, a few photographers even forgot their flash-bulbs. He stood and played in earnest, with intent. Perhaps it was a shepherd's tune he had played in his village, with his flock. Perhaps it was a melody he had prepared for the moment.

With his song, one live, shimmering spark flew out from under the anvil of our lives. For one whole day, from within the jarring dissonance of our inner sound system, we produced one true note, one clear, harmonious note; enough to evoke the entire melody.

INDEX

Page numbers in *italics* refer to illustrations.

PHOTO CREDITS

We especially wish to thank the following persons and institutions: Cissy Grossman and Reva G. Kirschberg/Judaica Collection of Congregation Emanu-El of the City of New York; David Harris; Susanne Kester/Hebrew Union College Skirball Museum, Los Angeles; Irene Lewitt/Israel Museum; Anton Kras/Jewish Historical Museum, Amsterdam; Barbara Treitel and Susan Chevlowe/Jewish Museum, New York; Sharon Lieberman-Mintz/Jewish Theological Seminary, New York; Malcolm Varon.

Color Illustrations: Agenzia Ricciarini/S Milan: cpl. 41; Art Resource, NY: cover, cpls. 32, 35, 42, 54, 62, 74, 76, 101, 109, 112, 122, 127; Artothek, Peissenberg, Germany: 115; Photo, Thomas Feist: cpl. 84; Photos, John Reed Forsman: cpls. 44, 72, 87, 88, 89, 91, 98, 100, 103, 104, 110, 114; Photo, Peter Goldberg: cpl. 68; Photos, © David Harris: cpls. 3, 5, 6, 12, 20, 27, 39, 48, 60, 65, 75, 81, 83, 92, 93, 97, 99, 105, 106, 107, 111, 113, 137, 138; Photo, Eric Hockley: cpl. 63; Photo IMJ/Moshe Caine: cpl. 125; Photos, IMJ/Pierre Alain Ferraz-zini: cpls. 8, 37, 43, 120; Photos, IMJ/David Harris: cpls. 36, 66, 73, 128; Photos, IMJ/Nachum Slapak: cpls. 51, 85; INDEX/Lufin: cpl. 45; Photos, courtesy Jewish Museum, New York: cpls. 68, 124; Photo, Suzanne Kaufman: cpl. 67; Photo, Jonathan Morris-Ebbs: cpl. 124; Photo, John Parnell/Art Resource, NY: cpl. 136; Princeton University Press/Art Resource, NY: cpl. 4; Photos, QuickSilver/Mark Gulezian, from "The Precious Legacy," organized by the Smithsonian Institution Traveling Exhibition Service, in cooperation with the Czechoslovak Socialist Republic: cpls. 30, 56, 57, 70, 71, 74; Robert Rubic: cpl. 121; Photo, Nicolas Sapieha/Art Resource, NY: cpl. 61; Photo, Lee Stalsworth: cpl. 126: Strenger, Osnabrück/Christian Grovermann: cpl. 129; Photos, © Malcolm Varon: cpls. 46, 47, 49, 50, 52, 53, 55, 58, 59, 69, 77, 78, 79, 80, 82, 86, 90, 94, 108, 132.

Black and White Illustrations: Art Resource, NY: pp. 35, 88, 132, 159, 185, 212, 226, 274, 279, 301, 324; The Bettmann Archive, NY: pp. 30, 82, 239, 327; Bildarchiv FotoMarburg/Art Resource, NY: p. 26; The Bund Archives, NY: p. 201; Photo courtesy, Collection Congregation Emanu-El of the City of New York: p. 236; Culver Pictures: pp. 203, 285; Photo, courtesy Terry Dintenfass, Gallery, Inc., NY: p. 33; Giraudon/Art Resource, NY: p. 107; Photos, © David Harris: pp. 156, 180, 348, 354; Photo, D. Hauser: p. 297; Suzanne Kaufman: pp. 57, 115, 137; Library of Congress: p. 281; Mansell Collection, London: p. 60; Photo, Marvin Newman: p. 71; Photos, © Barbara Pfeffer: pp. 377, 378, 380; Private collection: p. 330; Photo, QuickSilver/Mark Gulezian, from "The Precious Legacy," organized by the Smithsonian Institution Traveling Exhibition Service, in cooperation with the Czechoslovak Socialist Republic: p. 16; © Photo, R.M.N., Paris: p. 69; Robert Rubic: pp. 131, 163; Nicholas Sapieha/Art Resource, NY: p. 107; Photo, D. Porokhovnikov/Tass/Sovfoto, NY: p. 177; Photo, Jim Strong, Inc.: p. 188; Ullstein Bilderdienst, Berlin: p. 216; UPI/Bettmann Newsphotos: pp. 277, 321.